Entrepreneurship for Development:
A Business Model

Entrepreneurship for Development: A Business Model

Editor: Otto Thomson

New York

Published by NY Research Press
118-35 Queens Blvd., Suite 400,
Forest Hills, NY 11375, USA
www.nyresearchpress.com

Entrepreneurship for Development: A Business Model
Edited by Otto Thomson

International Standard Book Number: 978-1-64725-456-8 (Hardback)

Cataloging-in-Publication Data

Entrepreneurship for development : a business model / edited by Otto Thomson.
    p. cm.
Includes bibliographical references and index.
ISBN 978-1-64725-456-8
1. Entrepreneurship. 2. Economic development. 3. Business. I. Thomson, Otto.
HB615 .E544 2023
658.421--dc23

Contents

               Permissions

               List of Contributors

               Index

Preface

The main aim of this book is to educate learners and enhance their research focus by presenting diverse topics covering this vast field. This is an advanced book which compiles significant studies by distinguished experts in the area of analysis. This book addresses successive solutions to the challenges arising in the area of application, along with it; the book provides scope for future developments.

Entrepreneurship refers to the ability and willingness to create, organize, and run a business enterprise and take responsibility for dealing with all the uncertainties in order to gain a profit. There are various types of entrepreneurship including scalable startup entrepreneurship, social entrepreneurship, small business entrepreneurship, and large company entrepreneurship. It promotes economic growth and development by introducing innovative products and services that helps create jobs, increases the standard of living of people, and lead to the overall improvement of an economy. It expedites modernization and has the potential to play a critical role in promoting sustainable development. This book aims to shed light on the role of entrepreneurship in development. It consists of contributions made by international experts. This book, with its detailed analyses and data, will prove immensely beneficial to professionals and students interested in entrepreneurship.

It was a great honour to edit this book, though there were challenges, as it involved a lot of communication and networking between me and the editorial team. However, the end result was this all-inclusive book covering diverse themes in the field.

Finally, it is important to acknowledge the efforts of the contributors for their excellent chapters, through which a wide variety of issues have been addressed. I would also like to thank my colleagues for their valuable feedback during the making of this book.

Editor

Social Entrepreneurship and Regional Economic Development: The Case of Social Enterprise in South Korea

Soogwan Doh⊕

Faculty of Department of Public Administration, School of Social Sciences, University of Ulsan, Ulsan 44610, Korea; sgdoh@ulsan.ac.kr

Abstract: Although many discussions of regional economic development have been made to this day, the regional economic development sector is constantly looking for new models to address the many challenges of each region in a sustainable way. This study aims to empirically examine the relationship between social entrepreneurship and regional economic development, focusing on government-driven social enterprises in South Korea. I conduct an exploratory study of government support for social enterprises in South Korea at the local and central government level and empirically examine the relationship between social entrepreneurship and regional economic development by using time sequential panel data collected over an eight-year period from 2007 to 2014. Results from panel regression (fixed-effect and random-effect) models indicate that social entrepreneurship measured as the number of government-driven social enterprises has a positive relationship with regional economic development. As claimed in numerous previous studies on regional economic development, the fixed-effect regression results of this study also indicate that physical capital, human capital, knowledge capital, and entrepreneurship are all significant and important factors shaping regional economic output. The results of this study suggest a new direction for policy that focuses on instruments to promote social entrepreneurship. Thus, governments of each region need to make efforts to promote job creation in social enterprises because they possess the ability to efficiently respond to the immediate needs of local social enterprises. These government-driven social enterprises can contribute to regional economic development through creating new jobs in South Korea.

Keywords: social entrepreneurship; social enterprise; regional economic development; sustainable regional economic development

1. Introduction

This study aims to empirically examine the relationship between social entrepreneurship and regional economic development, using data on certified social enterprises in South Korea. For this purpose, research models were developed by first examining theoretical discussions on social entrepreneurship and regional economic development.

In response to the global financial crisis of 2008 and its impact on the economy, many countries increased their spending in order to promote economic growth and sustainable economic development. However, increased government spending caused massive financial deficits in many countries. Each country carried out multifaceted efforts to resolve massive financial deficits caused by increased government spending in the process of overcoming fiscal and financial crises [1–3]. Nevertheless, the measures taken, based on two extreme (dichotomous) approaches of existing state-led and market-driven methods, instigated market and government failures and led to heavy questioning concerning their effectiveness. Therefore, it became necessary to find new alternatives that could solve fiscal deficit issues, a stagnant market, and unemployment all at the same time. In particular, in the area of social welfare, the integrity of welfare provision spending emerged as an important issue. What developed as an alternative was the expansion of welfare service provisions and the creation of new jobs through stimulating the social economy and ultimately achieving sustainable economic development [4–9].

South Korea, an OECD member, has made direct investments in its social economy to mount a new response to the global economic crisis, welfare state decline, and social challenges. In particular, South Korea has mainly developed social enterprises among various operators in the social economy. Social enterprise is an organization established based on social entrepreneurship to pursue social and economic objectives. As a response to the global economic crisis and welfare state decline, the Korean government introduced a plan to support social enterprises. To provide services and work opportunities for socially excluded people, the Korean government enacted the Social Enterprise Promotion Act (SEPA) in 2007. Based on SEPA, a company or organization must go through seven steps before being certified as a social enterprise in South Korea.

According to a press release in 2020 by the Korea Social Enterprise Promotion Agency, the Korean government had approved 3125 social enterprises as of 30 September 2020. Because subsidies are typically required in the start-up phase of a social enterprise [10], South Korea increased the budget by about 53.348 million US dollars in 2016 (about 0.013% of the central government's total expenditure, equaling approximately 398.5 billion US dollars) to provide social enterprises with financial and managerial support. The Korean government is also actively promoting local government attempts to foster and support social enterprises that meet the specific needs of local communities by allowing local governments to identify preliminary social enterprises and establish regulations at the local level to foster them. Job creation, unemployment reduction, and regional economic development through vitalization of social enterprises had been emphasized more and more in correlation with the 'Creative Economy' measures of the Park Geun-hye administration. As a result, by the end of September 2020, there were 2626 certified social enterprises that were currently active, showing a remarkable growth from the 55 certified social enterprises that were active in 2007.

Despite the increasing numbers of government-driven social enterprises established based on social entrepreneurship and financial support from public and private organizations for them in South Korea, neither an evaluation of the performance of social enterprise programs, based on regional economic development, nor explicit strategies for social enterprises have been proposed. Because some of the Korean government's key roles are job creation and sustainable regional economic development, various forms of support including government subsidies are given to the social enterprises with official recognition. Since proving the effectiveness of external funding is critical in order to allocate limited resources as efficiently as possible, evaluation of the social enterprise policy of the Korean government is a necessary task to promote regional economic development. Despite the need for such research, experiential and empirical studies on this matter are quite scarce in South Korea. Existing studies on social enterprises in South Korea (e.g., [11–14]) focus on job creation using data on certified social enterprises. Such studies are crucial to government efforts to create new jobs for the underprivileged. However, these studies are limited in that they do not take into account the role(s) of social enterprises in regional economic development.

This study aims to address the limitations of prior studies by empirically examining the relationship between social entrepreneurship and regional economic development through focusing on the role of government-driven certified social enterprises in regional economic development in South Korea. To frame our query, this study considers prominent theories on regional economic development, focusing particularly on arguments related to physical capital, human capital, knowledge, and entrepreneurship, and on associated conceptualizations of social entrepreneurship. The result of the analysis in this study is expected to present important implications for establishing future directions for policies regarding social enterprise support for regional economic development.

This paper is structured as follows. The next Section reviews the literature on social economy, social entrepreneurship, social enterprise, the relationship between social entrepreneurship and regional economic development, and social enterprise policy initiatives implemented by the Korean government. The third Section explains the data, variables, and method for the empirical analysis. After interpreting the empirical results, we conclude with a discussion and list of policy implications.

2. Literature Review

2.1. Social Economy, Social Entrepreneurship, and Social Enterprises

Since the rise of the social economy has been recognized in political, economic, legal, administrative, and other circles, 'social economy' has become a useful term for academics and researchers. According to Spear (2013), "the social economy is typically understood as a family of different types of organizations: co-operatives, mutuals, associations, and foundations (CMAF)" [10: 8]. The social economy plays an important role in assisting the most disadvantaged in society in many countries. It has been expected to present a new alternative to government-provided public service initiatives and to contribute to resolving social issues such as unemployment and poverty [15–17].

In the social economy, active participation of social entrepreneurs has become increasingly important for social and economic development through the expansion of welfare service provisions and the creation of new jobs [18,19]. Social entrepreneurs have the capabilities and temperament for a set of exceptional behaviors. Since social entrepreneurs are searching for innovative solutions to meet new social needs and to develop a new response to social challenges, social entrepreneurship is often associated with social innovation [20–22]. Although the initiatives of social entrepreneurs result in the establishment of various kinds of innovative organizations, social enterprise can be seen as a general form of economic organization operating within the social economy [7,23,24] and it refers to one of the tangible outcomes of social entrepreneurship.

Many studies and discussions about social enterprises have taken place along with their rapid growth. However, despite the existence of research highlighting the cross-sectoral nature of social enterprise, scholars have conflicted over its definition [25–28]. This is largely due to the fact that social enterprise in each country has developed from different origins and in a different manner, thus creating a wide range of models [29,30]. Although it is difficult to clearly define a social enterprise, most scholars have generally agreed that a social enterprise denotes an economic agent that pursues public interest objectives of production and supply of social services, as well as the traditional corporate objective of maximum profit at the same time [31–34]. In other words, social enterprise can be viewed as economic entities creating social and economic value within the social economy [23,35,36]. Thus, a social enterprise is regarded as a hybrid between nonprofit organizations pursuing social goals and businesses pursuing economic goals [18,19,37] or a hybrid providing state services [30,38,39].

The OECD broadly defines a social enterprise as an organization established based on entrepreneurship to pursue social and economic objectives, which, in a narrower sense, promotes regional economic development by re-integrating the labor market through training of the poor and by consuming the products and utilizing services produced in the process [40]. Defourny (2001) explains the concept of social enterprise separately in terms of both economic and social dimensions [25]. He explains that a social enterprise, in the economic sense, should take some level of risk while continuously producing or selling goods and services, have a high degree of autonomy, and retain a minimum number of paid workers. He also describes that in the social sense, a social enterprise is formed based on citizens' voluntary participation; its decision-making authority should not be determined based on ownership of capital; parties affected by the social enterprise's activities should be able to participate in decision-making; and profit sharing should be limited. In this perspective, a social enterprise, unlike private companies, has public interest, and its concept of social enterprise is also clearly distinct from that of the social responsibility of corporations.

It has been said that social enterprises emerged as an alternative to resolve market and government failures [14]. In other words, it can be said that out of the three sectors of the economy, a social enterprise performs broad activities within the spectrum of the social economic sector, which is the third sector that has the properties of the first sector—public area (state)—and the second sector—private area (market). Therefore, it can be said that social enterprise seeks to achieve social goals through commercial activities [18,19,37,41–43] and plays a key role in providing the state services [38,39].

However, countries in Europe do not subscribe to this model and view both the third and fourth sectors as the social economic area. According to scholars who advocate a fourth sector distinct from the third (e.g., [44–49], the third sector represents citizen groups and non-government, non-profit organizations; whereas the fourth sector is defined as a new collective organizational model that simultaneously seeks profit and public interests, and combines the existing sectors to resolve social issues. These scholars include social enterprises in the fourth sector and suggest that social enterprise is an important economic agent that functions within the fourth sector. In addition, Williams (2008, 2010) presents the fourth sector as an area for non-official, volunteer activities and a form of citizen participation culture that can supplement the public activities of the third sector [44,45]. Jimenez and Morales (2011) also argue that it is a collective sphere that combines public, private, and civic sectors for the purpose of resolving social issues, and economic agents like social enterprises, cooperatives, and township enterprises are main constituents of the fourth sector [48].

Taken together, social enterprise is an important form of economic organization working within the social economy. Each country's government exerts multifaceted efforts to meet social service needs through vitalization of social enterprises, although the contents and methods of support differ by country [50–52].

2.2. Social Entrepreneurship and Regional Economic Development

Recent entrepreneurship literature has emphasized the innovative capacity of social entrepreneurs as new actors for social and economic development [20]. Thus, social entrepreneurship is an important factor for the development of the social economy and contributes to regional economic development. For example, social economy organizations are often the biggest employers in the area of economic crisis in East Germany; in fact, the organizations are some of the most important actors for regional economic development in almost all European crisis regions [53]. Therefore, the significance of social entrepreneurship for keeping some such thing as a locality or community alive has been emphasized in terms of regional economic development [53].

It is clearly not easy to identify the main actors in the social economy because of the marked diversity of national realities concerning the concepts and the level of recognition of the social economy [9]. Nevertheless, it can be said that nowadays, the organizations that represent the social economy in Europe are cooperative family, family of mutual societies, family of associations and social action organizations, and platforms for social enterprises [9]. These organizations can contribute to the creation of jobs and entrepreneurial ventures in disadvantaged regions [11]; therefore, they can have an influence on regional economic development.

As mentioned above, social enterprise can be seen as a general form of economic organization operating within the social economy [7,23,24] and it refers to one of the tangible outcomes of social entrepreneurship, although the initiatives of social entrepreneurs result in the establishment of various kinds of innovative organizations. The presence of social enterprises in regions where public services are poor or lacking is particularly important because it provides social services or jobs to the socially underprivileged while producing and selling goods and services; promotes social values that are difficult to provide through the market mechanism; and retains the attributes and profit-driven nature of a corporation and social nature that seeks to fulfill public interests [11]. Social enterprises seek to add to regional economic development through the creation of jobs and entrepreneurial ventures in disadvantaged regions. By helping to improve the overall skills of a local workforce, reducing inequalities in access to health and social care services, constructing good-quality housing for those living in sub-standard conditions, reducing social exclusion for the unemployed, creating wealth and adding benefits due to a multiplier effect, improving labor productivity due to skills investment, increasing tax revenues while reducing welfare payments, and enabling community-led rejuvenation and renewal, social enterprises can also provide economic development benefits to poor regions [54]. Thus, social enterprise was expected to present itself as one of the new alternatives to expand welfare service provisions, creation of new jobs, and reduction of unemployment and poverty in such regions through stimulating the social economy and ultimately achieving sustainable regional economic development [4–9,15–17,23,24]. Recent data from CIRIEC (2012) actually show that the social economy actors including social enterprise have increased their share of employment within Europe [55]. For this reason, some countries like South Korea have promoted supporting social enterprises and have increased the budget to provide social enterprises with financial and managerial support. The social enterprise of South Korea is a typical case of government-driven social enterprise because it has grown under the benefits of government-led development policies, mainly represented by government certification and support towards personnel expenses. In addition, infrastructure access, information, consultancy, and technical support are available for the certified social enterprises in South Korea.

In general, improvement in the efficiency of resource allocation, equity through redistribution, economic stability, and growth accomplishment can be considered as bases for government intervention in the private sector's economic activities [56]. Each government's active financial support of social enterprises can be interpreted as a pursuit of equity through redistribution and economic stability and development. For example, the Korean government actively fostered social enterprises in order to seek equity through redistribution by providing social services to the underprivileged, and to pursue sustainable economic development through regional economic vitalization by providing sustainable jobs, thereby promoting job creation and increased employment. The increase in employment and job creation represents economic stability. Since Korea's 1997 financial crisis, job creation and increased employment were imperative to alleviating the economic downfall at hand, so a fundamental goal for creating a comprehensive policy was in place. Based on the aggressive funding of social enterprise, it is possible to infer that the Korean government has regarded the objective of job creation as highly important.

Another way for evaluating the government's financial support for social enterprises is by measuring improvement in the efficiency of resource allocation. Identifying the two axes that make up modern society as the market and the government, we can say that efficient allocation of resources is primarily the responsibility of the market. Government interventions to achieve efficient resource allocation are justified only when the market fails to do so—that is, when a market failure occurs [57–59]. In this respect, the socially disadvantaged would be unable to obtain decent employment and continue to be placed in vulnerable situations, if their employment is determined solely by the market. Therefore, the government seeks to enhance equality by providing various welfare benefits to the socially disadvantaged through income redistribution policies. However, it is necessary to ultimately inspire the socially disadvantaged to desire to work and be independently active in the market. It is difficult, practically, for the government of a welfare state to afford the continually increasing costs of welfare in the face of a crisis. Hence, vitalization of social enterprises that can provide the socially disadvantaged with sustainable employment and social services at the same time can be an essential alternative for the government. In the case of Korea, such legitimacy of government intervention became the basis for state-led support for social enterprises, and as a result, enabled a rapid quantitative growth in a short time through certification and labor cost support. Moreover, the method of supporting labor costs was a practical way to recruit talent for the immediate implementation of certain projects and became the most powerful force behind the integration of labor among the underprivileged, development of social service providers, and the creation of jobs [60].

However, a social enterprise can also be regarded as a social venture that is operated based on the principles of profit generation and innovation typical of general for-profit corporations, while at the same time pursuing the social objectives of alleviating social problems and market failures or creating social values. Therefore, a social enterprise utilizes creative entrepreneurship, innovation, and market principles to create social values and encourage social changes. Considering these perspectives, the government's direct financial support for social enterprises, such as the support for labor costs, may contribute to job creation and social service provision through the establishment and maintenance of social enterprises in the short term. In the long term, though, it could act as a hindrance to the development of social enterprises or distort the fundamental attributes of a social enterprise. Under such conditions, it is difficult to promote independence and autonomy of social enterprises and the development of diverse social enterprises may also be inhibited. Sustainability issues have also been shown to exist for less competitive social enterprises, as most social enterprises have scaled down on employment once support for personnel expenses expired, while others disposed of their assets or even closed business. Despite these issues, there is a general consensus that financial support, such as support for personnel expenses, enables the establishment and maintenance of social enterprises in the short term, thereby contributing to job creation and regional economic development [4,27,32–34,61].

South Korea's support policy for social enterprises is expected to promote the quantitative and qualitative development of social enterprises and ultimately contribute to regional economic development. To corroborate such theoretical arguments, an empirical study on whether social enterprises are actually contributing to regional economic development is needed. So far, there are virtually no previous studies available.

Based on the limitations of previous studies and the above discussion, this study seeks to answer the following research question. Social entrepreneurship is a vital factor for promoting regional economic development and therefore I asked, "what effect does social entrepreneurship have on regional economic development?" Thus, this study addresses the following two hypotheses:

Hypothesis 1 (H1). *Regional economic development is positively affected by social entrepreneurship.*

Hypothesis 2 (H2). *After controlling physical capital, human capital, knowledge capital, and entrepreneurship, social entrepreneurship has a positive impact on regional economic development.*

This study uses a model to investigate the relationship between government-driven social enterprises and regional economic development. Before moving on to specific analyses of the relationship, support policies and the general status of social enterprises in Korea will be briefly examined below.

2.3. Social Enterprise Policy in South Korea

In Europe, interest towards social enterprises—along with the trend of privatization of social welfare and job creation—began to rise in the 20th century. In South Korea, on the other hand, the government did not begin to actively promote the expansion of social services and job creation until the 1997 financial crisis. At that time, it did so in an effort to overcome the economic crisis, to resolve social welfare problems, and to promote economic development [52]. The government's increased interest and investment in this area can be clearly seen in data from the years following that crisis: A budget of about 7.3 million US dollars created approximately 2000 social enterprise jobs in 2003, and a budget of about 1.3 billion US dollars created approximately 162,000 jobs in 2011 [62]. In other words, to overcome the economic crisis, to provide social welfare services, and to promote economic development in regions where public services are poor or lacking, the Korean government introduced the social enterprise model as an alternative. It even enacted a special 'Social Enterprise Promotion Act' in 2007.

With rapid aging and the dismantling of the traditional family structure, public demand for social services rapidly increased. Under the government's lead, certification of social enterprises began, and starting in August 2012, revised statutes of the 'Social Enterprise Promotion Act (SEPA) of 2007' were implemented. Financial and operational support was provided to certified social enterprises.

In December 2012, the Social Enterprise Promotion Agency was established. In addition to central government support, an 'ordinance on standards for social enterprise development support' was enacted to encourage local governments to enact ordinances to foster and support social enterprises at the regional level. By planning for quality improvement in certification services and supporting fair certification screening, the Korea Social Enterprise Promotion Agency (KoSEA) contributes to the expansion and invigoration of social enterprises. Figure 1 shows procedure for certification of social enterprises in South Korea.

Figure 1. Brief description of the steps necessary for the Korean social enterprise certification. Source: Korea Social Enterprise Promotion Agency (KoSEA) [63].

As activities of government-driven social enterprises are generally based on local governments' administrative districts, the enforcing agency was changed from the central government to local governments [11]. Hence, the central and local governments have been providing various types of support to social enterprises based on the SEPA and other relevant laws and ordinances. The Labor Department in particular aims to foster approximately 3000 social enterprises by 2017.

According to the revised SEPA, a social enterprise is a corporation that pursues social objectives, such as enhancing the quality of life of local residents, by providing social services or employment opportunities to the underprivileged or contributing to the local community, while simultaneously producing and selling goods and services that meet appropriate requirements and have been certified. The Korea Social Enterprise Promotion Agency provides specific examples of underprivileged groups, such as low-income individuals, the disabled, victims of sexual trafficking, the elderly, those who have been unemployed for a long period, and women who have taken a career break. Thus, a social enterprise in South Korea is different from that of Europe or other countries in terms of concept, characteristics, and function. Specifically, social enterprises in South Korea, unlike in other countries, have grown under the benefits of government-led development policies, mainly represented by government certification and support towards personnel expenses. Figure 2 roughly shows South Korea's development policy for social enterprises.

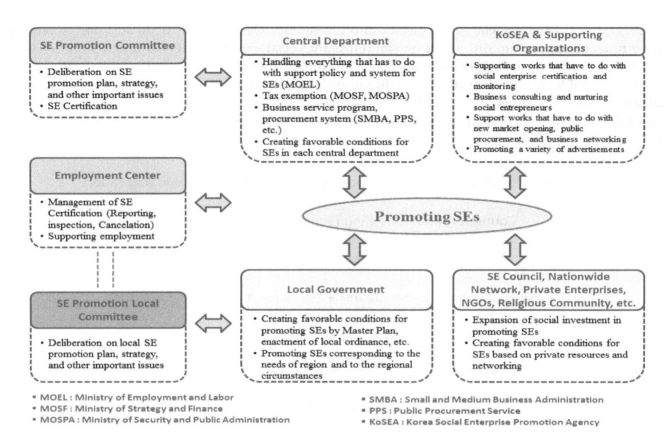

Figure 2. Korean social enterprise (SE) promotion system. Source: Adapted from Ministry of Employment and Labor (2012: 30) [64] and revised by author.

The support for social enterprises in Korea can be separated into the central government and the local government levels as follows. At the central government level, certified social enterprises are provided with management support, training support, facility cost support, priority purchase for public agencies, tax exemption, social insurance premium assistance, funding for social-service-providing enterprises, and employment liability exemption and tax reduction for affiliated companies. At the local government level, with some variation by logicality, various policy efforts are made to help region-based preliminary social enterprises meet the certification requirements at an early stage by providing management consulting, personnel expenses for new and professional recruitments, business development costs, priority purchases, and pro bono assistance. In addition, organizations such as the Korea Business Council of Social Enterprise, Work Together Foundation, Korea Foundation for Social Investment, and Social Solidarity Bank, provide support at the national level while social enterprise support centers of metropolitan municipalities or primary local governments provide assistance at the local level.

Although central and local governments provide a wide variety of support to certified social enterprises and region-based preliminary social enterprises, a majority of the associated budget is allocated for personnel expenses for creating jobs [11,52]. This trend has existed since support for social enterprises began, as they were aggressively fostered to alleviate unemployment and to provide decent employment opportunities to the underprivileged. Currently, the social enterprise development policies for both the central and local governments are focused on how many jobs will be created and on promoting regional economic development through future job creation. It implies that social enterprises are gaining attention as a viable means of job creation in an era of rising unemployment.

In South Korea, certification status is a particularly important element, considering the country's unique government-led development process by way of certification and personnel expense assistance. According to a study by Kim and Lee (2012a) [11], in the early phase of certification, a high percentage of organizations transitioning into social enterprises were ones that started in the job creation project led by the central government under the Ministry of Employment and Labor. However, more recently, related government agencies under the Memorandum of Understanding (MOU) with the Ministry of Employment and Labor are actively discovering and fostering social enterprises in the areas of agriculture and fishery and arts and cultures. As of the end of 2016, approximately 40% of all social enterprises were based and operated in the metropolitan areas of Seoul, Incheon, and Gyeonggi, all of which have large populations. Table 1 indicates the annual status of applications, certification rates, and maintenance rates since 2007 when the certification program was implemented.

Table 1. Overview of the number of social enterprise applications, certifications, and operations.

Year	Number of Applications	Number of Certified Social Enterprises (%)	Number of Certified Social Enterprises Operating in the Market as of 31 December 2016 (Persistency Rate, %)
Year 2007	166	55 (33.1)	40 (72.7)
Year 2008	285	166 (58.2)	125 (75.3)
Year 2009	199	77 (38.7)	63 (81.8)
Year 2010	408	216 (52.9)	169 (78.2)
Year 2011	224	155 (60.8)	125 (80.6)
Year 2012	317	142 (36.8)	133 (93.7)
Year 2013	469	269 (51.8)	247 (91.8)
Year 2014	481	265 (55.1)	256 (96.6)
Year 2015	427	295 (69.1)	290 (98.3)
Year 2016	326	265 (81.3)	265 (100.0)
Total	3302	1905 (57.7)	1713 (89.9)

Source: Korea Social Enterprise Promotion Agency annual reports on social enterprise certification.

3. Materials and Methods

3.1. Empirical Model: Regional Economic Development Model

Quite a number of theoretical discussions of regional economic development have been made to this day. In particular, the arguments made by a variety of social scientists, including economists, state that physical capital, human capital, knowledge capital, and entrepreneurship are important factors in regional economic development [65].

Physical capital, as emphasized from the primitive age to the information society of the modern era, is a fundamental element of personal and social development and economic growth. Human capital has developed as an important factor along with physical capital as the creative ideas of humans began to gain property value with the maturation of industrial society. Highlighting this, neoclassical economic growth theorists such as Robert Solow (1957) [66], advocated the diminishing marginal product of capital and labor and stressed the qualitative and quantitative enhancement of human and physical capital.

Endogenous growth theorists, such as P.M. Romer (1986) [67] and R. Lucas (1998) [68], advocated the importance of knowledge and changes in technology and attempted to explain a portion of the Solow residual—the part of growth that cannot be explained by capital accumulation or increased labor input. New knowledge creation and transfer through R&D investments are important for innovation and economic development. Scholars like T.W. Schultz (1967) [69] and G.S. Becker (1975) [70], who stressed the importance of human capital, claimed that the accumulation of human capital through education ultimately contributes positively to sustainable economic development and tried to explain another portion of the Solow residual. Moreover, they stated that innovation through entrepreneurship (as measured by new firm formation) is an essential factor that can lead to sustainable economic development and explain a certain portion of the Solow residual. Over the years, a variety of arguments have been put forth to address this issue. Each government, irrespective of country, has been accounting for regional and local factors that affect entrepreneurship. This is because entrepreneurship has been regarded as one of the important drivers of sustainable economic development and growth in this current knowledge-based economy [71–74].

The belief that social entrepreneurship can enable local communities to resolve their own issues and integrate underprivileged groups into the community is even more strongly held in the new governance era of today. In particular, each government puts great importance on the potential contribution of social enterprises towards economic development, as the third sector contributes to the creation of social and economic values through many kinds of activities [23,35,36]. Thus, this study examines the relationship between the level of regional economic development and social entrepreneurship (as measured by the number of social enterprises), focusing on government-driven certified social enterprises in each region. For this, the level of regional economic development is used as a dependent variable and the number of certified social enterprises in each region as an explanatory variable. Additionally, physical capital, human capital, knowledge capital, and entrepreneurship that may have an influence on regional economic development are used as control variables.

The physical capital, human capital, knowledge capital, and entrepreneurship, used as controls in this study, are variables that are chiefly used to describe regional economic development. Numerous existing studies have used values or ratios representing the natural logarithm of each variable. Thus, this study used natural logarithm values for physical capital, human capital, knowledge capital, and entrepreneurship.

This study examines the relationship between social entrepreneurship and regional economic development by using time-sequential panel data collected over an 8-year period from 2007 to 2014. In the course of the panel regression analysis, both a fixed-effect model and a random-effect model were used to interpret results and determine which model is more appropriate. Before exploring the relationship between social entrepreneurship and regional economic development by the panel regression analysis, this study also analyzes the relationship between social entrepreneurship and regional economic development by the pooled regression model. Equations (1) and (2) below indicate the pooled and panel regression analysis models used in this study. Using a specification of the Cobb–Douglas production function type generally used in previous empirical studies on regional economic development, this study augments a production function with social enterprise.

$$Y_{it} = \alpha SE_{it}^{\beta_1} P_{it}^{\beta_2} H_{it}^{\beta_3} K_{it}^{\beta_4} E_{it}^{\beta_5} e^{\varepsilon_{it}} \qquad (1)$$

$$Y_{it} = \alpha + \beta_1 SE_{it} + \beta_2 P_{it} + \beta_3 H_{it} + \beta_4 K_{it} + \beta_5 E_{it} + \varepsilon_{it} \qquad (2)$$

In Equations (1) and (2), Y_i indicates the level of economic development of region i, and SE_{it} represents social entrepreneurship measured as the number of certified social enterprise in region i during period t. β_1 represents the estimated coefficient values of regional certified social enterprise variables in the model; that is, an increase of the regional certified social enterprise variable by one percent correspondingly increases the left-hand side (regional economic development) by β_1 percent. β_2, β_3, β_4, and β_5 represent coefficient values of physical capital, human capital, knowledge capital, and entrepreneurship, respectively. Because the level of regional economic development can be affected by regional characteristic variables as well as regional social enterprise, this study includes physical capital, human capital, knowledge capital, and entrepreneurship as control variables in the model. Finally, ε_{it} represents the error term.

3.2. Data and Variables

The key variable for this study is government-driven certified social enterprises funded by central and local governments in South Korea. The Korean government started to support social enterprises with public funding in 2007. This study explores the relationship between government-driven certified social enterprises and regional economic development from 2007 to 2014. Due to the limitations in obtaining data, this study uses the data on the certified social enterprises generated by the Ministry of Employment and Labor of Korea in recent years.

The temporal scope of this study is from 2007, when certification of social enterprises began, up to the end of 2014. In this study, the analysis of the relationship between government-driven social enterprise and regional economic development centers around the period between 2007 and 2014. The spatial extent of this study is nationwide, including 16 key metropolitan region-levels.

Indicators for the other basic variables were drawn from a variety of sources. To collect data on other indicators that are not covered by the Ministry of Knowledge Economy of South Korea, this study uses data on gross regional domestic product per capita, gross fixed capital formation, human capital, knowledge capital, and entrepreneurship from the Korea National Statistical Office. For ease of reference, the basic variables are summarized in Table 2, which also shows a brief description and the data source of each variable.

Table 2. Brief description of variables and data sources.

Variables	Brief Description	Data Sources
Regional Economic Development	Natural log value of Gross Regional Domestic Product per Capita (Unit: 1000 US dollars)	Korea National Statistical Office (KNSO)
Physical Capital	Natural log value of gross fixed capital formation (GFCF) per 1000 economically active population (Unit: 1000 US dollars)	
Human Capital	Natural log value of the percentage of people with college or above degree among economically active population	
Knowledge Capital	Natural log value of total R&D investment (Unit: 1000 US dollars)	
Entrepreneurship	Natural log value of the number of new firm formation	
Social Entrepreneurship	Natural log value of the number of certified social enterprise	Ministry of Knowledge Economy of South Korea
Year 2007	1 = Year 2007; 0 = Others	
Year 2008	1 = Year 2008; 0 = Others	
Year 2009	1 = Year 2009; 0 = Others	
Year 2010	1 = Year 2010; 0 = Others	Calculation by Authors
Year 2011	1 = Year 2011; 0 = Others	
Year 2012	1 = Year 2012; 0 = Others	
Year 2013	1 = Year 2013; 0 = Others	
Year 2014	1 = Year 2014; 0 = Others	

Note: For ease of understanding, this study supposes that 1 US dollar is equal to 1000 Korean Won; the economically active population means aged 15 years and above.

4. Results

4.1. Descriptive Statistics

Before exploring the relationship between social entrepreneurship and regional economic development, this study discusses the descriptive statistics regarding the regional characteristic variables such as physical capital, human capital, knowledge capital, entrepreneurship, and social entrepreneurship as well as regional economic development. Table 3 summarizes descriptive statistics regarding the characteristics of each variable included in empirical models for regional economic development based on pooled data analysis and panel data analysis.

Table 3. Descriptive statistics of each variable by year: 2007–2014 year.

Variables	2007 Mean (S.D.)	2008 Mean (S.D.)	2009 Mean (S.D.)	2010 Mean (S.D.)	2011 Mean (S.D.)	2012 Mean (S.D.)	2013 Mean (S.D.)	2014 Mean (S.D.)	Total Mean (S.D.)
Regional Economic Development	9.938 (0.312)	9.986 (0.324)	10.025 (0.313)	10.116 (0.342)	10.168 (0.346)	10.197 (0.344)	10.225 (0.327)	10.260 (0.312)	10.114 (0.338)
Social Entrepreneurship	0.812 (0.885)	2.372 (0.659)	2.671 (0.647)	3.237 (0.615)	3.482 (0.634)	3.659 (0.613)	3.951 (0.573)	4.206 (0.523)	3.049 (1.206)
Physical Capital	16.570 (0.355)	16.550 (0.345)	16.542 (0.354)	16.582 (0.380)	16.565 (0.422)	16.564 (0.394)	16.594 (0.379)	16.592 (0.373)	16.570 (0.366)
Human Capital	3.463 (0.231)	3.514 (0.229)	3.536 (0.226)	3.558 (0.206)	3.588 (0.205)	3.616 (0.195)	3.653 (0.176)	3.675 (0.171)	3.575 (0.211)
Knowledge Capital	13.641 (1.317)	13.746 (1.284)	13.821 (1.279)	13.937 (1.311)	14.102 (1.275)	14.157 (1.301)	14.193 (1.314)	14.277 (1.280)	13.984 (1.278)
Entrepreneurship	10.491 (0.806)	10.433 (0.811)	10.396 (0.805)	10.407 (0.814)	10.467 (0.795)	10.431 (0.778)	10.395 (0.783)	10.535 (0.765)	10.444 (0.774)
Cases	16	16	16	16	16	16	16	16	128

Note: The number in parentheses (S.D.) represent standard deviation.

On the one hand, Table 3 shows overall descriptive statistics of each variable, where we can see that 16 regions, analyzed over a period of 2007–2014, have mean regional economic development (11.114) with standard deviation (0.338), mean social entrepreneurship (3.049) with standard deviation (1.206), mean physical capital (16.570) with standard deviation (0.366), mean human capital (3.575) with standard deviation (0.211), mean knowledge capital (13.984) with standard deviation (1.278), and mean entrepreneurship (10.444) with standard deviation (0.774). On the other hand, Table 3 shows descriptive statistics of each variable over time variation from 2007 to 2014. First, it is obvious that mean values of regional economic development and social entrepreneurship variables have increased every year since 2007. Second, mean values of control variables such as human capital and knowledge capital variables have increased every year since 2007, but we can see an increase or decrease of mean values of physical capital and entrepreneurship variables since 2007. Figure 3 includes four Geographic Information System (GIS) maps visualizing the number of social enterprises and GDP per capita of 16 regions in 2007 and 2014, respectively.

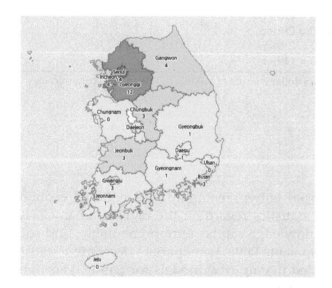

(A) The number of social enterprises in 2007

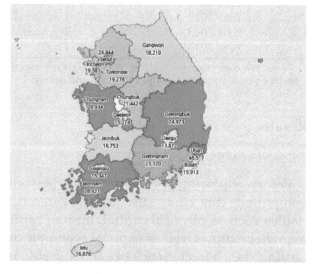

(C) GDP per capita in 2007, US dollar

Figure 3. *Cont.*

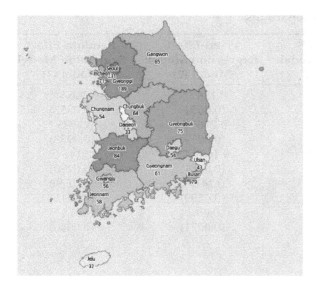
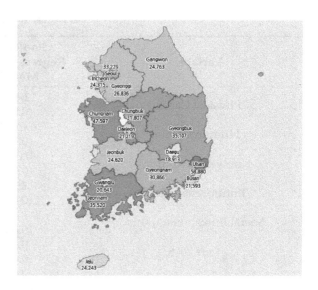

(**B**) The number of social enterprises in 2014   (**D**) GDP per capita in 2014, US dollar

Figure 3. The number of social enterprises and GDP per capita of each region in 2007 and 2014. Note: Sejong region exculded in each GIS map.

Data on GDP per capita and the number of social enterprises statistics that are spatially referenced has allowed a better understanding of the geography of different GDP per capita values and the number of social enterprises. If we look at map (**A**), map (**B**), map (**C**), and map (**D**), we can identify patterns and trends of the number of social enterprises and GDP per capita based on location. These four maps are data driven and use rules based on a number 'attribute' such as social enterprise or GDP per capita in order to style each feature. Each feature in the maps in Figure 3 is color coded based on GDP per capita and the number of social enterprises. In Figure 3, the darker color in each map indicates higher GDP per capita or higher number of social enterprises and lighter colors represent lower GDP per capita or a lower number of social enterprises. If we look at map (**A**) and (**B**), which visualize the number of social enterprises based on location, we can find Seoul, the capital of South Korea, had the highest number of social enterprises among the 16 regions. Gyeonggi province showed the second-highest number of social enterprises in both 2007 and 2014. Compared to the Seoul and Gyeonggi regions, other regions showed very low numbers of social enterprises in 2007; however, they had very high growth rates of the number of social enterprises between 2007 and 2014.

Figure 3 also includes GIS maps visualizing GDP per capita of 16 regions in 2007 and 2014. According to map (C) and (D), Ulsan province had the highest GDP per capita while Daegu province had the lowest GDP per capita in 16 regions. In terms of growth rate of GDP per capita, Chungnam province had the highest and Chungbuk province the second-highest growth rate from 2007 to 2014. Thus, this type of visualization is very useful for identifying patterns and trends of the number of social enterprises and GDP per capita based on location.

4.2. Regression Results: Pooled OLS Regression Resutls and Panel Regression Results

This study conducted a regression analysis using panel data to examine whether there is any relationship between the increase in the natural log value of the number of certified social enterprises and the level of regional economic development. A pooled OLS regression model, fixed-effect model, and random-effect models were used in this study. Table 4 presents specific results of the regression analysis on regional economic development.

Table 4. Regression results.

Variables	Pooled OLS Regression Model: Model (1)	Fixed-Effect Regression Model: Model (2)	Random-Effect Regression Model: Model (3)
Physical Capital	1.0457 *** (0.0602)	0.1769 ** (0.0534)	0.3667 *** (0.0553)
Human Capital	0.6157 *** (0.1102)	0.2561 ** (0.0859)	0.2005 * (0.0933)
Knowledge Capital	−0.0868 *** (0.0242)	0.1689 *** (0.0281)	0.1148 *** (0.0290)
Entrepreneurship	0.1901 *** (0.0498)	0.1418 * (0.0599)	−0.0596 (0.0515)
Social Entrepreneurship	−0.0395 (0.0380)	0.0496 *** (0.0071)	0.0614 *** (0.0080)
Year 2008	0.1186 (0.0805)		
Year 2009	0.1785 (0.0910)		
Year 2010	0.2435 * (0.1095)		
Year 2011	0.3075 ** (0.1168)		
Year 2012	0.3392 ** (0.1242)		
Year 2013	0.3345 * (0.1357)		
Year 2014	0.3499 * (0.1404)		
Constant	−10.3008 *** (1.3612)	2.2731 * (0.9267)	2.1514 * (1.0067)
Rho		0.9933	0.9421
F-value	46.28 ***	220.27 ***	
Wald χ^2			757.92 ***
R^2 Within		0.9114	0.8905
R^2 Between	0.8284	0.0134	0.3602
R^2 Overall		0.0411	0.4211
Number of Observations	128	128	128
Hausman Test		$\chi^2 = 344.12$ ***	

* $P < 0.05$, ** $P < 0.01$, *** $P < 0.001$; the numbers in parentheses represent standard errors.

According to regression results of Model (1) in Table 4, social entrepreneurship has a negative (−), statistically insignificant, effect on GDP per capita (−0.0395) at the 0.05 level. Among control variables, physical capital, human capital, and entrepreneurship have positive (+), statistically significant, effects on GDP per capita, however, knowledge capital has a negative (−), statistically significant, effect on GDP per capita at the 0.05 level. Regression results of Model (1) in Table 4 are not in line with those of previous empirical studies on regional economic development.

For a pooled OLS model to be accurate, some assumptions need to be tested, including no serial correlation, homoscedasticity, and no cross-sectional dependence. Thus, this study implemented the 'Wooldridge test' for serial correlation in panel data because the test requires relatively few assumptions and is easy to implement [75–77]. After employing the Wooldridge test, we found that the null hypothesis of no serial correlation is strongly rejected ($F = 57.081$, Prob $> F = 0.0000$). Also, the output from the first-differenced regression includes standard errors that account for clustering within the panels, therefore other estimators are needed to produce more efficient estimates.

For other estimators in this study, both fixed-effect and random-effect models were used for the regression analyses using panel data, and a Hausman Test was conducted to determine which model was more appropriate. Table 4 presents specific regression results of Model (2) and Model (3).

As indicated in Table 4, in the fixed-effect model (Model (2)), the value of the regression coefficient for regional social entrepreneurship measured as the number of social enterprises indicates statistical significance at the 0.01 level, implying that an increase in the natural log value of the number of regional certified social enterprises has a positive (+) impact on regional economic development. As claimed in numerous previous studies on regional economic development (i.e., [64–73], the regression coefficient values of variables like physical capital, human capital, knowledge capital, and entrepreneurship show statistical significance at the 0.05 level, indicating these variables are positively relevant to regional economic development.

Looking next at the random-effect model (Model (3)), the value of the regression coefficient for regional social entrepreneurship also indicates statistical significance at the 0.01 level, implying that an increase in the natural log value of the number of regional certified social enterprises has a positive (+) impact on regional economic development. Moreover, the regression coefficient values of variables like physical capital, human capital, and knowledge capital, but not entrepreneurship showed statistical significance at the 0.05 level, indicating these variables have a positive (+) impact on regional economic development. However, the regression coefficient values of the entrepreneurship variable indicated no statistical significance at the 0.05 level.

A Hausman Test was conducted to determine which of the two models—fixed-effect model or random-effect model—was more appropriate, and the value of χ^2 at 344.12 was found to be statistically significant at the 0.01 level, indicating the fixed-effect model to be more appropriate. In other words, the result of the Hausman Test shows that we can reject the null hypothesis, which implies that there is no correlation between the error term and the regressors. Thus, we can decide that fixed-effect model is preferred.

Previous studies on entrepreneurship (i.e., [65,78]) suggested the importance of the link of entrepreneurship to regional economic performance by using a production function model including several different measures of entrepreneurship. As claimed in numerous previous studies on regional economic development, the regression coefficient values of variables like physical capital, human capital, knowledge capital, and entrepreneurship in this study also indicate that physical capital, human capital, knowledge capital, and entrepreneurship are all significant and important factors shaping regional economic output. In addition, this study indicates that social enterprise start-up as well as new firm formation is a significant and important factor for regional economic development. The results of this study suggest a new direction for policy that focuses on instruments to enhance regional social entrepreneurship.

5. Discussion

While questions about social entrepreneurship effects can be answered only through conducting empirical studies in a variety of policy contexts, researchers in the area of social entrepreneurship have not adequately tested propositions related to social entrepreneurship effects in regional economic development and are still at an early stage in this research field. As one of only a few empirical studies that has examined social entrepreneurship effects in regional economic development, this study contributed to this research field by exploring effects of social entrepreneurship in regional economic development using objective measure such as gross regional domestic product per capita and the number of certificated social enterprise in South Korea. In particular, to explore the relationships between social entrepreneurship and regional economic development, this study presents a framework that illustrates the theoretical causal relationship between social entrepreneurship and regional economic development; and then analyzes the impact of social entrepreneurship on regional economic development by using data on certificated social enterprises in South Korea. The following summarizes the empirical results from pooled OLS, fixed-effect, and random-effect regression models, which simultaneously control for factors that are theorized to affect regional economic development.

First, results of the fixed-effect and random-effect regression models suggested that the regional GDP per capita increased as the number of regional certified social enterprises increased, indicating that a growth in the number of social enterprises contributes positively to regional economic development. It means that social enterprise start-up and operation contribute to promoting regional economic development. This result is in line with previous studies [4–9,15–17,23,24,27,32–34,61] on social enterprise. In this study, the use of longitudinal study designs helps us better understanding the impact of social entrepreneurship measure as the number of certified social enterprise on regional economic development. Evidence from this study could strengthen and modify the framework, as reliance of previous empirical studies on results from cross-sectional studies in its development is undoubtedly a limitation.

Second, based on results of fixed-effect and random-effect regression models, this study also found that regional economic development variables such as physical capital, human capital, knowledge capital, and entrepreneurship contribute to regional economic development. This supports arguments made by previous studies based on neoclassical economic growth theories (ex. [66]), endogenous growth theories (ex. [67,68]), human capital theories (ex. [69,70]), and entrepreneurship theories (ex. [71–74]). Therefore, the results from this study tie well with the argument made by the variety of social scientists, including economists, state that physical capital, human capital, knowledge capital, and entrepreneurship are important factors in regional economic development [65].

Third, the results suggest a new direction for policy that focuses on instruments to promote regional social entrepreneurship in a region. The results of this study also imply that governments of each region should put forth an effort to implement policies to promote sustainable regional economic development and growth by actively fostering social enterprises there. Because each local government possess the ability to efficiently respond to the immediate needs of social enterprises in their regions, they need to make efforts to promote regional economic development through social enterprise policies.

Since much of the importance of social enterprises comes from their ability to reintegrate into the workforce people from disadvantaged backgrounds, it would also be necessary to measure the impact of social enterprise on the general unemployment rate and, in particular, the rate of unemployment among people with lower levels of education. Because of data unavailability, it was not possible to measure the impact of social enterprise on the rate of unemployment among people with lower levels of education. Alternatively, this study tried to measure the impact of social enterprise on the general unemployment rate of each region by using pooled OLS regression model and panel regression models (fixed-effect and random-effect models). However, the coefficients of social enterprise in regression results by using all empirical models were not statistically significant at the 95% confidence level. Specifically, the value of the regression coefficients of social enterprise for regional unemployment rate were 8.7304 ($p = 0.055$) in pooled OLS regression result, -2.0664 ($p = 0.479$) in fixed-effect panel regression result, and -1.1162 ($p = 0.694$) in random-effect panel regression result, respectively, although the empirical results on the impact of social enterprise on regional unemployment rate were not provided in detail in this study. Thus, more empirical research on the relationship between social enterprise and regional unemployment rate and especially the rate of unemployment among people with lower levels of education is needed in the future.

In addition, it is recommendable to isolate the effect of social enterprise from the effect of other factors; therefore, author of this study included a set of interaction variables in all empirical models such as pooled OLS regression model and panel regression models (fixed-effect and random-effect models) after generating new variables that reflect interactions between social enterprise and physical capital, between social enterprise and human capital, between social enterprise and knowledge capital, and between social enterprise and entrepreneurship. However, all regression results show that social enterprise is not statistically significant at the 95% confidence level. For better understanding of the relationship between social enterprise and regional economic development, follow-up empirical studies considering a variety of interaction effects among social enterprise, physical capital, human capital, knowledge capital, and entrepreneurship are needed in the future.

The South Korean government borrowed the general policy direction and the particular regulatory device from UK social enterprise policy; however, it failed to learn about the specific contexts of the

UK policy and to attempt two-way communication with domestic stakeholders [30,39]. As a result of the failure, a distorted social enterprise policy transfer took place, and the Korean government's social enterprise policy has been biased toward the perspective of the government, not that of stakeholders such as the socially disadvantaged and vulnerable. As mentioned, South Korea has mainly developed social enterprises among various operators in the social economy in response to the global economic crisis and welfare state decline. Thus, the Korean government introduced a plan to support social enterprises and enacted the Social Enterprise Promotion Act (SEPA) in 2007 to provide services and work opportunities for socially excluded people such as the elders, low-income people, working poor, etc., and the ageing population. However, the South Korean social enterprise policy has been biased toward the perspective of the government. The distorted social enterprise policy transfer was caused by the centralized power structures, legacy of top-down control, and one-way communication of the Korean government [30]. A top-down approach with strict controls in centralized power structures is less likely to contribute to social entrepreneurship and innovation. Thus, the South Korean government needs to consider two-way communication with stakeholders to foster better understanding on both sides, although the government's current social enterprise policy has been shown to contribute to regional economic growth as it. The South Korean government needs to be more focused on social enterprise policies based on the needs of the socially disadvantaged and vulnerable rather than a broader response to unemployment in the future.

Finally, unlike in Europe and other countries, social enterprises in South Korea were institutionalized to solve employment and poverty issues of the working poor. They will likely be an alternative to labor market policy, which is inevitably underscored in an aging society with poverty issues among the elderly. Aging faster than western societies, South Korea is facing problems with employment and welfare, including workforce reduction, reduced productivity, and an increased fiscal burden. Therefore, an employment strategy for the elderly in the area of social economy is an important policy measure necessary for employment stability and social welfare. In this perspective, the development of regional social enterprise for the elderly is to be recommended as one possible method to help solve the problems of employment and welfare for the elderly in South Korea. Also, more empirical research on the role of senior social entrepreneurship in regional economic development is needed in the future.

References

1.   Taylor, J.B. The Financial Crisis and the Policy Responses: An Empirical Analysis of What Went Wrong. In *NBER Working Paper Series No. 14631*; National Bureau of Economic Research: Cambridge, MA, USA, 2009.

2.   Baldacci, E.; Gupta, S.; Granados, C. How Effective is Fiscal Policy Response in Systemic Banking Crises? In *IMF Working Paper No. 160*; International Monetary Fund: Washington, DC, USA, 2009.

3.   Claessens, S.; Dell'Ariccia, G.; Igan, D.; Laeven, L. Cross-country Experiences and Policy Implications from the Global Financial Crisis. *Econ. Policy* **2010**, *25*, 267–293. [CrossRef]

4.   European Commission. *White Book on Growth, Competitiveness, Employment*; Office for Publications: Luxembourg, 1993.

5.   Defourny, J.; Delveterre, P. *The Social Economy: The Worldwide Making of a Third Sector*; Centre d'Economie Sociale: Liege, Belgium, 1999.

6.   Evans, M.; Syrett, S. Generating Social Capital? The Social Economy and Local Economic Development. *Eur. Urban Reg. Studies* **2007**, *14*, 55–74. [CrossRef]

7.   Noya, A.; Clarence, E. *The Social Economy: Building Inclusive Communities*; OECD Publishing: Paris, France, 2007.

8.   Monzon, J.L.; Chavez, R. The European Social Economy: Concept and Dimensions of the Third Sector. *Ann. Public Coop. Econ.* **2008**, *79*, 549–577. [CrossRef]

9.   Monzon, J.L.; Chavez, R. *The Social Economy in the European Union*; Centre of Research and Information on the Public, Social and Cooperative Economy (CIRIEC): Liege, Belgium, 2012.

10.   Spear, R. *Social Economy: Laying the Groundwork for Innovative Solution to Today's Challenges*; Publications Office of the European Union: Luxembourg, 2013.

11.   Kim, J.H.; Lee, J.K. *Impact of Financial Support for Social Enterprises on Job Creation and Performance of Social Enterprises*; National Assembly Special Committee on Budget and Accounts: Seoul, Korea, 2012.

12.   Kim, J.H.; Lee, J.K. An Analysis on the Economic and Social Performance of the Social Enterprises in Korea: Focusing on the Effects of Governmental Subsidies. *Korean Public Adm. Q.* **2012**, *24*, 1037–1063.

13.   Jeon, B.Y.; Kim, S.K.; Bhan, J.H.; Shin, H.K.; Oh, C.H.; Lee, B.H.; Lee, H.J.; Lee, I.J.; Jang, J.I.; Jang, H.G.; et al. *A Field Study on Social Enterprises*; Korea Social Enterprise Promotion Agency: Gyeonggi, Korea, 2012.

14.   Doh, S.; Park, K. Social Enterprises and Job Creation in South Korea. *Korean Public Adm. Rev.* **2014**, *48*, 495–520.

15.   Aiken, M. *What is the Role of Social Enterprise in Finding, Creating and Maintaining Employment for Disadvantaged Groups?* A Social Enterprise Think Piece for the Office of Third Sector, Cabinet Office: London, UK, 2007.

16.   Mendell, M.; Nogales, R. Social Enterprises in OECD Member Countries: What are the Financial Streams? In *The Changing Boundaries of Social Enterprises*; Noya, A., Ed.; OECD Publishing: Paris, France, 2009.

17.   Fonteneau, B.; Neamtan, N.; Wanyama, F.; Pereira, L.; de Poorter, M.; Borzaga, C.; Galera, G.; Fox, T.; Ojong, N. *Social and Solidarity Economy: Our Common Road towards Decent Work*; International Training Center of the International Labor Organization: Turin, Italy, 2011.

18.   Dees, J.G. Enterprising Nonprofits. *Harv. Bus. Rev.* **1998**, *76*, 55–67.

19.   Dees, J.G. *The Meaning of "Social Entrepreneurship"*; Center for the Advancement of Social Entrepreneurship (CASE), Duke University: Durham, NC, USA, 1998.

20.   Defourny, J.; Nyssens, M. Conceptions of Social Enterprise and Social Entrepreneurship in Europe and the United States: Convergences and Divergences. *J. Soc. Entrep.* **2010**, *1*, 32–53. [CrossRef]

21.   Petrella, F.; Richez-Battesti, N. Social Entrepreneur, Social Entrepreneurship, Social Enterprise: Semantics and Controversies. *J. Innov. Econ. Manag.* **2014**, *14*, 143–156. [CrossRef]

22.   Cieslik, K. Moral Economy Meets Social Enterprise Community-based Green Energy Project in Rural Burundi. *World Dev.* **2016**, *83*, 12–26. [CrossRef]

23.   Kerlin, J.A. A Comparative Analysis of the Global Emergence of Social Enterprise. *Volunt. Int. J. Volunt. Non-Profit Organ.* **2010**, *21*, 162–179. [CrossRef]

24.   Smith, G.; Teasdale, S. Associate Democracy and the Social Economy: Exploring the Regulatory Challenge. *Econ. Soc.* **2012**, *41*, 151–176. [CrossRef]

25.   Defourny, J. 'Introduction'. In *The Emergence of Social Enterprise*; Borzaga, C., Defourny, J., Eds.; Routledge: London, UK, 2001; pp. 1–28.

26.   Westlund, H. Form or Contents? On the Concept of Social Economy. *Int. J. Soc. Econ.* **2003**, *30*, 1192–1206. [CrossRef]

27.   Nyssens, M. *Social Enterprise: At the Crossroads of Market, Public Policies and Civil Society*; Routledge: London, UK, 2006.

28.   Ridley-Duff, R. Social Enterprise as a Socially Rational Business. *Int. J. Entrep. Behav. Res.* **2008**, *14*, 291–312. [CrossRef]

29.   Heckl, E.; Pecher, I. *Study on Practices and Policies in the Social Enterprise Sector in Europe*; Austrian Institute for SME Research: Vienna, Austria, 2006.

30.   Park, C.; Lee, J.; Wilding, M. Distorted Policy Transfer? South Korea's Adaptation of UK Social Enterprise Policy. *Policy Studies* **2017**, *38*, 39–58. [CrossRef]

31.   Daly, H.; Cobb, J.B. *For the Common Good: Redirecting the Economy towards Community, the Environment and a Sustainable Future*; Green Print: London, UK, 1990.

32.   European Commission. *Local Initiatives for Economic Development and Employment*; Office for Publications: Luxembourg, 1995.

33.   Pearce, J. *Social Enterprise in Anytown*; Calouste Gulbenkian Foundation: London, UK, 2003.

34.   Birkhölzer, K. Development and Perspectives of the Social Economy or Third Sector in Germany. In *Nordic Civic Society Organizations and the Future of Welfare Services*; Matthies, A.L., Ed.; Nordic Council of Ministers: Copenhagen, Denmark, 2006; pp. 343–370.

35.   Defourny, J.; Nyssens, M. Defining Social Enterprise. In *Social Enterprise*; Nyssens, J., Ed.; Routledge: London, UK, 2006.

36. Doherty, B.; Foster, G.; Mason, C.; Meehan, J.; Meehan, K.; Rotheroe, N.; Royce, M. *Management for Social Enterprise*; Sage Publication: London, UK, 2009.
37. Young, D.R.; Salamon, L.M. Commercialization, Social Ventures, and For-profit Competition. In *The State of Nonprofit America*; Salamon, L.M., Ed.; Brookings Institution: Washington, DC, USA, 2002; pp. 425–448.
38. Aiken, M.; Slater, R. Feeling the Squeeze? Tabbies or Tigers: The Case of Social Enterprises Contracting in the Fields of Recycling and Work Integration. In Proceedings of the 4th Annual Social Enterprise Research Conference, London, UK, 4–5 July 2007.
39. Carmel, E.; Harlock, J. Instituting the Third Sector as a Governable Terrain: Partnership, Procurement and Performance in the UK. *Policy Politics* **2008**, *36*, 155–171. [CrossRef]
40. OECD. *Social Enterprises*; OECD Publishing: Paris, France, 1999.
41. Young, D.R. New Trends in the US Non-profit Sector: Towards Market Integration? In *The Non-profit Sector in a Changing Economy*; OECD Publishing: Paris, France, 2003; pp. 61–77.
42. Kerlin, J.A. (Ed.) A Comparison of Social Enterprise Models and Contexts. In *Social Enterprise: A Global Comparison*; Tuft University Press: Lebanon, 2009; pp. 184–200.
43. Moizer, J.; Tracey, P. Strategy Making in Social Enterprise: The Role of Resource Allocation and Its Effects on Organizational Sustainability. *Syst. Res. Behav. Sci.* **2010**, *27*, 252–266. [CrossRef]
44. Williams, C.C. Developing a Culture of Volunteering beyond the Third Sector Approach. *J. Volunt. Sect. Res.* **2008**, *1*, 25–44.
45. Williams, C.C. Harnessing Voluntary Work: A Fourth Sector Approach. *Policy Studies* **2010**, *23*, 247–260. [CrossRef]
46. Sabeti, H. *The Emerging Fourth Sector*; The Aspen Institute: Washington, DC, USA, 2009.
47. Cohen, R.J.; Hansen-Turton, T. The Birth of a Fourth Sector. *Phila. Soc. Innov. J.* **2009**, *1*, 81.
48. Jimenez, J.; Morales, A.C. Social Economy and the Fourth Sector, Base and Protagonist of Social Innovation. *CIRIEC Esp. Rev. Econ. Pulica Soc. Coop.* **2011**, *73*, 33–60.
49. Yoon, J.W.; Park, D.H.; Bahn, J.S. The Fourth Sector Driven Regional Development: A Case Study on the Hwacheon-County's Tourism Development. *Korea Local Adm. Rev.* **2013**, *27*, 317–352.
50. Bidet, E.; Spear, R. The Role of Social Enterprise in European Labour Markets. In *EMES Network Working Paper No. 03/10*; EMES International Research Network: Liege, Belgium, 2003.
51. Amin, A. Extraordinarily Ordinary: Working in the Social Economy. *Soc. Enterp. J.* **2009**, *5*, 30–49. [CrossRef]
52. Park, C.; Wilding, M. An Exploratory Study on the Potential of Social Enterprise to Act as the Institutional Glue of Network Governance. *Soc. Sci. J.* **2014**, *51*, 120–129. [CrossRef]
53. Birkhölzer, K. The Role of Social Enterprise in Local Economic Development. In Proceedings of the 2nd EMES International Conference on Social Enterprise, Trento, Italy, 1–4 July 2009.
54. Haugh, H.; Tracy, P. *Role of Social Enterprise in Regional Development*; Judge Institute of Management Studies: Cambridge, UK, 1997.
55. CIRIEC. *The Social Economy in the European Union*; The European Economic and Social Committee (EESC): Brussel, Belgium, 2012.
56. Musgrave, R.A.; Musgrave, P.B. *Public Finance in Theory and Practice*; McGraw-Hill: New York, NY, USA, 1984.
57. Arrow, K.J. An Extension of the Basic Theorems of Classical Welfare Economics. In Proceedings of the Second Berkeley Symposium on Mathematical Statistics and Probability, Statistical Laboratory of the University of California, Berkeley, USA, 31 July–12 August 1950; Neyman, J., Ed.; University of California Press: Berkeley, CA, USA, 1951; pp. 507–532.
58. Debreu, G. *The Theory of Value*; Yale University Press: New Haven, CT, USA, 1959.
59. Greenwald, B.; Stiglitz, J.E. Externalities in Economies with Imperfect Information and Incomplete Markets. *Q. J. Econ.* **1986**, *101*, 229–264. [CrossRef]
60. Park, C.I. Government Support to the Social Enterprises and their Development in South Korea. *Citiz. World* **2009**, *15*, 165–186.
61. Castelli, L. *European Social Entrepreneurs: Looking for a Better Way to Produce and to Live*; LE MAT Partnership: Ancona, Italy, 2005.
62. National Assembly Budget Office. *Evaluation on Social Enterprise Promotion Program*; National Assembly Budget Office: Seoul, Korea, 2012.

63. Korea Social Enterprise Promotion Agency (KoSEA). Available online: http://www.socialenterprise.or.kr/eng/certification/support.do (accessed on 3 October 2020).
64. Ministry of Employment and Labor. *The 2nd Social Enterprises Promotion Master Plan (2013–2017)*; Ministry of Employment and Labor: Sejong, Korea, 2012.
65. Doh, S.; McNeely, C. A Multi-dimensional Perspective on Social Capital and Economic Development: An Exploratory Analysis. *Ann. Reg. Sci.* **2012**, *49*, 821–843. [CrossRef]
66. Solow, R.S. Technical Change and the Aggregate Production Function. *Rev. Econ. Stat.* **1957**, *39*, 312–320. [CrossRef]
67. Romer, P.M. Increasing Returns and Long-run Growth. *J. Political Econ.* **1986**, *94*, 1002–1037. [CrossRef]
68. Lucas, R. On the Mechanics of Economic Development. *J. Monet. Econ.* **1988**, *22*, 3–42. [CrossRef]
69. Schultz, T.W. *The Economic Value of Education*; Columbia University Press: New York, NY, USA, 1967.
70. Becker, G.S. *Human Capital: A Theoretical and Empirical Analysis with Special Reference to Education*; National Bureau of Economic Research: New York, NY, USA, 1975.
71. Grossman, G.M.; Helpman, E. Endogenous Innovation in the Theory of Growth. *J. Econ. Perspect.* **1994**, *8*, 23–44. [CrossRef]
72. Kirzner, I.M. Entrepreneurial Discovery and the Competitive Market Process: An Austrian Approach. *J. Econ. Lit.* **1997**, *35*, 60–85.
73. Baumol, W.J. Entrepreneurial Enterprises, Large Established Firms and Other Components of the Free-market Growth Machine. *Small Bus. Econ.* **2004**, *23*, 9–21. [CrossRef]
74. Acs, Z.J. How is Entrepreneurship Good for Economic Growth. *Innovations* **2006**, *1*, 97–107. [CrossRef]
75. Wooldridge, J.M. *Econometric Analysis of Cross Section and Panel Data*; MIT Press: Cambridge, MA, USA, 2002.
76. Drukker, D.M. Testing for Serial Correlation in Linear Panel-data Models. *Stata J.* **2003**, *3*, 168–177. [CrossRef]
77. Grozdić, V.; Marić, B.; Radišić, M.; Šebestová, J.; Lis, M. Capital Investments and Manufacturing Firms' Performance: Panel-data Analysis. *Sustainability* **2020**, *12*, 1689. [CrossRef]
78. Audretsch, D.; Keilbach, M. Entrepreneurship Capital and Economic Performance. *Reg. Stud.* **2004**, *38*, 949–959. [CrossRef]

2

Type of Entrepreneurial Activity and Sustainable Development Goals

Ana Venâncio *⑩ and Inês Pinto⑩

ISEG-Lisbon School of Economics and Management, Universidade de Lisboa, and ADVANCE/CSG, 1200-781 Lisbon, Portugal; inespinto@iseg.ulisboa.pt
* Correspondence: avenancio@iseg.ulisboa.pt

Abstract: In this study, we conduct an exploratory study with the aim to investigate whether the type of entrepreneurial activity contributes to the achievement of sustainable development goals (SDGs) in its five dimensions (people, prosperity, planet, peace, and partnership). In addition, we evaluate whether foreign direct investment (FDI) strengthens or reduces these relations. To do so, we apply a multivariate analysis to a sample of 67 countries and find that entrepreneurship contributes negatively to the achievement of SDGs. This effect is mostly due to necessity and non-innovative entrepreneurships, and is evident in the people, prosperity, and partnership dimensions. Nonetheless, FDI helps to diminish this negative effect, as it improves the relation between entrepreneurships, particularly necessity entrepreneurships, and SDG achievement. The main dimension which experiences an improvement due to FDI is people.

Keywords: sustainable development goals; opportunity entrepreneurship; necessity entrepreneurship; innovative entrepreneurship; non-innovative entrepreneurship

---

1. Introduction

Today, the United Nations' Sustainable Development Goals (SDGs) provide a legitimate framework to guide the daily activities of businesses and society. The SDGs highlight the need to change the unsustainable path pursued up to now [1] and to address the main economic, social, and environmental challenges. Entrepreneurial activity may play a significant role in this change [2,3] by contributing to the three pillars of SDGs, namely, economic prosperity, social equity, and environmental protection.

Entrepreneurial action shapes the economic, social, and environmental context of a country. In fact, entrepreneurs create the change that incumbent firms fail to perform due to organisational inertia or the risk of cannibalising existing business models [4]. For this reason, entrepreneurship is usually associated with economic growth [5]. Nonetheless, the effects of entrepreneurship differ according to the type of activity, and in some cases, entrepreneurship only generates turbulence and deploys resources [6,7].

Different motivations exist for undertaking an entrepreneurial venture. Some studies distinguish between opportunity and necessity entrepreneurship activities: Positive factors, such as opportunities to socially develop or simply the desire to be independent; and negative motivations, such as unemployment or the general dissatisfaction with the current situation [8]. Other studies distinguish between innovative and non-innovative entrepreneurial activities and find that their effect on economic performance is different [9]. As the motivation to start a new venture affects its performance [8], the understanding of which type of entrepreneurial activity supports the transition towards sustainable development is of special interest [2].

Despite the increase in the sustainability-related entrepreneurship literature, the number of studies is still lacking, and those that exist remain mostly conceptual. The limited research on the role of start-ups in achieving SDGs is unfortunate, especially as the UN has identified entrepreneurship, together with innovation, as being key elements in addressing sustainable development challenges [10]. Therefore, a need exists for studies that empirically investigate the outcomes of entrepreneurship for sustainable development.

Our paper aims to fill this gap by exploring the relationship between the type of entrepreneurship and sustainability, contributing to the development of the theory of this phenomenon. We investigate whether and under what circumstances entrepreneurship can contribute to the economic, environmental, and social dimensions of SDGs. One of novelties of this study is that attention is devoted to evaluating the effect of the different types of entrepreneurial activity on SDGs. This study focuses on two classifications which have gained importance in classifying entrepreneurial motives; namely, opportunity versus necessity entrepreneurship [11] and innovative versus non-innovative entrepreneurship [12]. We also evaluate the role of foreign direct investment (FDI) in mediating the relation between the different types of entrepreneurial activity and SDGs. FDI plays a key role in financing the achievement of SDGs [13] and consequently, together with entrepreneurship, can contribute to achieving these goals. Additionally, our study contains countries under different economic conditions, which allow us to study the interactions of entrepreneurship with SDGs in different contexts.

Our research provides evidence that the type of entrepreneurship influences the achievement of the global index scores of SDGs, and that FDI may act as a moderator in these relations.

This study contributes to the sustainable development literature by attempting to respond to the call for a better understanding of the role of entrepreneurship in achieving SDGs. Hall, Daneke, and Lenox (2010) [14] find that although the UN recognizes entrepreneurship as an important driver of sustainable development, there is little knowledge about under what conditions entrepreneurs can simultaneously foster economic growth, advance environmental goals, and improve social conditions. Our study also contributes new insights to decision-makers for developing policies to support the achievement of SDGs. A better understanding of the conditions under which entrepreneurship can contribute to sustainable development is needed to enact better policies accordingly.

The paper is organised as follows: In the next section, we review the relevant literature. Section 3 presents the data, and in Section 4 we explain the empirical method. Section 5 presents the empirical results. Section 6 gives the conclusion and a discussion of the main results.

2. The Contribution of Entrepreneurship to the Sustainable Development

Entrepreneurship influences the achievement of SDGs in its three pillars: Economic prosperity, social equity, and environmental protection. Sustainable entrepreneurship intends to balance these three dimensions simultaneously, linking business and sustainable development [15,16]. Due to the difficulties inherent in trying to achieve these objectives simultaneously, sustainable entrepreneurship is a more complex phenomenon than entrepreneurship driven only by economic incentives [16].

Recently, researchers have applied the theory of planned behaviour [17] to explain intention formation in sustainable entrepreneurship [16,18]. According with this theory, an individual's attitudes, motivations, and beliefs together shape said individual's behaviours. Forming a new firm is usually triggered by profit expectations [19] or by the difference between expected profits and current wages [20,21]. However, certain individuals are reconsidering this economic motivation to strike a balance between the environment and society [22].

New ventures typically address the economic prosperity dimension, as they are considered as drivers of economic growth, employment generation, and technological upgrading [23,24]. New ventures exploit opportunities usually not well-understood by incumbent firms [25,26] that are displaced in a process of "creative destruction" [12]. Individual's beliefs can help them to uncover new sustainable opportunities and address the social and environmental dimensions of the SDGs. Therefore, entrepreneurs can change the business environment by redesigning industries toward a sustainable path [26–28].

Entrepreneurship contributes to most of the individual SDGs [15]. In fact, entrepreneurship has a strong direct engagement with industry, innovation, and infrastructure (SDG 9); good health and well-being (SGD 3); responsible consumption and production (SGD 12) [29]; and economic development (SGD 8) [3]. Other SDGs are addressed either indirectly, or in an aggregated term. For instance, new ventures can indirectly influence the following: Causes of poverty (SDG1), a lack of education (SDG 4), affordable energy (SDG 7), and climate action (SDG 13) [3,29]. For example, Cohen and Winn (2007) [26] show that market failures contributed to environmental degradation, but also provided opportunities to entrepreneurs to introduce new business models. Nevertheless, some goals are less suitable for entrepreneurial contributions than others; for example, SDG 17 (partnership for the goals) and SDG 16 (peace, justice, and strong institutions), because the underlining indicators depend largely on governmental action [29]. Nonetheless, Pacheco, Dean, and Payne (2010) [30] argue that entrepreneurs can also influence their institutional context. However, importantly, entrepreneurial activities for sustainable development may run the risk of achieving one goal at the expense of another one. Therefore, it is important to evaluate the effects of entrepreneurial activity globally and per goal.

However, many new ventures might not be agents of change with regards to sustainability, and some might actually create negative effects. Unsustainable businesses that are triggered by profit expectations [19] usually misuse resources, negatively affecting the environment [31,32]. In many industries, start-ups can simply originate "turbulence" [6,7]. Marginal start-ups with a low likelihood of survival displace incumbent firms and other marginal start-ups. These "revolving door" start-ups are continuously entering and exiting the market destroying jobs and deploying resources that could be used more efficiently by other firms. This situation is even more pronounced in countries with weak institutions, which incentivises unproductive entrepreneurship [33].

Empirically, few studies have examined whether and how entrepreneurship can foster sustainable development. The literature finds that entrepreneurship does not contribute positively to all dimensions of sustainable development. Indeed, Youssef et al. (2018) [32] and Dhahri and Omri (2018) [34] find that entrepreneurship does not contribute to the environmental dimension goal. According to Youssef et al. (2018) [32], formal and informal entrepreneurships increase pollution, particularly in low-income countries [35]. In high-income countries, [35] finds an inverted U-shaped relation between entrepreneurship and pollution. On a positive note, [34] suggest that entrepreneurship positively contributes to economic and social dimensions, and Pansera and Sarkar (2016) [36] argue that resource-scarce entrepreneurs derive the maximum value from limited resources contributing positively to the achievement of SDGs.

To sum up, as entrepreneurship can positively and negatively influence the achievement of SDGs, we posit that:

Hypothesis 1. *Entrepreneurship is likely to influence the achievement of SDGs.*

The prevalence of the effect depends on the type of entrepreneurial activity. Indeed, not every kind of entrepreneurship has the same impact in the economy and society. Entrepreneurship is rather heterogeneous and complex, in which innovative and opportunity entrepreneurs occur along with non-innovators and escapees from unemployment [37]. Accordingly, new firm creation is not necessarily associated with economic growth and innovation, particularly in less-developed countries. The positive relation between economic growth and entrepreneurial activity only occurs when "opportunity entrepreneurs" (those motivated by market opportunities) are separate from "necessity entrepreneurs" (those motivated by a lack of opportunities in the labour market) [38]. Indeed, opportunity entrepreneurs take advantage of market opportunities and introduce new products, services, or processes [39], and can also tackle sustainable opportunities. Fostering opportunity entrepreneurship leads to economic growth [40] and job creation in both developed and developing economies [41]. Opportunity entrepreneurship reflects the creation of knowledge and technology, which in the end positively affects economic growth and social development. Therefore, countries with a higher level of opportunity entrepreneurship achieve faster growth and higher economic prosperity. In developing countries, where inequalities are more pronounced, opportunity entrepreneurship increases employment and economic growth, while reducing inequalities. In addition, opportunity entrepreneurs might see sustainable opportunities (in production efficiency, energy, and education, for example) as being a competitive advantage [14]. In fact, Shepherd and Patzelt (2011) [15] and York and Venkataraman (2010) [42] argue that entrepreneurship can be a solution to the environmental challenges by contributing to their preservation and biodiversity. However, balancing the desire to make profits with maintaining economic efficiency and environmental protection is not simple [43]. Entrepreneurs often emphasise individual rewards over sustainability goals by adopting behaviours that are harmful to the environment [34].

In contrast, entrepreneurs who start their businesses out of necessity due to the lack of alternative employment opportunities have different characteristics [44]. For example, they have inferior human capital endowments (in terms of formal education and relevant experiences) that negatively affect start-ups' performance and economic growth [45]. As necessity entrepreneurship is replaced by opportunity entrepreneurship, the level of economic development increases [46]. Because necessity entrepreneurs are pushed into entrepreneurship, they usually have less time and fewer resources in terms of capital and knowledge [47,48]. Thereby, while opportunity entrepreneurship usually involves attempts to exploit new market opportunities, necessity entrepreneurship is more likely to be imitative ventures. Additionally, necessity and informal entrepreneurships make a higher contribution to environment pollution in comparison to opportunity and formal entrepreneurships [49].

To sum up, opportunity entrepreneurs are positively associated with economic prosperity and social equity, and contribute significantly to job creation, product innovation, and the exploitation of sustainable business opportunities. In contrast, necessity entrepreneurship can negatively affect the achievement of SDGs, because of their lower contribution to economic growth and social equity and their higher contribution to pollution. Therefore, we posit that:

Hypothesis 2a. *Opportunity-driven entrepreneurship is likely to positively influence the achievement of SDGs.*

Hypothesis 2b. *Necessity-driven entrepreneurship is likely to negatively influence the achievement of SDGs.*

By the same token, a new firm may not necessarily lead to a technological upgrade or industrial growth [50,51]. Therefore, it is important to distinguish between innovative entrepreneurs, (those who introduce product innovations, new processes, and new forms of organisations) and non-innovative entrepreneurs [12,52]. Further, Baumol (2005) [53] argues that most of the new firm entries are due to imitators or replicators, and that only a tiny minority are due to innovators.

Innovative and high growth entrepreneurs, also known as Schumpeterian entrepreneurs, positively affect economic growth [54]. These innovative entrepreneurs are distinguished by their ability to search for and create new market opportunities [55]. Their academic education allows them to develop knowledge-based technology or research-driven opportunities [56]. Innovative entrepreneurs thereby convert advances in knowledge into economic growth. In addition, innovative entrepreneurship can be a source of societal progress by reducing inequalities [57]. Nonetheless, the definition of innovative entrepreneurship highlights that these entrepreneurs temporarily take advantage of a monopoly position. In terms of environmental sustainability, Youssef et al. (2018) [32] argue that certain conditions have to be met to ensure the positive effect of entrepreneurship. Among these conditions, the authors show that the innovation when combined with entrepreneurship improves the quality of the environment.

Like necessity entrepreneurship, non-innovative entrepreneurship is less likely to foster economic growth and job creation. These entrepreneurs do not have the ability to introduce new production methods, such as technological products or services or even a new organisational form, because, in effect, they replicate previous ventures and mainly create "turbulence" in the market [6,7].

To sum up, innovative entrepreneurs positively contribute to the economic, environmental, and social dimensions of the SDGs; and non-innovative entrepreneurs make less of a contribution to economic growth and social equity. Therefore, we posit:

Hypothesis 3a. *Innovative entrepreneurship is likely to positively influence the achievement of SDGs.*

Hypothesis 3b. *Non-innovative entrepreneurship is likely to negatively influence the achievement of SDGs.*

3. The Role of FDI on the Relationship between the Type of Entrepreneurship and the Sustainable Development

Some studies provide conflicting evidence regarding the relation between FDI and entrepreneurship [58]. While Doytch and Epperson (2012) [59] find that FDI positively affects entrepreneurship, De Backer and Sleuwaegen (2003) [60] find that FDI discourages entry and even stimulates the exit of domestic entrepreneurs. On one hand, FDI can stimulate local entrepreneurship by reinforcing cooperation between foreign investors and host firms [61]. This cooperation contributes to the development of new products and new technology by diffusing knowledge and managerial practices [62]. These contributions help to create new markets and entrepreneurial opportunities that provide access to critical resources, such as financial capital [63]. FDI can also boost export competitiveness by bringing technical and knowledge externalities [64]. However, foreign investors can increase competition for local entrepreneurs that crowds out possible entrants and raises the barriers to entry, as foreign competitors are usually more technologically advanced and can better exploit economies of scale [65]. The prevalence of the effect depends on the structure of FDI inflows (inward versus outward FDI), types of entrepreneurship, and the technological gap or institutional support of the host country [65]. For example, Kim and Li (2014) [66] provide evidence that the positive impact of FDI on firm formation is most relevant in countries which are characterised by weak institutional support, particularly in the less-developed countries.

Turning now to the type of entrepreneurial activity, Albulescuab and Tămăşilă (2014) [65] conclude that the effect of FDI on the entrepreneurship depends on the motivations to start a new venture. FDI has a positive effect on opportunity entrepreneurs, as it leads to uncovering untapped market opportunities. Entrepreneurial activity can increase as multinational firms enter the market due to the demand effect. With regards to necessity entrepreneurs, while inward FDI does not influence this type of entrepreneurship, outward FDI can positively influence it. When capital leaves the country, it has a negative effect on job creation that stimulates the necessity of entrepreneurial activity.

Although the empirical literature presents mixed results regarding knowledge spill overs from FDI [67], the majority of empirical studies conclude that inward FDI has a positive influence on local innovative activities [68]. Using a large firm-level sample, Gorodnichenco, Svejanar, and Terrell (2020) [69] show that FDI has a positive spill over effect on product and technology innovations by domestic firms.

FDI influences entrepreneurship according to the motivations which underlie its activity, and in turn, entrepreneurship has an effect on sustainable development. Thus, we consider that it is relevant to assess the moderating effect that FDI might have between the type of entrepreneurship and the achievement of SDGs.

FDI plays a key role in providing access to capital and knowledge [64,68], and therefore foreign investors might reinforce the positive effect of opportunity and innovative entrepreneurship on SDGs. FDI can also reinforce the positive effect of entrepreneurship on the economic and social dimensions of SDGs. Furthermore, FDI brings about technical and informational externalities and promotes economic growth and fosters job creation. In addition, FDI can encourage new firms to develop new products due to increased demand in the host country [70].

FDI can offset the negative effect between necessity-driven entrepreneurs who have fewer capital- or knowledge-based resources available [47,48] and non-innovative entrepreneurs who are characterised by a lack of innovative products and services and the achievement of SDGs. Moreover, FDI can encourage knowledge diffusion and improve the managerial skills of both. This diffusion can occur directly when workers employed in foreign-owned firms transition to entrepreneurship. Additionally, both necessity and non-innovative entrepreneurs can offer comparable products by imitating their foreign competitors, while leveraging their local knowledge. With this knowledge, non-innovative entrepreneurs can more easily identify new markets, as they are comparatively more difficult and costly for foreign competitors to identify [70]. Overall, together with necessity entrepreneurship, FDI is likely to positively influence economic and social dimensions. Thus, we state the following hypotheses:

Hypothesis 4a. *FDI is likely to reinforce the positive effect between opportunity-driven and innovative entrepreneurship and the achievement of SDGs.*

Hypothesis 4b. *FDI is likely to reduce the negative effect between necessity and non-innovative entrepreneurship and the achievement of SDGs.*

Figure 1 shows the proposed model, including the hypothesised relationships. In this model, FDI has a moderating role between entrepreneurial activity and the achievement of SDGs.

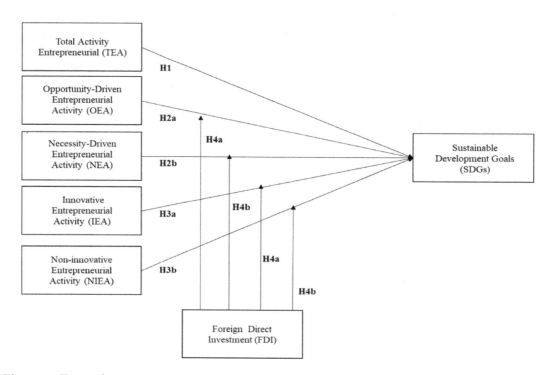

Figure 1. Type of entrepreneurial activity and Sustainable Development Goals (SDGs) model.

4. Data

To implement our empirical analysis, we match data from the Sustainable Development Goals Index (SDG Index) [71] with the GEM Adult Population Survey. We supplement these data with information from the World Bank and the OECD national accounts data. GEM is a cross-national survey that uses standardised definitions and procedures on entrepreneurship and has existed since 1999 [72]. Regarding the SDG score, we use the 2019 Sustainable Development Report [71], which provides a score for 193 countries on their achievement of SDGs. For each SDG, the index integrates a wide range of statistical indicators.

Due to the lack of data, we do not include in our sample low-income countries. Our sample captures the variance across 67 lower-middle, upper-middle, or high-income countries for the period from 2015 and 2018. Thus, the dataset is a cross-section of 67 countries averaged over the period of 2015 to 2018 for all independent variables. See Table 1 for the definitions of variables, and Table A1 in the Appendix A for a list of countries included in the sample.

Table 1. Variable definitions.

Variables	Definition
Panel A: Dependent Variables	
SDG Scores	SDG index on a country's performance on the 17 SDGs (Sachs et al., 2019) for the year of 2019.
People	SDGs' score for the following goals: No poverty, zero hunger, good health, quality education, gender equality, clean water, and sanitation.
Prosperity	SDGs' score for the following goals: Affordable and clean energy; decent work and economic growth; industry, innovation, and infrastructure; reduced inequality.
Planet	SDGs' score for the following goals: Sustainable cities and communities, responsible consumption and production, climate action, life below water, life on land.
Peace	SDGs' score for the following goals: Peace, justice, and strong institutions.
Partnership	SDGs' score for the following goal: Partnerships.
Panel B: Independent Variables	
Total Entrepreneurial Activity (TEA)	Proportion of 18–64 population who are nascent entrepreneurs or owner-managers.
Necessity Entrepreneurship (NEA)	Proportion of total entrepreneurial activity which reported no better option for work.
Opportunity Entrepreneurship (OEA)	Proportion of total entrepreneurial activity that is driven by opportunity.
Innovative Entrepreneurship (IEA)	Proportion of total entrepreneurial activity that offers new products or services to some or all customers and is offered by few or no other competitors.
Non-innovative Entrepreneurship (NIEA)	Proportion of total entrepreneurial activity that does not offer new products or services.
Government Expenditure (GOVEXP)	Sum of the general government's final consumption and military, health, and education expenditures as a percentage of the GDP.
Foreign Direct Investment (FDI)	Net inflows (new investment inflows less disinvestment) from foreign investors divided by the GDP.
Population (POP)	Country's population in millions.

Table 2 provides the descriptive statistics by country and income group.

Table 2. Descriptive Statistics.

	HIC	UMIC	LMIC	All Sample
	(1)	(2)	(3)	(4)
SDG SCORE	75.89	68.69	63.42	71.25
TEA	9.86	16.08	16.64	13.12
NEA	1.92	4.33	5.25	3.30
OEA	7.46	11.29	10.83	9.33
IEA	3.03	4.13	3.30	3.44
NIEA	6.82	11.95	13.34	9.67
FDI	−0.72	2.58	2.43	0.91
GOVEXP	29.90	18.62	23.94	25.92
POP (millions)	35.00	107.52	168.53	82.03
N° Countries	33	22	12	67

This table presents the mean of several variables by country income group (HIC—high income country; UMIC—upper-middle income country; LMIC—lower-middle income country). All variables are defined in Table 1. Independent variables are computed as the annual average over the period from 2015–2018.

High-income countries present the highest percentage level of achievement in SDGs (75.89%), yet a lower level of total entrepreneurial activity (9.86%). The SDG index score ranks a country between 0 (the worst performance) and 100 (the best performance). For example, the average index score for high-income countries is 75.89 out of 100, which indicates that on average, these countries are

76% of the way to achieving their SDGs across all 17 goals. As Column 4 in Table 2 shows, the main type of activity is opportunity entrepreneurship (9.33% for opportunity entrepreneurship (OEA) vs. 3.30% for necessity entrepreneurship (NEA)). However, the percentage of necessity entrepreneurship is higher for lower-middle and upper-middle countries (32 and 27% of total entrepreneurial activity for lower-middle and upper-middle countries). This percentage is reduced to 19% for high-income countries. Regarding innovation, Column 4 shows that the great majority of the entrepreneurs are non-innovative, (3.44% for innovative entrepreneurship (IEA) vs. 9.67% for non-innovative entrepreneurship (NIEA)). The percentage of innovative entrepreneurship is higher for high-income countries. It accounts for 31% of the total entrepreneurial activity in high-incomes countries; while in lower-middle and upper-middle countries, this percentage is reduced to 20 and 26%, respectively. High-income countries are also characterised by having lower populations, greater government expenditure, but less FDI.

5. Research Design

To investigate whether entrepreneurial activity contributes to the achievement of SDGs, we first estimate the following model:

$$SDG_i = \alpha + \beta TEA_i + \lambda FDI_i + X'_i \theta + \varepsilon_i \tag{1}$$

in which i refers to the country.

The dependent variable is the SDG Index, which tracks country performance on the 17 SDGs for the year 2019. All goals are equally weighted in this index [71].

Our variable of interest is total entrepreneurial activity (TEA), measured as the percentage of the adult population (aged 18–64) which is actively involved in entrepreneurial start-up activity averaged between 2015 and 2018. According to our first hypothesis, we postulate that entrepreneurial activity is likely to affect the achievement of SDGs, however, the direction of the effect depends on the type of entrepreneurial activity.

To test the predictions that necessity entrepreneurship negatively affects the achievement of SDGs and that opportunity entrepreneurship positively affects the achievement of SDGs, we re-estimate Equation (1) by splitting the TEA by necessity and opportunity entrepreneurship activities. NEA is the proportion of total entrepreneurial activity, which reports no better options for work averaged between 2015 and 2018. In contrast, OEA is the average proportion of total entrepreneurial activity in which the main driver for being involved in entrepreneurship is to be independent or increase income.

Additionally, we also distinguish between innovative and non-innovative entrepreneurships. IEA is the average proportion of total entrepreneurial activity which offers new products or services to some, or all customers, which is offered by few or no other competitors. We predict that IEA is positively related to sustainable development, while NIEA is negatively related.

Finally, we also evaluate the direct and indirect effects of FDI on the achievement of SDGs. FDI is the net new investment inflows less disinvestment from foreign investors that is divided by GDP [73].

Several control variables, which are included in the X vector, reflect key trends which could affect SDGs. In all countries, the transformation of SDGs requires a huge increase in public and private investment [13] and therefore, government expenditure, GOVEXP, plays a fundamental role in the achievement of SDGs. GOVEXP is the sum of the general government's final consumption and military, health, and education expenditures as a percentage of GDP. We also control for population, POP, which is measured as the natural logarithm of the population for each country. The variable of interest and control variables are averaged over the period from 2015 to 2018. By computing the average of the variables, we eliminate the short-to-medium term effects [74]. In addition, we include country income group (INCOMRG) fixed effects in order to control for countries' economic conditions.

6. Results

Table 3 presents the OLS regression results for Equation (1). Model (1) evaluates the effect of TEA, while Models (2) and (3) analyse the influence of OEA and NEA, and IEA and NIEA, respectively.

Table 3. Impact of entrepreneurial activity on the achievement of SDGs.

	Model 1 (TEA)	Model 2 (NEA and OEA)	Model 3 (NIEA and IEA)
TEA	−0.281 ***		
	(0.087)		
NEA		−0.721 ***	
		(0.270)	
OEA		−0.094	
		(0.137)	
NIEA			−0.377 **
			(0.137)
IEA			−0.034
			(0.197)
GOVEXPEND	0.231 *	0.229 *	0.234 **
	(0.126)	(0.126)	(0.124)
FDI	−0.019	−0.027	−0.027
	(0.047)	(0.045)	(0.047)
POP	0.318	0.320	0.375
	(0.278)	(0.298)	(0.291)
Constant	70.841 ***	70.210 ***	70.501 ***
	(4.369)	(0.270)	(4.289)
Dummy Income Level	Yes	Yes	Yes
Observations	67	67	67
R—squared	61.90%	63.20%	62.60%

This table presents the effect of different types of entrepreneurial activity on the achievement of SDGs. All variables are defined in Table 1. Independent variables are computed as the annual average over the period 2015–2018. Robust standard errors are in parentheses. *** $p < 0.01$; ** $p < 0.05$; * $p < 0.1$.

Model (1) shows that TEA has a negative effect on the achievement of SDGs. The coefficient is negative and is statistically significant at the 1% level. Model (2) presents the results for NEA and OEA. We find that the coefficient for NEA is negative and statistically significant at the 1% level. In Model (3), we divide the TEA into the IEA and NIEA. The results show that the coefficient associated with NIEA is negative and statistically significant at the 1% level. Our results are in line with Hypotheses 2b and 3b. The influence of entrepreneurial activity on SDGs is negative when entrepreneurs are pushed to entrepreneurship due to the lack of job opportunities or create non-innovative businesses. In all the models, the coefficient associated with FDI is not statistically significant.

Regarding the control variables, we find that they are all consistent with the literature. GOVEXP is fundamental in mobilising capital and finance activities which could enhance sustainable development and the achievement of SDGs [75]. In all models, the coefficient for GOVEXP is statistically significant at the 5 or 10% level.

Next, we evaluate the influence of entrepreneurship on the main SDGs. For this purpose, we classify the SDGs according to Sachs et al.'s (2019) [71] classifications: People, prosperity, planet, peace, and partnership. Each category goal score is computed as being the sum of each goal score, divided by the total number of goals. We therefore re-estimate the previous regressions by using five dependent variables. The results of this analysis are presented in Table 4. Panels A, B, and C present the results for Models (1), (2), and (3) of Table 3, respectively.

Entrepreneurship negatively and significantly affects the following SDG dimensions: People, posterity, and partnership. For the planet and peace goals, the effect is also negative, but not statistically significant (Panel A of Table 4).

Table 4. Impact of entrepreneurial activity on SDGs' five dimensions.

	Model 1 (People)	Model 2 (Prosperity)	Model 3 (Planet)	Model 4 (Peace)	Model 5 (Partnership)
Panel A—Model 1 of Table 3					
TEA	−0.087 *	−0.152 ***	−0.002	−0.004	−0.036 ***
	(0.053)	(0.028)	(0.035)	(0.014)	(0.009)
R—squared	48.80%	68.50%	12.00%	21.10%	66.60%
Panel B—Model 2 of Table 3					
NEA	−0.527 ***	−0.242 **	0.083	0.030	−0.066 **
	(0.153)	(0.111)	(0.103)	(0.042)	(0.031)
OEA	0.106	−0.123 **	−0.034	−0.020	−0.024 *
	(0.086)	(0.055)	(0.057)	(0.020)	(0.015)
R—squared	52.90%	69.00%	12.60%	21.70%	67.20%
Panel C—Model 3 of Table 3					
NIEA	−0.194 **	−0.184 ***	0.049	0.004	−0.051 ***
	(0.081)	(0.046)	(0.050)	(0.020)	(0.014)
IEA	0.189	−0.070	−0.134	−0.023	0.003
	(0.121)	(0.115)	(0.127)	(0.053)	(0.022)
R—squared	52.90%	69.00%	12.60%	21.70%	67.20%
Control Variables	Yes	Yes	Yes	Yes	Yes
Dummy Income Level	Yes	Yes	Yes	Yes	Yes
Observations	67	67	67	67	67

This table shows the effect of entrepreneurial activity on the five dimensions of SDGs: People, prosperity, planet, peace, and partnership. The dependent variables are the sum of SDG index scores in each category divided by the total number of goals. Panels A, B, and C present the results for Models (1), (2), and (3) of Table 3. All variables are defined in Table 1. Independent variables are computed as the annual average over the period 2015–2018. Control variables, intercept, and income level fixed effects are included but not reported. Robust standard errors in parentheses. *** $p < 0.01$; ** $p < 0.05$; * $p < 0.1$.

Similarly, NEA negatively and significantly affects the people and prosperity goals (Panel B of Table 4). Both coefficients are statistically significant, although the negative effect is larger for the people goal. Surprisingly, we do not find a significant and negative effect of NEA on the planet goal, as expected in the literature. For OEA, we find a negative and significant effect on the propensity dimension which suggests that opportunity-based start-ups can cause turbulence and therefore negatively affect economic growth. However, we do find a negative and significant effect on the partnership goal for both OEA and NEA. Although this goal depends primarily on the government, entrepreneurs can influence their institutional context.

By the same token, NIEA also negatively affects the partnership goal. Additionally, it negatively contributes to the achievement of the people and prosperity goals (Panel C of Table 4). Again, the negative effect is larger for the people goal, and we continue to not find any effect on the planet and peace goals. Surprisingly, IEA does not seem to have an effect on the goal of innovation. Nevertheless, it should be mentioned that the targets of goal 9 (industry, innovation, infrastructure) are mainly related to sustainable infrastructure and industrialisation, to an upgrade in the technological capabilities of industrial sectors, and an increase in access to information and communications technology. Considering that our sample of entrepreneurs includes mainly start-ups established in the retail sector, the effect on sustainable infrastructure and industrialisation is expected to be low.

Table 5 presents the results for the moderating role of FDI on the relation between entrepreneurial activities and the achievement of SDGs. For that purpose, we add several interaction terms between the variable FDI and the different types of TEA described above to Equation (1). Again, Model (1) gives the results for TEA, while Models (2) and (3) display the results for OEA and NEA, and IEA and NIEA, respectively. Due to its importance on raising capital and knowledge diffusion, FDI should positively affect the relation between entrepreneurship activities and the achievement of SDGs.

Table 5. The moderating role of FDI on the relationship between entrepreneurship activities and the achievement of SDGs.

	Model 1 (TEA)	Model 2 (NEA and OEA)	Model 3 (NIEA and IEA)
TEA	−0.294 ***		
	(0.075)		
TEAxFDI	0.024 *		
	(0.012)		
NEA		−0.833 ***	
		(0.238)	
OEA		0.030	
		(0.136)	
NEAxFDI		0.102 **	
		(0.036)	
OEAxFDI		−0.034	
		(0.024)	
NIEA			−0.340 **
			(0.141)
IEA			−0.106
			(0.294)
NIEAxFDI			0.028
			(0.023)
IEAxFDI			0.000
			(0.051)
FDI	−0.239 *	0.053	−0.194
	(0.113)	(0.155)	(0.156)
Intercept	70.509 ***	69.127 ***	70.071 ***
	(0.075)	(4.405)	(4.464)
Control Variables	Yes	Yes	Yes
Dummy Income Level	Yes	Yes	Yes
Observations	67	67	67
R—squared	63.00%	64.80%	63.40%

This table presents the moderating role of FDI on the relation between entrepreneurial activity and the achievement of SDGs. All variables are defined in Table 1. Independent variables are computed as the annual average over the period 2015–2018. Robust standard errors are in parentheses. *** $p < 0.01$; ** $p < 0.05$; * $p < 0.1$.

In Model (1), TEA continues to negatively affect the achievement of SDGs. Nevertheless, we find that the coefficient for the interaction term between FDI and TEA is positive and statistically significant at the 10% level, which means that in countries with a higher share of FDI, entrepreneurial activity promotes sustainable development. The same occurs with NEA. While the coefficient associated with NEA is negative, the coefficient for the interaction between FDI and NEA is positive, which indicates that FDI can motivate entrepreneurs to establish sustainable businesses when they have no alternative occupations. FDI could provide access to knowledge and capital. For NIEA, we continue to find a negative effect on sustainable development, although the interaction term between NIEA and FDI is positive, albeit non-significant. Thereby, we find partial support for Hypothesis 4b. We continue to find no significant effects for OEA and IEA on their interaction terms with FDI.

Table 6 shows the results for the interaction effects between FDI and entrepreneurship on the five SDG dimensions. Panels A, B, and C present the results for Models (1), (2), and (3) of Table 3, respectively.

In Panel A, we find that entrepreneurship continues to negatively affect the achievement of SDGs in the people, prosperity, and partnership dimensions. Nevertheless, the interaction effect between entrepreneurship and FDI is positive and significant for the people goal, which indicates that countries with more FDI and entrepreneurial activity are more likely to achieve the people index score. However, the total effect of entrepreneurship on the people goal is still negative.

Table 6. The moderating role of FDI on the relationship between entrepreneurship activities and the five dimensions of SDGs.

	Model 1 (People)	Model 2 (Prosperity)	Model 3 (Planet)	Model 4 (Peace)	Model 5 (Partnership)
Panel A—Model 1 of Table 3					
TEA	−0.099 **	−0.152 ***	−0.003	−0.004	−0.036 ***
	(0.038)	(0.027)	(0.034)	(0.014)	(0.009)
FDI	−0.236 ***	−0.017	−0.002	0.013	0.003
	(0.083)	(0.051)	(0.062)	(0.022)	(0.013)
FDIxTEA	0.022 ***	−0.001	0.002	−0.000	−0.000
	(0.008)	(0.005)	(0.005)	(0.002)	(0.001)
R-squared	51.70%	68.50%	12.10%	21.10%	66.60%
Panel B—Model 2 of Table 3					
NEA	−0.539 ***	−0.359 ***	0.148	0.026	−0.108 ***
	(0.133)	(0.130)	(0.150)	(0.057)	(0.038)
OEA	0.143	−0.031	−0.077	−0.014	0.009
	(0.092)	(0.063)	(0.092)	(0.037)	(0.023)
FDI	−0.066	0.081	−0.054	0.014	0.040 **
	(0.091)	(0.075)	(0.087)	(0.030)	(0.020)
NEAxFDI	0.054 **	0.032	−0.002	0.006	0.012 *
	(0.026)	(0.022)	(0.021)	(0.010)	(0.006)
OEAxFDI	−0.011	−0.024 *	0.011	−0.002	−0.009 **
	(0.017)	(0.012)	(0.015)	(0.007)	(0.004)
R-squared	54.50%	70.10%	13.30%	22.00%	69.70%
Panel C—Model 3 of Table 3					
NIEA	−0.204 **	−0.186 ***	0.071	−0.000	−0.056 ***
	(0.080)	(0.048)	(0.055)	(0.022)	(0.014)
IEA	0.271	−0.063	−0.252	−0.001	0.029
	(0.198)	(0.135)	(0.188)	(0.078)	(0.030)
FDI	−0.192 *	0.000	−0.034	0.010	0.012
	(0.097)	(0.054)	(0.051)	(0.021)	(0.012)
NIEAxFDI	0.032 *	−0.003	−0.002	0.002	0.001
	(0.017)	(0.009)	(0.007)	(0.005)	(0.002)
IEAxFDI	−0.032	−0.001	0.032	−0.006	−0.007
	(0.040)	(0.023)	(0.022)	(0.013)	(0.005)
R-squared	53.90%	68.90%	15.90%	21.70%	68.60%
Control Variables	Yes	Yes	Yes	Yes	Yes
Dummy Income Level	Yes	Yes	Yes	Yes	Yes
Observations	67	67	67	67	67

This table shows the moderating role of FDI on the relation between entrepreneurial activity and the five dimensions of SDGs: People, prosperity, planet, peace, and partnership. The dependent variables are the sum of SDG index scores in each category divided by the total number of goals. Panels A, B, and C present the results for Models (1), (2), and (3) of Table 3, respectively. All variables are defined in Table 1. Independent variables are computed as the annual average over the period 2015–2018. Control variables, intercept, and income level fixed effects are included but not reported. Robust standard errors in parentheses. *** $p < 0.01$; ** $p < 0.05$; * $p < 0.1$.

In Panel B, we divide entrepreneurship into NEA and OEA. NEA continues to negatively affect the achievement of people, prosperity, and partnership goals. Nevertheless, the interaction effect between NEA and FDI is positive and is statistically significant for the people and partnership goals. Although the total effect of NEA is still negative, the countries with more FDI and NEA are more likely to improve their SDGs in terms of the people and partnership dimensions. Moreover, FDI has a positive effect on the partnership goal, which means that foreign investors can create valuable networks by building inter- and intra-industry alliances or partnerships to improve countries' sustainability. Contrary to our expectation, the interaction effect between OEA and FDI is negative for the prosperity and partnership dimensions. This finding could be due to the fact that opportunity entrepreneurs want to take advantage of market opportunities and are reluctant to collaborate with foreign investors who could be responsible for the crowding effect that has a negative effect on economic growth and sustainable development [76]. In fact, foreign competitors crowd out entrepreneurial activity by absorbing potential entrepreneurs as employees [77].

By the same token, in Panel C, we find that NIEA negatively affects the achievement of the people, prosperity, and partnership goals. Like NEA, the interaction effect between FDI and OEA is positive for the people dimension. This result indicates that there is a positive spill over effect of FDI regarding ending poverty and enhancing the contribution of entrepreneurship for basic needs, such as nutrition, education, and access to water, sanitation, and electricity.

Although our study is explorative by nature, it is important to address an important issue, the endogeneity of the entrepreneurship variables. We estimated Equation (1) using OLS, however, there is a potential bi-directional relationship between entrepreneurship and sustainability. Entrepreneurship may influence SDGs, but SDGs may also have an impact on entrepreneurship. For example, SDGs may inspire entrepreneurs to launch new ventures with sustainable business models or products, which translates to more entrepreneurial activity. To account for this issue, in our previous analyses, we used the lagged proportion of individuals engaged in entrepreneurial activity averaged over the period 2015–2018 to explain the SDGs score achievement in 2019. Furthermore, we employ an instrumental variable (IV) approach. To instrument for the entrepreneurship variables, we used their lagged values averaged over the period 2012–2014. The reasoning is that the past prevalence of entrepreneurial activity in a country motivates potential entrepreneurs to move into entrepreneurship, but the past level of entrepreneurial activity is unlikely to account for the current SDGs' score. Entrepreneurship has only begun to gain ground as a concept to promote the three pillars of sustainable development after 2014 [1].

Table 7 presents the IV regression results for TEA, OEA, and NEA, and IEA and NIEA, respectively, in Models (1), (2), and (3).

Table 7. Impact of entrepreneurial activity on the achievement of SDGs.

	Model 1 (TEA)	Model 2 (NEA and OEA)	Model 3 (NIEA and IEA)
TEA	−0.266 **		
	(0.125)		
NEA		−0.893	
		(0.546)	
OEA		0.083	
		(0.190)	
NIEA			−0.353 **
			(0.170)
IEA			0.157
			(0.341)
Constant	70.570 ***	68.532 ***	69.045 ***
	(4.072)	(3.679)	(4.394)
Dummy Income Level	Yes	Yes	Yes
Observations	55	55	55
R—squared	68.50%	69.80%	67.90%
Kleibergen-Paap F-statistics	12.72	11.57	2.689

This table presents the effect of different types of entrepreneurial activity on the achievement of SDGs using instrumental variable (IV) regression. All variables are defined in Table 1. Independent variables are computed as the annual average over the period 2015–2018. TEA, NEA, OEA, NIEA, and IEA are instrumented using their lagged values averaged over the period 2012–2014. Control variables, intercept, and income level fixed effects are included but not reported. Robust standard errors are in parentheses. *** $p < 0.01$; ** $p < 0.05$; * $p < 0.1$.

Table 8 presents the results for the moderating role of FDI on the relation between entrepreneurial activities and the achievement of SDGs using IV approach.

Table 8. The moderating role of FDI on the relationship between entrepreneurship activities and the achievement of SDGs.

	Model 1 (TEA)	Model 2 (NEA and OEA)	Model 3 (NIEA and IEA)
TEA	−0.279 **		
	(0.124)		
TEAxFDI	0.036 *		
	(0.021)		
NEA		−1.125 **	
		(0.530)	
OEA		0.215	
		(0.196)	
NEAxFDI		0.105 *	
		(0.062)	
OEAxFDI		−0.028	
		(0.028)	
NIEA			−0.364 **
			(0.176)
IEA			0.126
			(0.370)
NIEAxFDI			0.039 *
			(0.022)
IEAxFDI			0.045
			(0.060)
FDI	−0.345 *	−0.035	−0.400 **
	(0.206)	(0.179)	(0.158)
Intercept	70.112 ***	67.946 ***	68.563 ***
	(4.272)	(3.657)	(4.556)
Control Variables	Yes	Yes	Yes
Dummy Income Level	Yes	Yes	Yes
Observations	55	55	55
R—squared	70.10%	71.70%	68.10%
Kleibergen-Paap F-statistics	10.92	17.06	5.355

This table presents the moderating role of FDI on the relation between entrepreneurial activity and the achievement of SDGs using IV regression. All variables are defined in Table 1. Independent variables are computed as the annual average over the period 2015–2018. TEA, NEA, OEA, NIEA, IEA, and the interactions variables are instrumented using their lagged values averaged over the period 2012–2014. Control variables, intercept, and income level fixed effects are included but not reported. Robust standard errors are in parentheses. *** $p < 0.01$; ** $p < 0.05$; * $p < 0.1$.

Tables 7 and 8 show that our IV results are very similar to previous findings using OLS estimation. As shown previously, entrepreneurship contributes negatively to the achievement of SDGs, and FDI helps to diminish this negative effect, as it improves the relation between NEA and NIEA and SDGs' achievement. The only difference in IV estimation is that the negative impact of NEA is not statistically significant in Model (2) of Table 7. This might be due to the substantial reduction in the number of observations (55 observations in IV vs. 67 observations in OLS). However, when we include the interaction effect between NEA and FDI, the coefficient associated with NEA becomes negative and statistically significant (see Model (2) of Table 8). The IV results for the five dimensions of the SDGs also maintain the same. The results are available by request.

For an instrument to be valid, the following conditions have to be satisfied. First, the instruments need to be correlated with the endogenous variables. In Appendix B, Table A8, we see that this condition is satisfied. Second, the lagged values of entrepreneurial activity should not be strongly correlated with the sustainability score in 2019, otherwise the estimated coefficient would still be biased. To test the relevancy of the instrument, we report the Kleibergen-Paap (2016) [78] wald F statistics. The results are reported on the bottom of Tables 7 and 8. The rejection of the Kleibergen-Paap rk LM statistics indicates the validity of the instruments used.

At this point, we have to address one shortcoming of OLS and IV regressions: These estimations provide only mean estimates and consequently they are unable to capture the full conditional distribution of SDGs scores. Additionally, the test for normality based on skewness and kurtosis rejected that the residuals from OLS estimation were normal distributed. Non-normal errors can be problematic in smaller samples. To account for this issue, we employ Quantile Regression (QR). QR provides more information on the relationship between SDG scores and entrepreneurship as it estimates the coefficients in any point of the conditional distribution of the SDG scores. Furthermore, it does not require a no-distribution assumption and it is more robust to non-normal errors.

Models (1), (2), and (3) in Table 9 present the QR estimates of Equation (1) evaluated at the 25th, 50th, 75th percentile, respectively.

Table 9. Impact of entrepreneurial activity on the achievement of SDGs.

	Model 1	Model 2	Model 3
	Q 25	Q 50	Q 75
Panel A—Model 1 of Table 3			
TEA	−0.285 **	−0.307 *	−0.130
	(0.114)	(0.171)	(0.130)
Pseudo R—squared	41.36%	43.66%	45.24%
Panel B—Model 2 of Table 3			
NEA	−0.694 **	−0.957 *	−0.639
	(0.323)	(0.494)	(0.558)
OEA	−0.108	−0.123	−0.033
	(0.201)	(0.254)	(0.160)
Pseudo R—squared	44.06%	43.92%	46.71%
Panel C—Model 3 of Table 3			
NIEA	−0.384 **	−0.462 *	−0.302
	(0.148)	(0.261)	(0.262)
IEA	0.077	−0.154	−0.074
	(0.292)	(0.274)	(0.252)
Pseudo R—squared	42.56%	44.41%	45.61%
Control Variables	Yes	Yes	Yes
Dummy Income Level	Yes	Yes	Yes
Observations	67	67	67

This table shows the effect of entrepreneurial activity using Quantile Regression (QR) estimation. Panels A, B, and C present the results for Models (1), (2), and (3) of Table 3, respectively. All variables are defined in Table 1. Independent variables are computed as the annual average over the period 2015–2018. Control variables, intercept, and income level fixed effects are included but not reported. Robust standard errors in parentheses. *** $p < 0.01$; ** $p < 0.05$; * $p < 0.1$.

Interestingly the negative marginal effect of TEA, NEA, and NIEA is only statistically significant for those countries that have a relatively lower SDG score. The marginal effect of TEA, NEA, and NIEA is not statistically significant for those countries that have achieved a higher SDGs score.

In Table 10, we present the results for the moderating role of FDI on the relation between entrepreneurship and the achievement of SDGs using QR estimation approach. Again, Models (1), (2), and (3) provides the estimates at the 25th, 50th, 75th percentile, respectively.

Table 10. Moderating role of FDI on the relationship between entrepreneurship activities and the achievement of SDGs.

	Model 1	Model 2	Model 3
	Q 25	Q 50	Q 75
Panel A—Model 1 of Table 3			
TEA	−0.234 *	−0.382 *	−0.123
	(0.140)	(0.223)	(0.186)
FDIxTEA	0.016	0.020	−0.004
	(0.031)	(0.043)	(0.064)
Pseudo R—squared	42.75%	44.42%	45.25%
Panel B—Model 2 of Table 3			
NEA	−0.862 *	−0.754 *	−0.921
	(0.463)	(0.434)	(0.572)
OEA	−0.003	−0.001	0.037
	(0.247)	(0.233)	(0.215)
NEAxFDI	0.124	0.113	0.091
	(0.111)	(0.091)	(0.155)
OEAxFDI	−0.026	−0.033	−0.022
	(0.056)	(0.045)	(0.058)
Pseudo R—squared	44.91%	47.01%	49.09%
Panel C—Model 3 of Table 3			
NIEA	−0.365 *	−0.495 *	−0.434
	(0.189)	(0.279)	(0.348)
IEA	−0.034	0.118	0.099
	(0.689)	(0.411)	(0.683)
NIEAxFDI	0.008	0.029	0.052
	(0.076)	(0.066)	(0.079)
IEAxFDI	0.014	−0.050	−0.081
	(0.142)	(0.102)	(0.133)
Pseudo R—squared	43.66%	45.75%	46.03%
Control Variables	Yes	Yes	Yes
Dummy Income Level	Yes	Yes	Yes
Observations	67	67	67

This table presents the moderating role of FDI on the relation between entrepreneurial activity and the achievement of SDGs using QR estimation. All variables are defined in Table 1. Independent variables are computed as the annual average over the period 2015–2018. Control variables, intercept, and income level fixed effects are included but not reported. Robust standard errors are in parentheses. *** $p < 0.01$; ** $p < 0.05$; * $p < 0.1$.

Like in the previous table, the negative marginal effect of TEA, NTEA, and NIEA is statistically significant for those countries that have a SDG score below the 50th percentile. Although we find positive coefficients for the interaction effects between FDI and TEA, NTEA, and NIE, these coefficients are not statistically significant. Overall, these results support Hypotheses 2b and 3b, while providing further understanding of the role of entrepreneurship across the SDGs score distribution. These results can be justified by the fact that the impact of entrepreneurship on economic growth depends on the level of economic development of a country [41]. Descriptive statistics show that lower SDGs' scores are registered in lower income countries. Thus, in relatively poor countries, where inequalities are more pronounced, necessity entrepreneurship may be more frequent with a negative effect on economic growth, contributing negatively to the achievement of SDGs.

7. Discussion and Conclusions

Research on entrepreneurship and sustainable development has experienced some progress over the last few years. However, the actual outcomes of entrepreneurship on sustainable development are largely unknown. We investigate the effects of entrepreneurship and its different types on the achievement of SDGs in a sample of 67 developed and developing countries. Additionally, as FDI plays a fundamental role in external finance for sustainable development [10] and leads entrepreneurial ventures towards SDGs, we also investigate the moderating role of FDI on the relation between entrepreneurship and sustainable development.

Although entrepreneurship is viewed as being a source of economic growth and employment creation [79], we conclude that entrepreneurship has an overall negative effect on the achievement of SDGs that harms sustainable development, particularly for countries with lower SDGs scores. Nevertheless, we observe that this negative effect is mainly due to necessity and non-innovative entrepreneurship. When entrepreneurs are motivated to start a new business by necessity, the influence of entrepreneurship on sustainable development is negative, because they have no other alternative occupations, or they introduce products or services which are very similar to those offered by other competitors. Thereby, they have a marginal contribution to economic prosperity dimension of the SDGs. When we disaggregate the results by the five dimensions goals of people, prosperity, planet, peace, and partnership, the negative effect is evident in the people and prosperity goals, while no type of entrepreneurship has any effect on the planet goals. Nevertheless, FDI helps diminish the negative effect of entrepreneurship and the achievement of SDGs, as it improves the relation between total and necessity entrepreneurships and the achievement of SDGs. This influence is particularly significant with regards to the goals of ending poverty and increasing basic needs, such as nutrition, education, access to water, sanitation, and electricity. These findings have mostly been confirmed by additional tests, namely by employing an instrumental variable (IV) approach and quantile egression (QR).

This study contributes to the literature in different ways. First, it provides empirical evidence of the effect that entrepreneurship has on countries´ sustainable development in a holistic way, by separating its effect for the five pillars of sustainable development. Second, by investigating the different types of entrepreneurship, this study highlights that the motivation underlying entrepreneurial activities can influence the ability of entrepreneurs to create sustainable businesses. Finally, it also highlights the role of foreign investors in the achievement of SDGs.

This study presents several limitations. First, our entrepreneurial measure is not limited to social or sustainable entrepreneurs, as it includes all types of entrepreneurship. Our entrepreneurship variables measure the proportion of individuals engaged in entrepreneurial activities without discriminating any social or sustainability orientation. Although we tried to measure social entrepreneurial activity, our results were not statistically significant. The results are available on request. Therefore, we are not able to effectively measure sustainability and social-oriented entrepreneurship. Second, measuring national SDG is challenging, as interaction effects, trade-offs, and vaguely defined goals exist [71]. Another limitation of this study is the relatively small number of countries considered in the analysis, and more specifically, the lack of low-income countries due to data unavailability. Considering that the low-income countries may be the ones that need the most investment in entrepreneurship and sustainable growth, further research should be conducted in this subject. Nevertheless, our results suggest that the negative impact of entrepreneurship is more prevalent in countries with lower SDGs scores. These countries are characterized by weak business environments and large skill gaps, therefore specific models and methodology should be applied in future works [80]. Nevertheless, this exploratory study advances the discussion of types of entrepreneurship and sustainability in countries with levels of development. Finally, we could have analysed the relationship between types of entrepreneurship and SDGs by grouping observations in a different way (e.g., countries grouped by population or income level). These types of analyses could potentially lead to different results, creating the modifiable areal unit problem, as described in [81]. Unfortunately, a lack of data prevents us from empirically testing these alternatives unit of analyses. Instead, we disaggregate SDGs in different dimensions (people, prosperity, planet, peace, and partnership) and evaluate the effect of entrepreneurship in points of the conditional distribution of the SDGs scores to ensure the stability of our data [81]. Empirical strategies using alternative units of analysis warrants further research when data becomes available.

Author Contributions: Conceptualization, A.V. and I.P.; methodology, A.V. and I.P.; software, A.V. and I.P.; writing—original draft preparation, A.V. and I.P.; writing—review and editing, A.V. and I.P. All authors have read and agreed to the published version of the manuscript.

Appendix A. List of Countries

Table A1. List of countries.

High Income Level	Upper-Middle Income Level	Lower-Middle Income Level
Argentina	Belize	Angola
Australia	Bosnia and Herzegovina	Cameroon
Austria	Botswana	Egypt, Arab Rep.
Belgium	Brazil	El Salvador
Canada	Bulgaria	Georgia
Chile	China	India
Croatia	Colombia	Indonesia
Cyprus	Ecuador	Morocco
Germany	Guatemala	Philippines
Greece	Iran, Islamic Rep.	Sudan
Hungary	Jamaica	Tunisia
Ireland	Jordan	Vietnam
Israel	Kazakhstan	
Italy	Lebanon	
Japan	Malaysia	
Latvia	Mexico	
Luxembourg	Peru	
Netherlands	Romania	
Norway	Russian Federation	
Panama	South Africa	
Poland	Thailand	
Portugal	Turkey	
Qatar		
Saudi Arabia		
Slovak Republic		
Slovenia		
Spain		
Sweden		
Switzerland		
United Arab Emirates		
United Kingdom		
United States		
Uruguay		
Total: 33 countries	**Total: 22 countries**	**Total: 12 countries**

Appendix B. Full Econometric Results Included in the Paper

Table A2. Econometric results of Panel A of Table 4.

	Model 1	Model 2	Model 3	Model 4	Model 5
	(People)	(Prosperity)	(Planet)	(Peace)	(Partnership)
TEA	−0.087 *	−0.152 ***	−0.002	−0.004	−0.036 ***
	(0.053)	(0.028)	(0.035)	(0.014)	(0.009)
FDI	−0.028	−0.023	0.016	0.013	0.003
	(0.028)	(0.025)	(0.034)	(0.011)	(0.005)
GOVEXPEND	0.101	0.059	0.006	0.064 **	0.003
	(0.083)	(0.049)	(0.046)	(0.027)	(0.010)
POP	0.158	0.074	0.251 *	−0.082	−0.083 **
	(0.187)	(0.130)	(0.143)	(0.063)	(0.035)
Constant	26.460 ***	17.814 ***	18.995 ***	2.221 **	5.351 ***
	(2.963)	(1.723)	(1.806)	(1.060)	(0.364)
Dummy Income Level	Yes	Yes	Yes	Yes	Yes
Observations	67	67	67	67	67
R-squared	0.488	0.685	0.120	0.211	0.666

This table shows the effect of entrepreneurial activity on the five dimensions of SDGs: People, prosperity, planet, peace, and partnership. The dependent variables are the sum of SDG index scores in each category divided by the total number of goals. All variables are defined in Table 1. Independent variables are computed as the annual average over the period from 2015–2018. Robust standard errors are in parentheses. *** $p < 0.01$; ** $p < 0.05$; * $p < 0.1$.

Table A3. Econometric results of Panel B of Table 4.

	Model 1	Model 2	Model 3	Model 4	Model 5
	(People)	(Prosperity)	(Planet)	(Peace)	(Partnership)
NTEA	−0.527 ***	−0.242 **	0.083	0.030	−0.066 **
	(0.153)	(0.111)	(0.103)	(0.042)	(0.031)
OTEA	0.106	−0.123 **	−0.034	−0.020	−0.024 *
	(0.086)	(0.055)	(0.057)	(0.020)	(0.015)
FDI	−0.036	−0.024	0.017	0.014	0.002
	(0.026)	(0.025)	(0.035)	(0.011)	(0.005)
GOVEXPEND	0.098	0.058	0.007	0.064 **	0.002
	(0.082)	(0.049)	(0.046)	(0.027)	(0.010)
POP	0.159	0.074	0.253 *	−0.083	−0.083 **
	(0.193)	(0.135)	(0.143)	(0.064)	(0.036)
Constant	25.866 ***	17.722 ***	19.034 ***	2.277 **	5.312 ***
	(2.906)	(1.722)	(1.816)	(1.074)	(0.358)
Dummy Income Level	Yes	Yes	Yes	Yes	Yes
Observations	67	67	67	67	67
R-squared	0.529	0.690	0.126	0.217	0.672

This table shows the effect of entrepreneurial activity on the five dimensions of SDGs: People, prosperity, planet, peace, and partnership. The dependent variables are the sum of SDG index scores in each category divided by the total number of goals. All variables are defined in Table 1. Independent variables are computed as the annual average over the period from 2015–2018. Robust standard errors are in parentheses. *** $p < 0.01$; ** $p < 0.05$; * $p < 0.1$.

Table A4. Econometric results of Panel C of Table 4.

	Model 1	Model 2	Model 3	Model 4	Model 5
	(People)	(Prosperity)	(Planet)	(Peace)	(Partnership)
NIEA	−0.194 **	−0.184 ***	0.049	−0.051 ***	0.004
	(0.081)	(0.046)	(0.050)	(0.014)	(0.020)
IEA	0.189	−0.070	−0.134	0.003	−0.023
	(0.121)	(0.115)	(0.127)	(0.022)	(0.053)
FDI	−0.036	−0.026	0.020	0.002	0.013
	(0.027)	(0.025)	(0.035)	(0.005)	(0.011)
GOVEXPEND	0.104	0.060	0.004	0.003	0.063 **
	(0.080)	(0.049)	(0.046)	(0.009)	(0.027)
POP	0.223	0.094	0.219	−0.074 **	−0.087
	(0.190)	(0.132)	(0.146)	(0.036)	(0.068)
Constant	26.068 ***	17.698 ***	19.191 ***	5.296 ***	2.248 **
	(2.877)	(1.734)	(1.819)	(0.351)	(1.084)
Dummy Income Level	Yes	Yes	Yes	Yes	Yes
Observations	67	67	67	67	67
R-squared	0.511	0.688	0.141	0.680	0.213

This table shows the effect of entrepreneurial activity on the five dimensions of SDGs: People, prosperity, planet, peace, and partnership. The dependent variables are the sum of SDG index scores in each category divided by the total number of goals. All variables are defined in Appendix A. Independent variables are computed as the annual average over the period from 2015–2018. Robust standard errors are in parentheses. *** $p < 0.01$; ** $p < 0.05$; * $p < 0.1$.

Table A5. Econometric results of Panel A of Table 6.

	Model 1	Model 2	Model 3	Model 4	Model 5
	(People)	(Prosperity)	(Planet)	(Peace)	(Partnership)
TEA	−0.099 *	−0.152 ***	−0.003	−0.004	−0.036 ***
	(0.038)	(0.027)	(0.034)	(0.014)	(0.009)
FDI	−0.236 ***	−0.017	−0.002	0.013	0.003
	(0.083)	(0.051)	(0.062)	(0.022)	(0.013)
FDI * TEA	0.022 ***	−0.001	0.002	0.000	0.000
	(0.008)	(0.005)	(0.005)	(0.002)	(0.002)
GOVEXPEND	0.105	0.059	0.006	0.003	0.063 **
	(0.083)	(0.049)	(0.046)	(0.010)	(0.028)
POP	0.210	0.073	0.255 *	−0.083 **	−0.083
	(0.196)	(0.130)	(0.147)	(0.035)	(0.065)
Constant	26.143 ***	17.824 ***	18.968 ***	2.222 ***	5.352 ***
	(2.944)	(1.720)	(1.825)	(1.077)	(0.362)
Dummy Income Level	yes	yes	yes	yes	yes
N° of Observations	67	67	67	67	67
R—squared	51.70%	68.50%	12.10%	21.10%	21.10%

This table shows the moderating role of FDI on the relation between entrepreneurial activity and the five dimensions of SDGs: People, prosperity, planet, peace, and partnership. The dependent variables are the sum of SDG index scores in each category divided by the total number of goals. All variables are defined in Table 1. Independent variables are computed as the annual average over the period from 2015–2018. Robust standard errors are in parentheses. *** $p < 0.01$; ** $p < 0.05$; * $p < 0.1$.

Table A6. Econometric results of Panel B of Table 6.

	Model 1	Model 2	Model 3	Model 4	Model 5
	(People)	(Prosperity)	(Planet)	(Peace)	(Partnership)
NEA	−0.539 ***	−0.359 ***	0.148	0.026	−0.108 ***
	(0.133)	(0.130)	(0.150)	(0.057)	(0.038)
OEA	0.143	−0.031	−0.077	−0.014	0.009
	(0.092)	(0.063)	(0.092)	(0.037)	(0.023)
FDI	−0.066	0.081	−0.054	0.014	0.040 **
	(0.091)	(0.075)	(0.087)	(0.030)	(0.020)
NEA * FDI	0.054 **	0.032	−0.002	0.006	0.012 *
	(0.026)	(0.022)	(0.021)	(0.010)	(0.006)
OEA * FDI	−0.011	−0.024 *	0.011	−0.002	−0.009 **
	(0.017)	(0.012)	(0.015)	(0.007)	(0.004)
GOVEXPEND	0.104	0.060	0.007	0.003	0.064 **
	(0.082)	(0.048)	(0.046)	(0.009)	(0.028)
POP	0.178	0.057	0.269 *	−0.089 ***	−0.082
	(0.192)	(0.129)	(0.145)	(0.032)	(0.065)
Constant	25.332 ***	17.304 ***	19.117 ***	2.217 **	5.157 ***
	(2.879)	(1.700)	(1.843)	(1.133)	(0.347)
Dummy Income Level	yes	yes	yes	yes	yes
N° of Observations	67	67	67	67	67
R—squared	52.90%	70.01%	13.30%	22.00%	69.70%

This table shows the moderating role of FDI on the relation between entrepreneurial activity and the five dimensions of SDGs: People, prosperity, planet, peace, and partnership. The dependent variables are the sum of SDG index scores in each category divided by the total number of goals. All variables are defined in Table 1. Independent variables are computed as the annual average over the period from 2015–2018. Robust standard errors are in parentheses. *** $p < 0.01$; ** $p < 0.05$; * $p < 0.1$.

Table A7. Econometric results of Panel C of Table 6.

	Model 1	Model 2	Model 3	Model 4	Model 5
	(People)	(Prosperity)	(Planet)	(Peace)	(Partnership)
NIEA	−0.204 **	−0.186 ***	0.071	0.000	−0.056 ***
	(0.080)	(0.048)	(0.055)	(0.022)	(0.014)
IEA	0.271	−0.063	−0.252	−0.001	0.029
	(0.198)	(0.135)	(0.188)	(0.078)	(0.030)
FDI	−0.192 *	0.000	−0.034	0.010	0.012
	(0.097)	(0.054)	(0.051)	(0.021)	(0.012)
NIEA * FDI	0.032 *	−0.003	−0.002	0.002	0.001
	(0.017)	(0.009)	(0.007)	(0.005)	(0.002)
IEA * FDI	−0.032	−0.001	0.032	−0.006	−0.007
	(0.040)	(0.023)	(0.022)	(0.013)	(0.005)
GOVEXPEND	0.114	0.060	0.000	0.004	0.064 **
	(0.082)	(0.049)	(0.047)	(0.009)	(0.029)
POP	0.229	0.091	0.236 *	−0.077 **	−0.089
	(0.186)	(0.132)	(0.141)	(0.035)	(0.069)
Constant	25.519 ***	17.736 ***	19.376 ***	2.188 *	5.252 ***
	(2.926)	(1.732)	(1.816)	(1.142)	(0.349)
Dummy Income Level	yes	yes	yes	yes	yes
N° of Observations	67	67	67	67	67
R—squared	51.10%	68.90%	14.10%	21.70%	68.60%

This table shows the moderating role of FDI on the relation between entrepreneurial activity and the five dimensions of SDGs: People, prosperity, planet, peace, and partnership. The dependent variables are the sum of SDG index scores in each category divided by the total number of goals. All variables are defined in Table 1. Independent variables are computed as the annual average over the period from 2015–2018. Robust standard errors are in parentheses. *** $p < 0.01$; ** $p < 0.05$; * $p < 0.1$.

Table A8. First stage results.

	(1)	(2)	(3)
Instrumented Variable	TEA	OEA	IEA
ivTEA	0.811 *** (0.132)		
ivOEA		0.995 ***	
		(0.131)	
ivNEA		−0.782 *	
		(0.399)	
ivIEA			0.763 ***
			(0.177)
ivNIEA			−0.089
			(0.061)
Observations	55	55	55

This table presents the first stage results for TEA, OEA, and IEA. The other results are available on request. All variables are defined in Table 1. Independent variables are computed as the annual average over the period 2015–2018. Control variables were included but not reported. Robust standard errors are in parentheses. *** $p < 0.01$; ** $p < 0.05$; * $p < 0.1$.

References

1. UN General Assembly. Transforming our World. In *The 2030 Agenda for Sustainable Development; Resolution Adopted by the General Assembly on 25 September 2015*; United Nations: New York, NY, USA, 2015.
2. Apostolopoulos, N.; Al-Dajani, H.; Holt, D.; Jones, P.; Newbery, R. Entrepreneurship and the sustainable development goals. In *Entrepreneurship and the Sustainable Development Goals, Contemporary Issues in Entrepreneurship Research*; Emerald Publishing Limited: Bradford, UK, 2018; Volume 8, pp. 1–7.
3. Filser, M.; Kraus, S.; Roig-Tierno, N.; Kailer, N.; Fischer, U. Entrepreneurship as Catalyst for Sustainable Development: Opening the Black Box. *Sustainability* **2019**, *11*, 4503. [CrossRef]
4. Hockerts, K.; Wüstenhagen, R. Greening Goliaths versus emerging Davids—Theorizing about the role of incumbents and new entrants in sustainable entrepreneurship. *J. Bus. Ventur.* **2010**, *25*, 481–492. [CrossRef]
5. He, J.; Nazari, M.; Zhang, Y.; Cai, N.; Jinjiang, H.; Yingqian, Z.; Ning, C. Opportunity-based entrepreneurship and environmental quality of sustainable development: A resource and institutional perspective. *J. Clean. Prod.* **2020**, *256*, 153–177. [CrossRef]
6. Beesley, M.E.; Hamilton, R.T. Small Firms' Seedbed Role and the Concept of Turbulence. *J. Ind. Econ.* **1984**, *33*, 217. [CrossRef]
7. Baptista, R.; Karaöz, M. Turbulence in growing and declining industries. *Small Bus. Econ.* **2009**, *36*, 249–270. [CrossRef]
8. Van Der Zwan, P.; Thurik, R.; Verheul, I.; Hessels, J. Factors influencing the entrepreneurial engagement of opportunity and necessity entrepreneurs. *Eurasian Bus. Rev.* **2016**, *6*, 273–295. [CrossRef]
9. Albert, M.G. Entrepreneurship, innovation and regional performance: Application for the Spanish regions. *Entrep. Reg. Dev.* **2016**, *29*, 271–291. [CrossRef]
10. UN General Assembly. *Entrepreneurship for Sustainable Development*; Resolution adopted by the General Assembly on 21 December 2016; United Nations: New York, NY, USA, 2016.
11. Reynolds, P.D.; Camp, S.M.; Bygrave, W.D.; Autio, E.; Hay, M. *Global Entrepreneurship Monitor Global 2001 Executive Report*; Kaufman Center: New York, NY, USA, 2001.
12. Schumpeter, J.A. *The Theory of Economic Development*; Harvard University Press: Cambridge, MA, USA, 1934.
13. UNCTAD. World Investment Report 2014—Investing in the SDGs: An Action Plan. Available online: https://unctad.org/en/PublicationsLibrary/wir2014_en.pdf (accessed on 8 April 2020).
14. Hall, J.K.; Daneke, G.A.; Lenox, M.J. Sustainable development and entrepreneurship: Past contributions and future directions. *J. Bus. Ventur.* **2010**, *25*, 439–448. [CrossRef]
15. Shepherd, D.A.; Patzelt, H. The New Field of Sustainable Entrepreneurship: Studying Entrepreneurial Action Linking "What Is to Be Sustained" With "What Is to Be Developed". *Entrep. Theory Pr.* **2011**, *35*, 137–163. [CrossRef]
16. Thelken, H.N.; De Jong, G. The impact of values and future orientation on intention formation within sustainable entrepreneurship. *J. Clean. Prod.* **2020**, *266*, 122052. [CrossRef]

17. Ajzen, I. The Theory of planned behavior. *Organ. Behav. Hum. Decis. Process.* **1991**, *50*, 179–211. [CrossRef]
18. Vuorio, A.M.; Puumalainen, K.; Fellnhofer, K. Drivers of entrepreneurial intentions in sustainable entrepreneurship. *Int. J. Entrep. Behav. Res.* **2018**, *24*, 359–381. [CrossRef]
19. Geroski, P. What do we know about entry? *Int. J. Ind. Organ.* **1995**, *13*, 421–440. [CrossRef]
20. Lucas, R.E. On the Size Distribution of Business Firms. *Bell J. Econ.* **1978**, *9*, 508. [CrossRef]
21. Parker, S.C. The Effects of Risk on Self-Employment. *Small Bus. Econ.* **1997**, *9*, 515–522. [CrossRef]
22. Porter, M.E.; Kramer, M.R. *Creating Shared Value. Managing Sustainable Business*; Springer: Dordrecht, The Netherlands, 2019; pp. 327–350.
23. Van Stel, A.; Carree, M.; Thurik, R. The Effect of Entrepreneurial Activity on National Economic Growth. *Small Bus. Econ.* **2005**, *24*, 311–321. [CrossRef]
24. Audretsch, D.B.; Keilbach, M.C.; Lehmann, E. *Entrepreneurship and Economic Growth*; Oxford University Press: Oxford, UK, 2006.
25. Carree, M.; Thurik, A.R. Understanding the role of entrepreneurship for economic growth. In *The Handbook of Entrepreneurship and Economic Growth*; Carree, M., Thurik, A.R., Eds.; Edward Elgar Publishing: Cheltenham, UK, 2006; pp. ix–xix.
26. Cohen, B.; Winn, M.I. Market imperfections, opportunity and sustainable entrepreneurship. *J. Bus. Ventur.* **2007**, *22*, 29–49. [CrossRef]
27. Dean, T.J.; McMullen, J.S. Toward a theory of sustainable entrepreneurship: Reducing environmental degradation through entrepreneurial action. *J. Bus. Ventur.* **2007**, *22*, 50–76. [CrossRef]
28. Hart, S.L.; Milstein, M.B. Global sustainability and the creative destruction of industries. *MIT Sloan Manag. Rev.* **1999**, *41*, 23.
29. Horne, J.; Recker, M.; Michelfelder, I.; Jay, J.; Kratzer, J. Exploring entrepreneurship related to the sustainable development goals—mapping new venture activities with semi-automated content analysis. *J. Clean. Prod.* **2020**, *242*, 118052. [CrossRef]
30. Pacheco, D.F.; Dean, T.J.; Payne, D.S. Escaping the green prison: Entrepreneurship and the creation of opportunities for sustainable development. *J. Bus. Ventur.* **2010**, *25*, 464–480. [CrossRef]
31. Gast, J.; Gundolf, K.; Cesinger, B. Doing business in a green way: A systematic review of the ecological sustainability entrepreneurship literature and future research directions. *J. Clean. Prod.* **2017**, *147*, 44–56. [CrossRef]
32. Youssef, A.B.; Boubaker, S.; Omri, A. Entrepreneurship and sustainability: The need for innovative and institutional solutions. *Technol. Forecast. Soc. Chang.* **2018**, *129*, 232–241. [CrossRef]
33. Baumol, W.J. Entrepreneurship: Productive, Unproductive, and Destructive. *J. Political Econ.* **1990**, *98*, 893–921. [CrossRef]
34. Dhahri, S.; Omri, A. Entrepreneurship contribution to the three pillars of sustainable development: What does the evidence really say? *World Dev.* **2018**, *106*, 64–77. [CrossRef]
35. Omri, A. Entrepreneurship, sectoral outputs and environmental improvement: International evidence. *Technol. Forecast. Soc. Chang.* **2018**, *128*, 46–55. [CrossRef]
36. Pansera, M.; Sarkar, S. Crafting Sustainable Development Solutions: Frugal Innovations of Grassroots Entrepreneurs. *Sustainability* **2016**, *8*, 51. [CrossRef]
37. Vivarelli, M. Is entrepreneurship necessarily good? Microeconomic evidence from developed and developing countries. *Ind. Corp. Chang.* **2013**, *22*, 1453–1495. [CrossRef]
38. Ghani, E.; Kerr, W.R.; O'Connell, S.D. Who Creates Jobs? *Econ. Premises* **2011**, *70*, 1–7.
39. Gaglio, C.M. The Role of Mental Simulations and Counterfactual Thinking in the Opportunity Identification Process*. *Entrep. Theory Pr.* **2004**, *28*, 533–552. [CrossRef]
40. Urbano, D.; Aparicio, S. Entrepreneurship capital types and economic growth: International evidence. *Technol. Forecast. Soc. Chang.* **2016**, *102*, 34–44. [CrossRef]
41. Van Stel, A.; Storey, D. The Link between Firm Births and Job Creation: Is there a Upas Tree Effect? *Reg. Stud.* **2004**, *38*, 893–909. [CrossRef]
42. York, J.G.; Venkataraman, S. The entrepreneur–environment nexus: Uncertainty, innovation, and allocation. *J. Bus. Ventur.* **2010**, *25*, 449–463. [CrossRef]
43. Zahra, S.A.; Gedajlovic, E.; Neubaum, D.O.; Shulman, J.M. A typology of social entrepreneurs: Motives, search processes and ethical challenges. *J. Bus. Ventur.* **2009**, *24*, 519–532. [CrossRef]

44. Block, J.H.; Wagner, M. Necessity and Opportunity Entrepreneurs in Germany: Characteristics and Earning s Differentials. *Schmalenbach Bus. Rev.* **2010**, *62*, 154–174. [CrossRef]

45. Kautonen, T.; Palmroos, J. The impact of a necessity-based start-up on subsequent entrepreneurial satisfaction. *Int. Entrep. Manag. J.* **2009**, *6*, 285–300. [CrossRef]

46. Acs, Z.J. Foundations of high impact entrepreneurship. In *Foundations and Trends in Entrepreneurship*; Now Publishers Inc.: Delft, The Netherlands, 2008; Volume 4, pp. 535–620.

47. Dencker, J.C.; Gruber, M.; Shah, S.K. Individual and Opportunity Factors Influencing Job Creation in New Firms. *Acad. Manag. J.* **2009**, *52*, 1125–1147. [CrossRef]

48. Solymossy, E. *Push/Pull Motivation: Does It Matter in Terms of Venture Performance?* Reynolds, P., Bygrave, W.D., Carter, N.C., Manigart, S., Mason, C., Meyer, G., Shaver, K., Eds.; Frontiers of Entrepreneurship Research: Babson Park, FL, USA; Babson College: Wellesley, MA, USA, 1997; pp. 204–217.

49. Omri, A.; Afi, H. How can entrepreneurship and educational capital lead to environmental sustainability? *Struct. Chang. Econ. Dyn.* **2020**, *54*, 1–10. [CrossRef]

50. Acs, Z.J.; Audretsch, D.B. *Innovation and Small Firms*; MIT Press: Cambridge, MA, USA, 1990.

51. Colombo, M.G.; Delmastro, M.; Grilli, L. Entrepreneurs' human capital and the start-up size of new technology-based firms. *Int. J. Ind. Organ.* **2004**, *22*, 1183–1211. [CrossRef]

52. Schumpeter, J.A. Business Cycles. In *A Theoretical, Historical and Statistical Analysis of the Capitalist Process*; McGraw-Hill: New York, NY, USA, 1939.

53. Baumol, W.J. Entrepreneurship and invention: Toward their microeconomic value theory. *AEI Brook. Jt. Cent. Regul. Stud. Relat. Publ.* **2005**, 5–38.

54. Shane, S. Why encouraging more people to become entrepreneurs is bad public policy. *Small Bus. Econ.* **2009**, *33*, 141–149. [CrossRef]

55. Wennekers, S.; Thurik, A. Linking Entrepreneurship and Economic Growth. *Small Bus. Econ.* **1999**, *13*, 27–56. [CrossRef]

56. Acs, Z.J.; Braunerhjelm, P.; Audretsch, D.B.; Carlsson, B. The knowledge spillover theory of entrepreneurship. *Small Bus. Econ.* **2009**, *32*, 15–30. [CrossRef]

57. Aghion, P.; Howitt, P. A Model of Growth through Creative Destruction. *Econometrica* **1992**, *60*, 323. [CrossRef]

58. Wach, K.; Wojciechowski, L. Inward FDI and entrepreneurship rate: Empirical evidence on selected effects of FDI in Visegrad countries. *J. Econ. Manag.* **2016**, *24*, 42–54. [CrossRef]

59. Doytch, N.; Epperson, N. FDI and Entrepreneurship in Developing Countries. *Glob. Sci. Technol. Forum Bus. Rev.* **2012**, *1*, 120–125.

60. De Backer, K.; Sleuwaegen, L. Does Foreign Direct Investment Crowd Out Domestic Entrepreneurship? *Rev. Ind. Organ.* **2003**, *22*, 67–84. [CrossRef]

61. Danakol, S.H.; Estrin, S.; Reynolds, P.; Weitzel, G. Foreign direct investment via M&A and domestic entrepreneurship: Blessing or curse? *Small Bus. Econ.* **2016**, *48*, 599–612. [CrossRef]

62. Javorcik, B.S. Does Foreign Direct Investment Increase the Productivity of Domestic Firms? In Search of Spillovers through Backward Linkages. *Am. Econ. Rev.* **2004**, *94*, 605–627. [CrossRef]

63. De Maeseneire, W.; Claeys, T. SMEs, foreign direct investment and financial constraints: The case of Belgium. *Int. Bus. Rev.* **2012**, *21*, 408–424. [CrossRef]

64. Meyer, K. Perspectives on multinational enterprises in emerging economies. *J. Int. Bus. Stud.* **2004**, *35*, 259–276. [CrossRef]

65. Albulescu, C.T.; Tămăşilă, M. The Impact of FDI on Entrepreneurship in the European Countries. *Procedia Soc. Behav. Sci.* **2014**, *124*, 219–228. [CrossRef]

66. Kim, P.H.; Li, M. Injecting demand through spillovers: Foreign direct investment, domestic socio-political conditions, and host-country entrepreneurial activity. *J. Bus. Ventur.* **2014**, *29*, 210–231. [CrossRef]

67. Rojec, M.; Knell, M. Why is there a lack of evidence on knowledge spillovers from foreign direct investment? *J. Econ. Surv.* **2017**, *32*, 579–612. [CrossRef]

68. Ascani, A.; Balland, P.-A.; Morrison, A. Heterogeneous foreign direct investment and local innovation in Italian Provinces. *Struct. Chang. Econ. Dyn.* **2020**, *53*, 388–401. [CrossRef]

69. Gorodnichenco, Y.; Svejnar, J.; Terrell, K. Do foreign investment and trade spur innovation? *Eur. Econ. Rev.* **2010**, *121*, 1–27. [CrossRef]

70. O'Malley, E.; O'Gorman, C. Competitive advantage in the Irish indigenous software industry and the role of inward foreign direct investment. *Eur. Plan. Stud.* **2001**, *9*, 303–321. [CrossRef]

71. Sachs, J.; Schmidt-Traub, G.; Kroll, C.; Lafortune, G.; Fuller, G. *Sustainable Development Report*; SDSN: New York, NY, USA, 2019.

72. Reynolds, P.; Bosma, N.; Autio, E.; Hunt, S.; De Bono, N.; Servais, I.; Lopez, P.-G.; Chin, N. Global entrepreneurship monitor: Data collecting design and implementation 1998–2003. *Small Bus. Econ.* **2005**, *24*, 205–231. [CrossRef]

73. Sarkodie, S.A.; Strezov, V. Effect of foreign direct investments, economic development and energy consumption on greenhouse gas emissions in developing countries. *Sci. Total. Environ.* **2019**, *646*, 862–871. [CrossRef]

74. Fölster, S.; Henrekson, M. Growth elects of government expenditure and taxation in rich countries. *Eur. Econ. Rev.* **2001**, *45*, 1501–1520. [CrossRef]

75. Aust, V.; Morais, A.I.; Pinto, I. How does foreign direct investment contribute to Sustainable Development Goals? Evidence from African countries. *J. Clean. Prod.* **2020**, *245*, 118823. [CrossRef]

76. Pathaka, S.; Laplume, A.; Xavier, E.-O. Crafting sustainable development solutions: Frugal innovations of grassroots entrepreneurs. *Entrep. Reg. Dev.* **2015**, *27*, 334–356.

77. Caves, R.E. *Multinational Enterprise and Economic Analysis, Cambridge Surveys of Economic Literature*, 2nd ed.; Cambridge University Press: Cambridge, UK, 1996.

78. Kleibergen, F.; Paap, R. Generalized Reduced Rank Tests Using the Singular Value Decomposition. *J. Econom.* **2006**, *133*, 97–126. [CrossRef]

79. Martínez-Rodriguez, I.; Callejas-Albiñana, F.E.; Callejas-Albiñana, A.I. Economic and Socio-Cultural Drivers of Necessity and Opportunity Entrepreneurship Depending on the Business Cycle Phase. *J. Bus. Econ. Manag.* **2020**, *21*, 373–394. [CrossRef]

80. Brixiova, Z.; Égert, B. Entrepreneurship, institutions and skills in low-income countries. *Econ. Model.* **2017**, *67*, 381–391. [CrossRef]

81. Buzzelly, M. Modifiable Areal Unit Problem. *Int. Encycl. Hum. Geogr.* **2020**, 169–173.

3

Entrepreneurial Competencies and Organisational Change—Assessing Entrepreneurial Staff Competencies within Higher Education Institutions

Jaana Seikkula-Leino [1,*] **and Maria Salomaa** [1,2]

[1] RDI and Business Operations, Tampere University of Applied Sciences, Kuntokatu, 33520 Tampere, Finland

[2] Lincoln International Business School, University of Lincoln, Brayford Pool, Lincoln LN6 7DQ, UK; maria.salomaa@tuni.fi

* Correspondence: jaana.seikkula-leino@tuni.fi

Abstract: Universities have become more entrepreneurial organisations in the past decades. However, the entrepreneurial competences needed for driving societal change have not been largely discussed in research literature. This paper sought to examine entrepreneurial staff competencies in the context of universities of applied sciences. A single case study from Finland, Tampere University of Applied Science, was selected. As the case institution has systematically developed an entrepreneurial strategy, the aim was to examine how entrepreneurial thinking and actions at individual and organisational levels were realised. The quantitative study involved 17 supervisors and 39 employees, and the survey took place in the Spring of 2020. The results indicate that the entrepreneurial strategy has been successfully implemented. Although both supervisors and employees evaluate themselves and the organisation to be entrepreneurial, internal communication should be further developed. Especially the provision of constructive feedback to support self-efficacy and self-esteem should be highlighted. As previous studies have stressed the challenges of integrating entrepreneurial behaviour in a 'traditional' academic context, these results provide insights for universities aiming to implement an entrepreneurial strategy, stressing psychological factors in the development of entrepreneurial competencies. Furthermore, we introduce a new theoretical approach to the discussion on the entrepreneurial university based on entrepreneurial competences.

Keywords: entrepreneurial competencies; sustainability; higher education; entrepreneurial university; organisational change

1. Introduction: Towards Entrepreneurial Organisation

Over the past decade, there has been a clear shift towards strengthening organisational culture through entrepreneurial competencies. The overarching aim to reinforce these competencies reflects the many recent socio-economic and politic changes in the society: In all sectors, new solutions for promoting innovation and creativity, aligned with social and economic well-being, are constantly been sought out [1,2]. However, investments in new knowledge do not automatically lead into increased competitiveness and growth, but the focus should be on commercialization and encouraging entrepreneurship [3], especially by strengthening the transition from 'latent' to 'emergent' entrepreneurship. In the latter, the entrepreneur has the needed strategic and managerial capacity to pursue change by turning knowledge spillovers into economic growth [4]. According to Chandler and Jansen [5] these entrepreneurial competencies are indeed fundamental for different kinds of organisations, so that they can perform and succeed well. In the context of corporate entrepreneurship, the development of an entrepreneurial organisation has been defined as a process whereby an individual or a group of individuals, in association with an existing organisation, together create a new organisation or investigate renewal or innovation within that organisation [6]. In practice, as argued by Bosman, Grard, and Roegiers [7], an individual, competence-based approach supporting entrepreneurship has become the most common structure for (staff) training programs and courses, e.g., in the field of entrepreneurial behaviour.

In parallel to the emergence of research literature focusing on entrepreneurial competencies, a lot has been written about universities' entrepreneurial and societal missions as well as their increasingly emphasised role in innovation systems. Hitherto, the academic literature has addressed the phenomenon through a myriad of overlapping concepts, including 'entrepreneurial university' [8], 'engaged university', see, e.g., [7,8], and the university 'third mission', see, e.g., [9,10], all of which widely refer to a range of different activities beyond education and research. These new roles played by universities have been increasingly articulated in higher education policies [11], which strengthen the university' role in the knowledge economy [12]. While many reform agendas have been created to support efficiency, effectiveness, and accountability within higher education institutions, e.g., by developing demand-based interdisciplinary research with businesses and industry partners [13], the entrepreneurial competencies needed for carrying out such initiatives has been less discussed in the context of higher education studies. Yet previous studies have indicated that reinforcing entrepreneurship education as well as entrepreneurial attitudes within the academic communities can be beneficial for producing highly skilled future entrepreneurs, allowing higher education systems to make a contribution to regional and national development [14].

It is obvious that both organisational and individual capacities to cope with uncertainty are increasingly important also in the higher education sector, especially in the time of the COVID-19 crises, which has challenged everyday operations of the higher education sector. Entrepreneurial capacities have been associated with organisational and individual abilities to cope in an uncertain and complex environment [15] in the context of entrepreneurial university [8]. As some scholars have even argued, that 'entrepreneurialism' can only be linked to individuals instead of organisations [16], and our paper seeks to generate in-depth knowledge on the entrepreneurial competencies needed for organisational change in the context of higher education institutions. Through a quantitative analysis based on a staff survey conducted in the Tampere University of Applied Sciences, we produce new insights on the different competence areas effectively driving change towards an entrepreneurial organisation.

The paper is structured as follows: Firstly, in the literature review, we summarise the shift towards entrepreneurial universities since the late 1990s, after which we present the chosen framework for assessing entrepreneurial competencies. Secondly, we provide an overview on the case study and a discussion on the methods. Thirdly, we present the results from the questionnaire. Lastly, we discuss on the key findings and make suggestions for further research.

2. Entrepreneurial Competencies Driving Organisational Change

2.1. From Entrepreneurial Universities to Entrepreneurial Competencies

It has been argued that 'entrepreneurial activity' can have a positive impact, not only to economic growth, but also to wealth and productivity [17]. Since the late 1990, the debate on the rise and impact of entrepreneurialism have been on the increase, also in regard to public organisations such as universities. In Clark's original conceptualisation of the 'entrepreneurial university' [8], 'entrepreneurialism' refers primarily to higher education institutions' internal dynamics and strategies [18]. The concept has been described as a framework for understanding organisational changes as 'dynamic, continuous, and incremental processes' based on collegial entrepreneurialism rather than direct top-down initiatives and/or management strategies [18]. However, the entrepreneurial university also underlines the commitment of the universities' personnel, being that reinforcing entrepreneurship demands 'department ownership' [8]. This can lead to the development of 'enterprise culture', which is open to change, as well as both creation and exploitation of innovations among students and staff members [14].

Overall, the research literature discussing entrepreneurship underlines that raising entrepreneurial efficacies will also raise perceptions of venture and entrepreneurial intentions in general [19]. Additionally, according to Wilson, Kickul, and Marlino [20] self-efficacy may play an important role in shaping and/or limiting perceived career options. Moreover, Neto et al. [21] found out in their study that self-efficacy actually predicts entrepreneurial behaviour of individuals. Thus, self-efficacy plays a key role in organisations' development, although it has been more associated with individual learning. As an example, Bandura [22] explains that students' beliefs about their efficacy regulate their learning, motivation, and mastering accomplishments. Moreover, teachers' beliefs about their personal efficacy and capacity to motivate and promote learning can affect the types of learning environments they create in practice for their students, as well as the level of academic progress they can accomplish in cooperation with their students. Furthermore, faculties' and schools' institutional beliefs about their collective instructional efficacy can contribute significantly to the schools' academic achievements and entrepreneurial activities as 'institutional determinants' increasing student entrepreneurship [14]. According to Borba [23,24], students and staff with high self-esteem and self-efficacy usually perform well, and they can better promote the development of their organisation towards goal-orientated actions, wider success, and collaborations.

Being so, we conclude that self-efficacy is not only an individual process, but it can be understood as a phenomenon formulated both through individuals and groups. Thus, self-efficacy, as a shared resource driving individual and organisational entrepreneurial competencies, is also our starting point for measuring the entrepreneurial organisation from the staff's perspective. In the following section, we present the framework for assessing entrepreneurial competencies within the context of higher education.

2.2. Framework for Assessing Entrepreneurial Competencies

According to Seikkula-Leino [25], the ground of entrepreneurial learning and behaviour involves a range of individual different competencies, such as: (1) Trust and respect, (2) each person is unique, (3) open interaction, (4) approaching goals and new opportunities, (5) competence and success oriented behaviour, (6) and working life, networks, and development. Seikkula-Leino's approach builds on Borba's [23,24] psychological and educational work focused on the development of self-esteem and self-empowerment, which can also be formed through group activities supporting staff self-esteem and self-efficacy—see also [22,26,27]—as well as through experiential learning, see, e.g., [28]. These elements, in combination, are also inherent in entrepreneurship research, e.g., through opportunity creation on both individual and organisational levels, see, e.g., [29,30].

Building on Seikkula-Leino's [25] and Ruskovaara et al.'s [31] previous work, we have chosen the following framework to assess entrepreneurial competencies (see Table 1) in the context of higher education. These entrepreneurial competencies form the theoretical basis of the research and designing of the survey, which was conducted for finding out how these entrepreneurial competencies are reflected in the thinking and everyday functions of both managers and employees within the chosen case university.

Table 1. Description of entrepreneurial competencies driving organisational change.

Competence Area	Description
Trust and respect within the working community	There is trust between the employees and the management, and in the organisation as a whole. There is trust enough to allow mistakes that may lead to new solutions or ideas.
Each person is unique	The personnel have an understanding of individual respect, and the personnel are given the space and opportunity to act individually. This also promotes new innovative ways to work in the organisation.

Table 1. *Cont.*

Competence Area	Description
Open interaction	A cooperative approach is encouraged at work. The personnel are proud of the team spirit in the workplace. The staff shares ideas. Furthermore, the organisation does not cooperate only internally. Interaction expands to communities outside of the organisation.
Approaching goals and new opportunities	The achievement of personal and group goals is supported in the workplace. The personnel are encouraged to seek out new opportunities and ways of doing things to achieve goals. The community participates in decision making. Changes in a working community bring improvements to the work.
Job satisfaction and competence	The personnel's skills are recognized, and the personnel have an opportunity to leverage their strengths in the workplace. There is a feeling that the staff is able to significantly influence one another's results. The staff evaluates whether objectives have led to results.
Working life, networks, development	The workplace supports the development of understanding of different fields and professions, and networking and partnerships with working life and the society around that. A workplace encourages the development/further development of ideas, solutions, or services for customers or other target groups. There is continuous development of competences. Moreover, understanding of entrepreneurship and/or entrepreneurial business is shared within the organisation.

Source: Authors' own elaboration after Seikkula-Leino [25] and Borba [23,24].

3. Case Study Overview

The Finnish Universities of Applied Sciences (UAS) actively conduct collaborative RDI activities with a range of different stakeholders, but these external linkages tend to be more often results of bottom-up initiatives rather than institutional bridging mechanisms (e.g., [32]). However, the Finnish UASs are considered to be significant promoters of innovation, particularly through their group-based and networked learning environments [33]. A strong entrepreneurial competence base of the UAS staff members could further reinforce the establishment of linkages with external partners and other collaborative initiatives [14]

The chosen case institution, namely the Tampere University of Applied Sciences (TAMK), is one of the biggest UASs in Finland, with well-established working life connections and a strategic aim to develop towards entrepreneurial organisation. It is a multidisciplinary UAS with 13,000 students and about 800 staff members, offering a range of BA and MA degree programmes in health and wellbeing, business studies, and technology. It's mission statement underlines the importance of developing collaboration with external partners and higher education's societal role: 'Our strong orientation towards working life ensures the best learning possibilities for our students. Furthermore, we are involved in research, development and innovation which specifically target the development needs of working life.' TAMK is also part of the newly established Tampere Higher Education Community, following the merger of the former University of Tampere and Tampere University of Technology in 2019, thus it represents a unique case in the Finnish UAS scene.

3.1. Research Design, Questions, and Target Group

Previous studies imply that the development of an entrepreneurial culture is not straightforward in an academic context [34]. This is argued, in particular, in the previous studies of Seikkula-Leino et al. [35,36] and Devici and Seikkula-Leino [37], discussing how entrepreneurship has been integrated into teachers' education. These studies underline that especially the development of entrepreneurial competencies and skills among the higher education staff members is not uncomplicated. These findings provided a profitable starting point for our study, allowing us to build on existing viewpoints related to entrepreneurial competencies in the context of higher education. Thus, we wanted to further investigate how different staff members working in a university perceive entrepreneurialism within the organisation, and how it could be reinforced while also examining individual employees' assessments of their entrepreneurial capacities. Furthermore, the entrepreneurial competencies of the supervisors were studies through both staff's evaluations and their own assessments.

It has been argued that the first step towards driving (organisational) change successfully is to ensure that the employees themselves have assimilated the strategic reform [35–37], thus we decided to limit our research to the academic personnel. The research questions of this study are the following:

1.   How are the entrepreneurial competencies assessed in a (higher education) organisation?
1.1   How do the employees evaluate the entrepreneurial competencies of their organisation?
1.2. How do the supervisors evaluate the entrepreneurial competencies of their organisation?
1.3. Are there any differences between the employees' and supervisors' evaluations of their organization's entrepreneurial competencies?

2.   How do personnel self-evaluate their entrepreneurial competencies?
2.1. How do the employees self-evaluate their entrepreneurial competencies?
2.2. How do the supervisors self-evaluate their entrepreneurial competencies?
2.3. Are there any differences between the employees' and the supervisors' self-evaluations of the entrepreneurial competencies?

3.   How are the entrepreneurial activities of the supervisors visible in the organisation?
3.1. How do the employees evaluate the entrepreneurial competencies of their supervisors?
3.2. How do the employees' evaluations of the supervisors' entrepreneurial competencies accord with the supervisors' self-evaluations of their entrepreneurial competencies?

As we explained above, the target group of the study includes different staff members working in higher education institutions (HEI). TAMK provided an interesting case HEI, as it has a strategic aim to strengthen entrepreneurial skills and competencies. Overall, the case study provided a suitable platform for investigating how these organisational goals can be detected in individual staff members' attitudes and beliefs. As Cohen, Manion, and Morrison [38] argue, the generalisability of such single experiments (e.g., case and pilot studies) can be extended through replication or multiple experiment strategies, allowing case studies to contribute to the development of a growing pool of data for eventually achieving a wider generalisability. Thus, the results obtained from our pilot study contribute to 'analytic' rather than 'statistical' generalisation to build on further studies.

The survey was conducted in Spring 2020 by sending the questionnaire to 198 respondents working at Tampere University of Applied Sciences by email. This specific group of staff member has been actively or, to some extent, actively involved in the development of an entrepreneurial organisation in TAMK. Altogether, 56 of the responses were received from 17 supervisors and 39 employees. In total, our response rate in this random sampling is about 29%, which can be considered reasonably good in this kind of quantitative research setting.

3.2. Assessment Tools and the Data Analysis

In our previous studies, the assessment tools have been successfully used in the corporate world (e.g., Wihuri Group, Property Management Association, Raisio, pharmacies etc.) between 2012–2015. These individual studies confirm the reliability of the assessment tools; as an example, Cronbach's alpha levels varied in different categories between 0.67–0.96, which can be interpreted as 'satisfactory' [39]. Minor changes were made to the metrics to increase its usability in the context of higher educational institutions; the assessment tools utilised in this study are based on Seikkula-Leino's [25] approach on entrepreneurial behaviour presented in the previous section. In addition, the SKILLOON student assessment tools, based on similar theoretical approach, were utilised in the development of the tools for this study. SKILLOON (www.skilloon.com), is an official education concept of Education Finland supported by the Finnish National Board of Education. SKILLOON involved assessment tools, entrepreneurial activities, and student mentoring programmes. SKILLOON is created in research cooperation with schools and universities, and it is used for education and research purposes.

The assessment tool targeted to personnel, the SKILLOON staff assessment survey, had four different assessment tools, each of which included six sets of research questions. The first assessment tool was targeted to both employees and supervisors, and it contained an evaluation of the different (entrepreneurial characteristics) of the organisation. The second and third assessment tool focused on self-assessment of the employers and the supervisors, and finally, the fourth assessment tool was targeted to employers, who assessed the employers. Each of these four sections contained between five to seven questions of claims. The respondents specified their level of agreement or disagreement on a symmetric agree/disagree scale between 1–10, whereas 1 meant that the respondent fully disagrees with the claim, and 10 that the respondent fully agrees. Each competence area forms an individual summation notation, by calculating each respondents' mean for each set of questions.

In order to assess the quality and representativeness of the data, we inspected the pattern and frequencies of missing values. One respondent was excluded from the analysis in the supervisors' self-evaluation section due to non-response. In addition, three respondents (employees) lacked an answer to one question in different sections, and these were treated as missing values in the analysis. The examples of survey questions and claims are summarised in Table 2.

Table 2. The examples of SKILLOON staff assessment tools and claims.

Competence Area, Examples	Evaluation of the Organisation (The 1st Assessment Tool)
Trust and respect within the working community	1. The staff share the same opinion about the common rules.
	2. There is open communication between the employees and the management, and this enables, for example, the proposal of 'crazy' ideas.
	3. There is trust between the employees and the management.
	4. Employees can count on the promises made by management.
	5. The rules governing employees are clear.
	6. We see that mistakes that are made lead to new solutions or ideas.
Open interaction	1. It is clear that the personnel are proud of the team spirit in the workplace.
	2. Cooperation is encouraged at work.
	3. The atmosphere in the workplace means that people keep ideas to themselves.*
	4. Employees want to work for the benefit of the whole organisation and not only to complete their own tasks.
	5. The employees have a feeling of unity.
	6. We actively develop network cooperation with parties outside our working community.
	Question number 3 was reversed. This was taken into account in our analysis by reversing the answers for this question.

Competence Area, Examples	Self-Evaluation of Supervisors (The 2nd Assessment Tool)	Self-Evaluation of Employees (The 3rd Assessment Tool)
Each person is unique	As a member of the management team … 1. I make an effort to get to know the personal lives of the employees. 2. I send personal messages (e.g., congratulations, condolences, thanks). 3. I regularly consider the uniqueness of each employee; 4. I take into account the efforts of employees. 5. I provide opportunities for employees to get to know each other's interests. 6. I allow space for employees to take risks when doing new things.	1. I will take note if my colleague or other member of the work community has succeeded in something. 2. I don't mind if I act differently to other employees. 3. I like to take into account the personal lives of others (birthday, hobbies, children, spouse, etc.). 4. I show my appreciation for others. 5. I am not afraid of failure, but I boldly try new things. 6. I encourage other employees to do new things.

Table 2. *Cont.*

Competence Area, Examples	Self-Evaluation of Supervisors (The 2nd Assessment Tool)	Self-Evaluation of Employees (The 3rd Assessment Tool)
Approaching goals and new opportunities	As a member of management team … 1. I strive to map employees' thoughts and ideas on development regularly. 2. I help staff develop a shared vision of what is most important in our workplace for the client or other target group. 3. I make sure that everyone is aware of our mission content. 4. I offer opportunities for shared responsibility. 5. I provide detailed feedback to help each employee achieve their goals. 6. I guide employees towards seeing the positive aspects of change.	1. I strive to find new opportunities in my work. 2. There are clear goals in my work. 3. I strive to reach my goals. 4. I try to influence decision-making. 5. I understand what the goals of our organisation are. 6. I am excited about new challenges in my work.

Competence Area, Examples	Evaluation of the Supervisors by Employees (The 4th Assessment Tool)	
Job satisfaction and competence	As an employee I think that the management … 1. Offers the support I need so I can fulfil the expectations set for me. 2. Enables me to demonstrate my competence. 3. Directs my improvement at work through various methods (e.g., through observation, discussion, leveraging customer feedback, etc.). 4. Clearly states what is good in my work and what could be improved. 5. Helps me to identify the significance of my activities regarding the personal activities of others (target groups/customers, other employees, etc.). 6. Evaluates how I have achieved results.	
Working life, networks, development	As an employee I think that the management … 1. Supports the development of my understanding of the various sectors and areas of working life. 2. Directs me towards networking in order to support the development of my work. (Networks include companies, educational institutions, organisations, social actors, etc.). 3. Encourages me to develop/further develop ideas, solutions, or services for customers. (A customer may also be a person or entity who does not pay for a service.) 4. Supports me in developing new solutions that improve my own operations. 5. Supports the continuous development of my own skills. 6. Contributes to strengthening my understanding of entrepreneurship and/or entrepreneurship business. 7. Encourages the search for partnerships from different sectors of society.	

4. Results

In this section, we present the key results from each of the four assessment tools of the survey.

4.1. How Are the Entrepreneurial Competencies Assessed in A (Higher Education) Organisation?

4.1.1. How Do the Employees Evaluate the Entrepreneurial Competencies of Their Organisation?

The sum variables were formed from the responses of 39 employees. The averages of the sum variables in every assessment tool are quite high, as we can see from Table 3. The highest average is in assessment tool 'Trust and respect within the working community' and the lowest average is in assessment tool 'Job satisfaction and competence'. Only the lowest average in assessment tool 'Job satisfaction and competence' is slightly smaller than in other assessment tools. This could be explained by the fact that in this assessment tool, one of the questions was reversed—there might be people that haven't noticed this. On the other hand, there is a reversed question also in assessment tool 'Open interaction', but there was no visible deviation within the results. Overall, the employees considered their organisation to be rather entrepreneurial.

4.1.2. How Do the Supervisors Evaluate the Entrepreneurial Competencies of Their Organisation?

The sum variables were formed from the responses of 17 supervisors. The highest average is in assessment tool 'Working life, networks, development' and the lowest average is in assessment tool 'Each person is unique'. The averages of every six sum variables were high and they were all at the same level. This can be verified from Table 3. In general, the supervisors highly evaluate the entrepreneurial competencies of their organisation.

4.1.3. Are There Any Differences between the Employees' and the Supervisors' Evaluations of the Entrepreneurial Competencies of Their Organisation?

Even though the averages of supervisors are slightly higher than the averages of employees in each assessment tool (Table 3), the boxplots in Figure 1 indicate that there is more dispersion in the responses of employees. Moreover, the employees have more extreme responses. In these boxplots, the orange and blue colours are for supervisors and employees, respectively. This could be explained by the fact that there were significantly more employees (n = 39) than supervisors (n = 17) among the respondents. Both the highest and the lowest averages of supervisors and employees are in different assessment tools. It was examined by analysis of variance (ANOVA) whether there were differences between the responses of supervisors and employees. The p-values in each assessment tool are in Table 3. Thus, based on these p-values, there was a statistically significant difference in assessment tool 'Job satisfaction and competence' between the answers of supervisors and the answers of employees: The supervisors evaluate the entrepreneurial competences in this assessment tool significantly higher than the employees.

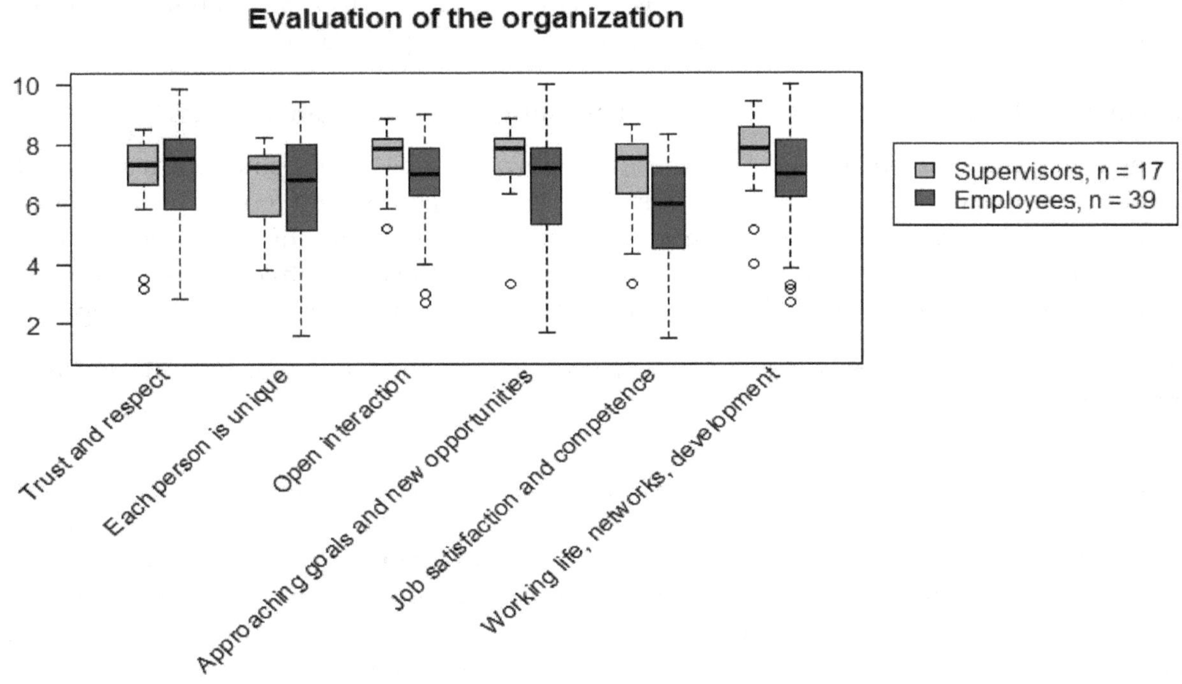

Figure 1. Evaluation of the organisation by each competency area, n = 56.

Altogether, the personnel's perception on the entrepreneurial competencies of their organisation is quite good, and there are no significant differences between the means of assessments of supervisors and the means of assessments of employees, except in assessment tool 'Job satisfaction and competence'. However, in this assessment tool, the supervisors evaluate the competencies of their organisation to be higher than the employees.

Table 3. Evaluation of the organisation, n = 56.

	Evaluation of the Organisation, Supervisors	Evaluation of the Organisation, Employees	Sig.
	Mean	Mean	
1. Trust and respect within the working community	6.98	6.9	0.9502
2. Each person is unique	6.58	6.43	0.768
3. Open interaction	7.52	6.82	0.1025
4. Approaching goals and new opportunities	7.24	6.46	0.1006
5. Job satisfaction and competence	6.99	5.73	0.008955 **
6. Working life, networks, development	7.6	6.86	0.127

*, **, *** indicate significant at the level of 5%, 1%, and 0,1% respectively.

4.2. How Do the Personnel Evaluate Their Own Entrepreneurial Competencies?

4.2.1. How Do the Employees Self-Evaluate Their Entrepreneurial Competencies?

The sum variables were formed from the answers of 39 employees. The averages in every assessment tool are very high as we can see from Table 4. The highest average is in assessment tool 'Open interaction', and the lowest average is in assessment tool 'Job satisfaction and competence'. In general, the employees evaluate themselves to be very entrepreneurial.

4.2.2. How Do the Supervisors Self-Evaluate Their Entrepreneurial Competencies?

The sum variables were formed from the responses of 16 supervisors, since one respondent among the supervisors did not answer any questions of the last two assessment tools. The averages are high or very high in all assessment tools, as we can see from Table 4. The highest average is in assessment tool 'Trust and respect within the working community', and the lowest average is in assessment tool 'Job satisfaction and competence'. The supervisors evaluate themselves to be very entrepreneurial.

4.2.3. Are There Any Differences between the Employees' and the Supervisors' Self-Evaluations of the Entrepreneurial Competencies?

Based on these results, we conclude that both the supervisors and the employees evaluate their entrepreneurial competencies to be rather high. Considering the assessment tool 'Trust and respect within the working community', the supervisors seem to evaluate themselves higher than the employees based on the means. In all other assessment tools, the employees have higher means. The highest average of employees and the highest average of supervisors are in different assessment tools. On the other hand, the lowest average of employees and the lowest average of supervisors are in the same assessment tool 'Job satisfaction and competence'. It was examined by analysis of variance whether there were differences between the means of supervisors' answers and the means of employees' answers in how they evaluate themselves. The differences are statistically significant in competency areas 'Each person is unique', 'Open collaboration', 'Approaching goals and new opportunities', and 'Job satisfaction and competence'. In each of these competence areas, the TAMK's employees seem to evaluate themselves higher than supervisors. The boxplots in Figure 2 also suggest the same conclusion obtained using statistical methods. By comparing Tables 3 and 4, we can conclude that the personnel evaluate their individual entrepreneurial competencies to be higher than the collective capacities of the organization. This applies to every assessment tool.

Self-evaluation

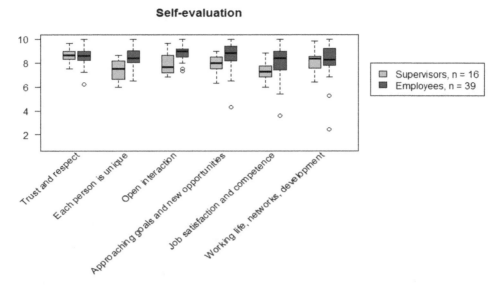

Figure 2. Self-evaluation by each competency area, n = 55.

Table 4. Self-evaluation, n = 55.

	Self-Evaluation, Supervisors,	Self-Evaluation, Employees,	Sig.
	Mean	Mean	
1. Trust and respect within the working community	8.63	8.52	0.9929
2. Each person is unique	7.48	8.41	0.000167 ***
3. Open interaction	7.95	8.83	0.0005413 ***
4. Approaching goals and new opportunities	7.9	8.62	0.002278 **
5. Job satisfaction and competence	7.28	7.98	0.009078 **
6. Working life, networks, development	8.11	8.26	0.504

*, **, *** indicate significant at the level of 5%, 1%, and 0,1% respectively.

4.3. How Are the Entrepreneurial Activities of the Supervisors Visible in the Organisation?

The supervisors' self-evaluation and the employees' assessment of the supervisors are both above average with overall means 7.89 and 6.34, respectively. Therefore, we can conclude that TAMK has a good entrepreneurial competence in particular amongst its supervisors.

4.3.1. How Do the Employees Evaluate the Entrepreneurial Competencies of Their Supervisors?

As summarised in Table 5, the employees evaluate the entrepreneurial competencies of their supervisors quite highly, with averages ranging from 5.97 to 7.14. The employees agree most in 'Trust and respect within the working community' and disagree most in 'Job satisfaction and competence'. Both the maximum mean, 7.14, and the maximum median, 7.50, is in 'Trust and respect within the working community', and the lowest mean is in 'Job satisfaction and competence'. Therefore, these assessment tools should be examined in more detail.

In the assessment tool 'Trust and respect within the working community', question 1. 'As an employee I think that the management is reliable (e.g., keeps its promises)' has a rather low dispersion, and the average of the question is 7.95, and the median is 8.0, which is a very good result. Thus, it can be concluded that the employees most often agree that the management is reliable. In 'Job satisfaction and competence', question 4. 'As an employee I think that the management clearly states what is good in my work and what could be improved' has the lowest score, a mean of 5.28, and median 5.00. The content of the question is worth paying attention to in the further development of the organisation.

Table 5. Employees evaluate supervisors, n = 39.

	Mean	Median	Standard Deviation
1. Trust and respect within the working community	7.14	7.5	1.99
2. Each person is unique	6.04	6.5	2.06
3. Open interaction	6.11	5.67	2.07
4. Approaching goals and new opportunities	6.15	6.83	2.25
5. Job satisfaction and competence	5.97	6.33	2.32
6. Working life, networks, development	6.6	7.14	2.06

4.3.2. How Do the Employees' Evaluations of the Supervisors' Entrepreneurial Competencies Accord with the Supervisors' Self-Evaluations of Their Entrepreneurial Competencies?

Supervisors evaluate their own entrepreneurial competencies to be higher compared to the employees' assessment on the entrepreneurial competencies of the supervisors. This can be seen in each of the assessment tools (Figure 3). Once again, the employees' responses are more dispersed, which may be due to the fact that there are significantly more employees (n = 39) than supervisors (n = 16) among the respondents. One supervisor lacked responses to self-evaluations assessment tools 5 and 6, reducing n to 16.

Otherwise, the results of sections 'Employees evaluation of supervisors' and 'Supervisors self-evaluation' are parallel in all the competence areas. The responses summarised in Table 6 indicates that 'Trust and respect within the working community' has the highest mean in both self-evaluation and evaluation of the supervisors, 8.63 and 7.14, respectively, while 'Job satisfaction and competence' has the lowest, 7.28 and 5.97, respectively.

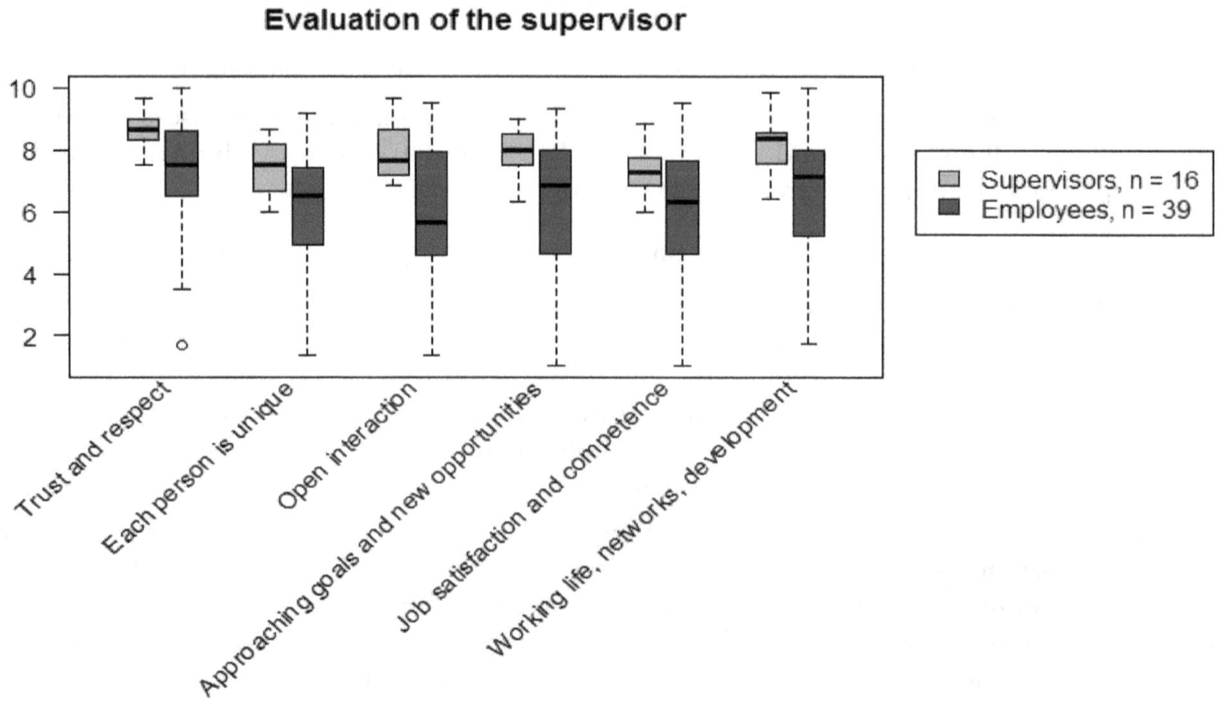

Figure 3. Evaluation of the supervisor by each competency area, n = 55.

Table 6. Comparison of the supervisors' self-evaluation and employees evaluating supervisors, n = 55.

	Supervisors' Self-Evaluation	Evaluation of the Supervisors	Sig.
	Mean	Mean	
1. Trust and respect within the working community	8.63	7.14	0.000111 ***
2. Each person is unique	7.48	6.04	0.000559 ***
3. Open interaction	7.95	6.11	2.63×10^{-5} ***
4. Approaching goals and new opportunities	7.9	6.15	6.77×10^{-5} ***
5. Job satisfaction and competence	7.28	5.97	0.002704 **
6. Working life, networks, development	8.11	6.6	0.000439 ***
Total	7.89	6.34	2.79×10^{-5} ***

*, **, *** indicate significant at the level of 5%, 1%, and 0,1% respectively.

Because of unequal variances and unbalanced data, the comparison of the two respondent groups' means was done using Welch's f-test. The differences in group means are statistically significant (see Table 6). Although in some sum variables the group means differed a lot, all are above 5.5, which can be considered a rather good result. But it should be noted that the average differences in the groups are at their highest 1.84 ('Open interaction'), which is a big deviation and may need some further examination. However, this can be partly explained by the different group sizes of the respondents, and perhaps the data is somewhat biased if, for example, more satisfied supervisors and less satisfied employees have responded to the survey.

When examining assessment tool 'Open interaction' question by question, it can be seen that the results are parallel, but the average responses of employees are, on average, almost two points lower than those of supervisors in questions 2–6. It can be concluded that supervisors and employees have different views on how well management invests in open interaction within the organisation. Also, the supervisors evaluate their entrepreneurial competencies in open interaction to be much higher than the employees do.

4.4. Consistency of the Assessment Tools

Internal consistency of the assessment tools was measured with Cronbach's alpha. These assessment tools have been used a lot, and they have been developed along the way. Furthermore, as presented before, they have been proven to work well in assessing entrepreneurial competencies in the context of private organisations. Table 7 indicates that all the alphas are good or excellent, ranging from 0.60 to 0.95, except in 'Employees self-evaluation', which is a new section. In assessment tools '1. Trust and respect within the working community', the alpha is 0.47, and in '3. Open interaction', the alpha is 0.52. However, considering that there are only 39 observations and that this section is in use for the first time, the alphas are sufficient for using the tool. This implies, that there are two questions within the two assessment tools that need to be reformulated for further use. There is also a new assessment tool 'Working life, networks, development', but it works very well, the alphas being between 0.79 and 0.95. Overall, there are a total of about 120 statements in all of our research metrics. Therefore, we do not consider this to compromise the results of the study, as only a few statements are not completely ideal. However, further examination of the tool is still needed.

Overall, we assess that the reliability and validity of the assessment tools are on a sufficient level for responding to the set research questions [39]. The phenomenon has been examined through a multidisciplinary approach, and with a range of different assessment tools and two different respondent groups. However, there is still room for further development of the assessment tools and research design, both of which are discussed in the following section together with the obtained results.

Table 7. Measuring the consistency of the assessment tools by Cronbach's alpha.

Evaluation of the Organisation	Cronbach's Alpha
1. Trust and respect within the working community	0.91
2. Each person is unique	0.87
3. Open interaction	0.83
4. Approaching goals and new opportunities	0.91
5. Job satisfaction and competence	0.88
6. Working life, networks, development	0.91
Supervisors Self-Evaluation	
1. Trust and respect within the working community	0.68
2. Each person is unique	0.61
3. Open interaction	0.7
4. Approaching goals and new opportunities	0.64
5. Job satisfaction and competence	0.6
6. Working life, networks, development	0.79
Employees Self-Evaluation	
1. Trust and respect within the working community	0.47
2. Each person is unique	0.69
3. Open interaction	0.52
4. Approaching goals and new opportunities	0.81
5. Job satisfaction and competence	0.77
6. Working life, networks, development	0.88
Employees Evaluating Supervisors	
1. Trust and respect within the working community	0.92
2. Each person is unique	0.89
3. Open interaction	0.89
4. Approaching goals and new opportunities	0.95
5. Job satisfaction and competence	0.95
6. Working life, networks, development	0.95

5. Discussion and Conclusion

In this paper, our aim was to investigate how entrepreneurial thinking and actions on both the individual and organisational levels were realized in practice after the case university's strategy reform. Our approach enabled analysing what kind of entrepreneurial competences are needed in the context of higher education to drive organisational change, which can have also a significant socio-economic impact in the long-term. Overall, the results obtained from our pilot study are positive in regard to the activities of the organisation and the individuals, both of which were estimated to be entrepreneurial. In regard to previous studies [34–37], it can be estimated that Tampere University of Applied Sciences has succeeded in implementing an efficient entrepreneurship strategy across the board, although there are also areas in which further development is needed.

The results indicate that the supervisors tend to estimate their entrepreneurial competencies higher than the employees. This implies, that the entrepreneurial strategies of the organisation are well communicated to different management levels, while the employees are less engaged and equipped to contribute to transformative change towards entrepreneurial organisation to support entrepreneurial attitudes within the university community [14]. However, as previous studies on the 'entrepreneurial university' have argued, top-down initiatives or organisational strategies alone are not sufficient for drivers of organisational change, but collegial entrepreneurialism should be supported through collegial entrepreneurialism [18]. The literature has also emphasized the role of the universities' personnel [8] in creating an 'enterprise culture'. Being so, identifying and further development of the entrepreneurial competencies among staff members would facilitate higher education institutions' path towards entrepreneurial organisations. As a practical recommendation, more attention could be paid to interaction and personal feedback of the employees. This is also likely to provide valuable feedback to the HR of organizations and the development of targeted management training programmes with an aim to equip the managers with new skills for providing constructive feedback, which supports open communication and raise further discussion on the organisational goals. Undoubtedly, the development of an entrepreneurial organisation also emphasises psychological starting points for meeting people, and thus also for strengthening the self-efficacy of individuals [26,27].

On the other hand, the number of participants in the pilot study is limited. The question also arises as to whether those persons who, in principle, have been more oriented towards entrepreneurialism, have responded to the survey. That is why, in the future, even more extensive organisational measurements are required to assess the entrepreneurial capacities effectively. Admittedly, qualitative research integration would also have the potential to generate a deeper understanding of the phenomenon. Similar measurements, also in different sectors and societal contexts, would provide more in-depth information on the extent to which entrepreneurialism appears as a contextual feature. Based on this knowledge, it would be possible to create even more customised development models or training programmes targeted for the development of an entrepreneurial organisation (e.g., management training and HR development).

Previous studies imply that the entrepreneurial culture is not given in the academic context [34–36], and thus future research is still needed in the area. Moreover, many studies aim to investigate the entrepreneurial culture within particular target groups (e.g., teachers) representing a part of the university personnel, although a more holistic view to the development of positive attitude towards entrepreneurial capacities can also increase student entrepreneurship [14] Being so, our research is even ground-breaking in the sense that we have not found any previous studies with a similar starting point—namely, identifying both employees' and supervisors' perceptions of their personal and their organisation's entrepreneurial capacities and exploring these aspects simultaneously.

As a part of the survey, employees also evaluated their supervisors. To that extent, our different assessment tools provide unique information on the phenomenon. The tools themselves triangulate [38] the manifestation of entrepreneurialism in an organisation through a variety of ways, even though our metrics provide only quantitative information. Furthermore, our tools are also based on an interdisciplinary premise integrating entrepreneurship, psychology, and behavioural science research, which contributes to the knowledge base of entrepreneurship research by 'borrowing' theoretical approaches from other research fields [40]. In this way, we have triangulated the phenomenon based on academic discussion within different disciplines, such as higher education studies.

In the future, we will also emphasise organisational development based on the Seikkula-Leino's competency model [25]. With these indicators, we will be able to study further, e.g., the effectiveness of different national and institutional development programmes. We estimate that our organisational development concept based on previous studies on entrepreneurial competencies (SKILLOON tool) could potentially contribute to the development of different entrepreneurial organisations and entrepreneurial culture, which is permissive, appreciative, and supports feelings of success and self-efficacy in all levels of the organisation. Furthermore, this approach can help to create a wider understanding of the theoretical basis of entrepreneurial organisation and its culture by identifying the elements that support effective managerial and strategic capacities to transform knowledge into entrepreneurial activity [3]. This type of culture does not only create a basis for entrepreneurial activity, but, at the same time, it promotes the wellbeing of management and employees, creating a solid foundation for building a sustainable organisational culture whilst also supporting student entrepreneurship [14]. Developing such a culture would contribute to the ability to operate more stably and in a more agile manner in a global and rapidly changing environment. It would also indirectly contribute to the strengthening of a sustainable society, in which people solve the challenges ahead and even find new and unpredictable innovative openings for the development of quality of life—allowing us to put into practice the latest global strategies driving entrepreneurship within the society (see, e.g., [1,2]).

6. Data Availability Statement

The dataset generated for this study will not be made publicly available because of the sensitive nature of the questions. All study participants were assured that the data will remain confidential and will not be shared. Therefore, all requests concerning the access to the dataset should be directed to the corresponding author.

Author Contributions: Conceptualization, J.S.-L. and M.S.; methodology, J.S.-L.; software, J.S.-L.; validation, J.S.-L.; formal analysis, J.S.-L.; writing—original draft preparation, J.S.-L. and M.S.; writing—review and editing, J.S.-L. and M.S. All authors have read and agreed to the published version of the manuscript.

References

1. Lackeus, M.; Lundqvist, M.; Middleton, K.W.; Inden, J. *The Entrepreneurial Employee in Public and Private Sector. What, Why, How*; European Commission, Joint Research Centre, Publications Office of the European Union: Luxembourg, 2020.
2. Global Entrepreneurship Monitor. *2020 Global Report*, Global Entrepreneurship Research Association: London, UK, 2020.
3. Audretsch, D.B.; Keilbach, M. Resolving the Knowledge Paradox: Knowledge-Spillover Entrepreneurship and Economic Growth. *Res. Policy* **2008**, *37*, 1697–1705. [CrossRef]
4. Caiazza, R.; Belitski, M.; Audretsch, D. From Latent to Emergent Entrepreneurship: the Knowledfe Spilloever Construction Circle. *J. Technol. Transfer* **2020**, *45*, 694–704. [CrossRef]
5. Chandler, G.N.; Jansen, E. The Founder's Self-Assessed Competence and Venture Performance. *J. Bus. Ventur.* **1992**, *7*, 223–236. [CrossRef]
6. Elfring, T. *Corporate Entrepreneurship and Venturing, ISEN International Studies in Entrepreneurship*; Springer: New York, NY, USA, 2005.
7. Bosman, C.; Grard, F.-M.; Roegiers, R. *Quel Avenir pour les Compétences?* De Boeck: Brussels, Belgium, 2000.
8. Clark, B. *Creating Entrepreneurial Universities: Organizational Pathways of Transformation*; Emerald Publishing: Bingley, UK, 1998.
9. Roper, C.; Hirth, M. A History of Change in the Third Mission of Higher Education: The Evolution of One-way Service to Interactive Engagement. *J. High. Educ. Outreach Engagem.* **2005**, *10*, 3.
10. Zomer, A.; Benneworth, P.; Boer, H.F. The Rise of the University's Third Mission. In *Reform of Higher Education in Europe*; Springer Science and Business Media: Berlin, Germany, 2011; pp. 81–101.
11. Vorley, T.; Nelles, J. Building Entrepreneurial Architectures: A Conceptual Interpretation of the Third Mission. *Policy Futur. Educ.* **2009**, *7*, 284–296. [CrossRef]
12. Göransson, B.; Maharajh, R.; Schmoch, U. New Activities of Universities in Transfer and Extension: Multiple Requirements and Manifold Solutions. *Sci. Public Policy* **2009**, *36*, 157–164. [CrossRef]
13. Etzkowitz, H.; Ranga, M.; Benner, M.; Guaranys, L.; Maculan, A.-M.; Kneller, R. Pathways to the Entrepreneurial University: Towards a Global Convergence. *Sci. Public Policy* **2008**, *35*, 681–695. [CrossRef]
14. Urbano, D.; Aparicio, S.; Guerrero, M.; Noguera, M.; Torrent-Sellens, J. Institutional Determinants of Student Employer Entrepreneurs at Catalan Universities. *Technol. Forecast. Soc. Chang.* **2017**, *123*, 271–282. [CrossRef]
15. Gibb, B.; Hannon, P. Towards Entpreneurial University? *Int. J. Entrep. Educ.* **2006**, *4*, 73–110.
16. Finley, I. Living in an 'Entrepreneurial' University. *Res. Post-Compuls. Educ.* **2004**, *9*, 417–434. [CrossRef]
17. Bjørnskov, C.; Foss, N. Institutions, Entrepreneurship, and Economic Growth: What do We Know and What so We Still Need to Know? *Acad. Manag. Perspect.* **2016**, *30*, 292–315. [CrossRef]
18. Rhoades, G.; Stensaker, B. Bringing Organisations and Systems Back Together: Extending Clark's Entrepreneurial University. *High. Educ. Q.* **2017**, *71*, 129–140. [CrossRef]
19. Shinnar, R.S.; Hsu, D.; Powell, B.C. Self-efficacy, Entrepreneurial Intentions, and Gender: Assessing the Impact of Entrepreneurship Education Longitudinally. *Int. J. Manag. Educ.* **2014**, *12*, 561–570. [CrossRef]
20. Wilson, F.; Kickul, J.; Marlino, D. Gender, Entrepreneurial Self-Efficacy, and Entrepreneurial Career Intentions: Implications for Entrepreneurship Education. *Entrep. Theory Pr.* **2007**, *31*, 387–406. [CrossRef]

21. Neto, R.; Rodrigues, V.; Stewart, D.; Xiao, A.; Snyder, J. The Influence of Self-Efficacy on Entrepreneurial Behaviour among K-12 Teachers. *Teach. Teach. Educ.* **2018**, *72*, 44–53. [CrossRef]

22. Bandura, A. Perceived Self-Efficacy in Cognitive Development and Functioning. *Educ. Psychol.* **1993**, *28*, 117–148. [CrossRef]

23. Borba, M. *A K-8 Self-Esteem, Curriculum for Improving Student Achievement, Behavior and School Climate*; Jalmar Press: Torrance, CA, USA, 1989.

24. Borba, M. *Staff Esteem Builders: The Administrator's Bible for Enhancing Self-Esteem*; Jalmar Press: Torrance, CA, USA, 1993.

25. Seikkula-Leino, J. (submitted): Developing Theory and Practice for Entrepreneurial Learning—Focus on Self-Esteem and Self-Efficacy. *Teach. Teach. Educ.* **2020**. submitted.

26. Bandura, A. *Self-Efficacy. The Exercise of Control*; W.H. Freeman and Company: New York, NY, USA, 1997.

27. Bandura, A. Self-Efficacy Beliefs in Adolescents. In *Guide for Constructing Self-Efficacy Scales*; Information Age Publishing: Greenwich, CT, USA, 2005.

28. Kolb, D. *Experiential Learning: Experience as the Source of Learning and Development*; Prentice Hall: Englewoord Cliffs, NJ, USA, 1984.

29. Schumpeter, J. *The Theory of Economic Development: An Inquiry into Profits, Capital, Credits, Interest, and the Business Cycle*; Transaction Publishers: Piscataway, NJ, USA, 1934.

30. Kirzner, I.M. *Competition and Entrepreneurship*; University of Chicago Press: Chicago, IL, USA, 1978.

31. Ruskovaara, E.; Rytkölä, T.; Seikkula-Leino, J.; Pihkala, T. Building a Measurement Tool for Entrepreneurship Education: A Participatory Development Approach. In *Entrepreneurship Research in Europe Series*; Edwaerd Elgar: Cheltenham, UK, 2015; pp. 40–58.

32. Maassen, P.; Spaapen, J.; Kallioinen, O.; Keränen, P.; Penttinen, M.; Wiedenhofer, R.; Kajaste, M. *Evaluation of Research, Development and Innovation Activities of Finnish Universities of Applied Sciences*; The Finnish Higher Education Evaluation Council: Helsinki, Finland, 2011.

33. Kettunen, J. Innovation Pedagogy for Universities of Applied Sciences. *Creative Educ.* **2011**, *2*, 56–62. [CrossRef]

34. Ilonen, S. *Entrepreneurial Learning in Entrepreneurship Education in Higher Education*; Painosalama: Turku, Finland, 2020.

35. Seikkula-Leino, J.; Satuvuori, T.; Ruskovaara, E.; Hannula, H. How do Finnish Teacher Educators Implement Entrepreneurship Education? *Educ. Train.* **2015**, *57*, 392–404. [CrossRef]

36. Seikkula-Leino, J.; Ruskovaara, E.; Hannula, H.; Saarivirta, T. Facing the Changing Demands of Europe: Integrating Entrepreneurship Education in Finnish Teacher Training Curricula. *Eur. Educ. Res. J.* **2012**, *11*, 382–399. [CrossRef]

37. Deveci, I.; Seikkula-Leino, J. A Review of Entrepreneurship Education in Teacher Education. *Malays. J. Learn. Instr.* **2018**, *15*, 105–148. [CrossRef]

38. Cohen, L.; Manion, L.; Morrison, K. *Research Methods in Education*; Routledge: Abington, UK, 2017.

39. Taber, K.S. The Use of Cronbach's Alpha When Developing and Reporting Research Instruments in Science Education. *Res. Sci. Educ.* **2017**, *48*, 1273–1296. [CrossRef]

40. Landström, H.; Harirchi, G.; Astrom, F. Entrepreneurship: Exploring the knowledge base. *Res. Policy* **2012**, *41*, 1154–1181. [CrossRef]

4

Social Entrepreneurial Intention and the Impact of COVID-19 Pandemic: A Structural Model

Inés Ruiz-Rosa [1,*], **Desiderio Gutiérrez-Taño** [2] **and Francisco J. García-Rodríguez** [2]

[1] Departamento de Economía, Contabilidad y Finanzas, Facultad de Economía, Empresa y Turismo, Universidad de La Laguna, 38071 San Cristóbal de la Laguna, Santa Cruz de Tenerife, Spain

[2] Departamento de Dirección de Empresas e Historia Económica, Facultad de Economía, Empresa y Turismo, Universidad de La Laguna, 38071 San Cristóbal de la Laguna, Santa Cruz de Tenerife, Spain; dgtano@ull.es (D.G.-T.); fgarciar@ull.es (F.J.G.-R.)

* Correspondence: ciruiz@ull.es

Abstract: The interest in promoting social entrepreneurship projects lies in their ability to develop innovative solutions to social and environmental problems. This ability becomes even more important in situations of global crises such as that arising from COVID-19. Based on the Theory of Planned Behavior (TPB), an explanatory structural model of social entrepreneurial intention was tested, and the impact of the COVID-19 crisis on this intention was evaluated. To do this, a quantitative investigation was conducted using a survey of Spanish university students, obtaining a total of 558 responses: 324 before the COVID-19 crisis and 234 during the crisis period (February and June 2020). The results obtained make it possible to validate the explanatory model of social entrepreneurial intention from the perspective of the TPB. In addition, it shows that social entrepreneurial intention decreases in times of deep socioeconomic crises and high uncertainty, such as that caused by COVID-19.

Keywords: social entrepreneurial intention; social entrepreneurship; COVID-19; theory of planned behavior

1. Introduction

The need to solve social and environmental problems in an innovative way and generate social value is increasingly necessary not only by the public sphere but also by private initiatives [1–3]. In this sense, Horne et al. [4] find that entrepreneurship has great potential to contribute to the Sustainable Development Goals (SDGs).

In this sense, social and environmental entrepreneurship refers to an enterprise project whose objective is to solve a social and/or environmental problem. Moreover, Maer and Noboa [5] understand social entrepreneurship as a process that involves people (social entrepreneurs) who show a tendency toward a specific type of behavior (social entrepreneurship behavior) and who try to carry out that behavior to achieve a tangible result (a social enterprise). The application of the talent, experience, and resources of entrepreneurs in solving social and environmental problems has become a great competitive advantage in many countries [6,7].

Despite growing interest in the concept of social entrepreneurship [8], there is still no clear academic consensus regarding the conceptual delimitation of the term itself, as well as the most appropriate theoretical approach for its analysis, including its antecedents [1,9–12]. Likewise, taking into account the importance of this type of entrepreneurship to mitigate the consequences of economic crises [13], it is necessary to know how such situations affect the behavior or social entrepreneurship intentions of individuals.

Considering the above, this study had a dual objective. On the one hand, to delimit an explanatory structural model of social entrepreneurial intention, analyzing the relationships between this variable and its antecedent variables. On the other hand, the study also aimed to test the effect of a socio-economic crisis with a high level of uncertainty, such as that posed by COVID-19 on social entrepreneurial intention.

To do this, this study first defined the concept and scope of social entrepreneurship. Next, the perspective of the Theory of Planned Behavior (TPB, hereafter) was used to try to delimit the formation of social entrepreneurial intention [14,15]. This theory proposes that entrepreneurial intention depends on the influence that three variables have on it: personal attitude, subjective norms, and perceived behavioral control [15].

The structural model defined was thus empirically tested using a sample of university students, as this population is considered one of the most sensitive to the development of social entrepreneurship projects [9]. The TPB was applied to social and/or environmental entrepreneurial intention, and the model was analyzed for two different periods: before the COVID-19 crisis, and during the pandemic period. A quantitative study was conducted using a survey of university students (University of La Laguna, Spain) obtaining a total of 558 responses: 324 before the COVID-19 crisis and 234 during the crisis period (February and June 2020). This allowed us to analyze whether the crisis had had a positive or negative impact on the social and/or environmental entrepreneurial intention of the sample.

This paper is organized as follows. In the next section, we present the theoretical context and the hypotheses to be tested in relation to the characterization of social entrepreneurial intention and the relation between crises and social entrepreneurial intentions. We subsequently describe the research model as well as sample selection and data collection before reporting the main results. Finally, we conclude with a discussion of results, theoretical and practical implications, limitations, and our main conclusions for further research.

2. Theory and Hypotheses

2.1. TPB and Social Entrepreneurial Intention

There is a growing interest, both by academic and government institutions, in promoting social and/or environmental entrepreneurship [3,5,11,16,17]. This is justified because these entrepreneurial projects can provide solutions to social and environmental problems in ways that are often more efficient and sustainable than those developed by the public sector [18]. Likewise, Ferri and Urbano [2] state that the social and/or environmental problems emerging in many countries, both developed and developing, have increased the importance of social and/or environmental entrepreneurship as an option to generate social value through social innovation [19,20].

However, despite this growing interest, there is still no clear academic consensus regarding the concept of social entrepreneurship and how to identify and measure it [1,9–12]. In this work, the concept of social entrepreneurship requires social and/or environmental entrepreneurs. The motivation of these entrepreneurs plays a fundamental role. Thus, while traditional entrepreneurship aims to generate profits, social entrepreneurship aims to solve a social and/or environmental problem [5,11,21]. These entrepreneurs are motivated by a strong desire to generate social value [5,22], they are able to identify opportunities focused on solving social and/or environmental problems [23,24] and, therefore, have a collective, and not an individualistic, view of reality [25]. This same author [25] introduces the term "sustainable social value". This concept of sustainability refers to the intention to maintain social activity over time, which, in turn, requires generating business activity with the aim of guaranteeing financial sustainability [26].

In short, social and/or environmental entrepreneurship projects are hybrid models [1,19,27–29] that function like traditional companies but incorporate an objective of a social and/or environmental nature [30]. Since social entrepreneurs are facing social and/or environmental challenges, it is important to understand the variables relating to social entrepreneurial intentions in order to stimulate those variables [31]. For this reason, it is a priority to know the formation process of social entrepreneurial intention, since it constitutes the previous step to the implementation of any entrepreneurship project and is the best predictor of actual entrepreneurship [14,15,32,33].

Along these lines, the TPB [14,15], used by Krueger and Carsrud [34] to build their entrepreneurial intention model, has become the model that best describes the entrepreneurial process [35] to the degree that it explains the entrepreneurial intention from the interaction, precisely, between personal and social factors. This same model has also been used by Forster and Grichnik [36] to explain the formation of social entrepreneurial intention. Prieto [37] defines social entrepreneurial intention as the purpose that a certain person manifests in starting a social company with the aim of generating social value through innovation.

The TPB proposes that entrepreneurial intention depends on the influence that three variables have on it: personal attitude, subjective norms, and perceived behavioral control [15]. Using this model, multiple academic studies have been carried out that try to analyze the formation of entrepreneurial intention and the relationship with its antecedents (e.g., [38–42]).

In this sense, personal attitude, according to the TPB [14], will depend on the assessment, positive or negative, that a certain person has in relation to the possibility of developing an entrepreneurial project. Indeed, there are several studies that find a positive relation between attitude and entrepreneurial intention (e.g., [39–41]). In our case, as we are analyzing social entrepreneurship, this assessment will be related to social entrepreneurial intention, thus it would be logical to think that:

Hypothesis 1 (H1). *There is a positive relationship between social entrepreneurship attitude and social entrepreneurial intention.*

On the other hand, subjective norms refer to the perceived social pressure to carry out, or not, a certain behavior, therefore this element becomes the main reflection of social and cultural values. An estimation of the subjective norm is obtained from the analysis of two variables: the beliefs about how other significant persons think that the individual should behave (normative beliefs) and the motivation that refers to the general tendency that exists in complying with the norms of a group taken as a reference [43]. In this sense, there is a diversity of results when it comes to justifying the relationship between subjective norms and entrepreneurial intention. While some studies have found a significant relation between both [44,45], others have not obtained any relation [46,47].

However, it would be reasonable to expect a positive relationship between this variable and social entrepreneurial intention to the extent that we understand that entrepreneurs are affected by the opinions of people linked to their closest environment about their social entrepreneurial intentions [48]. Following this reflection, the second hypothesis is proposed.

Hypothesis 2 (H2). *There is a positive relationship between subjective norms and social entrepreneurial intention.*

Finally, perceived behavioral control refers to the greater or lesser difficulty that a person perceives in performing the action in relation to his or her abilities to control the behavior [49]. Perceived behavioral control is linked to the self-perception of personal abilities and, therefore, is associated with the concept of self-efficacy [50]. In this sense, Smith and Woodworth [51] recognize that a person with a high social entrepreneurial self-efficacy will tend to act more persistently in their goal of creating social value. Therefore, it can be understood that the self-perception of the personal capacity to perform a certain action significantly influences the intention to do that action [44,47]. Following this logic of reasoning, the third hypothesis of this work is proposed.

Hypothesis 3 (H3). *Perceived behavioral control positively influences social entrepreneurial intention.*

Finally, following Heuer and Liñán [52] and Liñan and Santos [53], it can be understood that subjective norms represent a form of social capital that could influence the perception of the entrepreneurial person's personal attitudes and perceived behavioral control. It is for this reason that it seems logical to assume that there could be a positive relationship between subjective norms and social entrepreneurship attitude and between subjective norms and perceived behavioral control linked to the perception of the personal capacity to develop a project [35,48]. To measure these relationships, the fourth and fifth hypotheses of this paper are proposed.

Hypothesis 4 (H4). *There is a positive relationship between subjective norms and social entrepreneurship attitude.*

Hypothesis 5 (H5). *There is a positive relationship between subjective norms and perceived behavioral control.*

2.2. Crises and Social Entrepreneurship

For Hundt et al. [54], the intention to start up an entrepreneurial project is conditioned, in addition to individual characteristics, by the conditions of the economic context, an aspect that must be taken into account to explain entrepreneurial intention, as well as its antecedents [55].

On the other hand, the promotion of entrepreneurship is one of the measures usually considered as a response to situations of economic crises [9], although according to the results obtained by Devece et al. [55], entrepreneurship out of necessity in situations of economic recession is less effective than that arising from the recognition of opportunities. In this sense, Aparicio et al. [56] find a positive relationship between the generation of entrepreneurial projects by opportunity and the economic growth of a given territory. This is why the development of entrepreneurial projects that take advantage of opportunities generates regional economic growth that is greater than that of entrepreneurship for necessity, since, while the latter is limited to solving short-term problems, opportunities can have a long-term impact [55].

Therefore, it would be essential in periods of recession to promote the creation of new businesses, focused on identifying opportunities, with the aim of encouraging economic activity [57]. In the special circumstances of the impact of the COVID-19 crisis, Maritz et al. [58] recognize that entrepreneurs will be key figures during and after the health crisis. Along these lines, [59] point out that the health requirements arising from the pandemic have facilitated the emergence of new business opportunities such as flexible manufacturing, online education, food safety, emergency management, analysis of medical care, care of the elderly, interest in healthy living, telemedicine, cultural services, adaptation of supply chains, remote communication, entertainment or fitness platforms, and the design of smarter cities, among others. Many of these business options could become opportunities for the development of social entrepreneurship projects, in accordance with the definition given above, which focus on solving social and/or environmental problems [23,24].

In short, fostering social entrepreneurship in these circumstances becomes a fundamental tool for generating social and/or environmental change [13]. However, according to the results obtained by Hundt et al. [54] when analyzing the impact of the 2008/2009 crisis on entrepreneurship, the context in which the entrepreneurs find themselves can affect their behavior. Indeed, among the conclusions obtained from the Global Entrepreneurship Monitor project [60], the rate of nascent entrepreneurship decreased notably during the period of 2008-2010 in the countries most affected by the crisis. Devece et al. [55] also conducted a comparative study of new company creation in Spain between 2005 and 2007 and 2008 and 2010, observing that the number of new companies created fell from 400,000 in the first period to 300,000 in the second. Therefore, following Arrighetti et al. [61], the perception of a crisis as a barrier negatively affects entrepreneurial intention, which leads to the last hypothesis of this work:

Hypothesis 6 (H6). *Social entrepreneurial intention is lower during COVID-19 than before.*

3. Empirical Study

3.1. Research Model

Based on what was stated in the previous section, we tested, on the one hand, the suitability of a structural model of social entrepreneurship based on Ajzen's TPB [14] and, on the other hand, the impact of the COVID-19 crisis on social entrepreneurial intention.

In this sense, the construct "entrepreneurial intention" was conceptualized as a latent variable depending on three others: the attitude toward social entrepreneurship, subjective norms, and perceived behavioral control. Finally, the crisis variable COVID-19 was added to the model.

Thus, our research model includes five factors (see Figure 1): social entrepreneurship attitude, subjective norms, perceived behavioral control, social entrepreneurial intention, and crisis variable COVID-19. Each factor was measured with multiple items. All items were adapted from extant literature to improve content validity.

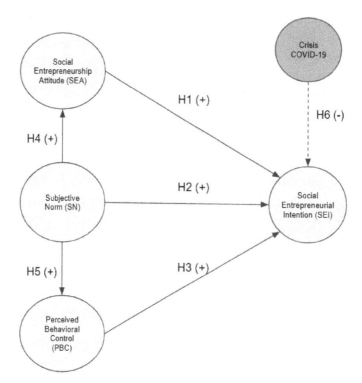

Figure 1. Research model.

3.2. Measures

A quantitative research design was used for this study through a survey of university students, as, according to the Global Entrepreneurship Monitor (GEM) Report on Social Entrepreneurship [62], this type of entrepreneurship is closely associated with young change-makers, who are idealistic in nature. In fact, the results of the GEM report show there is a greater representation of incipient social entrepreneurs than commercial entrepreneurs among young people between 18 and 34 years old. More specifically, according to Capella-Peris et al. [9], higher education students are one of the most relevant populations for the development of social and/or environmental projects.

The questionnaire developed for the study was structured in three parts. The first part introduced the context. The second part included the items of the constructs of the proposed model, which were measured by a 7-point Likert scale regarding the level of agreement (1 = Strongly disagree to 7 = Strongly agree). In the last part of the questionnaire, classification data were collected: gender, age, studies, and academic year. We included a definition of social and/or environmental entrepreneurship projects in the survey. We proposed that there could be hybrid models that function like traditional companies but incorporate an objective of a social and/or environmental nature.

The questionnaire was sent to the students by their teachers in February 2020 and in May 2020.

Regarding the items used (Table 1), Armitage and Conner [63] propose three different approaches to measure entrepreneurial intention. One of them is based on the desire to perform an action, another on the probability of performing the action, and the last one centered on the intention to perform said action. These authors corroborate that the latter is slightly more efficient in predicting behavior. To measure social entrepreneurship attitude and subjective norms, the scales proposed by Liñán and Chen [49] were used. The items used to measure social entrepreneurship attitude are supported both by affective considerations (developing social and/or environmental entrepreneurship projects can be an attractive activity that could generate satisfaction) and other more objective aspects. Those linked to subjective norms refer to the perception that entrepreneurs may have about what people close to their environment (family, friends, colleagues) think about their interest in developing a social and/or environmental entrepreneurship project. Finally, to measure perceived behavioral control, the six items proposed by Zhao et al. [64] were used; they refer to the entrepreneur's ability to identify opportunities, offer new products and services, manage projects, and have contact networks and leadership skills.

Table 1. Construct and associated items.

SEI	Social Entrepreneurship Intention
	Indicate your level of agreement with the following sentences
SEI1	I am willing to do anything to start a social project.
SEI2	My professional goal is to become a promoter of social projects.
SEI3	I am determined to create a social project in the future.
SEA	**Social Entrepreneurship Attitude**
	Indicate your level of agreement with the following sentences
SEA1	Being a social entrepreneur has more advantages than disadvantages for me.
SEA2	A career as a promoter of social projects is attractive to me.
SEA3	Promoting social projects would be a great satisfaction for me.
SN	**Subjective Norms**
If you decided to create a social project, would people in your close environment approve of that decision?	
SN1	Your closest family.
SN2	Your friends.
SN3	Your study partners.
PBC	**Perceived Behavioral Control**
To what extent do you agree with following statements regarding your entrepreneurial abilities?	
PBC1	Identify new opportunities.
PBC2	Create new products and services.
PBC3	Apply my personal creativity.
PBC4	Be a leader and communicator.
PBC5	Create a network of professional contacts.
PBC6	Successfully organise/manage a project.

Scale 1 to 7 (1 = Strongly disagree to 7 = Strongly agree).

3.3. Sample Selection and Data Collection

Data were obtained from the same students in two phases: the first one prior to the COVID-19 crisis in February 2020 and the second one in full crisis, in June 2020. The information was collected through a self-completed online questionnaire using the Lime Survey platform (version 3.6.3). Students at the University of La Laguna (Spain) were sent the links to the online questionnaire twice in each phase by email. These students belong to the following degrees: Building and Civil Engineering, Social Work, Industrial Relations, and Accounting and Finance. A total of 558 responses were obtained:

324 (58%) before the crisis (response rate 21%) and 234 (42%) responses in the crisis period (response rate 15%).

To verify that the sample size was sufficient, G*Power [65] was used, which suggests that for the test of the proposed model (Figure 1), a minimum sample of 129 individuals is required for a statistical power of 0.95. Therefore, it can be safely concluded that the sample size used was much larger than required for the purposes of this study.

Table 2 shows the profile of the respondents. Most of the responses obtained corresponded to women, 66.3%, and the largest number of questionnaires were completed by first-year students and the least in the last year of the degree, both of which correspond to the distribution of the analyzed population.

Table 2. Profile of respondents.

Gender	Total	Before (February) COVID-19	During (June) COVID-19
Female	66.3%	67.6%	64.5%
Male	33.7%	32.4%	35.5%
Degree studies			
Building and Civil Engineering	26.6%	23.7%	30.6%
Social Work	33.3%	36.1%	29.3%
Industrial Relations	18.4%	19.9%	16.4%
Accounting and Finance	21.7%	20.3%	23.7%
Academic year			
1st	54.3%	54.9%	53.4%
2nd	19.5%	20.7%	17.9%
3rd	22.4%	21.3%	23.9%
4th	3.8%	3.1%	4.7%
Total sample	558	324 (58%)	234 (42%)

3.4. Method of Analysis

To analyze the proposed theoretical model and test the hypotheses, the Partial Least Squares (PLS-SEM) technique was used, with the Smart PLS software v.3.3.2 [66]. The analysis of the measurement model involved the reliability and validity of the constructs, as well as the structural model through R^2, the path coefficients, the confidence intervals, and the values of the Standardized Root Mean Square (SRMR) as a measure of approximate fit of the model for PLS-SEM [67]. A Common Method Bias (CMB) assessment was also performed.

Likewise, to identify the differences between social entrepreneurial intention before and during the COVID-19 crisis, a Student's t-test was carried out for differences in the means of construct values.

4. Results

4.1. Descriptive Analysis

From a descriptive analysis of the results, it can be seen (Table 3) that there is a clear social entrepreneurial intention on the part of the investigated population, with the mean of the items of the construct being slightly above the midpoint of the scale, between 4.50 and 4.78 (scale from 1 to 7).

The subjective norms or level of perceived support of the social environment for social entrepreneurial intention is high, with the items of this latent variable being between 5.54 and 5.93. Table 3 shows the results of the descriptive analysis (mean and standard deviation) of the items of the constructs of the proposed model. Social entrepreneurship attitude is also above the midpoint of the scale, and the average of the items is between 4.66 and 5.17. Similarly, perceptions of self-capacity and competencies (perceived behavioral control) to implement social entrepreneurship initiatives are high, with the indicators measured for this latent variable being between 4.72 and 5.23, always above the midpoint of the scale, which ranges from 1 to 7.

Table 3. Descriptive analysis.

	Constructs and Associated Items	Mean	Standard Deviation
SEI	**Social Entrepreneurial Intention**		
	Indicate your level of agreement with the following sentences:		
SEI1	I am willing to do anything to start a social project.	4.68	1.336
SEI2	My professional goal is to become a promoter of social projects.	4.50	1.424
SEI3	I am determined to create a social project in the future.	4.78	1.335
SEA	**Social Entrepreneurship Attitude**		
	Indicate your level of agreement with the following sentences:		
SEA1	Being a social entrepreneur has more advantages than disadvantages for me.	4.66	1.283
SEA2	A career as a promoter of social projects is attractive to me.	4.76	1.366
SEA3	Promoting social projects would be a great satisfaction for me.	5.17	1.285
SN	**Subjective Norms**		
	If you decided to create a social project, would people in your close environment approve of that decision?		
SN1	Your closest family.	5.93	1.270
SN2	Your friends.	5.93	1.109
SN3	Your study partners.	5.54	1.259
PBC	**Perceived Behavioral Control**		
	To what extent do you agree with the following statements regarding your entrepreneurial abilities?		
PBC1	Identify new opportunities.	5.05	1.121
PBC2	Create new products and services.	4.73	1.169
PBC3	Apply my personal creativity.	5.23	1.194
PBC4	Be a leader and communicator.	5.05	1.305
PBC5	Create a network of professional contacts.	4.72	1.148
PBC6	Successfully administer/manage a project.	5.11	1.110

Scale 1 to 7 (1 = Strongly disagree to 7 = Strongly agree).

4.2. Assessment of the Global Model

The results revealed SRMR model fit values of 0.058, with values lower than 0.08 being considered acceptable for PLS-SEM [67].

Additionally, the CMB has been used along with Harman's single-factor approach [68]. A CMB is present if a single or general factor seems to represent the majority of the variance. A non-rotational factor analysis using the eigenvalue criterion greater than one revealed three different factors that represented 63.9 percent of the variance. The first factor captured 36.9 percent of the variance in the data. Since no single factor emerged and the first factor did not account for most of the variance, the CMB does not appear to be a problem.

It has also been verified that there are no indications of multicollinearity between the antecedent variables of each of the endogenous constructs since all the VIF (Variance Inflation Factor) values are less than 5.

4.3. Measurement Model Assessment

The individual reliability of the indicators of the constructs, formulated in the reflective Mode A, is assessed by examining the loadings (λ) of the indicators with their respective construct. As shown in Table 4, all item loadings in the final measurement model are greater than 0.707 [69]. In Table 4, the reliability of the construct is analyzed, and it is observed how all the values of Cronbach's Alpha and of the composite reliability [70] are above the minimum cut-off point of 0.70 [71].

Table 4. Assessment results of the measurement model.

Constructs and Associated Items		Loading	Cronbach's Alpha	Composite Reliability	Average Variance Extracted (AVE)
Social Entrepreneurial Intention			**0.893**	**0.934**	**0.824**
SEI1	I am willing to do anything to start a social project.	0.907			
SEI2	My professional goal is to become a promoter of social projects.	0.908			
SEI3	I am determined to create a social project in the future.	0.908			
Social Entrepreneurship Attitude			**0.853**	**0.911**	**0.773**
SEA1	Being a social entrepreneur has more advantages than disadvantages for me.	0.848			
SEA2	A career as a promoter of social projects is attractive to me.	0.910			
SEA3	Promoting social projects would be a great satisfaction for me.	0.878			
Subjective Norms			**0.823**	**0.895**	**0.739**
SN1	Your closest family.	0.845			
SN2	Your friends.	0.910			
SN3	Your study partners.	0.821			
Perceived Behavioral Control			**0.836**	**0.878**	**0.547**
PBC1	Identify new opportunities	0.815			
PBC2	Create new products and services.	0.799			
PBC3	Apply my personal creativity.	0.719			
PBC4	Be a leader and communicator.	0.701			
PBC5	Create a network of professional contacts.	0.734			
PBC6	Successfully administer/manage a project.	0.714			

All latent variables achieve convergent validity since their AVE measurements exceed the level of 0.5 [71]. The discriminant validity was assessed by using the recommended approach of Fornell and Larcker [71] and examining the heterotrait-monotrait (HTMT) of the correlations, which is considered a stricter criterion [72].

The results in Table 5 show that the constructs examined exceeded the requirements of Fornell and Larcker [71] since all the correlations were less than the square of the AVEs and also the heterotrait-monotrait (HTMT) of the correlations (values less than 0.85 [73], which is considered a stricter criterion [72]). Therefore, the measurement model was considered satisfactory and provided sufficient evidence in terms of reliability and convergent and discriminant validity.

Table 5. Result of discriminant validity.

Constructs	SEA	PBC	SN	SEI
Fornell–Larcher [69]				
SEA	**0.879**			
PBC	0.287	**0.739**		
SN	0.365	0.153	**0.860**	
SEI	0.727	0.349	0.358	**0.908**
Heterotrait-Monotrait Ratio (HTMT)				
SEA				
PBC	0.334			
SN	0.434	0.174		
SEI	0.829	0.389	0.418	

Note: The square root of AVEs is shown diagonally in bold.

4.4. Structural Model Assessment

The path coefficients (standardized regression coefficients) show the estimates of the structural model relationships, that is, the hypothesized relationships between constructs. The significance of the effects was assessed by bootstrapping [74]. Since the hypotheses specify the direction of the relationship of the variables, a one-tailed Student's t-distribution with n-1 degrees of freedom, where n is the number of subsamples, was used. There were 5000 samples made [75] with the number of cases equal to the number of observations in the original sample. To assess the significance of the relationships, in addition to bootstrapping, confidence intervals were analyzed [76].

As can be seen in Table 6 and Figure 2, the personal attitude toward social entrepreneurship has the greatest significant relationship with social entrepreneurial intention (H1: $\beta = 0.647, p < 0.001$). Subjective norms (H2: $\beta = 0.097, p < 0.01$) and perceived behavioral control (H3: $\beta = 0.147, p < 0.001$) also have a positive and significant relationship with social entrepreneurial intention, although the latter relationship has lower direct influence.

Table 6. Results of hypothesis testing.

		Path Coefficient	Sig.	T Statistics	Confidence Intervals	Confidence Intervals Bias	Supported
Hypothesis 1	SEA -> SEI	0.647	***	21.156	[0.594; 0.695]	[0.594; 0.695]	Yes/Yes
Hypothesis 2	SN -> SEI	0.097	**	2.96	[0.042; 0.151]	[0.041; 0.150]	Yes/Yes
Hypothesis 3	PBC -> SEI	0.147	***	4.271	[0.092; 0.205]	[0.089; 0.202]	Yes/Yes
Hypothesis 4	SN -> SEA	0.356	***	8.22	[0.283; 0.428]	[0.279; 0.423]	Yes/Yes
Hypothesis 5	SN -> PBC	0.156	***	3.357	[0.084; 0.235]	[0.077; 0.228]	Yes/Yes

Bootstrapping using 5000 subsamples one-tailed t Student: ns: non-significant; ** $p < 0.01$; *** $p < 0.001$; t (0.05; 4999) = 1.645; t (0.01; 4999) = 2.327; t (0.001; 4999) = 3.092; Confidence Intervals [5–95%].

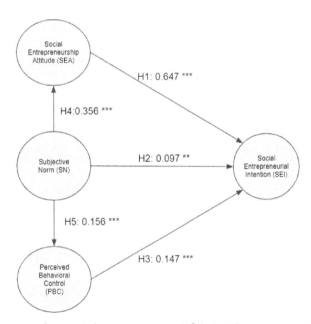

Figure 2. Results of analysis for social entrepreneurial intention. ns: non-significant; ** $p < 0.01$; *** $p < 0.001$.

The indirect relationship of subjective norms or social influence on social entrepreneurial intention was also tested through social entrepreneurship attitude (H4: $\beta = 0.356, p < 0.001$) and perceived behavioral control (H5: $\beta = 0.156, p < 0.001$) with indirect effects as seen in Table 7.

As stated above and in relation to the first aim of this work, to analyze the relationships between the variables identified as antecedents of social entrepreneurial intention, the hypotheses of the model are confirmed (H1, H2, H3, H4, and H5), although H2 is the weakest due to its low contribution and significance.

Therefore, we can affirm that there is a positive relationship between social entrepreneurship attitude, subjective norms, and perceived behavioral control and social entrepreneurial intention. In addition, there is a positive relationship between subjective norms and social entrepreneurial intention through the relationship with social entrepreneurship attitude and perceived behavioral control.

Table 7. Total, direct, and indirect effects.

	Direct Effects	Specific Indirect Effects	Total Effects
SEA -> SEI	0.647		0.647
PBC -> SEI	0.147		0.147
SN -> SEA -> SEI		0.230	
SN -> PBC -> SEI		0.023	
SN -> SEI	0.097		0.350
SN -> SEA	0.356		0.356
SN -> PBC	0.156		0.156

The coefficient of determination (R^2) represents a predictive power measure that indicates the amount of variance of a construct that is explained by the predictor variables of the endogenous construct in the model. The proposed model explains 55.4% of social entrepreneurial intention, 12.7% of social entrepreneurship attitude, and 2.4% of perceived behavioral control (Table 8).

Table 8. Decomposition of variance, predictive relevance, and effect size.

	Path Coefficient	Variable Correlation	R^2	Q^2	f^2
Social entrepreneurship intention			55.4%	0.451	
SEA -> SEI	0.647	0.724	46.8%		0.765
SN -> SEI	0.097	0.350	3.4%		0.018
PBC -> SEI	0.147	0.352	5.2%		0.044
Attitude toward social entrepreneurship			12.7%	0.096	
SN -> SEA	0.356	0.356	12.7%		0.145
Perceived behavioral control			2.4%	0.012	
SN -> PBC	0.156	0.156	2.4%		0.025

Effect f^2: <0.15 small; <0.35 moderate; ≥0.35 large.

Additionally, indicator f^2 (Table 8) evaluates the degree to which an exogenous construct contributes to explain a specific endogenous construct in terms of R^2 [77].

We observe that the relationship between subjective norms and entrepreneurial intention has a small effect size, thus its influence is limited. The relationships between subjective norms and perceived behavioral control, as well as between perceived behavioral control and social entrepreneurial intention, also have a small effect size.

On the other hand, as a criterion to measure the predictive relevance of the constructs, the Stone–Geisser test was used [78,79], observing in Table 8 that the Q^2 values are greater than zero, which indicates that the model has predictive potential.

4.5. Assessment of the Relationship between COVID-19 and Social Entrepreneurial Intention

To test the influence of the health crisis caused by COVID-19, a *t*-test was carried out for the mean differences of the items of the social entrepreneurial intention construct measured in two periods: before the crisis and during the crisis.

Table 9 shows that all the items that make up the latent variable have a significantly lower value during the crisis than before the crisis, thus it can be concluded that social entrepreneurial intention has decreased, confirming hypothesis 6.

Table 9. *t*-Test of the mean differences of the social entrepreneurial intention.

Social Entrepreneurial Intention	Before (February) COVID-19	During (June) COVID-19	Dif.	Sig.	
I am willing to do anything to start a social project.	4.78	4.55	−0.24	0.039	**
My professional goal is to become a promoter of social projects.	4.60	4.37	−0.23	0.063	*
I am determined to create a social project in the future.	4.91	4.62	−0.29	0.011	**

Scale 1 to 7 (1 = Strongly disagree to 7 = Strongly agree). Level of significance: <0.05 **; <0.1 *; no significance "ns".

5. Discussion and Conclusions

This work analyzed, using the perspective of Ajzen's TPB [14], the relationship between the antecedent variables that make up this model and social entrepreneurial intention. Subsequently, the impact of the COVID-19 crisis on social entrepreneurial intention was measured.

From the analysis of the relationships between the variables considered as predictors of social entrepreneurial intention (social entrepreneurship attitude, subjective norms, and perceived behavioral control) and the performance of the behavior (social entrepreneurial intention), it is observed that hypotheses 1, 2, and 3 are fulfilled, with hypothesis 2, regarding the incidence of subjective norms, being the one with a weaker significance.

This assumes that there is a positive relationship between the social entrepreneurship attitude of university students [80] and their social entrepreneurial intention. In addition, there is a positive relationship between the perceived behavioral control of university students' ability to carry out social projects and their social entrepreneurial intentions. This confirms that the more positive the perceptions about one's own abilities are, the stronger the social entrepreneurial intention will be.

Regarding the weak relationship between university students' subjective norms and social entrepreneurial intention, this result coincides with that obtained in previous works by various authors such as Liñan and Chen [49], Autio et al. [46], and Krueger et al. [47], who used the TPB to measure the relationship between the variables that predict entrepreneurial intention. Liñan and Chen [49] suggest the non-significance of the relationship between subjective norms and entrepreneurial intention is due to the impact that this motivational factor has on this type of decision. In this case, it seems that the altruism that motivates the development of social and/or environmental projects [21] is more intense than the importance that the entrepreneurs themselves give to the perception of the opinions that their immediate environment has on the development of their project.

Hypotheses 4 and 5 were intended to measure the influence of subjective norms on social entrepreneurial intention through their relationship with social entrepreneurship attitude and perceived behavioral control. Both hypotheses are fulfilled, observing that there is more influence of subjective norms on social entrepreneurship attitude than on perceived behavioral control. This indicates that the perception of the opinions that people close to the individual have regarding the implementation of social and/or environmental projects affects more the attitude toward the behavior than the perception of their own ability and training for carrying out the entrepreneurial behavior.

The results that confirm hypotheses 1, 3, 4, and 5 of this work coincide with those obtained by Kruse [35]. This author analyzes, among other things, the direct and indirect effects on social entrepreneurial intention of antecedent variables according to Azjen's TPB [14]. In the case of hypothesis 2, which analyzes the impact of subjective norms on entrepreneurial intention, Kruse [35] obtains a non-significant result. Kruse's [35] study is applied to a total of 335 German promoters of social entrepreneurship projects. However, in the work of Tiwari et al. [48], in which Ajzen's TPB is applied to a sample of 390 students from the main technical universities in India, a positive impact, but of weak significance, is obtained for subjective norms in relation to entrepreneurial intention. These two different results show that the effect of the opinions from the environment (family, friends, colleagues) on social entrepreneurial intention is more relevant in people with entrepreneurial experience than in university students, with attitudes more prone to this type of initiative, in the line pointed out by Capella-Peris et al. [9].

Regarding the impact of the COVID-19 health crisis, it is observed that social entrepreneurial intention decreases after the pandemic. This result is explained to the extent that, following Kasych et al. [81], among the external barriers that exist linked to the development of social projects are those of an economic nature. It also coincides with the results obtained for traditional entrepreneurship in times of crisis (e.g., Devece et al. [55]) for which a clear negative impact is manifested.

In summary, and according to our results and also those obtained by Kruse [35], it seems that Ajzen's TPB [14] constitutes an ideal perspective to explain the formation of social entrepreneurial intention, taking into account the incidence of its antecedents, both directly and indirectly. Moreover, it is verified that the impact of subjective norms on entrepreneurial intention through social entrepreneurship attitude is more important than through perceived behavioral control.

In addition, despite the importance of promoting the creation of social entrepreneurship projects with the aim of providing innovative solutions to social and environmental problems, a situation of economic recession becomes a relevant barrier in the implementation of this type of enterprise.

In practice, the results obtained suggest the desirability of promoting the development of social entrepreneurship projects within the educational field, especially in university education, to the extent that at these ages, the promotion of social motivation may have the greatest impact. In this sense, it has been proven that the altruism associated with the social entrepreneurial intention of young people is more intense than the perceived opinions of their immediate environment on the development of their project.

The above coincides with what was pointed out by Tiwari et al. [48] in the sense that social entrepreneurship attitude is one of the variables that should be promoted in educational systems since its impact on entrepreneurial intention is greater than perceived behavioral control.

At the same time, it is logical to think that in an economic and social crisis climate, entrepreneurial intention decreases, since uncertainty generates a negative impact on the development of such intentions. In this sense, it would be interesting to develop educational actions that promote, especially among university students, the ability to identify entrepreneurial opportunities in the social field, even in times of economic crisis, taking into account that entrepreneurship by opportunity generates a greater impact in the long-term [56].

On the other hand, in the paper of Zaremohzzabieh [82], two alternative models were proposed and then evaluated, suggesting alternative formulations of the antecedents of social entrepreneurial intention by modifying the relationships between key TPB constructs and intentions. The findings revealed that the strength of the two models enriches the TPB through additional factors. This could be an upcoming challenge for a future extension of our work.

Fiore et al. [83] show the importance of creating teams with different competencies, cognitive and decision-making skills in entrepreneurship education. The creation of multidisciplinary teams could also be a good option for subsequent studies on social entrepreneurship.

Finally, it would be valuable to train university students in the ability to identify business opportunities despite possible situations of economic and social crises. This effort must be accompanied by public policies focused on facilitating the implementation of this type of initiative.

This study has certain limitations that open new research avenues. First, the sample used was made up of university students from one European country, as is commonly used in research into entrepreneurial intention, taking into account that higher education students could be included in the millennial generation, who share similar attitudes, perceptions, and experiences. Thus, having similar characteristics, it is possible to generalize the conclusions obtained [84]. However, to add more value to this line of research, it is proposed to extend the analysis carried out here to broader samples in order to test the model of formation of social entrepreneurial intention among students not only from other nationalities but from different academic fields and cultural backgrounds. The results obtained would also help personalize the training linked to the development of social entrepreneurship projects to obtain better results. Second, the research has been transversally designed, obtaining data from two periods: before the COVID-19 crisis and during the pandemic period. To develop causal inferences, further empirical studies would be necessary that analyze the post-pandemic period. Finally, it would be useful to perform other studies including some control variables such as if students have previously participated in an entrepreneurship training course [85], entrepreneurial antecedents of their parents, etc.

Author Contributions: Conceptualization, I.R.-R. and F.J.G.-R.; methodology, I.R.-R., F.J.G.-R. and D.G.-T.; validation, D.G.-T.; formal analysis, I.R.-R., F.J.G.-R. and D.G.-T.; investigation, I.R.-R., F.J.G.-R. and D.G.-T.; resources, F.J.G.-R.; writing—original draft preparation, I.R.-R.; writing—review and editing, I.R.-R. All authors have read and agreed to the published version of the manuscript.

References

1. Crucke, S.; Decramer, A. The Development of a Measurement Instrument for the Organizational Performance of Social Enterprises. *Sustainability* **2016**, *8*, 161. [CrossRef]
2. Ferri, E.; Urbano, D. *Environmental Factors and Social Entrepreneurship*; Universitat Autónoma de Barcelona: Barcelona, Spain, 2010. Available online: http://hdl.handle.net/2072/97455 (accessed on 3 June 2020).
3. Certo, S.T.; Miller, T.L. Social entrepreneurship: Key issues and concepts. *Bus. Horiz.* **2008**, *51*, 267–271. [CrossRef]
4. Horne, J.; Recker, M.; Michelfelder, I.; Jay, J.; Kratzer, J. Exploring entrepreneurship related to the sustainable development goals-mapping new venture activities with semi-automated content analysis. *J. Clean. Prod.* **2020**, *242*, 118052. [CrossRef]
5. Mair, J.; Noboa, E. Social Entrepreneurship: How Intentions to Create a Social Enterprise Get Formed. *IESE Work. Pap.* **2003**. [CrossRef]
6. Fernández-Serrano, J.; Martínez-Román, J.A.; Romero, I. The entrepreneur in the regional innovation system. A comparative study for high- and low-income regions. *Entrep. Reg. Dev.* **2018**, *31*, 337–356. [CrossRef]
7. Kirby, D.A.; Ibrahim, N. The case for (social) entrepreneurship education in Egyptian universities. *Educ. Train.* **2011**, *53*, 403–415. [CrossRef]
8. Kraus, S.; Filser, M.; O'Dwyer, M.; Shaw, E. Social Entrepreneurship: An exploratory citation analysis. *Rev. Manag. Sci.* **2013**, *8*, 275–292. [CrossRef]
9. Capella-Peris, C.; Gil-Gómez, J.; Martí-Puig, M.; Ruiz-Bernardo, P. Development and Validation of a Scale to Assess Social Entrepreneurship Competency in Higher Education. *J. Soc. Entrep.* **2019**, *11*, 23–39. [CrossRef]
10. Urbano, D.; Toledano, N.; Ribeiro-Soriano, D. Analyzing Social Entrepreneurship from an Institutional Perspective: Evidence from Spain. *J. Soc. Entrep.* **2010**, *1*, 54–69. [CrossRef]
11. Martin, R.; Osberg, S. Social Entrepreneurship: The case for definition. *Stanf. Soc. Innov. Rev.* **2007**, *5*, 28–39.
12. Tan, W.L.; Williams, J.; Tan, T.-M. Defining the 'Social' in 'Social Entrepreneurship': Altruism and Entrepreneurship. *Int. Entrep. Manag. J.* **2005**, *1*, 353–365. [CrossRef]
13. Prabhu, G.N. Social entrepreneurial leadership. *Career Dev. Int.* **1999**, *4*, 140–145. [CrossRef]
14. Ajzen, I. The Theory of Planned Behavior. *Organ. Behav. Hum. Decis. Process.* **1991**, *50*, 179–211. [CrossRef]
15. Ajzen, I. Nature and Operation of Attitudes. *Annu. Rev. Psychol.* **2001**, *52*, 27–58. [CrossRef] [PubMed]
16. Sansone, G.; Andreotti, P.; Colombelli, A.; Landoni, P. Are social incubators different from other incubators? Evidence from Italy. *Technol. Forecast. Soc. Chang.* **2020**, *158*, 120132. [CrossRef]
17. Sassmannshausen, S.P.; Volkmann, C. The Scientometrics of Social Entrepreneurship and Its Establishment as an Academic Field. *J. Small Bus. Manag.* **2016**, *56*, 251–273. [CrossRef]
18. Kickul, J.; Lyons, T.S. *Understanding Social Entrepreneurship: The Relentless Pursuit of Mission in an Ever Changing World*; Routledge: New York, NY, USA; London, UK, 2012.
19. Austin, J.; Stevenson, H.; Wei-Skillern, J. Social and Commercial Entrepreneurship: Same, different or both? *Entrep. Theory Pract.* **2006**, *30*, 1–22. [CrossRef]
20. Leadbeater, C. Social enterprise and social innovation: Strategies for the next ten years. In *A Social Enterprise Think Piece for the Office of Third Sector*; Cabinet Office of the Third Sector: London, UK, 2007.
21. Auerswald, P. Creating Social Value. Stanford Social Innovation Review, Spring. 2009. Available online: https://ssrn.com/abstract=1376425 (accessed on 25 May 2020).

22. Arena, M.; Azzone, G.; Bengo, I. Performance Measurement for Social Enterprises. *Volunt. Int. J. Volunt. Nonprofit Organ.* **2014**, *26*, 649–672. [CrossRef]

23. Mair, J.; Martí, I. Social entrepreneurship research: A source of explanation, prediction, and delight. *J. World Bus.* **2006**, *41*, 36–44. [CrossRef]

24. Hibbert, S.A.; Hogg, G.; Quinn, T. Consumer response to social entrepreneurship: The case of the Big Issue in Scotland. *Int. J. Nonprofit Volunt. Sect. Mark.* **2002**, *7*, 288–301. [CrossRef]

25. Harding, R. Social Enterprise: The New Economic Engine? *Bus. Strat. Rev.* **2004**, *15*, 39–43. [CrossRef]

26. Doherty, B.; Haugh, H.; Lyon, F. Social Enterprises as Hybrid Organizations: A Review and Research Agenda. *Int. J. Manag. Rev.* **2014**, *16*, 417–436. [CrossRef]

27. Saebi, T.; Foss, N.J.; Linder, S. Social Entrepreneurship Research: Past Achievements and Future Promises. *J. Manag.* **2018**, *45*, 70–95. [CrossRef]

28. Santos, F.M. A Positive Theory of Social Entrepreneurship. *J. Bus. Ethics* **2012**, *111*, 335–351. [CrossRef]

29. Peredo, A.M.; McLean, M. Social entrepreneurship: A critical review of the concept. *J. World Bus.* **2006**, *41*, 56–65. [CrossRef]

30. Leborgne-Bonassié, M.; Coletti, M.; Sansone, G. What do venture philanthropy organisations seek in social enterprises? *Bus. Strat. Dev.* **2019**, *2*, 349–357. [CrossRef]

31. Lee, S.H.; Wong, P.-K. An exploratory study of technopreneurial intentions: A career anchor perspective. *J. Bus. Ventur.* **2004**, *19*, 7–28. [CrossRef]

32. Krueger, N.F.; Brazeal, D.V. Entrepreneurial Potential and Potential Entrepreneurs. *Entrep. Theory Pract.* **1994**, *18*, 91–104. [CrossRef]

33. Fishbein, M.; Ajzen, I. *Belief, Attitude, Intention and Behaviour: An Introduction to Theory and Research*; Addison-Wesley: Boston, MA, USA, 1975.

34. Krueger, N.F.; Carsrud, A.L. Entrepreneurial intentions: Applying the theory of planned behaviour. *Entrep. Reg. Dev.* **1993**, *5*, 315–330. [CrossRef]

35. Kruse, P. Can there only be one?—An empirical comparison of four models on social entrepreneurial intention formation. *Int. Entrep. Manag. J.* **2019**, *16*, 641–665. [CrossRef]

36. Forster, F.; Grichnik, D. Social Entrepreneurial Intention Formation of Corporate Volunteers. *J. Soc. Entrep.* **2013**, *4*, 153–181. [CrossRef]

37. Prieto, L. The Influence of Proactive Personality on Social Entrepreneurial Intentions among African American and Hispanic Undergraduate Students: The Moderating role of hope. Ph.D. Thesis, Louisiana State University, Baton Rouge, LA, USA, 2010. Available online: https://digitalcommons.lsu.edu/gradschool_dissertations/317 (accessed on 20 May 2020).

38. Vamvaka, V.; Stoforos, C.; Palaskas, T.; Botsaris, C. Attitude toward entrepreneurship, perceived behavioral control, and entrepreneurial intention: Dimensionality, structural relationships, and gender differences. *J. Innov. Entrep.* **2020**, *9*, 5. [CrossRef]

39. Rodríguez, F.J.G.; Gil Soto, E.; Rosa, I.R.; Sene, P.M. Entrepreneurial intentions in diverse development contexts: A cross-cultural comparison between Senegal and Spain. *Int. Entrep. Manag. J.* **2013**, *11*, 511–527. [CrossRef]

40. Paço, A.D.; Ferreira, J.J.; Raposo, M.; Rodrigues, R.G.; Dinis, A. Behaviours and entrepreneurial intention: Empirical findings about secondary students. *J. Int. Entrep.* **2011**, *9*, 20–38. [CrossRef]

41. Liñán, F.; Urbano, D.; Guerrero, M. Regional variations in entrepreneurial cognitions: Start-up intentions of university students in Spain. *Entrep. Reg. Dev.* **2011**, *23*, 187–215. [CrossRef]

42. Shook, C.L.; Bratianu, C. Entrepreneurial intent in a transitional economy: An application of the theory of planned behavior to Romanian students. *Int. Entrep. Manag. J.* **2008**, *6*, 231–247. [CrossRef]

43. Moriano León, J.A.; Gómez Jiménez, A.; Bohdan Roznowski, M.L. Validación de un cuestionario para medir la intención emprendedora: Una aplicación en España y Polonia. In *Método, Teoría e Investigación en Psicología Social*; Editorial Pearson Educación: Madrid, Spain, 2008; pp. 101–122.

44. Kolvereid, L.; Isaksen, E.J. New business start-up and subsequent entry into self-employment. *J. Bus. Ventur.* **2006**, *21*, 866–885. [CrossRef]

45. Tkachev, A.; Kolvereid, L. Self-employment intentions among Russian students. *Entrep. Reg. Dev.* **1999**, *11*, 269–280. [CrossRef]

46. Autio, E.; Keeley, R.H.; Klofsten, M.; Parker, G.G.C.; Hay, M. Entrepreneurial Intent among Students in Scandinavia and in the USA. *Enterp. Innov. Manag. Stud.* **2001**, *2*, 145–160. [CrossRef]

47. Krueger, N.F.; Reilly, M.D.; Carsrud, A.L. Competing models of entrepreneurial intentions. *J. Bus. Ventur.* **2000**, *15*, 411–432. [CrossRef]
48. Tiwari, P.; Bhat, A.K.; Tikoria, J. An empirical analysis of the factors affecting social entrepreneurial intentions. *J. Glob. Entrep. Res.* **2017**, *7*, 179. [CrossRef]
49. Liñán, F.; Chen, Y.-W. Development and Cross-Cultural Application of a Specific Instrument to Measure Entrepreneurial Intentions. *Entrep. Theory Pract.* **2009**, *33*, 593–617. [CrossRef]
50. Bandura, A.; Freeman, W.H.; Lightsey, R. Self-Efficacy: The Exercise of Control. *J. Cogn. Psychother.* **1999**, *13*, 158–166. [CrossRef]
51. Smith, I.H.; Woodworth, W.P. Developing Social Entrepreneurs and Social Innovators: A Social Identity and Self-Efficacy Approach. *Acad. Manag. Learn. Educ.* **2012**, *11*, 390–407. [CrossRef]
52. Heuer, A.; Heuer, A.; Liñán, F. Testing alternative measures of subjective norms in entrepreneurial intention models. *Int. J. Entrep. Small Bus.* **2013**, *19*, 35. [CrossRef]
53. Liñán, F.; Santos, F.J. Does Social Capital Affect Entrepreneurial Intentions? *Int. Adv. Econ. Res.* **2007**, *13*, 443–453. [CrossRef]
54. Hundt, C.; Sternberg, R. How Did the Economic Crisis Influence New Firm Creation? *Jahrbücher für Nationalökonomie und Statistik* **2014**, *234*. [CrossRef]
55. Devece, C.; Peris-Ortiz, M.; Rueda-Armengot, C. Entrepreneurship during economic crisis: Success factors and paths to failure. *J. Bus. Res.* **2016**, *69*, 5366–5370. [CrossRef]
56. Aparicio, S.; Urbano, D.; Audretsch, D. Institutional factors, opportunity entrepreneurship and economic growth: Panel data evidence. *Technol. Forecast. Soc. Chang.* **2016**, *102*, 45–61. [CrossRef]
57. Ahmed, I.; Nawaz, M.M.; Zafar, A.; Shaukat, M.Z.; Usman, A.; Rehman, W.; Ahmed, N. Determinants of students' entrepreneurial career intentions: Evidence from business graduates. *Eur. J. Soc. Sci.* **2010**, *15*, 14–22.
58. Maritz, A.; Perényi, A.; De Waal, G.; Buck, C. Entrepreneurship as the Unsung Hero during the Current COVID-19 Economic Crisis: Australian Perspectives. *Sustainability* **2020**, *12*, 4612. [CrossRef]
59. Isenberg, D.; Schultz, E.B. Opportunities for Entrepreneurs in the Pandemic and Beyond. Medium.com. 2020. Available online: https://medium.com/@disen2/opportunities-for-entrepreneurs-in-the-pandemicand-beyond-f92f5fa1997b (accessed on 9 June 2020).
60. Kelley, D.; Singer, S.; Herrington, M. Global Report 2015/2016. Available online: https://www.gemconsortium.org/file/open?fileId=49480 (accessed on 5 June 2020).
61. Arrighetti, A.; Caricati, L.; Landini, F.; Monacelli, N. Entrepreneurial intention in the time of crisis: A field study. *Int. J. Entrep. Behav. Res.* **2016**, *22*, 835–859. [CrossRef]
62. Bosma, N.; Thomas, S.; Terjesen, S.; Kew, P. Global Entrepreneurship Monitor 2015 to 2016: Special Topic Report on Social Entrepreneurship. 2016. Available online: https://ssrn.com/abstract=2786949 or http://dx.doi.org/10.2139/ssrn.2786949 (accessed on 22 May 2020).
63. Armitage, C.J.; Conner, M. Efficacy of the theory of planned behavior: A meta-analytic review. *Br. J. Soc. Psychol.* **2001**, *40*, 471–499. [CrossRef] [PubMed]
64. Zhao, H.; Seibert, S.E.; Hills, G.E. The Mediating Role of Self-Efficacy in the Development of Entrepreneurial Intentions. *J. Appl. Psychol.* **2005**, *90*, 1265–1272. [CrossRef] [PubMed]
65. Faul, F.; Erdfelder, E.; Buchner, A.; Lang, A.-G. Statistical power analyses using G*Power 3.1: Tests for correlation and regression analyses. *Behav. Res. Methods* **2009**, *41*, 1149–1160. [CrossRef]
66. Ringle, C.M.; Wende, S.; Becker, J.M. "SmartPLS 3." Boenningstedt: SmartPLS GmbH. 2015. Available online: http://www.smartpls.com (accessed on 4 June 2020).
67. Henseler, J.; Ringle, C.M.; Sarstedt, M. A new criterion for assessing discriminant validity in variance-based structural equation modeling. *J. Acad. Mark. Sci.* **2014**, *43*, 115–135. [CrossRef]
68. Podsakoff, P.M.; Organ, D.W. Self-Reports in Organizational Research: Problems and Prospects. *J. Manag.* **1986**, *12*, 531–544. [CrossRef]
69. Carmines, E.G.; Zeller, R.A. Reliability and validity assessment. In *Sage University Paper Series on Quantitative Applications in the Social Sciences*; Sage: Beverly Hills, CA, USA, 1979.
70. Dijkstra, T.K.; Henseler, J. Consistent Partial Least Squares Path Modeling. *MIS Q.* **2015**, *39*, 297–316. [CrossRef]
71. Fornell, C.; Larcker, D.F. Evaluating Structural Equation Models with Unobservable Variables and Measurement Error. *J. Mark. Res.* **1981**, *18*, 39–50. [CrossRef]

72. Henseler, J.; Hubona, G.; Ray, P.A. Using PLS path modeling in new technology research: Updated guidelines. *Ind. Manag. Data Syst.* **2016**, *116*, 2–20. [CrossRef]

73. Kline, R. Convergence of structural equation modeling and multilevel modeling. In *The SAGE Handbook of Innovation in Social Research Methods*; Williams, M., Vogt, W.P., Eds.; SAGE Publications Ltd.: London, UK, 2015; pp. 562–589. [CrossRef]

74. Hair, J.F., Jr.; Hult, G.T.M.; Ringle, C.; Sarstedt, M. *A Primer on Partial Least Squares Structural Equation Modeling (PLS-SEM)*; Sage Publications: Thousand Oaks, CA, USA, 2014.

75. Streukens, S.; Leroi-Werelds, S. Bootstrapping and PLS-SEM: A step-by-step guide to get more out of your bootstrap results. *Eur. Manag. J.* **2016**, *34*, 618–632. [CrossRef]

76. Henseler, J.; Ringle, C.M.; Sinkovics, R.R. The use of partial least squares path modeling in international marketing. *Adv. Int. Mark.* **2009**, *20*, 277–319. [CrossRef]

77. Lachenbruch, P.A.; Cohen, J. *Statistical Power Analysis for the Behavioral Sciences*, 2nd ed.; Erlbaum: Hillsdale, NJ, USA, 1998.

78. Stone, M. Cross-Validatory Choice and Assessment of Statistical Predictions. *J. R. Stat. Soc. Ser. B.* **1974**, *36*, 111–133. [CrossRef]

79. Geisser, S. The Predictive Sample Reuse Method with Applications. *J. Am. Stat. Assoc.* **1975**, *70*, 320–328. [CrossRef]

80. Ajzen, I.; Fishbein, M. *Understanding Attitudes and Predicting Social Behavior*; Prentice Hall: Englewood Cliffs, NJ, USA, 1980.

81. Kasych, A.; Kozhemiakina, S.; Vochozka, M.; Romanenko, O.; Glukhova, V. A world model of social entrepreneurship in a crisis. *J. Entrep. Educ.* **2019**, *22*, 1–6.

82. Zaremohzzabieh, Z.; Ahrari, S.; Krauss, S.E.; Abu Samah, A.; Meng, L.K.; Ariffin, Z.; Abu Samah, A. Predicting social entrepreneurial intention: A meta-analytic path analysis based on the theory of planned behavior. *J. Bus. Res.* **2019**, *96*, 264–276. [CrossRef]

83. Fiore, E.; Sansone, G.; Paolucci, E. Entrepreneurship Education in a Multidisciplinary Environment: Evidence from an Entrepreneurship Programme Held in Turin. *Adm. Sci.* **2019**, *9*, 28. [CrossRef]

84. Gurtner, S.; Soyez, K. How to catch the generation Y: Identifying consumers of ecological innovations among youngsters. *Technol. Forecast. Soc. Chang.* **2016**, *106*, 101–107. [CrossRef]

85. Secundo, G.; Mele, G.; Sansone, G.; Paolucci, E. Entrepreneurship Education Centres in universities: Evidence and insights from Italian "Contamination Lab" cases. *Int. J. Entrep. Behav. Res.* **2020**, *26*, 1311–1333. [CrossRef]

5

The Efficiency of R&D Expenditures in ASEAN Countries

Pawel Dobrzanski [1,*] **and Sebastian Bobowski** [2]

[1]   Department of Mathematical Economics, Wroclaw University of Economics and Business,
      53-345 Wroclaw, Poland
[2]   Department of International Economic Relations, Wroclaw University of Economics and Business,
      53-345 Wroclaw, Poland; sebastian.bobowski@ue.wroc.pl
*   Correspondence: pawel.dobrzanski@ue.wroc.pl

Abstract: The aim of this study is to determine whether funds spent on research and development are used efficiently in Association of Southeast Asian Nations (ASEAN) countries. Fifteen countries in the 2000-2016 period have been examined. Measuring the efficiency of research and development spending was performed using the non-parametric Data Envelopment Analysis (DEA) methodology, which allows for the assessment of input–output efficiency. The research includes the following input and output variables: annual public and private spending on innovation, high-technology exports as a percentage of manufactured exports, patent applications to the World Intellectual Property Organisation (WIPO) by priority year for million inhabitants, trademark applications (TA) for million inhabitants and information and communications technology (ICT) exports as a percentage of manufactured exports. Hong Kong and the Philippines are perhaps the most efficient with respect to research and development (R&D) when analysed using the constant return to scale (CRS) approach. However, according to the variable return to scale (VRS) approach, the most efficient ASEAN countries are Hong Kong, Indonesia, Singapore and the Philippines. The study also confirms that increased spending on innovation is resulting in non-proportional effects.

Keywords: Innovation; DEA Methodology; Relative efficiency

1. Introduction

The importance of innovation in shaping economic growth is fundamental to new growth theory, which assumes that long-term growth can be achieved through endogenous technological progress [1]. This theoretical concept has been confirmed in numerous empirical studies [2–5]. Improving innovation is particularly important for developing countries that are trying to improve their competitiveness and stimulate economic growth. As concluded in the study of Liu et Al. [6], the whole world is benefitting from the R&D inputs of advanced countries and international R&D spillovers help to improve technologies, but at the same time the worldwide technological gap is still enlarging.

Nowadays, governments focus on the development of innovation policies and strategies. This strategy assumes a steady increase in R&D spending; however, such spending does not necessarily go hand-in-hand with the efficient use of such funding. Such inefficiency may be one of the reasons for the deepening innovation gap.

The Association of Southeast Asian Nations (ASEAN) countries were selected for this analysis due to the dynamic growth of the region. Ten countries belonging to the ASEAN group are characterised by a wide variety of macroeconomic indicators, levels of development and innovation. Also, the experience of ASEAN countries in the areas of shaping and conducting innovation policies and creating national innovation systems are diverse.

Despite over 40 years of cooperation among ASEAN member states (AMS) in the fields of science, technology and innovation (STI), little has been achieved in the establishment of a region-wide innovation policy. Notwithstanding this, there have been many important initiatives at the regional level aimed at enhancing the innovation capacities of AMS. In 1978, the ASEAN Committee on Science and Technology (ASEAN COST) was established to promote and coordinate STI and human resource development policies across ASEAN, as well as to stimulate the intra- and extra-ASEAN transfer of technologies. Such technological transfer has been inscribed in the institutional framework of ASEAN summits and the ASEAN Ministerial Meetings on Science and Technology (AMMST). Both AMMST and ASEAN COST meet yearly to address STI policy issues, with the latter regularly hosting representatives of the European Union, China, Japan, South Korea and the United States. ASEAN COST has been instrumental in spearheading the creation of the first ASEAN Plan of Action on Science and Technology in 1985. At the second ASEAN Informal Summit on 15 December 1997 in Kuala Lumpur, the ASEAN Vision 2020 was announced, which pointed to STI policies as one of the pillars of a future technologically competitive ASEAN, with highly skilled workers and strong networks of R&D institutes. Shortly after the establishment of the ASEAN Economic Community (AEC) in December 2015, the ASEAN Plan of Action on Science, Technology and Innovation 2016–2025 was announced to promote an innovative, competitive, integrated and sustainable ASEAN by 2025. A set of strategic actions was aimed, among other things, at promoting cooperation between the public and private sector, small and medium entrepreneurship, skilled staff mobility, the transfer of R&D results and commercialisation. ASEAN COST has subsequently been relocated from the ASEAN Socio-Cultural Community (ASCC) to the AEC Blueprint 2025, thus stressing the role of innovation, investment in R&D and STI in improving productivity and industrial competitiveness of ASEAN. However, ASC Blueprint 2025 still addresses STI in the field of education to establish a creative, innovative and responsive ASEAN.

The aim of this research is to verify whether funds spent on R&D are used efficiently in ASEAN countries. Innovativeness is a popular topic discussed in numerous scientific articles, where it is studied through the prism of expenditure, its effects and innovation policy. However, the efficiency of R&D spending, while seldom addressed, is certainly worth exploring.

The rest of the paper is organised as follows. Section 2 presents a review of the literature regarding innovation policies in the ASEAN region and investigates innovation efficiency across ASEAN. Section 3 presents the research methodology. Section 4 describes the results of the data, while we discusses the meaning of these results in Section 5. Section 6 concludes this research.

2. Literature Review

2.1. Region-Wide Innovation Policy in ASEAN

To date, there have been few in-depth studies of innovation policies in ASEAN or their economic impacts. These studies include analyses by the Economic Research Institute for ASEAN and East Asia (ERIA). Hahn and Narjoko [7] studied innovation at the level of microenterprises and establishment in East Asian countries. Kuncoro [8] conducted research on innovation among medium and large enterprises in Indonesia under globalisation, finding a disorganised approach to R&D expenditure in the private sector between the mid-1990s and mid-2000s, with R&D declining in years 2000–2006. Ito [9] observed that many enterprises in Indonesia shifted from high-end to low-end products, which would suggest that the assumption of increased R&D expenditure and innovation might be inaccurate. Indonesia, like many AMS, has been challenged by the middle-income trap due to a development strategy relying on their cost advantage in the labour-intensive manufacturing/industrial market [10]. As argued by Ambashi et al. [11], the rapid rise in the cost of energy and related commodities upon which primary industries depend at the beginning of the 21st century has discouraged private sector innovation in many AMS and has led manufacturers to avoid high-end products. In this regard, there is a lack of incentive to spend on R&D and innovation in the long run by both public and private sectors in many AMS [9].

The *Global Innovation Index 2019* rankings recognise eight AMS among 129 countries/economies (except Lao PDR and Myanmar), with Singapore in the highest rated (8th) position, followed by Malaysia, Vietnam, Thailand, the Philippines, Brunei Darussalam, Indonesia and Cambodia (in 35th, 42nd, 43rd, 54th, 71st, 85th and 98th positions, respectively).

Malaysia was ranked second after China in the upper-middle income group, and Vietnam first in the lower-middle income group. Noteworthy, Singapore was ranked first in the Innovation Input Sub-Index 2019, surpassing, among others, Switzerland, the United States and the Scandinavian countries; however, with respect to the Innovation Output Sub-Index 2019, Singapore was only ranked in the 15th position. Noteworthy, South East Asia is described as a region of continuous improvement in innovation.

The United Nations Development Program (UNDP) assessed AMS in terms of the Technology Achievement Index (TAI), recognising an increase in regards to technological development and innovation in 1999–2008 in Brunei Darussalam, Malaysia, Singapore, Thailand, but especially in Vietnam.

The Asian Development Bank Institute divided AMS into two categories in terms of technological and innovation capacities based on data from 1999 to 2008: Singapore as the frontier and the rest of AMS. Interestingly, while Singapore's performance proved to be comparable to that of Japan and South Korea, followers were ranked similarly to China and India.

Ambashi et al. [11] stressed that ASEAN as a whole is characterised by economic growth, surpassing the technological and innovation achievements of most individual AMS. Intal et al. [12] categorised these AMS into five groups, taking into account their stages of innovation (Table 1).

Intal et al. [12], building upon the work of Rasiah [13], studied the innovation policies of AMS in regards to basic and high-tech infrastructure, network cohesion and global integration. Less developed AMS (e.g., Cambodia, Lao PDR and Myanmar) are encouraged to stabilise politically, inspire demand for innovation, competition and openness to foreign markets. Indonesia, the Philippines, Thailand and Vietnam—classified to learning phase—are expected to learn-by-doing and to imitate, advance social institutions to play the role of formal intermediaries between economic agents, and to be open to foreign markets and foreign direct investment (FDI). As argued by Ambashi et al. [11], AMS might establish and develop their own national innovation system (NIS) based on the typology described above, taking into account various capabilities and limitations.

A multidimensional approach to innovation policy could embrace both industrial and trade policy measures, R&D expenditure and incentives, as well as human resources development. Importantly, the national governments of AMS may consider seek for balance between market and non-market mechanisms of intervention to proceed with innovation-based industrialisation. In this regard, ASEAN as a whole might consider to work on a region-wide innovation policy that would induce synergy between the innovation policies of AMS.

Table 1. Typology of innovation policies in AMS.

Phase	Basic Infrastructure	High-Tech Infrastructure	Network Cohesion	Global Integration
(1) Initial conditions Cambodia, Lao PDR, Myanmar	Political stability and efficient basic structure	Emergence of demand for technology	Social bonds driven by the spirit to compete and achieve	Linking with regional and global markets
(2) Learning Thailand, Philippines, Indonesia, Vietnam	Strengthening of basic infrastructure with better customs and bureaucratic coordination	Learning-by-doing and imitation	Expansion of tacitly occurring social institutions to formal intermediary organisations to stimulate connections and coordination between economic agents	Access to foreign sources of knowledge, imports of material and capital goods, and inflows of foreign direct investmentIntegration in global value chain
(3) Catch-up Malaysia	Smooth links between economic agents	Creative destruction activities start through imports of machinery and equipment, licensing, and creative duplication	Participation of intermediary and government organisations in coordinating technologyinflows, initiation of commercially viable R&D	Licensing and acquisition of foreign capabilities, upgrading synergies through technology imports, emergence of strong technology-based exports
(4) Advanced	Advanced infrastructure to support meeting demands of economic agents	Developmental research to accelerate creative destruction activities. Frequent filing of patents in the United States starts	Strong participation of intermediary and government organisations in coordinating technology inflows, initiation of commercially viable R&D	Access to foreign human capital, knowledge links, and competitiveness in high-tech products and collaboration with R&D institutions
(5) Frontier Singapore	Novel infrastructure developed to save resource costs and stimulate short lead times	Basic research R&D labs to support creative accumulation activities generating knowledge. Technology shapers generate invention and design patents extensively	Participation of intermediary organisations in two-way flows of knowledge between producers and users	Connecting to frontier nodes of knowledge, and competitive exports of high-tech products

Sources: [11,12].

Both Japan and South Korea are examples of countries that have successfully established their NIS and developed domestic innovation with the support of properly designed industrial and trade policies, relying on strategic technological and knowledge resources imported from the Western economies [14]. In the case of Japan, licensing agreements, strategic alliances with Western businesses as well as reverse engineering have played a crucial role in their NIS. Using highly-skilled low-wage human resources, Japanese enterprises imitated Western products to create something new and unique as opposed to relying on the transfer of foreign technologies and knowledge through FDI, as has been the case in China and Singapore. Domestic industries were supported by the government through R&D and export incentive schemes. Similarly, instead of relying on inward FDI, South Korea developed an industrial policy aimed at the effective use of licensing agreements and arm's length connections with Western enterprises to build domestic innovation capacities, with strategic support dedicated to large business conglomerates. China's NIS has relied heavily on technology transfer through FDI since the late 1970s, attracting Western businesses with a network of economic and technological development zones supported by industrial policies and export promotion. Both central and local governments enhanced the development of industrial clusters through regulatory reforms, financial incentives and networking between SMEs, research institutes and universities [12]. In relation to China, India demonstrates relatively low manufacturing and innovation competitiveness, thus its innovation ecosystem has made less progress in such aspects as innovation and business sophistication and higher education. Inadequate R&D expenditure—far below the target of 2% of GDP set in 2013—has been dominated by the public sector, with special regard to the central government. On the other hand, while the private sector remains relatively active in R&D activities in pharmaceuticals, information and communications technology (ICT) and transportation, it is still only a relatively minor contributor [15]. Since the 1980s, India has attempted to become a kind of software hub, capitalising upon the prior success of South Korea and Taiwan. In 1990, the government established the Software Technology Parks (STPs), where Indian enterprises pioneered a Global Offshore Delivery Model.

2.2. National Innovation Policies in ASEAN

To date, six AMS have established NIS, categorised either to frontier phase of innovation policy (Singapore), catch-up phase (Malaysia) or learning phase (Indonesia, the Philippines, Thailand and Vietnam).

2.2.1. Indonesia

Indonesia has moved toward a service-led and knowledge-based economy since the mid-2000s. Previously, however, Indonesia's development strategy and economic growth used to rely heavily on natural resources and trade in the import-substitution industries, followed by the accumulation of labour and capital instead of science and technology. Key challenges included institutional and regulatory bottlenecks, as well as a deficit of highly-skilled workers. Importantly, both public and private R&D expenditure was government-centric and far below the average for the lower-middle income transitional economies. As observed by Ambashi et al. [11], foreign enterprises are discouraged from conducting R&D activities in Indonesia due to the relatively low quality of intellectual property rights (IPR) with no significant changes in this regard after 2010.

In 2010, the National Innovation Committee was established to make innovation policy more systematic and better governed; however, it was very soon dissolved under the guise of streamlining bureaucracy. The coordinating role of the Directorate General for Innovation Strengthening, under the supervision of the Ministry of Research, Technology and Higher Education (MRTHE), is highly questionable due to lack of political mandate in multilayered hierarchy. Despite the government-centric character of Indonesian R&D projects, they were historically poorly coordinated and short-lived because of a lack of any formal, integrated NIS with no governing framework. Indonesia's NIS (SINAS), which is still under implementation, was established on the basis of the Medium-Term Development

Plan 2015–2019, which aimed to increase Indonesia's capacities in STI. This initiative should be regarded as a step toward the implementation of more effective and formal innovation system.

2.2.2. Malaysia

In Malaysia, dynamic economic growth and technological development has been enhanced since the 1980s by inward FDI, moving this economy up in the value chain from primary to manufacturing products. Among key documents addressing science, technology and innovation development at both macro and micro level, there has been the First National Science and Technology Policy (NSTP1) 1986–1989; the Industrial Technology Development: A National Action Plan 1990–2001; Second National Science and Technology Policy (NSTP2) 2002–2010; and National Policy on Science, Technology and Innovation, 2013–2020. Among the key objectives of the strategies were enhancing national R&D capacities, the commercialisation of R&D results through the National Innovation Model, establishing partnerships between public universities and industries, and the development of new knowledge-based industries.

The Malaysian government failed to achieve two of the basic objectives of the NSTP2, assuming an increase in R&D expenditure (up to 1.5% of GDP) and personnel (up to 60 per 10,000 inhabitants) by 2010. The National Policy on Science, Technology and Innovation, 2013–2020 put an emphasis on sharing and communicating the objectives of STI policies among stakeholders, enhancing R&D capacities of both public and private sectors, and promoting good governance to secure high quality institutional and regulatory framework of STI. The New Economic Model (NEM), announced in 2010, emphasised innovation. The NEM (2010) departed from the strategy of manufacturing export based on low-cost labour immigration in favour of domestically-developed innovation capacities.

The Malaysian NIS has evolved gradually, with the Ministry of Science, Technology and Innovation (MOSTI) and Ministry of Higher Education (MOHE) playing key roles. MOSTI supervises several entities involved in biotechnology, ICT, industry, sea-to-space as well as ST, such as National Institutes of Biotechnology Malaysia (NIBM) and Academy of Sciences (ASM), while MOHE governs a network of centres of excellence with solid international reputation, mainly thanks to research results and publications [16]. Both MOSTI and MOHE are primary donors to R&D activities in public and private sector, however, other ministries such as Ministry of International Trade and Industry, Ministry of Energy, Green Technology and Water, the Ministry of Agriculture and Agro-based Industry, and the Ministry of Finance provide financing schemes to selected stakeholders.

As already noted, Malaysia is currently in the catching-up phase, thus still needs to improve and advance its NIS to follow frontiers, such as Singapore. Firstly, there is a need to consolidate the numerous departments, agencies and institutes inside the NIS to avoid overlaps and to make interconnections between the different schemes and initiatives, making these clearer and more transparent. Secondly, the availability of R&D incentives for industry are limited because of the administrative burden and information deficit. Thirdly, universities could be more active in knowledge transfer, spill-over and dissemination, and thus be more flexible and open to various stakeholders. Fourth, the number of patent applications might be increased, including involvement of SMEs and better IP governance.

2.2.3. The Philippines

The Philippines had no emphasis on innovation policy until the late 2000s; however, many STI plans and projects were launched following 1993 under the Ramos administration. The first National Innovation Strategy (2000–2010), or Filipinnovation, was focused on investment in human capital, STI and related management systems, and upgrading the Filipino mindset. There were four strategies in the Philippine Development Plan 2011–2016 aimed at making national industries and services sectors globally competitive and innovative. The Duterte administration (2016–2022) implemented a strategy of promoting and increasing innovation under four national programs: the Collaborative Research and Development to Leverage Philippine Economy Program (CRADLE), the Niche Centers in the Regions for R&D Program (NICER), the R&D Leadership Program (RDLead) and the Business Innovation through S&T for Industry Program.

The Philippines are currently classified as being in the learning phase; nevertheless, there are many important obstacles to implement and develop NIS. Firstly, there is a need to enhance cooperation and spill-over among various stakeholders, such as industry, government and academia, including specificity of sectors and companies involved. Secondly, intellectual property rights (IPR) could be better protected and effective, striking a balance between incentives and restrictions dedicated to FDI. Thirdly, regular cooperation between universities and the private sector is necessary to develop products and to commercialise R&D results. Fourth, both public and private R&D expenditure might be higher, including introduction of effective financing schemes dedicated to start-ups under internationally recognised standards.

2.2.4. Singapore

Singapore has experienced dynamic economic growth and technological development since 1965 due to inward FDI attracted by a business-friendly macroeconomic environment, low taxes and a highly-skilled labour force. In 2016, the Research, Innovation and Enterprise 2020 Plan was launched to increase the innovation capacities of the private sector. Financial resources are distributed within the white space under the supervision of the National Research Foundation.

An important component of Singapore's innovation policy is the development of knowledge-based industrial clustering [17]. The timing of government intervention depends on the maturity and specificity of a sector. The Economic Development Board (EDB) was established to serve as a one-stop shop to attract FDI and talents under the slogan of Singapore's innovation strategy: 'Home for Business, Home for Talent, Home for Innovation'. The geographical proximity of rapidly growing markets, such as China and India, has made Singapore a regional hub for many Western multinational corporations (MNCs) willing to tap into the economic dynamism in this part of the world.

It is critical for Singapore to maintain a competitive and consistent institutional regulatory framework for NIS, and to keep all relevant stakeholders, including the private sector, actively involved. As concluded by Ambashi et al. [11], Singapore is challenged nowadays by its transition from being a technology adopter to a technology innovator through the development of a technological entrepreneurial community. It seems then that knowledge-based industrial clustering is the key.

2.2.5. Thailand

Thailand experienced dynamic economic growth from the 1960s to the mid-1990s due to its successful transition from an agrarian to a manufacturing economy by attracting inward FDI. However, industrialisation with inadequate development of domestic technological capacities, accompanied by rising labour shortages and cost pressure, has resulted in a middle-income trap. This, in turn, has resulted in a growing emphasis on innovation to increase productivity and development through industrial upgrading instead of the diversification of export markets and sectors.

In institutional terms, Thailand's innovation policy is fragmented and ineffective, including the functioning of NSTI Policy Committee and the National Research Council. Next to tax incentives, under 12th National Economic and Social Development Plan, the government assumes an increase in the R&D expenditures up to 2% of GDP with private sector shares up to 70% by 2021. In order to increase R&D personnel, the Thai government has established a set of scholarship schemes serviced by the Ministry of Science and Technology (MOST), as well as selected government agencies, such as the Thailand Research Fund, the Office of the Higher Education Commission, and the Institute for the Promotion of Teaching Science and Technology.

Thailand, is currently categorised as being in the learning phase. As such, Thailand needs to increase the level of public investment in R&D and to make the system more demand-driven, to implement transparent systems of evaluation and monitoring of public R&D expenditure, to establish an institutional core/coordinator of innovation policy and to promote human resources development, considering, among others, unfavourable demographic trends.

2.2.6. Vietnam

Vietnam has evolved gradually from centrally planned to socialist market economy, experiencing high rates of growth in the 1990s and 2000s. The innovation-oriented *Đổi Mới* policy (Pillars of the policy were as follows: development of institutional frameworks of the market economy; macroeconomic stability; and economic integration at regional and global level) since the mid-1980s has addressed both micro and macro level innovation. Nevertheless, *Đổi Mới* has proved insufficient to maintain high quality growth and labour productivity in the long term.

The institutional frameworks underpinning Vietnam's innovation policy was strengthened by the establishment of, among others, the National Council for Science and Technology Policy, the State Agency for Technology Innovation and the National Foundation for Science and Technology Development. In 2005 and 2009, IPR regulations were updated to meet the standards of international innovation system. STI development and innovation were prioritised in Socio-economic Development Strategy 2011–2020 and the Socio-economic Development Plan 2016–2020.

In conclusion, there are a number of important obstacles needing to be overcome before making the transition from the learning to the catching-up phase in terms of innovation policy. Firstly, the institutional environment of innovation policy is inconsistent, with different agencies and institutions involved in the design and implementation of STI policy, including IPR. Secondly, systems of financing R&D are ineffective, primarily being sponsored by public expenditure. Thirdly, R&D personnel are limited and lack higher skills due to the poor performance of the tertiary education system in Vietnam. Fourthly, cooperation between industry and academia, including technology transfers and spill-overs, is limited and weak, mainly because of limited resources. While addressing these obstacles, the Vietnamese central government should put emphasis on enhancing the private sector's involvement in innovation.

As previously observed, three less developed AMS (i.e., Cambodia, Lao PDR and Myanmar) lack NIS, prioritising different economic and social development objectives, such as poverty reduction, as well as the modernisation of agriculture and infrastructure. In both the Lao PDR and Myanmar, the Ministry of Science and Technology (MOST) is responsible for STI policies and STI legislation, which is expected to provide the framework for the future NIS. Importantly, less developed AMS cooperate under such programs as Science and Technology Research Partnership for Sustainable Development (SATREPS) and e-ASIA Joint Research Program (e-ASIA JRP) with institutions from Japan and South Korea, including Japan International Cooperation Agency (JICA), Japan's Ministry of Education, Culture, Sports, Science and Technology (MEXT), Japan Science and Technology Agency (JST) and Korea International Cooperation Agency (KOICA) [18]. On the other hand, resource-abundant Brunei Darussalam, which has not been classified in terms of the innovation policy typology, is currently involved in two Japanese programs (e.g., ASEAN exchanges of the Institute of Advanced Energy at Kyoto University and solar energy generation experimental facility of Mitsubishi Corporation). Considering rising R&D expenditure and the construction plans for the Bio-Innovation Corridor in the National Development Plan, Brunei Darussalam seems to be preparing itself for the post-oil and -gas era in the economic development.

2.3. Studies on Innovation Efficiency for ASEAN

Data envelopment analysis (DEA) studies of R&D spending efficiency are an increasingly popular topic in the scientific literature. The choice of variables and models leads to different conclusions and recommendations. Nevertheless, empirical studies on R&D spending efficiency are still limited and need to be supplemented, especially with respect to the developing countries of ASEAN economies. Table 2 presents a cross-country analysis of DEA innovation studies, which include some of the ASEAN and Asia-Pacific countries.

Table 2. Cross-country innovation studies for Association of Southeast Asian Nations (ASEAN) and ASIA-PACIFIC countries using DEA methodology.

Input and Output Variables	DEA Model Used	List of Countries in the Studied Sample	Efficient Countries
	Nasierowski W., Arcelus F.J. [18]		
Input variables: imports of goods and commercial services, gross domestic expenditure on research, degree of private business involvement in R&D, Employment in R&D, Total educational expenditures. **Output variables:** External patents by resident, Patents by a country's residents, National productivity	CRS, input-oriented DEA model	46 countries; 14 from ASEAN and ASIA-PACIFIC: Australia, China, Hong Kong, India, Indonesia, Israel, Japan, Malaysia, New Zealand, Philippines, Singapore, South Korea, Taiwan, Thailand	Fully efficient (in all three models and all two periods of study): Japan, Taiwan Partially efficient (at least in one model or in one year): Hong Kong
	Cullmann A., Schmidt-Ehmcke J., Zloczysti P. [19]		
Input variables: BERD, GERD, GOVERD, HERD Researchers. **Output variables:** Weighted Patents, Unweighted Patents	VRS, output oriented DEA model	28 countries, 3 from ASEAN and ASIA-PACIFIC: China, Japan, South Korea.	Among Asia countries Japan was the most efficient, then South Korea. China was characterized by a very low rate of knowledge production, suggesting that they are still in the phase of imitating and replicating existing technologies.
	Abbasi F., Hajihoseini H., Haukka S. [20]		
Input variables: number of scientists in R&D, expenditure on education and R&D expenditures. **Output variable:** patent counts, royalty incomes and license fees, high-technology export and manufacturing exports.	Virtual DEA based innovation index on the basis of VRS, output oriented DEA model	42 countries, 10 from ASEAN and ASIA-PACIFIC: Australia, China, Hong Kong, Iran, Israel, Japan, Kyrgyzstan, New Zealand, South Korea, Thailand.	Study results are very unclear and hard to understand.
	Cai Y. [21]		
Input variables: General Expenditures on R&D (GERD), Total R&D personnel. **Output variables:** WIPO patents granted, Scientific and technical journal articles, High-technology and ICT services exports.	CRS, output oriented DEA model	22 countries, 4 from ASEAN and ASIA-PACIFIC: China, India, Japan, South Korea.	India and China have relatively high efficiency score and good ranking

Table 2. *Cont.*

Input and Output Variables	DEA Model Used	List of Countries in the Studied Sample	Efficient Countries
		Chen C.P., Hu J.L., Yang C.H. [22]	
Input variables: R&D expenditure stocks (million US dollars in year 2000); Total R&D manpower (full-time equivalent units). **Output variables:** patents applied for in the EPO and USPTO, Scientific journal articles, Royalty and licensing fees. (million US dollars in year 2000).	CRS, output oriented DEA model	24 countries, 3 from ASEAN and ASIA-PACIFIC: Japan, Singapore, South Korea.	South Korea was efficient in some years of period of study.
		Guan J., Chen K. [23]	
Input variables: prior accumulated knowledge stock participating in downstream knowledge commercialization with incremental knowledge; consumed full-time equivalent labor for non-R&D activities; number of full-time equivalent scientists and engineers; incremental R&D expenditure funding innovation activities; prior accumulated knowledge stock breeding upstream knowledge production. **Output variables:** Number of patents granted by United States Patent and Trademark Office; international scientific papers; added value of industries; export of new products in high-tech industries.	VRS and CRS, output-oriented DEA model; Super-efficiency DEA model	22 countries, 3 from ASEAN and ASIA-PACIFIC: Japan, Singapore, South Korea.	Japan was efficient in two models.

Source: Authors' own study on literature review.

Nasierowski and Arcelus [19] studied the NIS efficiency of 46 countries, reporting differences in efficiency and the components of NIS policies (i.e., scale and congestion). This assessment of the impact of R&D on a country's productivity led the authors to conclude that most of the economies subjected to analysis were operating under a variable return to scale (VRS) model. Authors remarked at the dichotomy among countries in terms of their commitment to technological efforts; while some overinvested in certain technological domains, negatively impacting their overall efficiency, others underinvested in R&D, recording reduced returns. The latter empirical result seemed to confirm many of the finding present in the literature.

Cullmann, Schmidt-Ehmcke and Zloczysti [20] investigated the relative efficiency of knowledge production in OECD countries based on intertemporal frontier estimation. The authors addressed the impact of the regulatory environment using the single bootstrap procedure described by Simar and Wilson (2007). The authors confirmed the hypothesis that limited competition, encouraged by entry barriers in regulatory dimensions, negatively impacts R&D efficiency due to the ineffective allocation of resources and eroding incentives to innovate because of the lack of pressure imposed on existing companies by new market entrants, with special regard to entrepreneurs.

Abbasi, Hajihoseini and Haukka [21] proposed a DEA-based virtual index consisting of three input and four output indicators to measure the relative innovativeness of economies, further adopting a multi-stage virtual benchmarking process to propose best and rational benchmarks for NISs assessed as inefficient. The authors found the Tobit and ordinary least squares (OLS) regression model as a useful instrument for providing an empirical explanation of changes in the performances of individual economies with inefficient NIS. It was concluded that there is a potential to improve the efficiency of individual economies without additional inputs to NISs. Moreover, a rapid increase in the contribution of these countries to R&D would not improve their performance. Abbasi et al. [11] stress that innovation may be found as business-driven rather than technology-driven, taking into account that both the increased trade in goods and services in terms of shares in GDP and women's participation in industry might improve the efficiency of NIS.

Cai [22] adopted an NIS approach and new growth theory to calculate the efficiency of 22 economies, including BRICS and the G7. The author found that the first of these groups were highly diversified in respect to NIS performance, with China and India ranking relatively high. Key determinants of NIS efficiency include ICT infrastructure, education system, market environment, economies of scale, governance, natural resources, external links and enterprise R&D. The latter was identified as the most important in the context of the efficiency of NIS. On the other hand, Cai [22] also appreciated the impacts of ICT infrastructure, economies of scale and openness as critical for the diffusion of technologies and knowledge, and thus the efficiency of NIS. The BRICS economies were characterised as natural resources-dependent, with low quality of governance, threaten by the middle-income trap. Therefore, a set of reforms was recommended to enhance transformation into the innovation-driven growth pattern.

Chen et al. [23] investigated the efficiency of R&D using a panel dataset of 24 countries with selected output-oriented indices. An empirical study indicated that economies differed in terms of journal publications, whereas the results of R&D efficiency in patents and royalties proved to be quite similar. Chen et al. [23] noted considerably positive impacts of an innovation environment's components, such as R&D intensity, protection of IPRs, as well as knowledge stock and human capital accumulation on R&D efficiency indices. Furthermore, enterprise R&D, both funded by the private business sector and foreign capital, proved to be an important trigger of improvement on the R&D efficiency index in respect to licensing fees, royalties and patents. On the other hand, the journal-oriented R&D efficiency index was positively influenced by the R&D intensity of higher education institutions.

Guan and Chen [24] proposed a relational network DEA model to measure the efficiency of NIS through the decomposition of the innovation process into a network with a two-stage innovation production framework, consisting of an upstream knowledge production process (KPP) and a downstream knowledge commercialisation process (KCP). Furthermore, the authors studied the effects of a policy-based institutional environment on innovation efficiency using a second step, partial least squares regression, to address such problems as multicollinearity, small datasets and a limited number of distribution assumptions. In the case of most OECD countries studied in the paper, a non-coordinated relationship between upstream R&D efficiency and downstream commercialisation efficiency was identified, resulting in significant rank differences. It was found that the overall innovation efficiency of NIS was considerably impacted by downstream commercialisation efficiency performance, thus this component of the innovation production network should be addressed by the future innovation-oriented policies in OECD economies. The empirical results of partial least squares regression analysis led to the formulation of a set of recommendations in terms of public policy interventions by the government aimed at improvements in NIS performance. Specifically, in the case of countries assessed as innovation leaders in terms of CRS efficiency measures (i.e., with relatively higher KPP and KCP efficiency performance), an improvement in innovation output may be difficult to achieve without increasing innovation input, while in the case of countries categorised as innovation followers (i.e., those with relatively lower KPP and KCP efficiency performance), both components require improvement. Without appropriate policies in place, an increase in innovation input will not improve innovation outputs or outcomes in these second group of countries. As a result, improved efficiency of the country may result in higher output and outcomes without additional innovation inputs. On the other hand, countries with diversified KPP and KCP efficiencies are recommended to introduce more stage-specific innovation policies; for instance, in the case of lower KPP and higher KCP efficiency performance, it might be useful to strengthen the protection of IPRs and to finance schemes for R&D projects, while countries with higher KPP and lower KCP should enhance market-driven innovation.

While the study of R&D spending efficiency is not in terms of economic analysis, empirical evidence still a fundamental requirement. This paper makes a number of contributions to the existing R&D spending efficiency literature. Firstly, this article provides a study of R&D efficiency in the context of ASEAN economies. We found no prior R&D efficiency studies published in the ASEAN or Asia Pacific context; as such, this paper fills a gap in the literature. The studies presented in Table 2 took into account only some of the ASEAN and Asia Pacific countries together with other economies from around the world. An analysis of countries from the same region will allow for the identification of regional innovative frontiers. Secondly, this analysis focuses on a long period of 17 years, from 2000 to 2016. Other studies usually took into account significantly shorter periods. Such a long period will allow for the identification of efficiency trends in the analysed economies.

3. Methodology

The main research method used in this study is the DEA methodology, which is a nonparametric method that relies on linear programming benchmarking to assess the relative efficiency of decision-making units (DMUs) with multiple outputs and multiple inputs. This methodology was introduced by Farrell [25] and developed by Charnes et al. [26]. The maximum performance value for each DMU relative to all DMUs in the studied group can be calculated with DEA. DEA constructs the efficiency production frontier over the data points which serves as a benchmark for efficiency measures. DEA is used to determine which DMUs operate as efficiency frontiers and which DMUs do not; moreover, this approach allows for the benchmarking of distance from the frontier at the nearest point [27]. Efficient DMUs are not necessarily production frontiers, but rather best-practice frontiers [28]. It is important to note that DEA measures relative technical efficiency, because DEA measures are based on a reference group of units that are compared with each other and engaged in the same production process.

DEA can use input or output oriented models. An input-oriented model seeks to identify technical efficiency as a proportional reduction in input usage with outputs remaining unchanged. Efficiency in an output-oriented model is represented by a proportional increase in outputs, while the proportion of inputs remains unchanged [29]. DEA models can use constant return to scale (CRS) or variable return to scale (VRS). However, the interpretation of VRS is much more complex than CRS, with VRS used only to control increasing or decreasing returns [30]. Slack-based context-dependent DEA is important extension of DEA methodology, which illustrate target of improvement for the inefficient DMUs. Step-by-step improvement is a useful way to improve performance, and the benchmark target for each step is provided based on the evaluation context at each level of efficient frontier. The slack-based context-dependent DEA allows for a more complete evaluation of the inefficiency of a DMU's performance [31].

Relative efficiency is calculated as the ratio of the weighted sum of outputs to the weighted sum of inputs [32]. The principle of the CRS model is maximisation of this ratio, shown below in Equations (1)–(3) [26]:

$$Max\theta_0 = \frac{\sum_{s=1}^{S} u_r \ y_{rj}}{\sum_{m=1}^{M} v_m x_{mj}}, \tag{1}$$

subject to:

$$\frac{\sum_{s=1}^{S} u_r \ y_{rj}}{\sum_{m=1}^{M} v_m x_{mj}} \leq 1, \tag{2}$$

$u_r, v_m \geq 0; s = 1, \ldots, S; m = 1, \ldots, M$

where:

u_s—weight of output
v_m—weight of input
y_{rj}—output
x_{mj}—input

VRS calculation requires an additional constraint equation [33]:

$$\sum n_{i=1} \lambda j = 1 \tag{3}$$

where θ is the efficiency score calculated for each DMU, λ is the corresponding solution vector for the optimisation and n is the number of DMUs.

The DEA methodology has many advantages. There is no need to define the function form of the relationship between input and outputs, and it can be used for the analysis of processes where the relationship between variables is of an unknown nature [34]. Secondly, DEA allows for the analysis of multiple inputs and outputs at the same time. Also, there is no need for a priori information regarding which inputs and outputs are the most important in the efficiency assessment [35]. Moreover, the causes of inefficiency can be analysed and quantified for each DMU [36].

Nevertheless, the DEA methodology also has some limitations. DEA does not take into account qualitative variables, which may result in some important factors being omitted from the analysis. Some authors are critical of DEA as overestimating efficiency, underlining that DEA provides information more about dominant DMUs [34]. Zhang and Bartels [37] also described a negative correlation between efficiency and the number of DMUs, with an increase in the number of DMUs reducing technical efficiency. Therefore, DEA necessitates the careful interpretation of results.

These issues also present certain limitations with respect to the current research. Firstly the variables we focused on were chosen based on available international statistics. The selected group of inputs and outputs have a crucial impact on the results of the efficiency measurement. Secondly, we initially selected only ASEAN economies for analysis, which gave us a smaller number of DMUs. To increase number of DMUs, additional Asia Pacific economies were selected for analysis. The analysis would be more complex if this study had analysed additional indicators, such as scientific and technical journal articles, human capital in innovation, etc. Nevertheless, expanding the number of indicators would also reduce the discriminatory power of the DEA. Lastly, it is necessary to observe that in the analysed case, DEA is only an assessment of relative efficiency for the selected group of 15 countries. Expanding the research group may render the DMUs analysis ineffective.

4. Data

Calculations for the purposes of examination of the relationship between innovation expenditure and innovation results were performed in a Microsoft Excel spreadsheet and DEA Frontier software. From the ASEAN group, only seven (i.e., Indonesia, Cambodia, Malaysia, Philippines, Singapore, Thailand, and Vietnam) out of 10 countries were analysed due to a lack of available statistics. To obtain comparable peer groups and an appropriate number of DMUs, the study was extended to an additional eight countries from the Asia Pacific region (i.e., Australia, China, Hong Kong, India, Japan, Korea, Sri Lanka, New Zealand). The research period is inclusive of 17 periods from 2000 to 2016. The research methodology was DEA.

Diagnostic variables were selected based on available data from the World Bank. Input indicators included annual public and private spending on innovation (as % of GDP), represented by RDE. The four output indicators chosen for analysis were as follows: (a) high-technology exports as a percentage of manufactured exports, (b) patent applications (PA) according to WIPO by priority year for million inhabitants, (c) TA for million inhabitants, and (d) ICT exports as a percentage of manufactured exports. We took into consideration a number of important principle with respect to the selection of variables [38].

$$n \geq 3 * (s + m) \tag{4}$$

where

s—number of inputs
m—number of outputs
n—numbers of DMUs

Given the limited data with respect to ASEAN countries, we added data from several Asia Pacific economies so as to produce more reasonable results via the DEA methodology. Based on the aforementioned formula, at least 15 DMUs should be analysed. It is important to take this rule into account otherwise the results may be erroneous, with some countries appearing more efficient when in reality they are not. In some cases, if the number of DMUs cannot be increased due to a lack of data, DEA window analysis can be applied. Another important rule in DEA is the coincidence between the inputs and outputs. Correlation coefficients between inputs and outputs should be verified. Output variables with a positive correlation to input variables can remain in the model. Pearson's linear correlation coefficient was also calculated [39]:

$$r_{ij} = \frac{cov \ (X_i \ Y_i)}{s_i s_j} \tag{5}$$

where:

$cov \ (X_i \ Y_i)$—covariance between i-variable and j-variable
s_i—standard deviation of variable X_i
s_j—standard deviation of variable X_j.

All selected variables fulfilled this assumption for all years from 2000 to 2016.

Table 3 presents the final set of analysed variables with their descriptions. Table 4 shows the input and output data for ASEAN and Asia Pacific countries in 2016. Due to the lack of available data, some indicators are marked '*', indicating that the values had been taken from the preceding or the following period, or their average.

Table 3. Indicators and sources.

Variable	Full Indicator Name	Units	Source
RDE	The annual public and private spending on innovation	(as % GDP)	World Bank
PA	Number of patent applications, total *	(Per million inhabitants)	World Bank
TA	Trademark applications, total *	(Per million inhabitants)	World Bank
HTE	Exports of high-tech products	(% of exports)	World Bank
ICT	Exports of ICT products	(% of exports)	World Bank

Note: WIPO. Source: [40]. * lack of available data, some indicators are marked.

Table 4. Diagnostic data of inputs and outputs–ASEAN and ASIA-PACIFIC countries in 2016.

2016	Country/Indicators (2016)	RDE	HTE	TA	PA	ICT
1	AUS	1.58	14.78	2986.31	1172.78	1.31
2	CHN	2.11	25.24	1526.41	970.87	26.50
3	HKG	0.76	12.12	4931.58	1920.78	49.99
4	IDN	0.07	5.79	241.04	32.70	3.37
5	IND	0.63	7.13	223.76	172.56	0.95
6	JPN	3.14	16.22	1283.39	2507.05	8.31
7	KHM	0.12	0.43	104.43	4.12	1.90
8	KOR	4.23	26.58	3548.96	4075.07	22.27
9	LKA	0.10	0.84	510.68	27.02	0.39
10	MYS	1.30	42.97	1253.94	232.02	30.53
11	NZL	1.23	10.14	4824.00	1360.69	1.03
12	PHL	0.14	55.10	317.23	33.09	43.21
13	SGP	2.20	48.85	4055.44	1958.17	33.64
14	THA	0.63	21.51	749.50	113.56	15.79
15	VNM	0.37	26.93	517.24	55.28	31.24
16	Average for ASEAN countries	0.69	28.80	1034.12	346.99	22.81
17	Average for ASIA-PACIFIC countries	1.24	20.98	1804.93	975.72	18.03

Note: AUS—Australia, CHN—China, HKG—Hong Kong, IDN—Indonesia, IND—India, JPN—Japan, KHM—Cambodia, KOR—Korea, Rep., LKA—Sri Lanka, MYS—Malaysia, NZL—New Zealand, PHL—Philippines, SGP—Singapore, THA—Thailand, VNM—Vietnam. Source: Authors' own study based on [40].

5. Empirical Results and Discussion

The authors have chosen the input-oriented model to verify whether a DMU under evaluation can reduce its inputs while keeping the outputs at their current levels. The authors used the CRS and VRS methods. CRS reflects the fact that outputs will change by the same proportion as inputs are changed. In contrast, VRS reflects the fact that production technology can exhibit increasing, constant and decreasing returns to scale. The results of CRS are presented in Table 5, while the VRS results are shown in Table 6.

Table 5. The efficiency of spending on innovation in 2016 (constant return to scale (CRS).

DMU No.	DMU Name	Input-Oriented CRS Efficiency	Sum of λ	RTS	Optimal Lambdas (λ) with Benchmarks	BDMU	λ	BDMU
1	AUS	0.30563	0.743	Increasing	0.608	dmu3	0.134	dmu12
2	CHN	0.20323	0.848	Increasing	0.499	dmu3	0.348	dmu12
3	**HKG**	**1.00000**	1.000	Constant	1.000	dmu3		
4	IDN	0.67610	0.138	Increasing	0.043	dmu3	0.096	dmu12
5	IND	0.13098	0.198	Increasing	0.088	dmu3	0.110	dmu12
6	JPN	0.31664	1.312	Decreasing	1.305	dmu3	0.007	dmu12
7	KHM	0.15226	0.041	Increasing	0.020	dmu3	0.021	dmu12
8	KOR	0.38256	2.137	Decreasing	2.121	dmu3	0.016	dmu12
9	LKA	0.78184	0.104	Increasing	0.104	dmu3		
10	MYS	0.19970	0.941	Increasing	0.207	dmu3	0.734	dmu12
11	NZL	0.60543	0.978	Increasing	0.978	dmu3		
12	**PHL**	**1.00000**	1.000	Constant	1.000	dmu12		
13	SGP	0.39107	1.673	Decreasing	1.008	dmu3	0.665	dmu12
14	THA	0.23610	0.491	Increasing	0.129	dmu3	0.362	dmu12
15	VNM	0.36884	0.713	Increasing	0.063	dmu3	0.650	dmu12

Source: Authors' calculations in DEAFrontier.

Table 6. The efficiency of spending on innovation in 2016 (VRS).

DMU No.	DMU Name	Input-Oriented VRS Efficiency	λ	DMU	λ	BDMU	λ	BDMU
1	AUS	0.31339	0.604	HKG	0.291	IDN	0.105	PHL
2	CHN	0.20667	0.497	HKG	0.173	IDN	0.331	PHL
3	**HKG**	**1.00000**	1.000	HKG				
4	**IDN**	**1.00000**	1.000	IDN				
5	IND	0.19176	0.074	HKG	0.908	IDN	0.018	PHL
6	JPN	0.54461	0.723	HKG	0.272	KOR	0.004	SGP
7	KHM	0.57225	1.000	IDN				
8	**KOR**	**1.00000**	1.000	KOR				
9	**LKA**	**1.00000**	1.000	LKA				
10	MYS	0.20083	0.200	HKG	0.065	LKA	0.735	PHL
11	NZL	0.60586	0.976	HKG	0.024	LKA		
12	**PHL**	**1.00000**	1.000	PHL				
13	**SGP**	**1.00000**	1.000	SGP				
14	THA	0.25647	0.070	HKG	0.564	LKA	0.366	PHL
15	VNM	0.39229	0.048	HKG	0.309	IDN	0.643	PHL

Source: Authors' calculations in DEAFrontier.

Among Asia-Pacific counties, only two were found to be efficient in 2016 under the CRS assumption for the overall process: Hong-Kong and the Philippines. The Philippines was found to be the only an efficiency frontier among ASEAN countries. The remaining countries scored between 0 and 1, and according to DEA methodology can be identified as inefficient. These countries can improve their efficiency or reduce their inefficiencies proportionately by reducing their inputs. In 2016, India obtained the worst result (0.131); while among ASEAN countries, we found that Cambodia, scored only 0.152. Both economies could improve their efficiency by reducing R&D expenditure up to 86.90% (1–0.131) and 84.80% (1–0.152), respectively. The DEA methodology also allow us to identify benchmarks (BDMU), which are effective units. Ineffective units should follow the innovation polices of benchmark DMUs or develop organisational solutions in order to recognise the best practices and their possible adaptation to improve their expenditure transformation processes. For example, the benchmark for New Zealand is Hong-Kong, while the benchmark for Thailand is Hong-Kong and the Philippines. Thailand should attempt to become more like the Philippines than as Hong-Kong, as suggested by higher lambda weight, respectively $\lambda = 0.362$, $\lambda = 0.129$. For overall process in 2016, two countries (i.e., Hong-Kong and the Philippines) are scale efficient, and have optimal returns-to-scale. This can be seen in Table 3 in the RTS column. In addition, 10 countries (i.e., Australia, China, Indonesia, Cambodia, Sri Lanka, Malaysia, New Zealand, Thailand and Vietnam) have an increasing returns-to-scale, while three countries (i.e., Japan, Korea and Singapore) have a decreasing returns-to-scale.

Under VRS, we make the assumption that there are six efficient countries: Hong-Kong, Indonesia, Korea, Sri Lanka, Philippines and Singapore. From the ASEAN region, the efficiency frontiers include Singapore, the Philippines and Indonesia. Similar to the CRS model, India and China were the least efficient (0.19176 and 0.20667, respectively). It is noteworthy that more countries are efficient under the VRS assumption, as all relatively CRS efficient DMUs are scale efficient too.

The DEA methodology allows us to investigate potential improvements, which is presented in Table 7 for all indicators in 2016 for both CRS and VRS methodologies. Less efficient countries might become more efficient by implementing proposed improvements. In terms of inputs, potential improvement refers to the percentage difference between the target amount and the actual amount of input and output for each country. In order to improve efficiency, a country can increase its outputs or decrease its inputs. It is noteworthy to mention that improvement suggestions obtained by countries for CRS and VRS models are not the same. In CRS, two out of 15 countries (i.e., Hong Kong and the Philippines) are efficient. Based on potential improvements results from DEA model can be concluded that Australia, China, Indonesia Japan, Korea and Singapore in order to improve the efficiency index should concentrate on increasing their number of trademark applications. In order to become more efficient Australia, China, Indonesia, India, Japan, Korea, Sri Lanka, Malaysia, New Zealand, Singapore and Thailand need to focus on increasing their ICT exports. Similar recommendations can be deduced from the second model (VRS). Also, inefficient countries can become efficiency frontiers by decreasing their R&D expenditure; this is especially true when these expenditures are very high and the country is not able to use all of them due to, for example, a lack of technology. However, it is worth paying attention to the pressure of politics.

To expand the analysis, the authors assessed the efficiency of spending on innovation for an additional 16 years (2000–2016), for which a similar procedure was carried out. The final results are presented in Tables 8–10.

The analysis calculated efficiency indicators for several ASEAN and Asia Pacific economies. The research input-oriented model was chosen using CRS and VRS methodology for analysis. In addition, the average efficiency indicator was calculated for a change in indicator between 2000 and 2016. The average efficiency score is the arithmetic average of efficiency scores across 17 years. Table 8 shows the final efficiency index for CRS and Table 9 for VRS.

Table 7. Potential improvement in outputs at the current level of inputs and inputs at the current level of outputs for ASEAN and ASIA-PACIFIC countries in 2016.

Input-Oriented/ CRS Model Slacks		Input Slacks		Output Slacks			CRS Model Target		Efficient Input Target		Efficient Output Target			Potential Improvement for Inputs or Outputs (%)					Potential Improvement for Inputs or Outputs (Values)				
DMU No.	DMU Name	RDE	HTE	TA	PA	ICT	DMU No.	DMU Name	RDE	HTE	TA	PA	ICT	RDE	HTE	TA	PA	ICT	RDE	HTE	TA	PA	ICT
1	AUS	0.00	0.00	56.02	0.00	34.91	1	AUS	0.48	14.78	3042.33	1172.78	36.22	-69.44%	0.00%	1.88%	0.00%	2670.43%	-1.09	0.00	56.02	0.00	34.91
2	CHN	0.00	0.00	1047.14	0.00	13.52	2	CHN	0.43	25.24	2573.55	970.87	40.01	-79.68%	0.00%	68.60%	0.00%	51.01%	-1.68	0.00	1047.14	0.00	13.52
3	HKG	0.00	0.00	0.00	0.00	0.00	3	HKG	0.76	12.12	4931.58	1920.78	49.99	0.00%	0.00%	0.00%	0.00%	0.00%	0.00	0.00	0.00	0.00	0.00
4	IDN	0.00	0.00	0.00	52.53	2.90	4	IDN	0.05	5.79	241.04	85.23	6.27	-32.39%	0.00%	0.00%	160.66%	86.03%	-0.02	0.00	0.00	52.53	2.90
5	IND	0.00	0.00	244.83	0.00	8.20	5	IND	0.08	7.13	468.59	172.56	9.15	-86.90%	0.00%	109.41%	0.00%	860.77%	-0.55	0.00	244.83	0.00	8.20
6	JPN	0.00	0.00	5155.10	0.00	57.25	6	JPN	0.99	16.22	6438.49	2507.05	65.56	-68.34%	0.00%	401.68%	0.00%	688.61%	-2.15	0.00	5155.10	0.00	57.25
7	KHM	0.00	0.97	0.00	34.64	0.00	7	KHM	0.02	1.40	104.43	38.76	1.90	-84.77%	224.68%	0.00%	839.97%	0.00%	-0.10	0.97	0.00	34.64	0.00
8	KOR	0.00	0.00	6917.40	0.00	84.46	8	KOR	1.62	26.58	10466.36	4075.07	106.73	-61.74%	0.00%	194.91%	0.00%	379.25%	-2.61	0.00	6917.40	0.00	84.46
9	LKA	0.00	0.41	0.00	171.88	4.79	9	LKA	0.08	1.26	510.68	198.90	5.18	-21.82%	48.89%	0.00%	636.01%	1222.70%	-0.02	0.41	0.00	171.88	4.79
10	MYS	0.00	0.00	0.00	189.94	11.55	10	MYS	0.26	42.97	1253.94	421.96	42.09	-80.03%	0.00%	0.00%	81.86%	37.83%	-1.04	0.00	0.00	189.94	11.55
11	NZL	0.00	1.71	0.00	518.19	47.87	11	NZL	0.74	11.86	4824.00	1878.88	48.90	-39.46%	16.88%	0.00%	38.08%	4630.64%	-0.49	1.71	0.00	518.19	47.87
12	PHL	0.00	0.00	0.00	0.00	0.00	12	PHL	0.14	55.10	317.23	33.09	43.21	0.00%	0.00%	0.00%	0.00%	0.00%	0.00	0.00	0.00	0.00	0.00
13	SGP	0.00	0.00	1126.54	0.00	45.49	13	SGP	0.86	48.85	5181.98	1958.17	79.12	-60.89%	0.00%	27.78%	0.00%	135.23%	-1.34	0.00	1126.54	0.00	45.49
14	THA	0.00	0.00	0.00	145.60	6.30	14	THA	0.15	21.51	749.50	259.16	22.08	-76.39%	0.00%	0.00%	128.22%	39.88%	-0.48	0.00	0.00	145.60	6.30
15	VNM	0.00	9.65	0.00	87.38	0.00	15	VNM	0.14	36.58	517.24	142.66	31.24	-63.12%	35.81%	0.00%	158.06%	0.00%	-0.24	9.65	0.00	87.38	0.00

Table 7. Cont.

Input-Oriented/ VRS Model Slacks		Input Slacks		Output Slacks			VRS Model Target		Efficient Input Target		Efficient Output Target			Potential Improvement for Inputs or Outputs (%)					Potential Improvement for Inputs or Outputs (Values)				
DMU No.	DMU Name	RDE	HTE	TA	PA	ICT	DMU No.	DMU Name	RDE	HTE	TA	PA	ICT	RDE	HTE	TA	PA	ICT	RDE	HTE	TA	PA	ICT
1	AUS	0.00	0.00	94.91	0.00	34.39	1	AUS	0.49	14.78	3081.22	1172.78	35.70	-68.66%	0.00%	3.18%	0.00%	2630.60%	-1.08	0.00	94.91	0.00	34.39
2	CHN	0.00	0.00	1070.18	0.00	13.21	2	CHN	0.44	25.24	2596.59	970.87	39.70	-79.33%	0.00%	70.11%	0.00%	49.84%	-1.67	0.00	1070.18	0.00	13.21
3	HKG	0.00	0.00	0.00	0.00	0.00	3	HKG	0.76	12.12	4931.58	1920.78	49.99	0.00%	0.00%	0.00%	0.00%	0.00%	0.00	0.00	0.00	0.00	0.00
4	IDN	0.00	0.00	0.00	0.00	0.00	4	IDN	0.07	5.79	241.04	32.70	3.37	0.00%	0.00%	0.00%	0.00%	0.00%	0.00	0.00	0.00	0.00	0.00
5	IND	0.00	0.00	366.05	0.00	6.58	5	IND	0.12	7.13	589.82	172.56	7.53	-80.82%	0.00%	163.59%	0.00%	690.38%	-0.51	0.00	366.05	0.00	6.58
6	JPN	0.00	0.00	3268.09	0.00	34.06	6	JPN	1.71	16.22	4551.49	2507.05	42.38	-45.54%	0.00%	254.64%	0.00%	409.75%	-1.43	0.00	3268.09	0.00	34.06
7	KHM	0.00	5.35	136.61	28.57	1.47	7	KHM	0.07	5.79	241.04	32.70	3.37	-42.78%	1238.31%	130.82%	692.92%	77.02%	-0.05	5.35	136.61	28.57	1.47
8	KOR	0.00	0.00	0.00	0.00	0.00	8	KOR	4.23	26.58	3548.96	4075.07	22.27	0.00%	0.00%	0.00%	0.00%	0.00%	0.00	0.00	0.00	0.00	0.00
9	LKA	0.00	0.00	0.00	0.00	0.00	9	LKA	0.10	0.84	510.68	27.02	0.39	0.00%	0.00%	0.00%	0.00%	0.00%	0.00	0.00	0.00	0.00	0.00
10	MYS	0.00	0.00	0.00	178.75	11.26	10	MYS	0.26	42.97	1253.94	410.77	41.79	-79.92%	0.00%	0.00%	77.04%	36.88%	-1.04	0.00	0.00	178.75	11.26
11	NZL	0.00	1.70	0.00	514.01	47.75	11	NZL	0.75	11.85	4824.00	1874.70	48.79	-39.41%	16.78%	0.00%	37.78%	4619.38%	-0.48	1.70	0.00	514.01	47.75
12	PHL	0.00	0.00	0.00	0.00	0.00	12	PHL	0.14	55.10	317.23	33.09	43.21	0.00%	0.00%	0.00%	0.00%	0.00%	0.00	0.00	0.00	0.00	0.00
13	SGP	0.00	0.00	0.00	0.00	0.00	13	SGP	2.20	48.85	4055.44	1958.17	33.64	0.00%	0.00%	0.00%	0.00%	0.00%	0.00	0.00	0.00	0.00	0.00
14	THA	0.00	0.00	0.00	48.35	3.77	14	THA	0.16	21.51	749.50	161.91	19.56	-74.35%	0.00%	0.00%	42.58%	23.88%	-0.47	0.00	0.00	48.35	3.77
15	VNM	0.00	10.86	0.00	69.14	0.00	15	VNM	0.15	37.79	517.24	124.42	31.24	-60.77%	40.33%	0.00%	125.06%	0.00%	-0.23	10.86	0.00	69.14	0.00

Source: Authors' calculations in DEAfrontier.

Table 8. The efficiency of spending on innovation for ASEAN and ASIA-PACIFIC in 2000–2016 (CRS).

CRS	CRS Effectivness Index	2000 CRS	2001 CRS	2002 CRS	2003 CRS	2004 CRS	2005 CRS	2006 CRS	2007 CRS	2008 CRS	2009 CRS	2010 CRS	2011 CRS	2012 CRS	2013 CRS	2014 CRS	2015 CRS	2016 CRS	Avarage	Change 2000–2016	Rank
3	**HKG**	1.000	1.000	1.000	1.000	1.000	1.000	1.000	1.000	1.000	1.000	1.000	1.000	1.000	1.000	1.000	1.000	1.000	**1.000**	0.000	1
12	**PHL**	1.000	1.000	1.000	1.000	1.000	1.000	1.000	1.000	1.000	1.000	1.000	1.000	1.000	1.000	1.000	1.000	1.000	**1.000**	0.000	1
4	IDN	0.689	0.798	0.747	0.845	1.000	0.917	1.000	0.769	0.789	0.792	0.732	0.717	0.734	0.712	0.569	0.564	0.676	0.768	−0.013	3
11	NZL	0.625	0.833	0.869	1.000	0.862	0.919	0.939	0.888	0.707	0.653	0.576	0.516	0.540	0.522	0.614	0.523	0.605	0.717	−0.019	4
14	THA	0.537	0.546	0.657	0.685	0.739	0.764	0.644	0.736	0.708	0.629	0.486	0.368	0.333	0.313	0.269	0.233	0.236	0.522	−0.301	5
9	LKA	0.253	0.276	0.330	0.367	0.413	0.475	0.502	0.488	0.543	0.425	0.411	0.498	0.594	0.600	0.584	0.631	0.782	0.481	0.529	6
13	SGP	0.443	0.426	0.439	0.531	0.543	0.597	0.569	0.486	0.302	0.393	0.457	0.366	0.398	0.382	0.408	0.442	0.391	0.445	−0.052	7
8	KOR	0.371	0.381	0.423	0.535	0.564	0.572	0.486	0.449	0.410	0.457	0.446	0.362	0.374	0.369	0.415	0.450	0.383	0.438	0.012	8
7	KHM	0.353	0.424	0.478	0.225	0.472	0.450	0.366	0.559	0.549	0.514	0.521	0.488	0.485	0.502	0.375	0.090	0.152	0.412	−0.201	9
6	JPN	0.425	0.471	0.471	0.533	0.534	0.471	0.388	0.351	0.335	0.383	0.385	0.313	0.335	0.293	0.323	0.347	0.317	0.393	−0.108	10
15	VNM	0.163	0.172	0.183	0.244	0.295	0.354	0.420	0.473	0.426	0.453	0.416	0.476	0.379	0.388	0.323	0.342	0.369	0.346	0.206	11
1	AUS	0.272	0.301	0.314	0.349	0.412	0.440	0.433	0.406	0.358	0.355	0.323	0.282	0.298	0.314	0.311	0.354	0.306	0.343	0.034	12
10	MYS	0.532	0.455	0.395	0.432	0.472	0.448	0.446	0.398	0.305	0.246	0.242	0.234	0.220	0.206	0.192	0.188	0.200	0.330	−0.333	13
2	**CHN**	0.081	0.095	0.110	0.126	0.138	0.127	0.125	0.122	0.112	0.110	0.125	0.132	0.135	0.150	0.170	0.199	0.203	**0.133**	0.122	14
5	IND	0.033	0.043	0.046	0.053	0.061	0.068	0.072	0.079	0.076	0.091	0.102	0.094	0.106	0.113	0.134	0.151	0.131	**0.085**	0.098	15

Source: Authors' calculations.

Table 9. The efficiency of spending on innovation ASEAN and ASIA-PACIFIC in 2000–2016 (VRS).

	VSR	2000	2001	2002	2003	2004	2005	2006	2007	2008	2009	2010	2011	2012	2013	2014	2015	2016	Avarage	Change 2000–2016	Rank
		VRS	VRS	VRS	VRS	VRS	VRS	VRS	VRS	VRS	VRS	VRS	VRS	VRS	VRS	VRS	VRS	VRS			
3	HKG	1.000	1.000	1.000	1.000	1.000	1.000	1.000	1.000	1.000	1.000	1.000	1.000	1.000	1.000	1.000	1.000	1.000	1.000	0.000	1
4	IDN	1.000	1.000	1.000	1.000	1.000	1.000	1.000	1.000	1.000	1.000	1.000	1.000	1.000	1.000	1.000	1.000	1.000	1.000	0.000	1
12	PHL	1.000	1.000	1.000	1.000	1.000	1.000	1.000	1.000	1.000	1.000	1.000	1.000	1.000	1.000	1.000	1.000	1.000	1.000	0.000	1
13	SGP	1.000	1.000	1.000	1.000	1.000	1.000	1.000	1.000	1.000	1.000	1.000	1.000	1.000	1.000	1.000	1.000	1.000	1.000	0.000	1
8	KOR	0.780	0.726	0.832	1.000	1.000	1.000	1.000	1.000	1.000	1.000	1.000	1.000	1.000	1.000	1.000	1.000	1.000	0.961	0.220	5
7	KHM	1.000	1.000	1.000	1.000	1.000	1.000	0.897	0.892	0.857	0.821	0.843	0.813	0.773	0.798	0.746	0.572	0.572	0.858	−0.108	6
11	NZL	1.000	1.000	1.000	1.000	1.000	1.000	1.000	1.000	1.000	1.000	0.577	0.519	0.546	0.527	0.614	0.529	0.606	0.819	0.000	7
6	JPN	1.000	1.000	1.000	1.000	1.000	1.000	0.761	0.707	0.737	0.734	0.738	0.652	0.684	0.531	0.585	0.583	0.545	0.780	−0.293	8
9	LKA	0.469	0.455	0.481	0.543	0.485	0.589	0.573	0.658	0.755	0.649	0.636	0.771	0.864	0.920	0.991	1.000	1.000	0.696	0.189	9
10	MYS	1.000	1.000	1.000	1.000	1.000	0.449	0.446	1.000	0.310	0.247	1.000	1.000	0.278	0.242	0.264	0.189	0.201	0.625	0.000	10
14	THA	0.564	0.569	0.690	0.703	0.752	0.798	0.663	0.780	0.755	0.678	0.519	0.401	0.366	0.345	0.305	0.261	0.256	0.553	0.216	11
15	VNM	0.352	0.349	0.331	0.382	0.375	0.449	0.461	0.565	0.536	0.567	0.522	0.561	0.419	0.396	0.358	0.376	0.392	0.435	0.213	12
1	AUS	0.274	0.304	0.318	0.354	0.412	0.441	0.433	0.409	0.360	0.360	0.334	0.291	0.307	0.321	0.317	0.359	0.313	0.348	0.135	13
5	IND	0.090	0.101	0.104	0.120	0.128	0.129	0.133	0.138	0.130	0.142	0.153	0.144	0.157	0.161	0.183	0.204	0.192	0.142	0.048	14
2	CHN	0.103	0.107	0.118	0.130	0.139	0.131	0.127	0.124	0.114	0.113	0.125	0.135	0.140	0.153	0.174	0.202	0.207	0.138	0.022	15

Source: Authors' calculations.

Table 10. Efficiency ranking for ASEAN and ASIA-PACIFIC in 2000–2016.

Country	Average CRS Effectiveness Index	Average VRS Effectiveness Index	Average Effectiveness Index	Rank
HKG	1.000	1.000	1.000	1
PHL	1.000	1.000	1.000	2
IDN	0.768	1.000	0.884	3
NZL	0.717	0.819	0.768	4
SGP	0.445	1.000	0.723	5
KOR	0.438	0.961	0.700	6
KHM	0.412	0.858	0.635	7
LKA	0.481	0.696	0.589	8
JPN	0.393	0.780	0.586	9
THA	0.522	0.553	0.538	10
MYS	0.330	0.625	0.478	11
VNM	0.346	0.435	0.390	12
AUS	0.343	0.348	0.345	13
CHN	0.133	0.138	0.135	14
IND	0.085	0.142	0.114	15
Average for ASEAN countries	0.579	0.782	0.680	
Average for ASIA-PACIFIC countries	0.494	0.690	0.592	

Source: Authors' calculations.

The results from Tables 8 and 9 were used to calculate final efficiency index and efficiency ranking presented in Table 10. It is necessary to highlight that presented results are only in the short-term view. Table 10 identifies Hong Kong and the Philippines as the most efficient countries, both being efficient for each year under both CRS and VRS. According to the VRS model, Indonesia (1.00) and Singapore (1.00) are efficiency frontiers; however, these countries scored worse results under the CRS model, thus explaining why these countries assume the third and fifth places in the ranking. Seven out of 15 analysed countries obtained scores above the average 0.592: Hong Kong, the Philippines, Indonesia, New Zealand, Singapore, Korea and Cambodia. Other countries obtained scores below the average efficiency index: Sri Lanka, Japan, Thailand, Malaysia, Vietnam, Australia, China, India. The worst efficiency index was obtained by China and India. At the beginning of the research period, China spent < 1%, although the value has since come to in excess of 2% since 2014. China's average spending on R&D in 2016 was 1.52% of the country's GDP. India, on the other hand, spent less than 1% on R&D. Conversely, the position of Japan may be surprising, because it is seen as one of the most innovative countries in the Asia Pacific region; however, it has among the highest R&D spending, which is more than 3% of GDP. As confirmed by quantitative research, high R&D spending funds does not produce proportionally larger results. This study additionally proves that increased spending on innovation causes non-proportional effects. R&D spending should be increased gradually to obtain optimal results. It is also worth to noting that the DEA methodology calculates relative efficiency, which examines the degree to which R&D expenditure has been transformed into potential innovation.

6. Conclusions

The results of the study complement the comparative analysis of ASEAN economies and provides new empirical material with which we can explain the innovation gap between countries. The paper gives a general overview of the level of innovation in ASEAN countries as compared with other Asia Pacific countries. Among all analysed countries, the CRS approach revealed the efficiency frontier as being Hong Kong and, in the case of ASEAN countries, the Philippines. The analysis also showed that among the ASEAN countries, the closest to being an efficiency frontier using the CRS approach are Indonesia, Thailand and Singapore, with Vietnam and Malaysia being less efficient. According to the VRS approach, however, the most efficient countries were Hong Kong, Indonesia, Singapore and the Philippines. According to the VRS model, Korea (0.961) is the closest to an efficiency frontier, and needs reduce its resource usage to 0.039% to become fully efficient. However, Korea also achieved a poor result in the CRS model, which is why it sits in sixth place in the ranking. Hong Kong, as argued by Wang [41], is an example of a country with a positive non-intervention policy aiming to minimise the government's influence on the market. Thus, while industry innovation is less active in Hong Kong, local industry nonetheless possesses a dynamic innovation base provided by smaller enterprises, most of which develop self-financed spontaneous innovation to provide a solid foundation in an innovation-based economy. Therefore, while lagging behind the other economies, starting with Singapore in terms of R&D expenditure and patent statistics, enterprises in Hong Kong demonstrate high innovation potential. Empirical results for China and India proved to be comparatively poor; although the first of these ranked second in absolute terms, with an annual contribution of over 2% of GDP, China lags behind other developed economies in terms of technology and innovation, especially when considering payments for intellectual property. As outlined in the Made in China 2025 development plan, there is a need to respond to the revolution in such fields as big data, artificial intelligence, the digitisation of conventional industries, robotics and cloud computing through joint efforts by the government, academia and industry, as well as smart manufacturing [11]. Such efforts might help to advance the country from the status of an imitative latecomer in technology, to an innovation-driven knowledge economy. On the other hand, the Make in India program emphasises the creation of clusters to synergise the potential of numerous smaller entities in India; however, there is still a problem with the lack of any long-term strategy or policy for higher education. As a result, there are many obstacles related to a lack of autonomy in governance, employment, intersecting disciplines, creativity bottlenecks, the segregation of teaching and research in STI-related institutions in India, accompanied by inadequate R&D expenditure.

ASEAN as a whole attempts to establish a region-wide innovation policy to make South East Asia an innovation hub. An important platform of cooperation is the ASEAN Committee on Science and Technology, under which there is the possibility of promoting innovation entailing cross-regional synergies. Potential initiatives include:

innovation surveys or censuses for the use of innovation infrastructure across AMS;

R&D platforms and databases to be used by regional agencies and institutes to promote and exchange findings; and

the coordination of R&D scholarship/grant/subsidies schemes, training and education programs across AMS.

This should enhance less-developed AMS to establish NIS. Furthermore, it is necessary to further liberalise and deregulate goods, services and the flow of capital (including ASEAN Framework Agreement on Services, ASEAN Trade in Services Agreement, ASEAN Plus FTAs and RCEP) to stimulate R&D expenditure under international competitive pressure. Last but not least, the freer movement of natural persons would encourage innovation development in ASEAN thanks to knowledge spill-overs. In this regard, regulatory reforms in the field of engineering services are crucial, as well as closer cross-regional collaboration among universities to strengthen the innovation ecosystem of South East Asia.

Despite the many efforts of ASEAN countries, several factors limit their capacity to improve their innovativeness, and hence their economic and social development. For example, with the exception of Singapore, funding across ASEAN countries is consistently low. The Philippines is among the most efficient of ASEAN countries, which was the first to implement NIS in the late 2000s. Indonesia also is close to an efficiency frontier. On the other hand, the position of Singapore, which is the most advanced in terms of NIS implementation and is one of the most developed counties in ASEAN, may be surprising. The evidence presented in this research documents the relative underperformance of the ASEAN region in innovation efficiency. Despite the small amounts spent on innovation, the results are not proportional. As mentioned previously in the methodology section, the research efficiency indicator explores the efficiency of R&D funding usage; therefore, countries with the highest efficiency score do not necessarily achieve the best innovative results. In ASEAN and the Asia Pacific countries, innovative capacities are still limited, and it would thus seem reasonable to gradually increase R&D spending, which in turn may produce better conditions for innovation-driven growth. The results of this study offer important insights for assessing and shaping innovation policies across the ASEAN region. However, it should be noted that results are very general to make concrete recommendations for the development of the NIS in the specific country. Individual country recommendation should also consider the impact of the development level of the country, the sectoral structure of the economy and time lag factor on the innovation input-output relationship.

International institutions are increasingly working towards extending the current statistics on innovation inputs, such as the stock of knowledge, human resources and research infrastructure. However, the current statistics tend to disregard actual innovation outcomes. Enterprises can transform innovation inputs into intermediate outputs, such as patents, and then into innovation outcomes. Innovation outcomes are the economic results of the introduction of innovation and should be taken into consideration, as patent applications themselves do not automatically result in economic outcomes. Ensuring the adequate measurement of innovation outcomes at the country level may require significant structural upgrading [42]. Moreover, the correct estimation of the time lag between transforming inputs into outputs should be taken into consideration. Such statistics, however, are not currently available. Should they become available, their inclusion in the DEA methodology may provide more a reliable overview of the level of efficiency in the economy.

Author Contributions: Conceptualization, P.D. and S.B.; methodology, P.D. and S.B.; formal analysis, P.D. and S.B.; investigation, P.D. and S.B.; data curation, P.D. and S.B.; writing—original draft preparation, P.D. and S.B.; writing—review and editing, P.D. and S.B.; visualization, P.D. and S.B.; supervision, P.D. and S.B.; All authors have read and agreed to the published version of the manuscript.

Acknowledgments: We would like to thank the chairperson, Jingfeng Lu from National University of Singapore (NUS), and the seminar participants at the Singapore Economic Review Conference in August 2019 for useful comments. We also feel grateful to Pete Tyler (University of Cambridge), Philip Arestis (University of Cambridge), Alan Barrell (Cambridge Innovation Academy), Tatsuyoshi Miyakoshi (HOSEI University), Ly Slesman (University of Brunei Darussalam) and to the anonymous referees for their helpful comments and suggestions, which contributed to the quality of the paper.

References

1.   Romer, P.M. Increasing Returns and Long Run Growth. *J. Political Econ.* **1986**, *98*, 71–102. [CrossRef]
2.   Taylor, M.S.; Grossman, G.M.; Helpman, E. Innovation and Growth in the Global Economy. *Economica* **1993**, *60*, 373. [CrossRef]
3.   Ulku, H. *R&D, Innovation, and Economic Growth: An Empirical Analysis*; IMF Working Papers. 04; International Monetary Fund: Washington, DC, USA, 2004. [CrossRef]

4. Hirooka, M. *Innovation Dynamism and Economic Growth*; Edward Elgar Publishing: Cheltenham, UK, 2006. [CrossRef]

5. Fagerberg, J.; Srholec, M. National innovation systems, capabilities and economic development. *Res. Policy* **2008**, *37*, 1417–1435. [CrossRef]

6. Liu, J.; Lu, K.; Cheng, S. International R&D Spillovers and Innovation Efficiency. *Sustainability* **2018**, *10*, 3974.

7. Hahn, C.H.; Narjoko, D. Globalization and Innovation in East Asia, ERIA Research Project Report 2010. Available online: http://www.eria.org/publications/research_project_reports/globalization-and-innovation-in-east-asia.html (accessed on 1 June 2019).

8. Kuncoro, A. Globalization and Innovation in Indonesia: Evidence from Microdata on Medium and Large Manufacturing Establishments. Available online: http://www.eria.org/publications/research_project_reports/images/pdf/y2010/no4/CH06_Microdata_Y2010.pdf (accessed on 1 June 2019).

9. Ito, K. Globalisation and Innovation in ASEAN: Suggestions from Micro Data Analysis. Available online: http://www.jftc.or.jp/shoshaeye/pdf/201311/201311_15.pdf (accessed on 1 June 2019). (In Japanese)

10. Griffith, B. Middle-income Trap. In *Frontier in Development Policies: A Primer on Emerging Issues*; Nallari, R., Yusuf, S., Griffith, B., Bhattacharya, R., Eds.; World Bank: Washington, DC, USA, 2011; pp. 39–43. [CrossRef]

11. Ambashi, M. (Ed.) *Innovation Policy in ASEAN*; Economic Research Institute for ASEAN and East Asia: Jakarta, Indonesia, 2018.

12. Intal, P., Jr.; Fukunaga, Y.; Kimura, F.; Han, P.; Dee, P.; Narjoko, D.; Oum, S. Competitive and Dynamic ASEAN. In *ASEAN Rising: ASEAN and AEC beyond 2015*; Economic Research Institute for ASEAN and East Asia: Jakarta, Indonesia, 2014; pp. 165–211.

13. Rasiah, R. Simulating Innovation in ASEAN Institutional Support, R&D Activity and Intellectual Property Rights. Available online: http://www.eria.org/ERIA-DP-2013-28.pdf (accessed on 15 June 2019).

14. Fagerberg, J.; Srholec, M.; Verspagen, B. Innovation and Economic Development. In *Handbook of the Economics of Innovation*; Hall, B.H., Rosenberg, N., Eds.; Elsevier: Amsterdam, The Netherlands, 2010; Volume 2, pp. 834–872.

15. Sandhya, G.D. India's Science, Technology and Innovation Policy: Choices for Course Correction with Lessons Learned from China. *STI Policy Manag. J.* **2018**, *3*, 1–16. [CrossRef]

16. Day, N.; Amran, M. *Malaysia: The Atlas of Islamic World Science and Innovation, Country Case Study No. 1*; Creative Commons: San Francisco, CA, USA, 2011.

17. Wong, P.K.; Ho, Y.P.; Singh, A. Industrial Cluster Development and Innovation in Singapore. In *From Agglomeration to Innovation: Upgrading Industrial Clusters in Emerging Economies*; Kuchiki, A., Tsuji, M., Eds.; Palgrave Macmillan: London, UK, 2010.

18. Hayashi, Y. (Ed.) *Current Status on Science and Technology in ASEAN Countries*, Tentative ed.; Center for Research and Development Strategy, Japan Science and Technology Agency: Tokyo, Japan, 2015.

19. Nasierowski, W.; Arcelus, F.J. On the efficiency of national innovation systems. *Socio Econ. Plan. Sci.* **2003**, *37*, 215–234. [CrossRef]

20. Cullmann, A.; Schmidt-Ehmcke, J.; Zloczysti, P. Innovation, R&D Efficiency and the Impact of the Regulatory Environment: A Two-Stage Semi-Parametric DEA Approach. *SSRN Electron. J.* **2009**. [CrossRef]

21. Abbasi, F.; Hajihoseini, H.; Haukka, S. Use of Virtual Index for Measuring Efficiency of Innovation Systems: A Cross-Country Study. *Int. J. Technol. Manag. Sustain. Dev.* **2010**, *9*, 195–212. [CrossRef]

22. Cai, Y. *Factors Affecting the Efficiency of the BRICS' National Innovation Systems: A Comparative Study Based on DEA and Panel Data Analysis*; Kiel Institute for the World Economy: Kiel, Germany, 2011.

23. Chen, C.P.; Hu, J.L.; Yang, C.H. An international comparison of R&D efficiency of multiple innovative outputs: The role of the national innovation system. *Innovation* **2011**, *13*, 341–360. [CrossRef]

24. Guan, J.; Chen, K.H. Modeling the relative efficiency of national innovation systems. *Res. Policy* **2012**, *41*, 102–115. [CrossRef]

25. Farrell, M.J. The measurement of productive efficiency. *J. R. Stat. Soc.* **1957**, *120*, 253–290. [CrossRef]

26. Charnes, A.; Cooper, W.W.; Rhodes, E. Measuring the efficiency of decision making units. *Eur. J. Oper. Res.* **1978**, *2*, 429–444. [CrossRef]

27. Cooper, W.W.; Seiford, L.M.; Tone, K. *Data Envelopment Analysis: A Comprehensive Text with Models, Applications, References and DEA-Solver Software*; Kluwer Academic Publishers: Boston, MA, USA, 2000.

28. Cook, W.D.; Tone, K.; Zhu, J. Data envelopment analysis: Prior to choosing a model. *Omega* **2014**, *44*, 1–4. [CrossRef]

29. Thanassoulis, E. Using Data Envelopment Analysis in Practice. In *Introduction to the Theory and Application of Data Envelopment Analysis*; Kluwer Academic Publishers: Norwell, MA, USA, 2001; pp. 89–121. [CrossRef]

30. Kao, C.; Liu, S.T. Efficiencies of Two-Stage Systems with Fuzzy Data. *Fuzzy Sets Syst.* **2011**, *176*, 20–35. [CrossRef]

31. Morita, H.; Zhu, J. Context-Dependent Data Envelopment Analysis and its Use. In *Modeling Data Irregularities and Structural Complexities in Data Envelopment Analysis*; Springer: Boston, MA, USA, 2007; pp. 241–259. [CrossRef]

32. Cooper, J.O.; Heron, T.E.; Heward, W.L. *Applied Behavior Analysis*, 2nd ed.; Pearson: Upper Saddle River, NJ, USA, 2007.

33. Simar, L.; Wilson, P. Non-parametric tests of returns to scale. *Eur. J. Oper. Res.* **2002**, *139*, 115–132. [CrossRef]

34. Alirezaee, M.R.; Howland, M.; van de Panne, C. Sampling size and efficiency bias in data envelopment analysis. *J. Appl. Math. Decis. Sci.* **1998**, *2*, 51–64. [CrossRef]

35. Wober, K.W. Data Envelopment Analysis. *J. Travel Tour. Mark.* **2007**, *21*, 91–108. [CrossRef]

36. Thanassoulis, E. *Introduction to the Theory and Application of Data Envelopment Analysis*; Kluwer Academic Publishers: Norwell, MA, USA, 2003. [CrossRef]

37. Zhang, Y.; Bartels, R. The Effect of Sample Size on the Mean Efficiency in DEA with an Application to Electricity Distribution in Australia, Sweden and New Zealand. *J. Prod. Anal.* **1998**, *9*, 187–204. [CrossRef]

38. Banker, R.D.; Charnes, A.; Cooper, W.W.; Swarts, J.; Thomas, D. *An Introduction to Data Envelopment Analysis with Some of Its Models and Their Uses*; Research Government and Nonprofit Accounting, JAI Press: Greenich, CT, USA, 1989; Volume 5.

39. DeVolpi, A. *Understanding Correlation Coefficients in Treaty Verification*; Argonne National Laboratory: Lemont, IL, USA, 1991. [CrossRef]

40. World Bank Data Base. 2019. Available online: https://data.worldbank.org/ (accessed on 1 June 2019).

41. Wang, J. Innovation and government intervention: A comparison of Singapore and Hong Kong. *Res. Policy* **2018**, *47*, 399–412. [CrossRef]

42. Dobrzanski, P. Innovation expenditures efficiency in Central and Eastern European Countries. *Zb. Rad. Ekon. Fak. U Rijeci* **2018**, *36*, 827–859. [CrossRef]

6

Relationship between Entrepreneurial Team Characteristics and Venture Performance in China: From the Aspects of Cognition and Behaviors

Xue-Liang Pei [1,2], Tung-Ju Wu [3,*], Jia-Ning Guo [1] and Jia-Qi Hu [1]

[1] College of Business Administration, Huaqiao University, Quanzhou 362021, China; peixueliang@hqu.edu.cn (X.-L.P.); 1716112005@stu.hqu.edu.cn (J.-N.G.); 1416111024@stu.hqu.edu.cn (J.-Q.H.)

[2] East Business Management Research Centre, Huaqiao University, Quanzhou 362021, China

[3] School of Management, Harbin Institute of Technology (HIT), Harbin 150001, China

* Correspondence: tjwu@hit.edu.cn

Abstract: Entrepreneurial and innovative activities are becoming a global economic and social phenomenon, especially in emerging economies. This study focuses on a typical emerging economy, China, and its entrepreneurial and innovative activities. On the basis of current research, the literature review and the chain of "cognition–behavior–outcome" are used for constructing the theoretical model for the relationship among entrepreneurial team cognition characteristics, behavior characteristics, and venture performance. A total of 101 valid copies of questionnaire are collected from entrepreneurial team members, as the research objects, and the structural equation modeling (SEM) method is applied to test the theoretical hypotheses. The research results reveal (1) significant effects of entrepreneurial team cognition characteristics and behavior characteristics on venture performance and (2) partial mediating effects of entrepreneurial team behavior characteristics on the relationship between cognition characteristics and venture performance. The research results are the expansion of research on entrepreneurial teams as well as the important reference for entrepreneurial team management and behavioral practice.

Keywords: entrepreneurial team; cognition characteristics; behavior characteristics; venture performance

1. Introduction

The effective implementation of sustainable growth and the development of organizations through entrepreneurship and innovation is a pressing matter for countries around the world, especially among those with emerging economies. According to the data of the National Development and Reform Commission of China from 2015, when the China government proposed the slogan of "mass entrepreneurship brings a mass of innovations" and implemented national policies that encouraged innovative entrepreneurship. Until to 2018, it already had 11,808 entrepreneur incubation organizations countrywide, with over 6.7 million new registered companies in 2018. Moreover, 3.5 million related jobs were created in total [1]. Innovative entrepreneurship is increasingly becoming an important driver of Chinese economic growth and sustainable development. Therefore, entrepreneurial and innovative activities are becoming a global economic and social phenomenon, one that is increasingly drawing the attention of theoretical and practical fields alike [2].

Moreover, the current contribution rate of emerging economies to the global economy is continuously increasing and is becoming the main source of the global economy's stability. Because of this, entrepreneurial and innovative activities within emerging economies should be given more attention. However, Singh and Gaur [2] believe that most of the present literature on entrepreneurship and innovation management focus on the research of relatively developed economies (e.g., North America and Europe), and that literature focusing on entrepreneurship and innovation management in emerging economies is scarce and not frequently published. Furthermore, owing to the higher level of obscurity and uncertainty in the business environments of emerging economies, it is imperative that the rules of entrepreneurial and innovative activities within these economies are more carefully uncovered [3]. On the basis of the foregoing, this study focuses on a typical emerging economy, China, and its entrepreneurial and innovative activities.

In the innovative and entrepreneurial activities of emerging economies, entrepreneurial ventures play an important role in the national economy and social development [4]; particularly, under the rapid development of information technology and the constant change of customer needs, entrepreneurial ventures, with the characteristics of flexibility, innovation, closeness to customers, and prompt responses, became critical economic power [5]. In the establishment and development process of entrepreneurial ventures, team entrepreneurship showed higher success rate than individual entrepreneurship, and the leadership and management patterns gradually changed from individual to team entrepreneurship [6]. In this case, research on the relationship among entrepreneurial team characteristics, the composition, and venture performance in entrepreneurial venture management became topics in the past years [7].

In China, "Fujian Merchants" are a unique group of businessmen who are characterized by "dedicate yourself and you will win", which is the most intuitive embodiment of entrepreneurship [8]. For example, the China Mass Entrepreneurship Index in 2016 (MEI-2016) released by Southwest Jiaotong University shows that Fujian Province ranks among the top ten provinces in terms of innovation and entrepreneurship in China [9]; the 6th Fujian Merchants Forum in 2019 is themed with "condensing the mind, condensing the intelligence; innovating, creating, and entrepreneurship" [10]. Among the innovation and entrepreneurship activities of Fujian Merchants, Quanzhou is the city with the highest economic aggregate, the largest contribution, the largest number of overseas Chinese businessmen, and the oldest history of entrepreneurship. It is also the starting point of the ancient "Maritime Silk Road", with enrich entrepreneurial culture accumulation [11]. Moreover, Xiamen is one of the earliest special economic zones in China, and it is also one of the cities with the best innovation and entrepreneurship environment in China now [12]. On the basis of above, this article selects the "Fujian Merchants" that are most typical with innovation and entrepreneurship in China, and takes the entrepreneurial teams of Quanzhou and Xiamen as the research objects to survey the entrepreneurial activities in emerging economies represented by China from a sustainable perspective.

The high risks, high failure rate, and high uncertainties of entrepreneurial ventures revealed the difference in entrepreneurial team characteristics from traditional businesses [13]. For instance, capital chain break, core technician loss, and external macro environment change might appear in the process of entrepreneurial venture development to result in entrepreneurial team loss and even disbandment [14], while in traditional businesses, they do not. Hence the necessities to further research the relationship between entrepreneurial team characteristics and venture performance [7].

Meanwhile, current research on the relationship between entrepreneurial teams and venture performance has focused on the internal mechanism of the structure and characteristics of entrepreneurial teams (e.g., heterogeneity, knowledge sharing, conflict resolution, and innovation ability) affecting venture performance, while the theoretical regulation behind the effect of entrepreneurial team characteristics on venture performance is yet to be interpreted [15]. In this case, team cognition theory is introduced to this study, wherein entrepreneurial team characteristics are divided into cognition characteristics and behavior characteristics, and the chain of "cognition–behavior–outcome" is followed to analyze the relationship between entrepreneurial team characteristics and venture performance [7,16].

Furthermore, owing to the higher degree of ambiguity and uncertainty in the business environment of emerging economies, it is more necessary to carefully explore the rules of entrepreneurship and innovation activities from a sustainable perspective in both theory and practice. It can promote the development of innovation and entrepreneurship activities.

2. Theoretical Basis and the Proposal of Research Hypothesis

2.1. Definition of Related Concepts

2.1.1. Entrepreneurial Teams and Their Characteristics

There is no universal definition of an entrepreneurial team within the academe. However, in the context of academic literature, the most widely accepted definition is that proposed by Kamm et al. [4], wherein they believe that an entrepreneurial team is a group of two or more people based on common prospects and interests who cooperate to establish a new enterprise for the purpose of gaining better economic profits. After this, Gartner et al. [17] expanded the concept of entrepreneurial teams, believing that the concept not only includes the multiple individuals who cooperated to start the enterprise, but also those individuals who have direct and important impacts on the formulation of the strategy of the company. Ensley and Carland [18] and Mol, Khapova, and Elfring [7] combined the afore-stated views and defined the characteristics of individuals within the entrepreneurial team from the perspectives of economic profit, team cooperation, and strategy formulation. Therefore, we proposed that the term "entrepreneurial team" refers to a group formed in the early establishment period of the company made up of individuals with shared responsibility, who have complementary talents and common entrepreneurial goals and prospects, and is a group wherein these individuals cooperate to set and implement business strategies.

There are many different schools of thought when it comes to the structure and characteristics of entrepreneurial teams [15]. On the basis of the objectives of this research, we divide entrepreneurial characteristics into cognitive characteristics and behavioral characteristics based on team cognition theory.

2.1.2. Venture Performance

Venture performance is the goal behind the establishment and development of entrepreneurial companies, and is also a focal point of discussion in the entrepreneurial research field [7,19]. Scholars believe that the impact on the behavior of the entrepreneur mainly manifests itself in the form of venture performance [16]. Furthermore, venture performance is not just the enumeration of various related indicators, but rather a more systematic whole that should yield related indicators through the analysis of the environment of the company, the entrepreneurial team, and the individuals composing that team [20]. Furthermore, venture performance should also include the results of entrepreneurship as well as the entrepreneurship process [21]. On the basis of the foregoing, this study holds that venture performance refers to an important reference indicator that evaluates the degree to which firms are able to complete certain tasks or reach certain goals throughout the entire entrepreneurial process.

2.2. Theoretical Analysis of the Relationship between the Cognition Characteristics and Venture Performance of an Entrepreneurial Team

Cognition characteristics of an entrepreneurial team refer to cognition basis and emotion difference among entrepreneurial team members. From the aspect of an organization, an entrepreneurial team is the establishment stage of a traditional business organization. Traditional research on the high management team of an enterprise indicated that the heterogeneity of background and experiences among high management team members would result in different cognition bases, thereby causing cognitive conflict. The cognitive conflict of such high management teams could improve the strategic decision making of an enterprise to further improve the business performance [22]. On the other hand, researchers considered that the different works engaged by high-level management team members would result in task conflict, which, essentially, is a kind of cognitive conflict to improve business performance [23]. According to the research on entrepreneurial teams, Roure and Maidique [24] indicated that an entrepreneurial team with higher skill heterogeneity could better improve the business performance with strategic decision making. Kamm and Nurick [25] mentioned that an entrepreneurial team with higher skill heterogeneity could effectively cope with risks and uncertainties in the entrepreneurial process. Carpenter [26] further determined the direct effects of the cognition characteristics of the heterogeneous skills, background, and experiences of an entrepreneurial team on venture performance. Accordingly, it is proposed that H1: cognitive conflict in the cognition characteristics of an entrepreneurial team presents remarkably positive effects on venture performance.

From the viewpoint of emotion difference in cognition characteristics of an entrepreneurial team, researchers considered that the heterogeneity among entrepreneurial team members not being reasonably used would not encourage team members to pursue creative conflict. Further, it will affect the positive emotion among members. In this study, normal communication channels might be blocked to form emotional conflict and further hinder teamwork [27]. Emotional conflict was generally regarded as negative. Chen [16] indicated that the emotional conflict of an entrepreneurial team would weaken the cooperation among its entrepreneurial team members, thereby negatively influencing venture performance. Accordingly, it is also proposed that H2: emotional conflict in cognition characteristics of an entrepreneurial team shows notable negative effects on venture performance.

2.3. Theoretical Analysis of the Relationship between the Behavior Characteristics and Venture Performance of an Entrepreneurial Team

The behavior characteristics of an entrepreneurial team refer to the behavioral performance of the same. In comparison with traditional businesses, entrepreneurial ventures have to do better on innovation ability and strategic sustainability in order to survive in the environment with rapid changes and uncertainties; the importance thus is higher. In terms of innovation ability, Kuratko, Ireland, & Hornsby [28] stated that an entrepreneurial team would form the innovation ability through exploring new problems or opportunities to enhance venture performance. Regarding strategic continuity, Covin and Miles [29] stated that an entrepreneurial team should purposively re-define the organization and market and confirm strategic objectives to further improve venture performance. On the basis of the foregoing, it is proposed that H3: innovation ability in behavior characteristics of an entrepreneurial team reveals significantly positive effects on venture performance and H4: strategic sustainability in behavior characteristics of an entrepreneurial team presents remarkably positive effects on venture performance.

2.4. Theoretical Analysis of the Relationship between the Cognition Characteristics and Behavior Characteristics of an Entrepreneurial Team

The cognitive and behavioral characteristics of entrepreneurial teams originated from the cognitive behavioral theory of psychology. In the field of entrepreneurial management, research scholars believe that the cognitive conflict of entrepreneurial team members can increase the individual confidence and ability of members, and, therefore, solve various problems encountered during the entrepreneurial process, with the overall effect of increasing the innovation ability of the entrepreneurial team [30]. On the basis of the foregoing, we propose that H5: the cognitive conflict of the cognitive characteristics of an entrepreneurial team has a notable positive influence on innovation ability.

The cognitive conflict aspect of an entrepreneurial team can also accelerate the processes of considering and solving problems within the entrepreneurial team, thereby increasing the ability of the entrepreneurial team in setting strategies and improving strategic sustainability [31]. Hence, we propose that H6: the entrepreneurial team cognitive characteristic of cognitive conflict has a notable positive influence on strategic sustainability.

At the same time, because the entrepreneurial team cognitive characteristic of emotional conflict will weaken the normal sentiments between team members, it is deemed, therefore, to have a negative influence on the innovation ability of the entrepreneurial team [16]. Thus, this we propose that H7:

the entrepreneurial team cognitive characteristic of emotional conflict has a notable negative influence on innovation ability.

Furthermore, the entrepreneurial team cognitive characteristic of emotional conflict damages the emotional bonds between team members, thereby putting obstacles in the way of normal communication channels among them. This impairs the ability of members to understand each other and weakens their understanding of the environment and decisions of the company. This, in turn, makes decision quality and company efficiency low to the point that the strategic sustainability of the entrepreneurial team is affected negatively [32]. Thus, we propose that H8: the entrepreneurial team cognitive characteristic of emotional conflict has a markedly negative influence on strategic stability.

The intermediary role played by entrepreneurial team behavioral characteristics in the relationship between cognitive characteristics and venture performance has not been directly discussed in the current literature. However, indirectly, scholars in the field of organization team research have researched and demonstrated the intermediary effect produced by organization team behavior on the relationship between cognitive characteristics and team performance [33,34]. Taking this view and applying it to the field of entrepreneurial companies, while also adhering to the theoretical framework of "cognition–behavior–performance", this study holds that there is a marked intermediary effect produced by the behavioral characteristics of entrepreneurial teams on the relationship between cognitive characteristics and venture performance. On the basis of the foregoing theoretical foundation, the researchers interviewed entrepreneurial team members online, one-on-one, from 20 different entrepreneur incubation parks. These interviews extracted factors related to the research of this study that influence team productivity and company performance. The researchers found that the innovation ability and strategic sustainability of entrepreneurial teams are important factors that have an impact on the relationship between entrepreneurial team cognition and venture performance. To summarize the theoretical analysis and the practical research, we hold that the cognitive conflict of teams can have an impact on venture performance and also influence the behavioral characteristics of entrepreneurial teams, including innovation ability and strategic sustainability, thereby affecting venture performance.

As the cognitive characteristics of entrepreneurial teams have a notable impact on innovation ability and on venture performance, we propose that H9: the innovation ability of entrepreneurial teams plays a pronounced intermediary role in the relationship between cognitive characteristics and venture performance. In addition to the foregoing, cognitive characteristics of entrepreneurial teams have a notable impact on strategic sustainability and the latter has a notable impact on venture performance. Therefore, on the basis of the "cognition–behavior–performance" framework, we propose that H10: the strategic sustainability of entrepreneurial teams plays a pronounced intermediary role in the relationship between cognitive characteristics and venture performance.

Hence, Figure 1 demonstrates the theoretical model of this study.

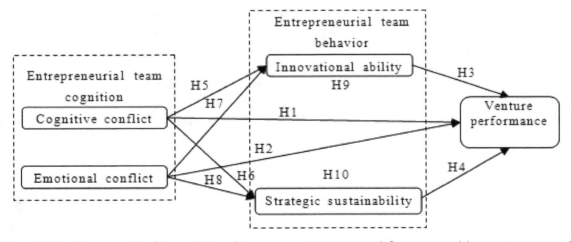

Figure 1. The framework of the relationship among entrepreneurial team cognition, entrepreneurial team behavior, and venture performance.

3. Research Method and Data Survey

3.1. Source and Process of Questionnaire Survey

The research subjects are entrepreneurial and innovative activities within emerging economies, mostly within the context of China. The Fujian province area is located in the southwest coast of China, an area with some of the most dynamic entrepreneurial and innovative activities outside of the major cities of Beijing, Shanghai, and Guangzhou. According to statistics from the Fujian province government, there were over 807,000 newly registered entrepreneurial companies in 2018, a 27.6% increase from 2017. Within Fujian, the cities of Quanzhou and Xiamen are some of the most economically developed areas and their entrepreneurial and innovative activities are among the most dynamic. According to statistics from the Fujian province government for the first half of 2019, the gross domestic products (GDPs) of Quanzhou and Xiamen make up almost 40% of the total GDP of the province [35]. It was for the foregoing reasons that the entrepreneurial companies within the entrepreneur incubation parks of Quanzhou and Xiamen were chosen as the subject of investigation.

Furthermore, "Fujian Merchants" are one of the most famous merchant groups, since a long time ago, and their typical characteristic is "dedicate yourself and you will win", which is the most intuitive embodiment of entrepreneurship. Therefore, we select Quanzhou, which is the oldest traditional city in Fujian [11], and Xiamen which is the most rapidly developing and potential emerging city, as our research area [12]. Then, we surveyed the entrepreneurial teams and collected the research data from these two cities.

Since 2015, the China government has proposed the slogan of "mass entrepreneurship brings a mass of innovations", and it intensively issued various policies to promote innovation and entrepreneurship activities in the same time. However, the relevant policies of innovation and entrepreneurship activities in Fujian Province are concentrated from the beginning to the end of 2015, and it will take time for the policies to be implemented. According to the data of innovation and entrepreneurship policy base of National Development and Reform Commission, Fujian Province is in the implementation stage of the policy between November 2015 and December 2017 [1]. Therefore, we chose to survey during November 2017 to May 2018.

Using online/offline questionnaire, entrepreneurial ventures in entrepreneur incubation parks in Quanzhou and Xiamen in Fujian Province were selected for data collection. A total of 225 copies of questionnaire were distributed from November 2017 to May 2018. By excluding the ones that were not seriously answered and the lack of data, a total of 101 valid copies were retrieved, with the retrieval rate of 44.88%. The valid sample characteristic statistics reveal that most respondents (62.38%) are female and aged between 21 and 30 (46.54%) and 30and 50 (38.61%), and the market channels of the supervisors focus on physical stores (45.55%) and online(30.69%).For descriptive statistics regarding the research subject of this study, see Table 1.

Table 1. Descriptive statistics of research sample characteristics.

Characteristic	Categories	Sample Number	Percentage Value
Sex	Male	38	37.62%
	Female	63	62.38%
Whether or Not the Individual is a Founding Member of the Company	Is a Founding Member	69	68.32%
	Is Not a Founding Member	32	31.68%
Age	0–20	9	8.91%
	21–30	47	46.54%
	30–50	39	38.61%
	50+	6	5.94%

Table 1. *Cont.*

Characteristic	Categories	Sample Number	Percentage Value
How Long the Company has been Established	0–1	27	26.73%
	2–5	59	58.42%
	5–10	14	13.86%
	10+	1	0.99%
Main Market Channel for Company Operations	Internet	31	30.69%
	Direct-to-Customer	13	12.87%
	Storefront	46	45.55%
	Other	11	10.89%

3.2. Variable Measurement

3.2.1. Measurement of Entrepreneurial Team Characteristics

Different scholars have different methods for measuring the entrepreneurial cognitive characteristic of cognitive conflict. Jehn believes that task conflict exists in the circumstance where team members have different views on the content of a task currently being carried out. She uses four factors to measure task conflict: (1) the number of times team members have differing views on the work being carried out, (2) the frequency of differing views within the team, (3) the level of conflict in regard to the task, and (4) the level of difference between the various views [23]. Amason holds that cognitive conflict refers to a difference in task orientation that originates from differing viewpoints, and uses the following three questions to measure cognitive conflict: (1) "how much disagreement is there in regard to different ways of thinking?", (2) "how many differences are there in decision content?", and (3) "how many different types of views are there in the group?" [27]. Chen et al. [16], on the other hand, sees the task as the center of cognitive conflict, with differences regarding the various methods of arrival at the task objective as the most important force. Therefore, he uses the two criteria of "differences in thought" and "differences in decision content", among others, to measure the cognitive conflict within entrepreneurial groups. We combine different measurement methods of cognitive conflict found within the existing literature, design question items to address the various necessary aspects (i.e., task conflict, differing views, differing management styles, and differing strategic plans), and measure such question items through a preliminary test. By calculating the Cronbach's alpha after deleting a given question item, unreasonable items are omitted. In the end, three question items are used to measure the cognitive conflict of entrepreneurial team members. The specific items can be found in Table 2.

In measuring the entrepreneurial team cognitive characteristic of emotional conflict, this study mainly used the measurement method within Jehn's intragroup conflict scale (ICS), specifically that part referring to the measurement of emotional conflict [23], and combined it with some practical adjustments made by Chinese scholars to make it appropriate to Chinese circumstances. We designed questions that measure emotional conflict from perspectives such as individual characteristics, relationships, emotions, and identification, and deleted unreasonable questions through the preliminary test. In the end, three question items were used to measure the emotional conflict of entrepreneurial teams, which can be found in Table 2.

Regarding the measurement of the entrepreneurial team behavioral characteristic of innovation ability, the most classic analysis is presently Schumpeter's definition of innovation, wherein he holds that forms of innovation within a firm include the methods for the development of new products, the acquisition of new markets, and the procurement of new resources. On the basis of this view, Miller and Friesen measure innovation through the following three criteria: (1) emphasis on research and development, cutting-edge technology, and innovative sales; (2) the number of new products and or services sold; and (3) the level of change in products and or services [36]. Karagozoglu and Brown measure team innovation by asking managers about their willingness to abandon old ideas and explore new choices [37]. This study combines the research of these two scholars and borrows from practical adjustments made to this measurement to make it more appropriate for Chinese circumstances. This research designed question items that measure team innovation by looking at products and services, market development, whether or not teams are keeping abreast of current trends, and the desire to innovate. Furthermore, unreasonable items were deleted through the preliminary test. In the end, three question items were used to measure the innovation ability of entrepreneurial teams, which can be found under Table 2.

Considering the impact of long-term position-making behaviors of entrepreneurial teams and implementing strategies on corporation performance. We measured the long- and short-term perspectives of behavioral characteristics by the entrepreneurial team behavioral characteristic of strategic sustainability. Moreover, Taneja and Chenault's work focused heavily on the issue of sustainable development for entrepreneurial firms [38]. We consider the concepts of long- and short-term orientation within Hofstede's theory of cultural dimensions, and put them in the context of the sustainable implementation of strategies of entrepreneurial firms. It measures strategic sustainability by looking at market share, business plans, and repeated innovation. There were no question items deleted through the preliminary test [39]. The specific items can be found in Table 2.

Meanwhile, the coefficient of internal consistency (Cronbach's Alpha, CA) and corrected item-total correction coefficient (CITC) are used for evaluating the reliability of the questionnaire. The reliability analysis results reveal that the team characteristics reliability coefficient (0.805) satisfies the basic reliability requirement. Applying statistical product and service solutions (SPSS) 19.0 to exploratory factor analysis, the results show that the cumulative variance explained that the extracted factors are at 67% and the factor loadings are higher than 0.5 that the validity conformity to the basic requirement.

3.2.2. The Measurement of Venture Performance

In evaluating venture performance, scholars have determined four main representative indicators: (1) arriving at a specified milestone, such as a new company completing the development of a product [40]; (2) the entrepreneurial firm made progress over the course of two or more stages of preparatory activities [41]; (3) whether or not the entrepreneurial process can be characterized as shutting down, still struggling, or operating normally [42]; and (4) the entrepreneurial firm made the first or second profit on a sale [19]. When this study evaluates venture performance, it is mainly concerned with consulting the measurement method laid out by Venkatraman and Ramanujam, which combines the aforementioned four indicators [43]. No items were deleted through the preliminary test. The specific items are found in Table 2.

Meanwhile, the reliability analysis results reveal the reliability coefficient of venture performance (0.890) satisfying the basic requirement for reliability. The exploratory factor analysis result shows the cumulative variance showed the extracted factors 56% and that the factor loadings are higher than 0.5, reaching the basic requirement for validity.

Table 2. Items used to measure entrepreneurial team characteristics.

Variable	Item
The Cognitive Conflict of Team Members	Members of the original entrepreneurial team frequently have different opinions on how to manage the company
	Disagreements among members of the original entrepreneurial team are, to a large extent, about work tasks
	Members of the original entrepreneurial team frequently have differing opinions on what course to take in managing the new company
The Emotional Conflict of Team Members	There is obvious personality conflict among members of the original entrepreneurial team
	Among members of the original entrepreneurial team, we see ourselves as partners who are collectively pushing our company towards success
	Members of the original entrepreneurial team do work tasks as if they are their own tasks

Table 2. Cont.

Variable	Item
Innovation Ability	We are the first company to introduce this product/service to the market
	We are always looking for new opportunities related to our business
	Our team frequently keeps abreast of recent trends
Strategic Sustainability	We are willing to sacrifice profits to increase market share
	We take time to set a comprehensive business plan and then ensured that it is strictly administered
	We frequently test our business model on the market and adjust according to market feedback
Venture Performance	Overall, we provided satisfactory investment returns to our founds and investors and arrived at our anticipated goal(s)
	Our company reached our anticipated product or service development goal(s)
	Our company reached our anticipated user-based or customer-based goal(s)
	Our company reached our anticipated regional market entry goal(s)

This study further evaluated the overall measurement model through the use of confirmatory factor analysis (CFA). The results of this analysis show that the measurement model has a relatively good degree of fit ($\chi 2$ = 125.42, df = 94, p = 0.017, $\chi 2$/df = 1.334, GFI (goodness-of-fit index) = 0.905, AGFI (adjusted goodness-of-fit index) = 0.958, CFI (comparative fit index) = 0.973, NFI (non-normed fit index) = 0.948, RMSEA (root mean square error of approximation) = 0.040, SRMR (standard root mean-square residual) = 0.037). The load factor of each measurement item fell between 0.707 and 0.947, and all had a p-value greater than $p < 0.001$. The construct reliability (CR) results yielded values greater than 0.7, showing that the underlying variables all have good internal consistency. The values of the average variance extracted (AVE) results all are greater than 0.5, which demonstrates that the average ability of the measurement indicators to explain the underlying variables is good. Therefore, it can be seen that the underlying variables have good construct reliability and validity. When a measurement model has differentiated validity, the correlation coefficients between its underlying variables must be smaller than the internal correlation coefficient of the underlying variables. This study utilized the correlation matrix between the underlying variables to verify that such was the case. The results show that the square root average of the average variance extracted estimate is higher than the correlation coefficient between the underlying variables, which demonstrates that the differentiated validity is good, as shown in Table 3, which depicts the average values of each variable, their standard variation, the square root of the AVE, and the correlation coefficients between each variable. As can be seen in Table 3, the square root of the AVE is greater than any other correlation coefficient in any row or column.

Table 3. Means, standard deviation, correlation coefficient, and discriminative validity

Variable	Average Value	Standard Deviation	1	2	3	4	5
1 Cognitive Conflict	3.16	1.02	**0.68**				
2 Emotional Conflict	3.46	0.86	−0.32 **	**0.66**			
3 Innovation Ability	2.88	1.09	0.54 **	−0.10 *	**0.69**		
4 Strategic Sustainability	3.67	0.78	0.42 **	−0.230 **	0.54 ***	**0.70**	
5 Venture Performance	3.84	0.83	0.469 ***	−0.154	0.343 ***	0.503 ***	**0.72**

Note: * means $p < 0.05$, ** means $p < 0.01$, *** means $p < 0.001$. Bold data are square root, which explains the variance. Data underneath the diagonal line are the correlation coefficient between the variables, all are two-tailed tests.

4. Results

This study used the structural equation modeling (SEM) method to test the previously proposed hypotheses. According to the SEM approach, the coefficient analysis results are as follows (seen in Figure 2): (1) the entrepreneurial team cognitive characteristic of cognitive conflict has a significant positive influence on venture performance (standardized regression weight = 0.496, $p < 0.001$), thereby confirming hypothesis 1; (2) the entrepreneurial team cognitive characteristic of emotional conflict had no significant influence on venture performance(standardized regression weight = −0.082, $p > 0.1$), thereby eliminating hypothesis 2; (3) the entrepreneurial team behavioral characteristic of innovation ability had a significant impact on venture performance (standardized regression weight = 0.343, $p < 0.001$), thereby confirming hypothesis 3; (4) the entrepreneurial team behavioral characteristic of strategic sustainability had a significant positive influence on venture performance(standardized regression weight = 0.501, $p < 0.001$), thereby confirming hypothesis 4; (5) the entrepreneurial team cognitive characteristic of cognitive conflict had a significant positive influence on innovation ability(standardized regression weight = 0.562, $p < 0.001$), thereby confirming hypothesis 5; (6) the entrepreneurial team cognitive characteristic of emotional conflict had a significant negative influence on innovation ability (standardized regression weight = −0.101, $p < 0.05$), thereby confirming hypothesis 6; (7) the entrepreneurial team cognitive characteristic of cognitive conflict had a significant positive influence on strategic sustainability (standardized regression weight = 0.421, $p < 0.001$), thereby confirming hypothesis 7; and (8) the entrepreneurial team cognitive characteristic of emotional conflict had a significant negative influence on strategic sustainability (standardized regression weight = −0.233, $p < 0.001$), thereby confirming hypothesis 8.

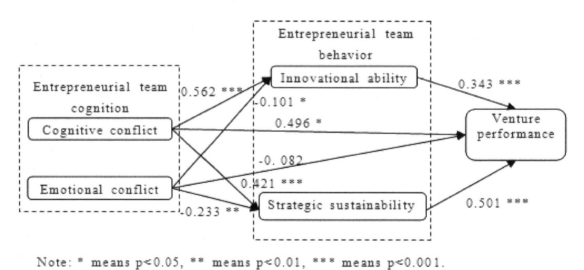

Note: * means p<0.05, ** means p<0.01, *** means p<0.001.

Figure 2. Path graph and standardized parameter estimation.

In order to further test the intermediary effects of entrepreneurial team behavioral characteristics, this study undertook an intermediary effect test according to Brown's multifactor mediating model [44]. In accordance with Brown's view, the effects of the model were separated into direct effects, total effects, total indirect effects, and individual indirect effects. Firstly, the entrepreneurial team cognitive characteristic of emotional conflict had no significant effect on venture performance. Furthermore, the entrepreneurial team cognitive characteristic of cognitive conflict significantly impacts innovation ability. The path coefficients between the entrepreneurial team cognitive characteristic of cognitive conflict, innovation ability, and venture performance were all significant, and in the case of innovation ability, its individual indirect effect of 0.193 (0.562 × 0.343) was smaller than its direct effect of 0.496, which shows that there is a partial intermediary effect produced by innovation ability, thereby partially confirming hypothesis 9. Finally, the entrepreneurial team cognitive characteristic of cognitive conflict will significantly impact strategic sustainability. Moreover, the path coefficients between the entrepreneurial team cognitive characteristic of cognitive conflict, strategic sustainability, and venture performance were all significant, and in the case of strategic sustainability, its individual indirect effect of 0.211 (0.421 × 0.501) was smaller than its direct effect of 0.496, demonstrating the partial intermediary effect produced by strategic sustainability, thereby partially confirming hypothesis 10.

5. Discussion

This study focuses on entrepreneurship and innovation within emerging economies and delves into the relationship between the characteristics of entrepreneurial firms and venture performance from the perspective of cognition and behavior. Furthermore, it explores the mechanism by which the cognitive and behavioral characteristics of entrepreneurial team impact venture performance. The research design of this study is based on two primary foundations: (1) regard for entrepreneurship and innovation within emerging economies and (2) emphasis on the sustainable development of entrepreneurial companies. As such, the study is in accordance with the views put forth by Taneja and Chenault [38]. Applying the theoretical framework of "cognition–behavior–performance" to the relationship between entrepreneurial team behavior and cognitive characteristics and venture performance, this study proposes a theoretical framework wherein the behavioral characteristics of entrepreneurial teams serve an intermediary role in the relationship between the entrepreneurial team cognitive characteristics and venture performance. After this, the SEM approach was used to analyze data from 101 entrepreneurial teams in the entrepreneur incubation parks of Xiamen and Quanzhou in Fujian Province. The research results show that, in the context of entrepreneurial companies, the cognitive characteristic of cognitive conflict has a significant positive influence on venture performance, but the cognitive characteristic of emotional conflict has no influence on innovation ability. In addition, in the context of entrepreneurial companies, the behavioral characteristics of innovation ability and strategic sustainability both have a significant positive influence on venture performance. Furthermore, in the context of entrepreneurial companies, the cognitive characteristic of cognitive conflict has a significant positive influence on innovation ability, and the cognitive characteristic of emotional conflict has a significant negative influence on innovation ability. Moreover, in the context of entrepreneurial companies, the cognitive characteristic of cognitive conflict has a significant positive influence on strategic sustainability, and the cognitive characteristic of emotional conflict has a significant negative influence on strategic sustainability. Finally, in the context of entrepreneurial teams, the behavioral characteristics of innovation ability and strategic sustainability both play an intermediary role in the relationship between the cognitive characteristic of cognitive conflict and venture performance. The theoretical and practical contributions of this study, as well as the limitations of this research, are summarized below.

5.1. Theoretical Contributions

The relationship between entrepreneurial team characteristics and venture performance is an important issue within the field of entrepreneurial management research. Past research has tended to focus on the impact of entrepreneurial team heterogeneity on the development and competitive advantage of entrepreneurial firms [27]. The section of this study that explored the impact of cognitive and behavioral characteristics of entrepreneurial teams on venture performance confirmed this previously held view. Moreover, in the context of an emerging economy such as China, the cognitive conflict, innovation ability, and strategic sustainability of entrepreneurial teams all markedly increase venture performance. At the same time, however, research results also discovered that, in the context of entrepreneurial teams, the cognitive characteristic of emotional conflict has no obvious negative influence on venture performance. This result is consistent with Chen's view [16]. The relationship between emotional conflict and venture performance must be researched further.

Moreover, the influence of the entrepreneurial team behavioral characteristics of innovation ability and strategic sustainability on venture performance is further discussed. Current research has tended to focus on the relationship between the innovation of entrepreneurial teams and venture performance.

This study's research also confirmed this close relationship in the context of entrepreneurial and innovative activities within emerging economies and further verified the markedly positive impact of innovation ability on venture performance. In addition, we focused on the positive influence of strategic sustainability behavior on venture performance. This both reflected and confirmed the theoretical value and meaning of long-term orientation in entrepreneurial management, a finding consistent with the most recent research.

Finally, the notable intermediary role played by entrepreneurial team behavioral characteristics in the relationship between entrepreneurial team cognitive characteristics and venture performance also reflects the importance of the innovation ability and strategic sustainability of entrepreneurial teams to the firm. Just as Taneja and Chenault expressed a focus on the sustainable development of entrepreneurial firms, entrepreneurial teams that possess innovation ability and have a long-term orientation are better able to lead the entrepreneurial firm to success [38]. Furthermore, the resulting discovery of this intermediary effect produced by entrepreneurial team behavioral characteristics is a theoretical extension and application of the "cognition–behavior–performance" theoretical framework within the entrepreneurial management field.

5.2. Implications for Practice

In the management process of entrepreneurial companies, entrepreneurial teams play an important role. Entrepreneurial teams that possess different cognitive structures notably increase the innovation ability of the entrepreneurial company, and thereby make the company more adaptive in responding to market and environmental changes, thereby increasing venture performance and leading to the accumulation of competitive advantages. In addition to this, entrepreneurial teams that possess different cognitive structures give the entrepreneurial company a more long-term orientation when setting strategy, developing markets, and settling on a business model, thereby increasing the sustainable development of the firm.

This research also revealed the role played by behavioral characteristics of entrepreneurial teams in the development process of the entrepreneurial firm. This is especially the case in emerging economies where, owing to the vagueness and uncertainty present in these business environments, entrepreneurial teams must deal with external markets and adapt to them. Moreover, in the context of emerging markets, where there are rapid changes in both the technological environment and the imperfect institutional environment, entrepreneurial teams must combine innovation ability and strategic sustainability in order to allow the entrepreneurial firm to better respond to the external environment and achieve sustainable development.

5.3. Limitations and Future Research

This research has the following limitations. (1) This research only focused on the cognitive and behavioral characteristics of entrepreneurial teams and does not take into consideration other characteristics. (2) This research's consideration of the impact of other factors on venture performance is not comprehensive. (3) Although this research focuses on innovative and entrepreneurial activities within emerging economies, the study lacks an in-depth look into the selection of its research subject and a concrete definition of the circumstances of emerging economies. These all must be explored further in future research.

6. Conclusions

This study explored the relationship between entrepreneurial team cognitive characteristics, behavioral characteristics, and venture performance in the context of China, a representative emerging economy, based on the theoretical framework of "cognition–behavior–performance". It analyzed the notable impact of entrepreneurial team cognitive and behavioral characteristics on venture performance. In addition to this, this research also demonstrated the intermediary effect produced by entrepreneurial team behavioral characteristics on the relationship between entrepreneurial team cognitive characteristics and venture performance. The theoretical contributions of this study are as follows: (1) we examined the relationship between entrepreneurial team characteristics and entrepreneurial performance in the context of emerging economies from the perspective of sustainability, and extended the traditional theory of the relationship between those; (2) we revealed the partial mediating effect of entrepreneurial team's innovation ability and strategic sustainability on the relationship between entrepreneurial team cognition and entrepreneurial performance. It showed the impact of entrepreneurial team's long-term strategy on entrepreneurial performance, and enriched the current theory of the relationship between entrepreneurial team's behavior and entrepreneurial performance. The practical contribution of this article is to propose that the entrepreneurial team should pay more attention to the long-term strategy making and ability cultivation, in order to enable entrepreneurial enterprises to achieve sustainable development.

Author Contributions: Conceptualization, X.-L.P. and T.-J.W.; methodology, J.-N.G.; software, J.-N.G.; validation, T.-J.W., X.-L.P., and J.-N.G.; formal analysis, X.-L.P.; investigation, J.-Q.H.; resources, T.-J.W.; data curation, J.-Q.H.; writing—original draft preparation, X.-L.P.; writing—review and editing, T.-J.W.; visualization, J.-N.G.; supervision, T.-J.W.; project administration, T.-J.W.; funding acquisition, X.-L.P. and T.-J.W. All authors have read and agreed to the published version of the manuscript.

References

1. Innovation and Entrepreneurship Policy Base. Available online: http://sc.ndrc.gov.cn/zhengceku.html (accessed on 26 December 2019).
2. Singh, S.; Gaur, S. Entrepreneurship and innovation management in emerging economies. *Manag. Decis.* **2018**, *56*, 2–5. [CrossRef]
3. Marcotte, C. Entrepreneurship and innovation in emerging economies: Conceptual, methodological and contextual issues. *Int. J. Entrep. Behav. Res.* **2014**, *20*, 42–65. [CrossRef]
4. Kamm, J.B.; Shuman, J.C.; Seeger, J.A.; Nurick, A.J. Entrepreneurial teams in new venture creation: A research agenda. *Entrep. Theory Pract.* **1990**, *14*, 7–17. [CrossRef]
5. Wang, L.; Tan, J.; Li, W. The impacts of spatial positioning on regional new venture creation and firm mortality over the industry life cycle. *J. Bus. Res.* **2018**, *86*, 41–52. [CrossRef]
6. Kollmann, T.; Stöckmann, C.; Meves, Y.; Kensbock, J.M. When members of entrepreneurial teams differ: Linking diversity in individual-level entrepreneurial orientation to team performance. *Small Bus. Econ.* **2017**, *48*, 843–859. [CrossRef]
7. Mol, E.D.; Khapova, S.N.; Elfring, T. Entrepreneurial team cognition: A review. *Int. J. Manag. Rev.* **2015**, *17*, 232–255. [CrossRef]
8. Peng, X.L.; Huang, B.J.; Chen, H.P. Decoding the Spirit of Fujian Merchants. *Fujian Daily.* 18 June 2019. Available online: http://fjrb.fjsen.com/fjrb/html/2019-06/18/content_1190687.htm?div=-1 (accessed on 20 December 2019).
9. Chen, S.S.; Liu, F. China Mass Entrepreneurship Index in 2016 (MEI-2016). *Southwest Jiaotong University News.* 12 September 2016. Available online: https://news.swjtu.edu.cn/ShowNews-12903-0-1.shtml (accessed on 25 December 2019).
10. Jiang, Q.L. The 6thFujian Merchants Forum in 2019 Open. *Xinhua Net.* 18 June 2019. Available online: http://www.fj.xinhuanet.com/yuanchuang/2019-06/18/c_1124640094.htm (accessed on 20 December 2019).
11. Introduction to Quanzhou, The People's Government of Quanzhou Municipality Home Page. Available online: http://www.quanzhou.gov.cn/zfb/zjqz/qzgk/ (accessed on 26 December 2019).
12. Introduction to Xiamen, The People's Government of Xiamen Municipality Home Page. Available online: http://www.xm.gov.cn/zjxm/ (accessed on 26 December 2019).
13. Iacobucci, D.; Rosa, P. The growth of business groups by habitual entrepreneurs: The role of entrepreneurial teams. *Entrep. Theory Pract.* **2010** *34*, 351–377. [CrossRef]
14. Klotz, A.C.; Veiga, S.P.D.M.; Buċkley, M.R.; Gavin, M.B. The role of trustworthiness in recruitment and selection: A review and guide for future research. *J. Organ. Behav.* **2013**, *34*, 104–119. [CrossRef]
15. Maschke, K.; Knyphausen-Aufseβ, D. How the entrepreneurial top management team setup influences firm performance and the ability to raise capital: A literature review. *Bus. Res.* **2012**, *5*, 83–123. [CrossRef]

16.   Chen, M.H.; Chang, Y.Y.; Chang, Y.C. The trinity of entrepreneurial team dynamics: Cognition, conflicts and cohesion. *Int. J. Entrep. Behav. Res.* **2017**, *23*, 934–951. [CrossRef]
17.   Gartner, W.B.; Shaver, K.G.; Gatewood, E. Finding the entrepreneur in entrepreneurship. *Entrep. Theory Pract.* **1994**, *18*, 5–10. [CrossRef]
18.   Ensley, M.D.; Carland, J.A.C. Exploring the existence of entrepreneurial teams. *Int. J. Manag.* **1999**, *16*, 276–281.
19.   Newbert, S.L. New Firm formation: A dynamic capability perspective. *J. Small Bus. Manag.* **2010**, *43*, 55–77. [CrossRef]
20.   Wdowiak, M.A.; Schwarz, E.J.; Breitenecker, R.J.; Wright, R.W. Linking the cultural capital of the entrepreneur and early performance of new ventures: A cross-country comparison. *J. East Eur. Manag. Stud.* **2012**, *17*, 149–183. [CrossRef]
21.   Mcgee, J.E.; Dowling, M.J.; Megginson, W.L. Cooperative strategy and new venture performance: The role of business strategy and management experience. *Strateg. Manag. J.* **2010**, *16*, 565–580. [CrossRef]
22.   Amason, A.C.; Sapienza, H.J. The effects of top management team size and interaction norms on cognitive and affective conflict. *J. Manag.* **1997**, *23*, 495–516. [CrossRef]
23.   Jehn, K.A.; Mannix, E.A. The dynamic nature of conflict: A longitudinal study of intragroup conflict and group performance. *Acad. Manag. J.* **2001**, *44*, 238–251.
24.   Roure, J.B.; Maidique, M.A. Linking prefunding factors and high-technology venture success: An exploratory study. *J. Bus. Ventur.* **2006**, *1*, 295–306. [CrossRef]
25.   Kamm, J.B.; Nurick, A.J. The stages of team venture formation: A decision-making model. *Entrep. Theory Pract.* **1993**, *17*, 17–27. [CrossRef]
26.   Carpenter, M.A. The implications of strategy and social context for the relationship between top management team heterogeneity and firm performance. *Strateg. Manag. J.* **2002**, *23*, 275–284. [CrossRef]
27.   Amason, A.C. Distinguishing the effects of functional and dysfunctional conflict on strategic decision making: Resolving a paradox for top management teams. *Acad. Manag. J.* **1996**, *39*, 123–148.
28.   Kuratko, D.F.; Ireland, R.D.; Hornsby, J.S. Improving firm performance through entrepreneurial actions: Acordia's corporate entrepreneurship strategy. *Acad. Manag. Perspect.* **2001**, *15*, 60–71. [CrossRef]
29.   Covin, J.G.; Miles, M.P. Corporate entrepreneurship and the pursuit of competitive advantage. *Entrep. Theory Pract.* **1999**, *23*, 47–63. [CrossRef]
30.   Kurtzberg, T.R.; Mueller, J.S. The influence of daily conflict on perceptions of creativity: A longitudinal study. *Int. J. Confl. Manag.* **2005**, *16*, 335–353.
31.   Banerjee, S.B. Organisational strategies for sustainable development: Developing a research agenda for the new millennium. *Aust. J. Manag.* **2018**, *27*, 105–117. [CrossRef]
32.   Poblete, C.; Sena, V.; Fernandez de Arroyabe, J.C. How do motivational factors influence entrepreneurs' perception of business opportunities in different stages of entrepreneurship? *Eur. J. Work Organ. Psychol.* **2019**, *28*, 179–190. [CrossRef]
33.   Dechurch, L.A.; Marks, M.A. Maximizing the benefits of task conflict: The role of conflict management. *Int. J. Confl. Manag.* **2001**, *12*, 4–22. [CrossRef]
34.   Chen, Y.; Pan, J. Do entrepreneurs' developmental job challenges enhance venture performance in emerging industries? A mediated moderation model of entrepreneurial action learning and entrepreneurial experience. *Front. Psychol.* **2019**, *10*, 1371. [CrossRef]
35.   Fujian Provincial Bureau of Statistics, Fujian Statistical Yearbook. In *Fujian Provincial People's Government*; 11 September 2019. Available online: http://tjj.fujian.gov.cn/tongjinianjian/dz2019/index.htm (accessed on 7 December 2019).
36.   Miller, D.; Friesen, P.H. Innovation in conservative and entrepreneurial firms: Two models of strategic momentum. *Strateg. Manag. J.* **1982**, *3*, 1–25. [CrossRef]
37.   Karagozoglu, N. Adaptive responses by conservative and entrepreneurial firms. *J. Prod. Innov. Manag.* **1988**, *5*, 269–281. [CrossRef]
38.   Taneja, H.; Chenault, K. Building a startup that will last. *Harv. Bus. Rev.* **2019**, *7*, 23–27.
39.   Hofstede, G. *Culture and Organization: Software of the Mind*; McGraw-Hill Press: New York, NY, USA, 2004.
40.   Delmar, F.; Shane, S. Legitimating first: Organizing activities and the survival of new ventures. *J. Bus. Ventur.* **2004**, *19*, 385–410. [CrossRef]
41.   Davidsson, P.; Honig, B. The role of social and human capital among nascent entrepreneurs. *J. Bus. Ventur.* **2003** *18*, 301–331. [CrossRef]

42. Parker, S.C.; Belghitar, Y. What happens to nascent entrepreneurs? An econometric analysis of the PSED. *Small Bus. Econ.* **2006**, *27*, 81–101. [CrossRef]
43. Venkatraman, N.; Ramanujam, V. Measurement of business economic performance: An examination of method convergence. *J. Manag.* **1986**, *8*, 7858–7864. [CrossRef]
44. Brown, R.L. Assessing specific mediational effects in complex theoretical models. *Struct. Equ. Model.* **1997**, *4*, 142–156. [CrossRef]

7

The Impact of the Family Background on Students' Entrepreneurial Intentions: An Empirical Analysis

Maria-Ana Georgescu [1] **and Emilia Herman** [2,*]

[1] Faculty of Sciences and Letters, "George Emil Palade" University of Medicine, Pharmacy, Sciences and Technology of Tirgu-Mures, 540139 Tirgu Mures, Romania; maria.georgescu@umfst.ro

[2] Faculty of Economics and Law, "George Emil Palade" University of Medicine, Pharmacy, Sciences and Technology of Tirgu-Mures, 540139 Tirgu Mures, Romania

* Correspondence: emilia.herman@umfst.ro

Abstract: In the current economic and social environment, a real challenge for youth is the acquisition and development of the relevant skills in entrepreneurship in order to consider entrepreneurship as a desirable employment choice. Given this aspect, the purpose of this paper is to investigate the main factors influencing students' entrepreneurial intentions, paying particular attention to their entrepreneurial family background. Additionally, the paper aims to explore the effect of entrepreneurial family background on the relationship between effectiveness of entrepreneurship education and entrepreneurial intention. We conducted a study where results were based on the outcomes of a survey among Romanian high school and university students in the final year (N = 617). Our four main hypotheses were tested through independent samples t-tests, correlation analysis, and hierarchical multiple regression analysis. The findings highlighted that the students with an entrepreneurial family background reported a higher entrepreneurial intention than those without such a background. The variables that positively influenced the entrepreneurial intentions of the students were entrepreneurial family background, effectiveness of entrepreneurship education, and entrepreneurial personality traits. Furthermore, this entrepreneurial family background negatively moderated the relationship between effectiveness of entrepreneurship education and entrepreneurial intention. For this reason, emphasis should be placed on both formal and informal entrepreneurial education, which will increase the propensity of young people to choose an entrepreneurial career.

Keywords: entrepreneurial intentions; self-employment; entrepreneurship education; entrepreneurial family background; entrepreneurial personality traits; students; hierarchical multiple regression analysis

---

1. Introduction

Unemployment is one of the biggest challenges for young people, taking into account that at EU level and elsewhere unemployment among young individuals (aged 18 to 24) is two to three times higher than the overall unemployment rate [1]. Choosing an entrepreneurial career is recognized as a plausible option for successfully integrating young people into the labour market and reducing the risk of social exclusion among youth [2–4]. Thus, an increase in employment through entrepreneurial activity among young people from different countries could achieve at least one of the 17 Sustainable Development Goals included in the 2030 Agenda for Sustainable Development [5]: Goal 8—"Promoting sustained, inclusive and sustainable economic growth, full and productive employment and decent work for all".

Although there is plenty of evidence available that a fairly large segment of young people intends to develop an entrepreneurial career, statistical data [1,6] prove that there is a low level of entrepreneurial activity among young people, measured both by the young self-employed and total early stage entrepreneurship activity (TEA) for those aged between 18 and 24. Therefore, the central question of entrepreneurship research is why individuals, especially young ones, choose or do not choose an entrepreneurial career, self-employment, or starting their own business.

Theoretical and empirical studies point out that intentionality is a central concept in understanding the reasons for individuals' careers [7]. In particular, entrepreneurial intention is considered a key aspect that explains the determination to start a business or to become self-employed. Entrepreneurial intentions (EIs), defined as "desires to own or start a business" [8], represent the antecedent of entrepreneurial behaviour in most career choice models [9], being a prerequisite for entrepreneurial behaviour [10].

Prior studies [4,7,11] have found that EIs of individuals can be determined by different factors (environmental or contextual factors and personal background factors), which can have a positive or negative influence, a direct or indirect influence, respectively. Also, a specific combination and interaction of the determinants of EI can drive entrepreneurial career choice [12–14]. Moreover, according to Dyer's model [15] of entrepreneurial careers, there are three important factors that can influence the entrepreneurial career choice. These are social factors, including educational experiences (formal and informal); individual factors such as entrepreneurial attitudes and traits; and economic factors, like the availability of network resources and economic resources. As regards the social factors, based on the social learning theory [16], researchers found that social influence via parents is an essential determinant of entrepreneurial career decisions. Thus, parental roles within the family business, observed from an early age, influence "the children's attitude towards becoming self-employed themselves" [13] (p. 122).

Based on these premises, the aim of this paper is to highlight the impact of Romanian students' exposure to prior family business as informal education, both directly, on students' entrepreneurial career intentions, and indirectly, on the entrepreneurship education–entrepreneurial intention relationship. The objectives of the research focus on analysing student entrepreneurial intentions and identifying differences between EI students in terms of entrepreneurial family background (EFB); identifying the direct effect of an EFB, effectiveness of entrepreneurship education (EEE), and entrepreneurial personality traits on students' entrepreneurial intentions; and emphasizing the moderating effects of an EFB on the EEE–EI relationship.

The topic is of real interest because the totalitarian regime in Romania, which lasted over 40 years, led to the drastic limitation of private initiative and the cessation of family business, in favour of large state-owned enterprises, based on common property. Moreover, a sustainable market economy is based on entrepreneurship, and Romania took this direction after the change of political regime in December 1989. Therefore, we are interested in the extent to which the family inheritance of entrepreneurial initiatives in the last three decades influenced the career intentions of the youth, and, at the same time, what types of young people show entrepreneurial intentions and to what extent entrepreneurial intentions are influenced by entrepreneurial education.

As for novelty, this paper fills the gap in the available research because it focuses on the moderating effect of entrepreneurial family background on the relationship between entrepreneurship education and the entrepreneurial intention of students. Also, the novelty of the paper lies in the socioeconomic context of the research, taking into account that in Romania, a former communist country, there is no other study that explores this moderating effect. Other Romanian studies [17,18] in the field highlighted the extent to which entrepreneurial intentions are influenced by certain psycho-behavioural traits of individuals and evaluated the influence of different types of education on these intentions or on the important determinants of venture creation among young students, such as locus of control, that are needed for achievement and entrepreneurial education.

2. Theoretical Background and Research Hypotheses

Scholars have recognized a broad influence of entrepreneurial family background (EFB) on the entrepreneurial intentions of offspring: modeling career options [12,19], acquiring human capital—especially entrepreneurial knowledge and skills [20]—providing better access to knowledge about entrepreneurial opportunities [21], and transferring financial and social capital to their children [21–23].

Empirical research [20,24–27] highlighted that the children from families with entrepreneurial backgrounds are more likely to start their own businesses or to join the family business. Sørensen [21] found that children with self-employed parents are twice as likely to become self-employed, but there is little evidence (from Danish data) to show that these young people become independent because they have privileged access to the financial or social capital of their parents, or because they have superior entrepreneurial abilities [21]. The most recent international report of the GUESSS Project–Global Student Entrepreneurship 2018 [26], based on 208,000 completed responses from 54 countries and 3000 universities, highlighted that the higher intention to become an entrepreneur among students with entrepreneurial parents, as opposed to students without entrepreneurial parents, depends on the parents' entrepreneurial performance.

According to social learning theory [16], which emphasizes that new patterns of behaviour can be acquired either through direct experience or by observing the behaviour of others, individuals learn (the informal learning) by observing the actions of their parents. In the context of role identification and social learning theories, Bosma et al. [28] state that four functions of entrepreneurial role models can be formulated that are interrelated: inspiration and motivation, increasing self-efficacy, learning by example, and learning by support.

The mechanisms of social influence via parents may include the transmission of skills gained through experience, tacit knowledge, and modeling of career options [20]. Walter and Dohse [29] argue that social networks play an important role in transferring tacit knowledge regarding how to seize entrepreneurial opportunities, with parental role models serving as a substitute for tacit knowledge obtained through entrepreneurial experience [28]. As Faas et al. [30] point out, parents with jobs requiring managerial skills, training and communication skills are able to transfer these skills to their children through a number of direct resources and indirect behaviours [30].

There have been studies [21,31] that explained the intergenerational transmission of self-employment, suggesting different mechanisms such as the influence of parental characteristics on children's aspirations and values and on the development of human capital (entrepreneurial skills). In addition, other potential sources of closure fostering the inheritance of self-employment are the financial and social capital of self-employed parents.

In order to highlight how the family business can impact, encourage, or constrain the EI of children, it is also important to take into consideration the main characteristics of the family business. Researchers [32] pointed out a high heterogeneity among family firms caused by a series of factors such as type of goal (economic vs. non-economic, and family-centred vs. business-centred) [33,34], resources, the involvement in and influence of the family upon the business [35–37]. As regards the entrepreneurial behaviours of family firms, entrepreneurship research identified significant differences among these firms that are determined by multiple factors. Thus, the feeling of family unity around their own firm [38], as well as the financial and social capital of the family [21] can explain why some family firms are more entrepreneurial than others. The organizational culture of family firms that fosters decentralization, a long-term orientation, as well as the ability to perceive technological opportunities and the desire for change [39,40] is also an important determinant of entrepreneurship in family firms. There are studies that claim entrepreneurship in family firms may be influenced by genetic factors [41] and by "role modeling by entrepreneurial parents" [27], suggesting that transgenerational inheritance is another driver factor of entrepreneurship in family firms. According to Jaskiewicz et al. [42], entrepreneurial heritage as a rhetorical reconstruction by the family of past entrepreneurial achievements or resilience helps to explain transgenerational entrepreneurship [42]. In addition, the same authors stated that children are taking over the inherited entrepreneurial legacies through active involvement in the family business and through storytelling in large and cohesive families. Exceeding common succession, entrepreneurial heritage motivates owners of the current and next generation to engage in three strategic activities feeding the transgenerational entrepreneurship, namely—strategic education, entrepreneurial bridging, and strategic succession [42].

Regarding students from this particular family background who inherit the atmosphere of a business environment that could influence their future career intentions, this aspect seems to induce optimism about their resources and abilities to follow an entrepreneurial career. Thus, an entrepreneurial career path can be feasible, but not necessarily desirable [22]. Also, the same authors pointed out that education received from parents who are firm owners might have a negative impact on their offspring's entrepreneurial career through their understanding of locus of control.

Entrepreneurial values and know-how can be taken up by children from parental role models, both during primary socialization and in later stages of life [29]. Based on the effect of parental role models, the decision to become an entrepreneur is positively correlated, according to some studies [13,24,27,43], with having parents who are or have been entrepreneurs or self-employed. According to Chlosta et al. [13], the EI analysis done on students from eight German universities showed that there is a positive relationship between the presence of parental role models of self-employment and the self-employment of the offspring, this relationship being moderated by aspects of their personality, such as the openness of the individual. According to Athayde [44], both EE and EFB positively influence high school students' intentions to become self-employed in the UK.

Entrepreneurial intentions can be indirectly influenced by the family business background [45,46], which has implications for antecedents of EI (perceptions of venture feasibility and desirability, attitude, and subjective norms). Peterman and Kennedy's research [46], based on a sample of Australian high school students, found a significant positive relationship between prior exposure to family business and entrepreneurship education, and the antecedents of entrepreneurial intention. Carr and Sequeira [12] found a significant, direct as well as indirect, influence of previous exposure to the existence of family businesses on entrepreneurial intention, by means of variables such as attitude towards starting a business, perception of family support, and entrepreneurial self-efficacy.

Empirical evidence regarding the EFB–EI relationship remains mixed, and there are also studies that highlight the existence of negative parental role models [9] or insignificant ones [47] for EI. Turkur and Selcuk [48], analysing the EI of students from universities in Turkey as a function of entrepreneurial educational, relational, and structural support, showed that only educational support (entrepreneurship education) and structural support influence the entrepreneurial intentions of students, whereas relational support (family background) does not affect entrepreneurial career choice. Mungai and Velamuri [31] emphasized that parental influence may not exist in case of parents' economic failure in self-employment, and the choice of an entrepreneurial career depends on the performance of self-employed parents. Criaco et al. [19] found, based on a large sample of 21,895 people from 33 countries, that the perceived performance of parents in entrepreneurship acts as a "double-edged sword". Thus, this perception, on the one hand, enriches the entrepreneurial desire and the feasibility of the descendants through mechanisms of exposure, but, on the other hand, inhibits the transposition of both the desires and the perceptions of feasibility regarding the entrepreneurial career intentions because of the ascending mechanisms of social comparison. Moreover, Murphy and Lambrechts [49] suggested that the family business involvement of the next generation, through the activity of helping, not only influences, but in some cases alters the career decisions of the next generation family members. Also, the same authors underlined the fact that these members strive to make "pure" career choices, because they are divided between helping and doing what is best for the family business, and following their own careers.

Educational experiences (formal and informal) as social factors can influence the decision to pursue a career [15], including an entrepreneurial career. The fact that entrepreneurial skills associated with entrepreneurial behaviour can be taught and learned is proven by the research of several authors [50]. Therefore, the main role of EE is to increase student awareness and to emphasize that entrepreneurship is a viable career choice [51]. Entrepreneurship education represents an important driver of the development of entrepreneurial attitudes of both potential and nascent entrepreneurs [51,52]. Different empirical researches [4,9,11,23,53,54] focused on the EE–EI relationship among university students from different countries (e.g., China, USA, Spain, Ukraine, UK, France, Poland, Romania) and found that EE's effect on students' EI is positive, but that its intensity varies among different countries. This positive impact was also confirmed by a university student sample from Hungary and Estonia [55]. Similar results were obtained by other studies [8,56], based on comprehensive qualitative and quantitative reviews, including meta-analyses of the EE–EI relationship.

Other researches [57–59] showed that the relationship between EE and EI is negative, a fact that can be explained by students' awareness of the risks associated with entrepreneurship because of higher education. This relationship is significantly influenced by the effectiveness of different types of entrepreneurship programmes and the field of study [4,26,60]. In a recent study, Herman and Stefanescu [4] stressed that the impact of EE in university on EI is higher in the case of Romanian business students than in engineering students. Solesvik [61] obtained similar results in the case of Ukraine university students, concluding that entrepreneurship education enhances entrepreneurial skills and competencies, as well as entrepreneurial intentions. Some researchers underlined the fact that providing only an adequate education may foster the entrepreneurial intention of individuals [48,62].

Therefore, taking into account that a large part of the empirical results highlights that an EFB provided as informal education and EE provided as formal education positively affect the EI, the following hypotheses can be formulated:

Hypotheses H1a. *Students who have previous entrepreneurial exposure within the family will demonstrate greater entrepreneurial intention.*

Hypotheses H1b. *Students' prior family entrepreneurial exposure positively influences the EI of students.*

Hypotheses H2. *Effectiveness of EE positively influences the EI of students.*

Prior researches [11,63–65] considered certain personality traits as important factors that influence students' EI. According to Rauch and Frese [64], personality traits are "dispositions to exhibit a certain kind of response across various situations" [64] (p. 355). The impact of the individual personality dimensions (conscientiousness, openness to experience, emotional stability, extraversion, and agreeableness) of the Big Five model (developed by Goldberg [66]) on entrepreneurial intention was largely analysed by several studies [65,67]. Şahin et al. [67] highlighted that "the multiple configurations of the big five personality traits and entrepreneurial self-efficacy" [67] (p. 1188) can generate a high level of entrepreneurial intention among Turkish students. Rauch and Frese [64], based on a meta-analysis of the relationship between business owners' personality traits and business creation, found that innovativeness, generalized self-efficacy, and proactive personality are significantly correlated with entrepreneurial behaviour. The risk-taking propensity and the locus of control have a strong impact on the attitude towards self-employment [63,65]. Ahmed et al. [68] found significant but small indirect effects of innovativeness and risk propensity on entrepreneurial intentions in the case of a sample of final year MBA students. According to Giacomin et al. [47], students who are more optimistic are more likely to intend to pursue an entrepreneurial career.

Zellweger and Sieger [69] emphasized that autonomy, innovativeness, risk taking, proactiveness, and competitive aggressiveness reflect only a partial picture of entrepreneurial orientation. Thus, the authors highlighted a real need to extend the entrepreneurial orientation scale in order to provide entrepreneurial behaviours in long-lived family businesses [69]. The research results of other authors [17], using four personality traits (innovativeness, propensity for taking risks, the need for achievement, and the locus of control), pointed out that risk-taking propensity and the need for achievement positively influence the entrepreneurial intention among Romanian university students. Although many personality traits were identified as having a significant effect on entrepreneurial intention, based on the EU report [70] we focused on the five student entrepreneurial personality traits, namely, innovativeness, risk-taking propensity, sense of self-confidence, optimism, and competitiveness. Therefore, we hypothesize:

Hypotheses H3. *Students' entrepreneurial personality traits positively influence their entrepreneurial intention.*

Entrepreneurial intentions represent the result of interrelated contextual factors [7,9,43], such as EE and EFB. Fayolle and Gailly [51] highlighted that students with prior exposure to entrepreneurship will benefit disproportionally from attending an EE programme. Thus, highly exposed students will be marginally or even negatively influenced by EE, whereas less exposed students could be impacted in a positive way. For the French students, their research results showed that the impact of EE on entrepreneurial intention is strongly affected by students' prior exposure to entrepreneurship, illustrating that this impact "on the variables of planned behaviour tend to supersede the impact of the training itself" [51] (p. 87). Bae et al. [8] reviewed 73 studies, analysing their results with a total sample size of 37,285 people, and identifying a significantly positive but weak correlation between EE and EI, which may explain EFB as a moderator of the EE–EI relationship.

Taking into account that students from entrepreneurial families are more likely than those without a similar background to have access to the human, financial, and social capital [22,24,27,43], and to learn techniques taught at universities, such as business planning or market analysis [29], their requirements for additional inputs from entrepreneurship education are reduced [8]. In the same line of ideas, Eesley and Wang [20] highlighted that, because the students who come from entrepreneurial families are already exposed to start-up norms, formal education such as EE in school has a marginal impact on EI. Additionally, exposed students can interpret the materials offered by EE more critically than others. Thus, EE may be less effective toward entrepreneurial intentions for students with an entrepreneurial family background than for those from non-entrepreneurial families [8]. Walter and Dohse [29] examined how the effect of entrepreneurial education on the entrepreneurial career intentions of German students is complemented by role models. Their study showed that parent role models motivate and qualify students for independent activity, significantly increasing entrepreneurial intentions. At the same time, role models surpass the effect of entrepreneurial education by simultaneously raising attitudes towards behaviour, subjective norms, and perceived behavioural control. Therefore, we hypothesize:

Hypotheses H4. *The intensity of the impact of EE on EI depends on the student's entrepreneurial family background.*

Figure 1 provides an illustration of our proposed conceptual model.

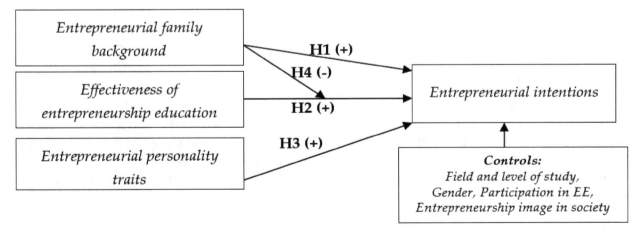

Figure 1. Conceptual model.

In summary, this study mainly hypothesizes that the EFB of students has both a direct effect and a moderating effect on the entrepreneurial intentions of students.

3. Methodology and Research Design

3.1. Studied Population and Sample

An empirical explorative research was conducted based on a questionnaire that was applied to final year undergraduate students, high school and university students. Two high schools (economics and non-economics) and two faculties were selected (the Faculty of Economics and the Faculty of Engineering of "G.E. Palade" University of Medicine, Pharmacy, Sciences and Technology of Tirgu-Mures (former "Petru Maior" University of Tirgu-Mures)), Romania. Our selection was limited to final year students, considering that these could be characterized as ready to launch into their professional careers and express their own choices, "as at this stage of life entrepreneurial conscience and attitude towards entrepreneurial career are formed" [14] (p. 387). Data for this study were collected using a non-random sampling technique, on quotas, according to the fields of study.

According to the records of the Faculties of Engineering and Economic Sciences of the university and the two targeted high schools, there were 880 students enrolled in the final years. Of these, we obtained valid questionnaires from 617 subjects, the sample (N) representing over 70% of the total number of young people in the last year of study, of the mentioned faculties (bachelor level) and of the two high schools. This fact indicates the representativeness of the sample.

From the total of 617 respondents, 57.9% were university students, 58.3% were female, and 17.8% had one or both parents self-employed or entrepreneurs. A total of 46.5% of students studied economics, and 74.7% of students considered that EE was included in their programmes of study (Table 1).

Table 1. Sample description (N = 617).

Respondents' Characteristics	Absolute Frequencies (N)	Absolute Frequencies (%)
Gender:		
Male	257	41.7
Female	360	58.3
Field of study:		
Economics students	287	46.5
Non-economics students	330	53.5
Level of study:		
High school	260	42.1
University	357	57.9
Students whose parents are self-employed or entrepreneurs (EFB)	110	17.8
Students' participation in entrepreneurship education (PEE)	461	74.7

3.2. Measures

3.2.1. Dependent Variables

To identify students' entrepreneurial intentions (EIs)—a dependent variable—we adapted two items from Sieger et al. [26] and EC [70]. Thus, respondents were asked the two following questions linked to: self-employment choice (If you could choose between different kinds of jobs after graduation, which would you prefer? employee = 0; self-employed = 1) and intention to become an entrepreneur (Do you want to become an entrepreneur or to start a business after graduation? yes = 1; no = 0). EI was assessed by averaging the individual mean of each question.

3.2.2. Independent Variables

In order to measure the students' EFB—Entrepreneurial family background—based on prior studies [13,26], we took into consideration the occupational status of the respondents' parents (employees or other category = 0; self-employed or entrepreneur = 1).

We assessed effectiveness of EE (EEE) using a four-item score (according to [70]) based on the self-assessment of the following statements by students (Education: has helped me to develop my sense of initiative; has helped me to better understand the role of entrepreneurs in society; has given me the skills and know-how to enable me to run a business; has made me interested in becoming an entrepreneur). In this study, EE was defined according to the EU report [71] as an education that equips individuals with key entrepreneurial competences, including entrepreneurial attitude, entrepreneurial skills, and entrepreneurship knowledge. Each response was given on a Likert scale from 1 (totally disagree) to 4 (totally agree). We calculated the total EEE score by taking the average of the four items.

The entrepreneurial personality traits (EPTs) of students were measured subjectively (from a student perspective) using five statements (according to [70]) concerning assertions linked to: innovativeness (I am an inventive person who has ideas), the risk-taking propensity (In general, I am willing to take risks), sense of self-confidence (Generally, when facing difficult tasks, I am certain that I will accomplish them), willingness to compete with others (I like situations in which I compete with others), and optimism (I am optimistic about my future). For the answers, a 4-point Likert scale was provided, where 1 = "completely disagree" and 4 = "completely agree". The final EPT score was calculated by averaging the scores of the five statements. Cronbach's alpha for EEE (of 0.68) and EPT (of 0.72) were above the acceptable threshold by 0.6, according to Aiken and West [72], a fact that proved the internal reliability of EEE and EPT.

3.2.3. Control Variables

We used a total of five control variables (Table 1) that potentially influenced the results of this research: participation in EE, field of study (non-economics = 0 and economics = 1), level of study (high school = 0 and university = 1), the student perception of the entrepreneurship's image in society and gender (male = 0 and female = 1). We assessed the students' participation in EE (PEE) based on the responses to the question: "Are there courses in the curricula which might be considered a form of entrepreneurship education?" (yes = 1; no = 0). The student perception of the image of entrepreneurs in society (positive entrepreneurship image–PEI) was assessed based on the self-assessment of two positive statements: "Entrepreneurs are job creators"; "Entrepreneurs create new products and services and benefit us all" (according to [70]) on a Likert scale that ranged from 1 = totally disagree to 4 = totally agree.

In terms of gender differences, there are studies [23,26] which showed that men have a stronger preference for self-employment than women. Moreover, statistical data report that women are less likely to be involved in entrepreneurial activity than men [1,6]. Block et al. [73] showed that the higher the level of education, the more likely the possibility of starting a business. There are significant differences in EI according to field of study [4,26,53], EI being higher among business students than among other students (engineering sciences and social sciences students). On the contrary, other empirical research [9] proved that science students have higher EI than students from other majors based on a higher risk-taking propensity, which was explained by the advantage created by their technical skills generating a higher sense of self-efficacy. As regards students' participation in EE, the EU report [71], based on a large sample of 2582 students from different European higher education institutions, found that entrepreneurship alumni had a higher preference for being self-employed than those who did not participate in EE. Moreover, we used the image of entrepreneurs in society as a control variable, taking into account that the favourable cultural attitudes of society towards entrepreneurship may also influence entrepreneurial intentions [6,25].

3.3. Methods for Data Analysis

From a methodological point of view, we used descriptive statistics, correlations, and a hierarchical analysis of multiple regression.

To find out if there were or were not significant differences between students in relation to the EI, t-test statistics (independent samples t-test for equality of means) were used. The intensity of the relationship between variables was analysed based on Pearson correlation coefficient (r).

To identify the functional relationship between the independent variable (EI) and the dependent and control variables, we used hierarchical multiple linear regression analysis ($Y = \alpha + \beta_1 \times X_1 + \beta_2 \times X_2 + ... + \beta_n \times X_n + \varepsilon$; Y—dependent variable, X—explanatory variables, α and β—regression coefficients, and ε—residual error). The regression coefficients were estimated based on the least-squares method [74]. We chose to use the hierarchical multiple linear regression analysis in this research, taking into account that, in recent years, this statistical analysis method was widely applied to empirical research [12,14,23,48] in order to analyse the influence of various factors (such as perceived family support, perceived educational support, entrepreneurial self-efficacy, EE, risk propensity, etc.) on entrepreneurial intentions. The hierarchical multiple regression analysis was conducted in three steps. Firstly, the control variables were regressed on student entrepreneurial intention (Model 1). Secondly, the direct effects of EFB, EEE, and EPT were added to regression (Models 2–5). Finally, we added the interaction effect between EFB and EEE to investigate the moderator effect of EFB on the EEE–EI link (Models 6–7). Significant interaction was probed with the simple effects approach [75], and was plotted by using a moderator variable (EFB) and one standard deviation above and one below the mean of the predictor (EEE). Fisher Snedecor (F) statistics was used to assess the validity of the models. For checking if the results were affected by multicollinearity, the variance inflation factors (VIFs) were tested. To avoid multicollinearity, according to Aiken and West [72], all independent variables were centred (the mean subtracted). We also examined multicollinearity by calculating the variance inflation factor (VIF) for the explanatory variables in multiple regressions. According to Hair et al. [76], there is a high multicollinearity if the VIF has a value which is higher than 10. The data were analysed with SPSS 18.0.

4. Results and Discussions

Our results showed a high level of student EI (60.5% of students intended to become entrepreneurs or self-employed). For Romania, this finding was in line with [6], according to which, on average, two-thirds of the adult population in the efficiency-driven economies (including Romania) consider starting a business a good career choice. This unexpected high level of student EI showed the desire for self-employment more than the feasibility of self-employment. Thus, according to the most recent EC Report [77], there is significant difference between the desire for and the feasibility of self-employment among Romanian young respondents (58% against 31%, respectively). Also, statistical data [1] show that in Romania in 2018, young self-employment accounted for only 11.4% of the employed persons aged between 20 and 24, and 10.08% of the employed persons aged between 25 and 29. There were large gaps in self-employment in the 25–29 age group among EU countries. Thus, developed countries like Germany (3.42%), Ireland (3.92%), Sweden (3.96%), and Ireland (3.96%) had the lowest values, while some CEE countries (Slovakia—11%; Czechia—10.9%; Poland—10.8%), as well as Italy (14.6%) and Greece (14.06%), showed the highest percentages of young self-employed among employed persons. These data should be viewed in a national context, taking into account the socioeconomic situation of each country, the size of the public and private sectors, the type of self-employment, etc. For example, in the case of Romania, the higher value of young self-employed (10.08%) can be partially explained by a high propensity for necessity-driven entrepreneurship [78], as young people choose self-employment out of necessity in the absence of other employment opportunities. In addition, Romania still has a high share of the self-employed population in agriculture, and this economic aspect is not at all in favour of a predominantly productive entrepreneurship [78].

For the analysed variables, the Pearson (r) correlations shown in Table 2 reflected low values, even if they were significant. The correlation results indicated that EI is positively low correlated with the field of study ($r = 0.096$), EFB ($r = 0.145$), EEE ($r = 0.142$), and EPT ($r = 0.201$), and is negatively correlated with the level of study. EFB is negatively correlated with PEE ($r = -0.099$) and EEE ($r = -0.115$).

Table 2. Correlations [1] matrix of dependent variables and independent variables (n = 617).

Variables	1	2	3	4	5	6	7	8	9
1. EI	1.00	0.016	0.096 *	−0.091 *	0.029	−0.017	0.145 **	0.142 **	0.201 **
2. PEE		1.00	0.288 **	−0.089 *	0.083 *	0.076	−0.099 *	0.311 **	0.079
3. Field of study			1.00	−0.106 **	0.094 *	0.056	−0.069	0.443 **	−0.009
4. Level of study				1.00	−0.003	−0.109 **	−0.048	0.072	0.016
5. PEI					1.00	0.023	0.007	0.145 **	0.064
6.Gender						1.00	−0.019	0.035	−0.099 *
7. EFB							1.00	−0.115 **	0.041
8. EEE								1.00	0.230 **
9. EPT									1.00

Note: [1] Pearson correlations (r); * $p < 0.05$ (2-tailed); ** $p < 0.01$ (2-tailed); EI = Entrepreneurial intention; PEE = Participation in EE; PEI = Positive entrepreneurship image; EEE = Effectiveness of EE; EFB = Entrepreneurial family background; EPT = Entrepreneurial personality trait.

A positive correlation (r = 0.311, $p < 0.01$) was identified between effectiveness of EE (with an average score of 2.725) and participation in EE, which emphasizes that the students who participate in EE access a higher level of the effectiveness of EE and vice versa. Also, EEE was positively associated with the field of study (economics vs. non-economics students) and students' positive perceptions of the image of entrepreneurs in society (the average score of PEI is 3.2), which suggests that students who have a high positive entrepreneurship image and are economics students report a high effectiveness of EE.

Our results showed that 74.7% of students appreciated that there were courses in the curricula that might be considered forms of entrepreneurship education. This very high percentage was surprising, taking into account that only 46.5% of respondents were economics students whose curricula contained entrepreneurship courses or entrepreneurship-related courses. However, this can be explained by the existence of economics or management courses in the curriculum of non-economics university students that might develop some entrepreneurship skills. Although, entrepreneurship education should not be confused with general business and economic studies [79]. We have to mention that in Romania, "Entrepreneurship education" is included in the high school curricula as elective courses in the second or third year of study, no matter the high school profile, and the subjects probably considered those hours as an equivalent of entrepreneurship education.

All significant correlations between the independent variables were modest and ranged from 0.115 to 0.443, showing a low probability that multicollinearity would affect the regression analysis.

Table 3 summarizes the results of the independent t-tests of the samples, from which it appeared that there was a positive difference in EI between students with an EFB and students without an EFB (t(615) = −3.864; $p = 0.000$). This implies that the inclination to choose an entrepreneurial career by students whose parents are self-employed is greater than among students whose parents are employees or other categories (73.6% against 57.6%). These results confirm hypothesis H1a.

Table 3. Results of independent samples t-test: EFB group vs. non-EFB group.

Variables	Mean		Levene's Test [1]		t-Test [2]	
	Non-EFB (N = 507)	EFB (N = 110)	F	Sig.	t	Sig. [3]
EI	0.576	0.736	4.716	0.030	−3.864	0.000
EEE	2.763	2.550	0.176	0.675	2.859	0.004
EPT	3.317	3.367	0.003	0.958	−1.012	0.312

Note: [1] Levene's test for equality of variances delivered a significance value higher than 0.05 for all the variables except EI, for which the "equal variances not assumed" option was used; df = 615; [2] t-test for equality of means; [3] 2-tailed; EI—entrepreneurial intention; EEE—effectiveness of EE; EPT—entrepreneurial personality trait.

Additionally, results pointed out that EEE differed significantly according to EFB (t(615) = 2.859; $p = 0.004$), which means that students with an EFB have a lower EEE score than students who do not have prior entrepreneurial family exposure (2.55 against 2.76). Thus, students who have entrepreneurial experience in the family context (EFB) consider that they already have entrepreneurial competences acquired from home and, therefore, EE in university and in high school is less effective. It means that the education offered by the education system helps them less to develop their sense of initiative, better understand the role of entrepreneurs in society, gain the necessary skills and knowledge to run a business, or arouse their interest in becoming an entrepreneur.

Regarding EPTs of students (with an average score of 3.326), no significant differences were identified between the two groups of subjects ($t(615) = -1.012; p = 0.312$).

Results obtained from the hierarchical regression analysis are presented in Table 4. In the first step, the control variables PEE, field of study, level of study, students' positive perception of the image of entrepreneurs in society (PEI), and gender were entered into the prediction model and two of them emerged as significant predictors. This baseline control variable model (Model 1) was significant at the 0.1 level ($F (5, 611) = 2.18, p < 0.1$). The level of study (high school vs. university) and field of study (economics vs. non-economics) significantly influenced students' EI. Therefore, those students from the field of economics ($\beta = 0.091, p < 0.05$) and at high school level ($\beta = -0.087, p < 0.05$) reported a higher EI. Our results do not support research findings [73], which indicated a positive link between level of education and the possibility of starting a business. However, there is an inconsistency regarding this link. For instance, another research finding [80] showed, for a Romanian sample, that the level of education does not influence significantly the perceived desirability of self-employment.

Table 4. Results of hierarchical multiple regression analysis for students' entrepreneurial intentions.

Independent Variables	Model 1	Model 2	Model 3	Model 4	Model 5	Model 6 [1]	Model 7 [1]
	Controls		Direct Effects			Interaction Effects	
PEE [a]	-0.018	-0.004	-0.036	-0.023	-0.043	-0.037	
Field of study [a]	0.091 *	0.099 *	0.036	0.105 *	0.061	0.035	
Level of study [a]	-0.087 *	-0.077 +	-0.098 *	-0.080 *	-0.094 *	-0.098 *	
PEI [a]	0.022	0.019	0.004	0.007	-0.002	0.007	
Gender [a]	-0.030	-0.028	-0.029	-0.007	-0.011	-0.029	
EFB [a]		0.147 **	0.157 **	0.138 **	0.146 **	0.151 **	0.158 **
EEE [a]			0.163 **		0.113 *	0.164 **	0.162 **
EPT [a]				0.198 **	0.173 **		
EEE*EFB [a]						-0.031	-0.041 +
Intercept	0.587	0.546	0.375	-0.010	-0.059	0.663	0.603
R^2	0.018	0.039	0.058	0.077	0.086	0.059	0.047
Adjusted R^2	0.009	0.029	0.047	0.066	0.074	0.047	0.043
R^2 Change	0.018	0.021	0.020	0.038	0.027	0.001	
Sig. F Change	0.055 +	0.000	0.000	0.000	0.000	0.438	
F value	2.180	4.096	5.381	7.248	7.120	4.781	10.144

Note: Dependent Variable: EI; [a] Standardized β-regression coefficients; + $p < 0.10$; * $p < 0.05$; ** $p < 0.001$; [1] Moderator: EFB.

We found that gender and the students' positive perception of image entrepreneurship in society had no significant effect on EI. Thus, our sample could not confirm the widespread belief that men have a higher propensity for an entrepreneurial career than women, but it confirmed the results of other studies [7].

Based on this model (Model 1), we added step by step independent variables for testing hypotheses H1b–H3: EFB (Model 2), EEE (Model 3), EPT (Model 4) and all three together (Model 5). As compared with the base model, R^2 improved to 3.9% (Model 2), 5.8% (Model 3), 7.7% (Model 4), and 8.6% (Model 5). These models were significant at the 0.01 level. Also, VIF scores (values ranged between 1.03 and 1.45) suggested that these models were not distorted by multicollinearity. As for the control variables, the level of study exhibited a negative relation to EI in the case of Models 2–5, while the field of study revealed a positive effect on EI, but only in the case of Model 2 and Model 4. For the other control variables, an insignificant effect was found in all models.

Table 4 shows that Model 2 was statistically significant (F (6, 610) = 4.096, $p < 0.01$), representing 3.9% of the EI variation ($R^2 = 0.039$, adjusted $R^2 = 0.029$), the change of R^2 was 0.021. By analysing beta (β) weights, it was found that EFB had a positive influence on EI ($\beta = 0.147, p < 0.001$). Therefore, H1b is supported. These aspects noted by us are consistent with the results of other studies [12,21,24], which revealed a positive direct influence of the entrepreneurial parental role model on the EI of the students. For instance, according to Carr and Sequeira [11], from an intergenerational point of view, children's experiences within business families have a great influence on entrepreneurial intention. This experience is an essential element in meeting informational and behavioural requirements as skills necessary for independent activities, regardless of whether this exposure happens within the family's existing business or not.

The results of Model 3 indicated that a higher level of EEE is predicted to be positively associated with a higher likelihood that the young people will choose an entrepreneurial career ($\beta = 0.163$, $p < 0.001$). Thus, hypothesis H2 is supported, confirmed by [11,23,53,81], which highlights the positive and direct effect of effectiveness of EE, as formal education, on students' entrepreneurial intentions.

In Model 4, EPT was identified as a significant determinant of EI ($\beta = 0.163, p < 0.001$). In the case of Model 5, all three independent variables, which were added at the same time, were statistically significant ($p < 0.01$), having a positive influence on EI. EPT received the strongest weight in the model ($\beta = 0.173, p < 0.01$), followed by EFB ($\beta = 0.146, p < 0.01$), and EEE ($\beta = 0.113, p < 0.05$), implying that EPT has a greater impact on EI. Thus, hypothesis H3 is confirmed and supported by the findings of other authors [47,64,65,80], hence entrepreneurial personality traits such as innovativeness, risk-taking propensity, sense of self-confidence, optimism, and competitiveness positively influence entrepreneurial career intentions.

We continued adding the interaction effect between EFB and EEE to verify hypothesis H4. (Model 6). This model did not improve significantly in comparison with the direct effect model (Model 3) according to its R^2 of 5.9% (Model 6: R^2 change = 0.001, $p = 0.438$), indicating that the interaction variable explained only a very small percentage of EI variation. The moderator variables EFB ($\beta = 0.151$, $p < 0.01$) and EEE ($\beta = 0.164, p < 0.01$) were significantly positively associated with the EI, as can be seen in Table 4 (Model 6). Also, we found an insignificant negative interaction effect between EFB and EEE ($\beta = -0.031, p = 0.438$, Model 6). Taking these results into account, in order to better identify the interaction effect between EFB and EEE on EI, the impact of the EFB moderator on the EEE–EI relationship was retested by adding the interaction term between EEE and EFB in the model without the control variables (Model 7). Model 7 was statistically significant (F (3613) = 10.144, $p < 0.001$) and accounted for over 4% of the variance of EI ($R^2 = 0.047$, Adjusted $R^2 = 0.043$). EEE received the strongest weight in the model ($\beta = 0.162, p < 0.01$), followed by EFB ($\beta = 0.158, p < 0.01$), which suggests that EEE influences EI positively and its influence is stronger than the EFB of students. In this model, the interaction effect between EFB and EEE was significantly negative, but marginal ($\beta = -0.041$, $p < 0.10$, Model 7). Moreover, based on the unstandardized coefficients of the regression model (Model 7), according to Preacher et al. [75], the moderating effect of EFB on the EEE–EI relationship is plotted in Figure 2. EI is on the y-axis of the dependent variable and EEE is plotted on the x-axis of the independent variable, representing low EEE (one standard deviation below mean) vs. high EEE (one standard deviation above mean).

In Figure 2, we can see that the link between EEE and EI was more pronounced for students who had no previous family entrepreneurial exposure than for students who had prior family entrepreneurial exposure, supporting hypothesis H4. Thus, the intensity of the impact of EEE on EI depends on the students' EFB being stronger for students without prior entrepreneurial family exposure. These results are in line with previous studies [24,51] that suggested that individuals coming from entrepreneurial families are already exposed to informal entrepreneurship learning (learning by doing and learning by example or modeling), providing an important opportunity for the acquisition of human capital related to running a successful business. As Carr and Sequeira [11] (p. 67) pointed out, family business can be seen as a "business incubator for future business".

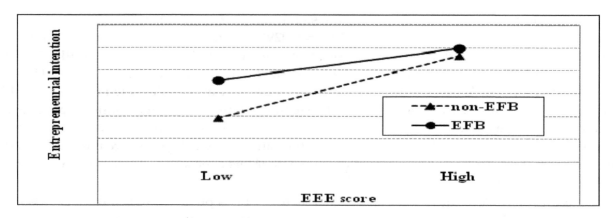

Figure 2. Interaction between EFB and EEE (Model 7).

Our study revealed other challenges faced by Romanian young people who aim to become entrepreneurs. Some of the most important are the lack of financial resources and the unfavourable business conditions in Romania. Thus, our results pointed out that the first reason why Romanian students do not want to become entrepreneurs is the lack of financial resources, whereas the second reason is the unfavourable business conditions in Romania. These results are in line with data provided by World Bank's Doing Business 2020 report [82], which showed that according to the Ease of doing business ranking, Romania ranked 55th out of 190 countries, after other CEE countries such as Poland (40th), Czechia (41st), Slovakia (45th), and Hungary (52nd). The place occupied by Romania is an argument that, in this country, the institutional environment represents a significant barrier to entrepreneurship.

Although students gave EEE a high score (2.73 out of 4), the lack of entrepreneurship knowledge was reported as the third reason why they do not want to become entrepreneurs. These results highlighted, once again, the need to increase the impact of primary, secondary, and tertiary education on entrepreneurship. Consequently, a strategic approach is highly needed, at both national and European levels. We emphasize that Romania is included among those EU countries that do not have a specific EE national strategy, although it has a broader strategy related to EE, especially economic development strategy [83].

5. Conclusions and Main Implications

In the current economic and social environment, the acquisition and development of the relevant skills in entrepreneurship is a real challenge for youth. These skills can offer them the path to an entrepreneurial career as a viable and sustainable alternative for them to successfully integrate into the labour market. In this context, the paper highlights the influence of the main social factors on entrepreneurial career intention by focusing on the impact of the EFB of students, aiming to improve their entrepreneurial intentions and to consider entrepreneurship as a desirable employment choice.

Following the completion of an exploratory research, which used a sample of 617 final year undergraduate Romanian students, the results highlight, on the one hand, a high level of Romanian students' entrepreneurial intentions, and, on the other hand, significant differences between the desire for and feasibility of self-employment, accompanied by a low number of young people actually being self-employed. Consequently, more attention needs to be paid in order to "improve the entrepreneurship key competence so that the desire for an entrepreneurial career turns into a real career choice" [4] (p. 320). Moreover, the research findings support the hypothesis that the students who have an entrepreneurial family background benefit from this informal education and exhibit a higher entrepreneurial intention than students without such a background.

Surprisingly, the effect of the level of study (high school vs. university) on EI is negative, university students having lower EI than high school students. These results can be explained, according to Oosterbeek et al. [57], by the fact that university education provides students with a more realistic perspective on the feasibility of entrepreneurship, creating an awareness of the risks associated with an entrepreneurial career path. Moreover, the research results prove that economics students have a higher propensity for an entrepreneurial career than non-economics students. This fact shows that entrepreneurship education, especially in the non-economic field, is necessary and must be ensured in order to meet the specific needs of students and thus improve the integration of young people into the labour market.

The hierarchical multiple regression analysis results show that students' entrepreneurial intentions are directly and positively influenced by EFB and EEE. These findings point out that the informal and formal education received by the students from their entrepreneur parents and from school improved their entrepreneurship key competence and enhanced entrepreneurial career intentions. The research results also prove that entrepreneurial personality traits positively influence the entrepreneurial intentions of students, highlighting the fact that high levels of innovativeness, risk-taking propensity, sense of self-confidence, optimism, and competitiveness increase the likelihood that young people will choose an entrepreneurial career.

By corroborating informal and formal education, our results, based on the moderator effect, show that the influence of EEE on students' entrepreneurial intentions is marginally negatively affected by the EFB. Thus, for our sample the greater the prior entrepreneurial family exposure, the lower the impact of the EEE on students' EI. Therefore, in order to foster and nurture entrepreneurial intentions among students with an EFB for a higher level of effectiveness of EE, education institutions, especially those with a large proportion of students with an entrepreneurial family background, should include special courses promoting the interests of students in their family business and not only in the curricula.

We consider that both formal and informal entrepreneurship education must act together, complementing each other, in order to increase the propensity of young people for choosing an entrepreneurial career, taking into account that "Europe needs more entrepreneurs" [3], including Romania, which, as an EU member state, must generate inclusive economic growth and more and better jobs.

The students pointed out some unfavourable barriers to starting a business in Romania, such as the lack of financial resources and the rather difficult access to them, an institutional framework that requires a lot of bureaucracy, and even insufficient knowledge in the entrepreneurial field. These barriers have negative consequences for young people's desires to start a business.

Therefore, in order to turn entrepreneurial intentions into a real motivation to start a business and become an entrepreneur, there are at least three issues that policy makers need to address for their practical implications. First, an improvement in the "Ease of Doing Business" context regarding the resources (such as easier access to credit, lower minimum capital to start a business) is needed. Second, at the level of bureaucracy, a shorter time for registering a firm, simpler procedures, and an online system for filing and paying taxes are necessary [82]. Finally, at the educational level, a specific EE national strategy must be developed.

The findings from our research have implications for those who pursue actual or potential entrepreneurship, the teaching staff who teach entrepreneurship, and the decision makers responsible for improving and sustaining entrepreneurship.

We recognize as a limitation of this study the fact that it focuses on intentionality, expressing an intention to pursue an entrepreneurial career, and not on the actual behaviour of entrepreneurs. Taking into account that intentions may not turn into actual behaviour in the future, even if some respondents expressed a high entrepreneurial intention in the survey, their career paths in the future can be completely different. Therefore, future longitudinal studies would be appropriate to find out to what extent the intentions of students with prior exposure to formal and informal education actually evolve into action. Another limitation is the fact that our findings represent only a partial picture of the issues related to the influence of an EFB on students' entrepreneurial intentions. In this context, further research should focus on a deeper analysis of the impact of an EFB on EI in order to find out if the EI is due to the transfer of human capital (entrepreneurial skills) and/or financial and/or social capital from self-employed parents to their children. Moreover, an interesting aspect to be further explored is to what extent parental economic success can influence the choice of an entrepreneurial career by young people.

Author Contributions: Both authors M.-A.G. and E.H. have contributed equally to this paper, both being considered as first authors. All authors have read and agreed to the published version of the manuscript.

References

1.   Eurostat Database. 2020. Available online: http://ec.europa.eu/eurostat/data/database (accessed on 20 May 2020).

2.   Thurik, A.R.; Carree, M.A.; van Stel, A.; Audretsch, D.B. Does self-employment reduce unemployment? *J. Bus. Ventur.* **2008**, *23*, 673–686. [CrossRef]

3.   EC. Entrepreneurship 2020 Action Plan. Reigniting the Entrepreneurial Spirit in Europe. 2013. Available online: http://ec.europa.eu/enterprise/policies/sme/public-consultation/files/report-pubcons-entr2020-ap_en.pdf (accessed on 18 March 2018).

4.   Herman, E.; Stefanescu, D. Can higher education stimulate entrepreneurial intentions among engineering and business students? *Educ. Stud.* **2017**, *43*, 312–327. [CrossRef]

5.   UN. Transforming Our World: The 2030 Agenda for Sustainable Development. A/RES/70/1. 2015. Available online: https://sustainabledevelopment.un.org/content/documents/21252030%20Agenda%20for%20Sustainable%20Development%20web.pdf (accessed on 19 May 2020).

6.   Global Entrepreneurship Research Association (GERA). Global Entrepreneurship Monitor. 2019/20 Global Report. 2020. Available online: https://www.gemconsortium.org/file/open?fileId=50443 (accessed on 19 May 2020).

7.   Franco, M.; Haase, H.; Lautenschläger, A. Students' entrepreneurial intentions: An inter-regional comparison. *Educ. Train.* **2010**, *52*, 260–275. [CrossRef]

8.   Bae, T.J.; Qian, S.; Miao, C.; Fiet, J.O. The relationship between entrepreneurship education and entrepreneurial intentions: A meta-analytic review. *Entrep. Theory Pr.* **2014**, *38*, 217–254. [CrossRef]

9.   Zhang, Y.; Duysters, G.; Cloodt, M. The role of entrepreneurship education as a predictor of university students' entrepreneurial intention. *Int. Entrep. Manag. J.* **2014**, *10*, 623–641. [CrossRef]

10. Fayolle, A.; Gailly, B.; Lassas-Clerc, N. Assessing the impact of entrepreneurship education programmes: A new methodology. *J. Eur. Ind. Train.* **2006**, *30*, 701–720. [CrossRef]

11. Pruett, M.; Shinnar, R.; Toney, B.; Llopis, F.; Fox, J. Explaining entrepreneurial intentions of university students: A crosscultural study. *Int. J. Entrep. Behav. Res.* **2009**, *15*, 571–594. [CrossRef]

12. Carr, J.C.; Sequeira, J.M. Prior business exposure as intergenerational influence and entrepreneurial intent: A theory of planned behavior approach. *J. Bus. Res.* **2007**, *60*, 1090–1098. [CrossRef]

13. Chlosta, S.; Patzelt, H.; Klein, S.B.; Dormann, C. Parental role models and the decision to become self-employed: The moderating effect of personality. *Small Bus. Econ.* **2012**, *38*, 121–138. [CrossRef]

14. Shirokova, G.; Osiyevskyy, O.; Bogatyreva, K. Exploring the intention-behavior link in student entrepreneurship: Moderating effects of individual and environmental characteristics. *Eur. Manag. J.* **2016**, *34*, 386–399. [CrossRef]

15. Dyer, G.W., Jr. Toward a theory of entrepreneurial careers. *Entrep. Theory Pr.* **1995**, *19*, 7–21. [CrossRef]

16. Bandura, A. *Social Learning Theory*; Prentice-Hall: Englewood Cliffs, NJ, USA, 1977; ISBN 978-0138167448.

17. Popescu, C.C.; Bostan, I.; Robu, I.B.; Maxim, A. An analysis of the determinants of entrepreneurial intentions among students: A Romanian case study. *Sustainability* **2016**, *8*, 771. [CrossRef]

18. Vodă, A.I.; Florea, N. Impact of personality traits and entrepreneurship education on entrepreneurial intentions of business and engineering students. *Sustainability* **2019**, *11*, 1192. [CrossRef]

19. Criaco, G.; Sieger, P.; Wennberg, K.; Chirico, F.; Minola, T. Parents' performance in entrepreneurship as a "double-edged sword" for the intergenerational transmission of entrepreneurship. *Small Bus. Econ.* **2017**, *49*, 841–864. [CrossRef]

20. Eesley, C.E.; Wang, Y. *Social Influence in Entrepreneurial Career Choice: Evidence from Randomized Field Experiments on Network Ties*; Research Paper No. 2387329; Boston University School of Management: Boston, MA, USA, 2016. [CrossRef]

21. Sørensen, J.B. Closure and Exposure: Mechanisms in the intergenerational transmission of self-employment. In *The Sociology of Entrepreneurship*; Research in the Sociology of Organizations; Martin, R., Lounsbury, M., Eds.; Emerald Group Publishing Limited: Bingley, UK, 2007; Volume 25, pp. 83–124. ISBN 978-0-7623-1433-1.

22. Zellweger, T.; Sieger, P.; Halter, F. Should I stay or should I go? Career choice intentions of students with family business background. *J. Bus. Ventur.* **2011**, *26*, 521–536. [CrossRef]

23. Solesvik, Z.M.; Westhead, P.; Matlay, H.; Parsyak, N.V. Entrepreneurial assets and mindsets. *Educ. Train.* **2013**, *55*, 748–762. [CrossRef]

24. Fairlie, R.; Robb, A. Families, human capital and small business: Evidence from the characteristics of business owners survey. *Ind. Labor Relat. Rev.* **2007**, *60*, 225–245. [CrossRef]

25. Ozaralli, N.; Rivenburgh, N.K. Entrepreneurial intention: Antecedents to entrepreneurial behavior in the USA and Turkey. *J. Glob. Entrep. Res.* **2016**, 6. [CrossRef]

26. Sieger, P.; Fueglistaller, U.; Zellweger, T.; Braun, I. Global Student Entrepreneurship 2018: Insights from 54 Countries. International Report of the GUESSS Project 2019. St.Gallen/Bern: KMU-HSG/IMU. Available online: http://www.guesssurvey.org/resources/PDF_InterReports/GUESSS_Global_2018.pdf (accessed on 20 May 2020).

27. Laspita, S.; Breugst, N.; Heblich, S.; Patzelt, H. Intergenerational transmission of entrepreneurial intentions. *J. Bus. Ventur.* **2012**, *27*, 414–435. [CrossRef]

28. Bosma, N.; Hessels, J.; Schutjens, V.; Praag, M.V.; Verheul, I. Entrepreneurship and role models. *J. Econ. Psychol.* **2012**, *33*, 410–424. [CrossRef]

29. Walter, S.G.; Dohse, D. The Interplay between Entrepreneurship Education and Regional Knowledge Potential in Forming Entrepreneurial Intentions. (No.1549). Kiel Working Paper. 2009. Available online: https://www.files.ethz.ch/isn/106013/kwp_1549.pdf (accessed on 30 March 2018).

30. Faas, C.; Benson, M.J.; Kaestle, C.E. Parent resources during adolescence: Effects on education and careers in young adulthood. *J. Youth Stud.* **2013**, *16*, 151–171. [CrossRef]

31. Mungai, E.; Velamuri, S.R. Parental entrepreneurial role model influence on male offspring: Is it always positive and when does it occur? *Entrep. Theory Pr.* **2011**, *35*, 337–357. [CrossRef]

32. Chua, J.H.; Chrisman, J.J.; Steier, L.; Rau, S.B. Sources of heterogeneity in family firms: An introduction. *Entrep. Theory Pr.* **2012**, *36*, 1103–1113. [CrossRef]

33. Chrisman, J.J.; Chua, J.H.; Pearson, A.W.; Barnett, T. Family involvement, family influence, and family–centered non–economic goals in small firms. *Entrep. Theory Pract.* **2012**, *36*, 267–293. [CrossRef]

34. Chrisman, J.J.; Patel, P.C. Variations in R&D investments of family and nonfamily firms: Behavioral agency and myopic loss aversion perspectives. *Acad. Manag. J.* **2012**, *55*, 976–997.

35. Kotlar, J. State of the art of family business research. In *Family Business Studies: An Annotated Bibliography*; De Massis, A., Sharma, P., Chua, J.H., Chrisman, J.J., Eds.; Edward Elgar: Cheltenham Glos, UK, 2012; pp. 10–46.

36. De Massis, A.; Frattini, F.; Majocchi, A.; Piscitello, L. Family firms in the global economy: Toward a deeper understanding of internationalization determinants, processes, and outcomes. *Glob. Strat. J.* **2018**, *8*, 3–21. [CrossRef]

37. Chrisman, J.J.; Chua, J.H.; De Massis, A.; Minola, T.; Vismara, S. Management processes and strategy execution in family firms: From "what" to "how". *Small Bus. Econ.* **2016**, *47*, 719–734. [CrossRef]

38. Eddleston, K.A.; Kellermanns, F.W.; Zellweger, T.M. Exploring the entrepreneurial behavior of family firms: Does the stewardship perspective explain differences? *Entrep. Theory Pr.* **2012**, *36*, 347–367. [CrossRef]

39. Zahra, S.A.; Hayton, J.C.; Salvato, C. Entrepreneurship in family vs. non-family firms: A resource-based analysis of the effect of organizational culture. *Entrep. Theory Pract.* **2004**, *28*, 363–379. [CrossRef]

40. Kellermanns, F.W.; Eddleston, K.A. Corporate entrepreneurship in family firms: A family perspective. *Entrep. Theory Pr.* **2006**, *30*, 809–830. [CrossRef]

41. Nicolaou, N.; Shane, S. Can genetic factors influence the likelihood of engaging in entrepreneurial activity? *J. Bus. Ventur.* **2009**, *24*, 1–22. [CrossRef]

42. Jaskiewicz, P.; Combs, J.G.; Rau, S.B. Entrepreneurial legacy: Toward a theory of how some family firms nurture transgenerational entrepreneurship. *J. Bus. Ventur.* **2015**, *30*, 29–49. [CrossRef]

43. Mueller, P. Entrepreneurship in the region: Breeding ground for nascent entrepreneurs? *Small Bus. Econ.* **2006**, *27*, 41–58. [CrossRef]

44. Athayde, R. Measuring enterprise potential in young people. *Entrep. Theory Pr.* **2009**, *33*, 481–500. [CrossRef]

45. Krueger, N. The impact of prior entrepreneurial exposure on perceptions of new venture feasibility and desirability. *Entrep. Theory Pr.* **1993**, *18*, 5–21. [CrossRef]

46. Peterman, N.E.; Kennedy, J. Enterprise education: Influencing students' perceptions of entrepreneurship. *Entrep. Theory Pr.* **2003**, *28*, 129–144. [CrossRef]

47. Giacomin, O.; Janssen, F.; Shinnar, R.S. Student entrepreneurial optimism and overconfidence across cultures. *Int. Small Bus. J.* **2016**, *34*, 925–947. [CrossRef]

48. Turker, D.; Selcuk, S. Which factors affect entrepreneurial intention of university students? *J. Eur. Ind. Train.* **2009**, *33*, 142–159. [CrossRef]

49. Murphy, L.; Lambrechts, F. Investigating the actual career decisions of the next generation: The impact of family business involvement. *J. Fam. Bus. Strateg.* **2015**, *6*, 33–44. [CrossRef]

50. Støren, L.A. Entrepreneurship in higher education: Impacts on graduates' entrepreneurial intentions, activity and learning outcome. *Educ. Train.* **2014**, *56*, 795–813. [CrossRef]

51. Fayolle, A.; Gailly, B. The impact of entrepreneurship education on entrepreneurial attitudes and intention: Hysteresis and persistence. *J. Small Bus. Manag.* **2015**, *53*, 75–93. [CrossRef]

52. De Jorge-Moreno, J.; Laborda Castillo, L.; Sanz-Triguero, M. The effect of business and economics education programs on students' entrepreneurial intention. *Eur. J. Train. Dev.* **2012**, *36*, 409–425. [CrossRef]

53. Souitaris, V.; Zerbinati, S.; Al-Laham, A. Do entrepreneurship programmes raise entrepreneurial intention of science and engineering students? The effect of learning, inspiration and resources. *J. Bus. Ventur.* **2007**, *22*, 566–591. [CrossRef]

54. Baran, M.; Jiménez Moreno, J.J.; Oliveras, G. Entrepreneurship Attitudes of Students in the Information Society Era with and Without Entrepreneurship Training: Exploratory Study. *Probl. Zarządzania* **2018**, *73*, 170–180. [CrossRef]

55. Hartsenko, J.; Venesaar, U. Impact of entrepreneurship teaching models on students' entrepreneurial intentions: The case of Estonia and Hungary. *Res. Econ. Bus. Cee* **2017**, *9*, 72–92.

56. Martin, B.; McNally, J.J.; Kay, M. Examining the formation of human capital in entrepreneurship: A meta-analysis of entrepreneurship education outcomes. *J. Bus. Ventur.* **2013**, *28*, 211–224. [CrossRef]

57. Oosterbeek, H.; van Praag, M.; Ijsselstein, A. The impact of entrepreneurship education on entrepreneurship skills and motivation. *Eur. Econ. Rev.* **2010**, *54*, 442–454. [CrossRef]

58. Von Graevenitz, G.; Harhoff, D.; Weber, R. The effects of entrepreneurship education. *J. Econ. Behav. Organ.* **2010**, *76*, 90–112. [CrossRef]

59. Lima, E.; Lopes, R.M.; Nassif, V.; Silva, D. Opportunities to improve entrepreneurship education: Contributions considering Brazilian challenges. *J. Small Bus. Manag.* **2015**, *53*, 1033–1051. [CrossRef]

60. Lans, T.; Gulikers, J.; Batterink, M. Moving beyond traditional measures of entrepreneurial intentions in a study among life sciences students in the Netherlands. *Res. Post-Compuls. Educ.* **2010**, *15*, 259–274. [CrossRef]

61. Solesvik, M.Z. Entrepreneurial competencies and intentions: The role of higher education. *Forum Sci. Oeconomia* **2019**, *7*, 9–23.

62. Rachwał, T.; Kurek, S.; Bogu's, M. Entrepreneurship education at secondary level in transition economies: A Case of Poland. *Entrep. Bus. Econ. Rev.* **2016**, *4*, 61–81. [CrossRef]

63. Lüthje, C.; Franke, N. The 'making' of an entrepreneur: Testing a model of entrepreneurial intent among engineering students at MIT. *RD Manag.* **2003**, *33*, 135–147. [CrossRef]

64. Rauch, A.; Frese, M. Let's put the person back into entrepreneurship research: A meta-analysis on the relationship between business owners' personality traits, business creation, and success. *Eur. J. Work Organ. Psychol.* **2007**, *16*, 353–385. [CrossRef]

65. Zhao, H.; Seibert, S.E.; Lumpkin, G.T. The relationship of personality to entrepreneurial intentions and performance: A meta-analytic review. *J. Manag.* **2010**, *36*, 381–404. [CrossRef]

66. Goldberg, L.R. An alternative description of personality: The big-five factor structure. *J. Pers. Soc. Psychol.* **1990**, *59*, 1216–1229. [CrossRef]

67. Şahin, F.; Karadağ, H.; Tuncer, B. Big five personality traits, entrepreneurial self-efficacy and entrepreneurial intention: A configurational approach. *Int. J. Entrep. Behav. Res.* **2019**, *25*, 1188–1211. [CrossRef]

68. Ahmed, T.; Klobas, J.E.; Ramayah, T. Personality traits, demographic factors and entrepreneurial intentions: Improved understanding from a moderated mediation study. *Entrep. Res. J.* **2019**, 20170062. [CrossRef]

69. Zellweger, T.; Sieger, P. Entrepreneurial orientation in long-lived family firms. *Small Bus. Econ.* **2012**, *38*, 67–84. [CrossRef]

70. EC. Entrepreneurship in the EU and Beyond. Flash Eurobarometer 283. 2010. Available online: http://ec.europa.eu/public_opinion/flash/fl_283_en.pdf (accessed on 20 May 2016).

71. EU. Effects and Impact of Entrepreneurship Programmes in Higher Education. 2012. Available online: http://ec.europa.eu/enterprise/policies/sme/promotingentrepreneurship/files/education/effects_impact_high_edu_final_report_en.pdf (accessed on 20 May 2016).

72. Aiken, L.S.; West, S.G. *Multiple Regression: Testing and Interpreting Interactions*; Sage: Newbury Park, CA, USA, 1991; ISBN 0803936052.

73. Block, J.H.; Hoogerheide, L.; Thurik, R. Education and entrepreneurial choice: An instrumental variables analysis. *Int. Small Bus. J.* **2011**, *31*, 23–33. [CrossRef]

74. Landau, S.; Everitt, B.S. *A Handbook of Statistical Analyses Using SPSS*; Chapman & Hall/CRC Press LLC: Boca Raton, FL, USA, 2004; ISBN 1-58488-369-3.

75. Preacher, K.J.; Curran, P.J.; Bauer, D.J. Computational tools for probing interactions in multiple linear regression, multilevel modeling, and latent curve analysis. *J. Educ. Behav. Stat.* **2006**, *31*, 437–448. [CrossRef]

76. Hair, J.F., Jr.; Black, W.C.; Babin, B.J.; Anderson, R.E. *Multivariate Data Analysis*, 7th ed.; Prentice-Hall: Upper Saddle River, NJ, USA, 2010; ISBN 978-0138132637.

77. EC. Entrepreneurship in the EU and Beyond. 2012 Flash Eurobarometer on Entrepreneurship. 2012. Available online: http://ec.europa.eu/public_opinion/flash/fl_354_en.pdf (accessed on 20 May 2016).

78. Herman, E.; Szabo, Z.K. Considerations on Romania's entrepreneurial profile: Barriers to productive entrepreneurship. *Proc. Econ. Financ.* **2014**, *15*, 1740–1750. [CrossRef]

79. EC. Entrepreneurship in Vocational Education and Training, Best Procedure Project, Enterprise Directorate-General, Brussels. 2009. Available online: http://ec.europa.eu/enterprise/policies/sme/files/smes/vocational/entr_voca_en.pdf (accessed on 24 May 2020).

80. Păunescu, C.; Popescu, M.C.; Duennweber, M. Factors determining desirability of entrepreneurship in Romania. *Sustainability* **2018**, *10*, 3893. [CrossRef]

81. Zamfir, A.M.; Mocanu, C.; Grigorescu, A. Resilient Entrepreneurship among European Higher Education Graduates. *Sustainability* **2018**, *10*, 2594. [CrossRef]

82. World Bank. *Doing Business 2020: Comparing Business Regulation in 190 Economies*; World Bank: Washington, DC, USA, 2020; Available online: http://documents.worldbank.org/curated/en/688761571934946384/pdf/Doing-Business-2020-Comparing-Business-Regulation-in-190-Economies.pdf (accessed on 20 May 2020).

83. European Commission/EACEA/Eurydice. Entrepreneurship education at school in Europe. 2016. Available online: https://op.europa.eu/en/publication-detail/-/publication/74a7d356-dc53-11e5-8fea-01aa75ed71a1 (accessed on 22 March 2020).

8

Flourishing Women through Sustainable Tourism Entrepreneurship

Murude Ertac * and Cem Tanova

Faculty of Tourism, Eastern Mediterranean University, 99628 Gazimagusa, North Cyprus, via Mersin 10, Turkey;
cem.tanova@emu.edu.tr
* Correspondence: murude.ertac@emu.edu.tr

Abstract: As a small island in the Mediterranean Sea, Cyprus must develop a sustainable tourism model. Although the ongoing political problems in Cyprus provide additional challenges, the number and activities of women ecotourism entrepreneurs demonstrated an inspiring growth over the last decade in the northern part of Cyprus. The well-being and flourishing of these women entrepreneurs influence their participation and further involvement in the sector. Psychological empowerment plays a significant role in achieving a flourishing society, and our results reveal that ecotourism can be used to create positive change in women's lives. We study how the mindsets and flourishing levels of these ecotourism entrepreneurs are related and how empowerment can change the direction of this relationship. Our research model was developed based on the self-Determination theory. Surveys were distributed to 200 women ecotourism entrepreneurs in rural areas of Northern Cyprus. We demonstrate that women who have growth mindsets, i.e., those that believe people's characteristics such as abilities are not fixed, experience lower levels of flourishing, perhaps contrary to what some might expect. This result may be due to the presence of gender inequality and may be an outcome of living in a region where a frozen conflict places additional external constraints on women entrepreneurs. However, as we predict, psychological empowerment changes the direction of this relationship. When psychological empowerment is high, women with a higher level of growth mindset experience a greater level of flourishing, even in an unfavorable context. This is the first study which analyzes women ecotourism entrepreneurs in Northern Cyprus. Moreover, this is the first study that focuses on the relationship between growth mindset, flourishing and psychological empowerment. The results can be used by governmental and non-governmental organizations as a source in their decision-making processes while managing and coordinating microfinance opportunities for rural development to support women's empowerment and well-being.

Keywords: ecotourism; women entrepreneurship; self-determination theory; psychological empowerment; flourishing; growth mindset

---

Highlights

Growth mindset and the flourishing level of women ecotourism entrepreneurs have a significantly negative relationship in Northern Cyprus.

Psychological empowerment has an interaction effect that changes the direction of this relationship, toward a significantly positive relationship.

Ecotourism is a tool to empower women living in rural areas.

1. Introduction

As a Mediterranean island with ample sunshine and beautiful beaches, Cyprus has long been a tourism destination. Although the political problem that divides the north and south has resulted in two separate administrations, both sides had focused on mass tourism strategies for rapid economic results but have recently become increasingly concerned with the potential damage that mass tourism may have on the environment and the issue of sustainability. In the past, policy makers developed incentive systems to attract large-scale investments, but now there is more interest in encouraging smaller-scale and sustainable tourism offerings which involve the local population. Northern Cyprus has seen an increase in women ecotourism entrepreneurs, who have been encouraged by community development programs and festivals [1].

Tourism is one of the routes through which women can be integrated into economic and social life [2], and entrepreneurship may help women, particularly those who live in rural areas where the job opportunities are limited, to increase their self-reliance and empowerment. Especially for the women who live in rural areas, the development of ecotourism can provide work opportunities. Taking part in ecotourism activities gives those women the freedom to earn their own money and be economically independent, which also enhances their social condition [3].

Although there has been increased interest in academic studies of ecotourism and entrepreneurship in general, we still lack an understanding of the factors that lead to well-being among ecotourism entrepreneurs [4]. In particular, the factors influencing the success of women ecotourism entrepreneurs whose empowerment and involvement can have significant social impact have not received adequate attention in the existing literature. To provide a better understanding of the impact of ecotourism on the lives of the women ecotourism entrepreneurs who typically did not have prior professional experience, we investigated how their mindsets, based on how empowered they feel, influence their well-being and feelings of flourishing.

Studies on mindset have generally argued that those with a growth mindset will perceive social and personal attributes as changeable, will have more positive emotional experiences and thus will have higher levels of thriving, flourishing and fulfillment [5,6]. However, more recent research has revealed that the positive results of growth mindset require certain contexts in which these positive outcomes could be possible [7]. In the current study, in the context of Northern Cyprus, where gender inequality and a frozen conflict place restrictions on women, we expect to see a negative relationship between growth mindset and the level of flourishing due to these restrictions. Based on the previous studies [8–10] we expect that women entrepreneurs who believe in themselves and want to take actions to control their lives will be more frustrated if they are held back as a result of these external factors and their flourishing level is lessened.

Contribution of the Study

The current study examines the mindset and flourishing relationship among ecotourism entrepreneurs in Northern Cyprus and explores how psychological empowerment through sustainable tourism can enable them to reach higher levels of thriving and flourishing. The study provides findings from a context that may be considered less supportive for growth mindset women entrepreneurs. Furthermore, by investigating how the impact of empowerment may influence the mindset–flourishing relationship, the study contributes to the theoretical discussions in the mindset literature.

2. Theoretical Background and Hypotheses Development

2.1. Theoretical Background

2.1.1. Well-Being and Flourishing

Flourishing means having a good life. It is a feeling of well-being, both physical and mental. It means the highest level of psychological well-being [11–13]. The concept of well-being can be defined as a multi-dimensional construct that considers hedonic (experience of pleasure) and eudemonic (the experience of meaning or accomplishment) ideas of prosperity [14]. However, the eudemonic and hedonic dimensions work simultaneously. A life rich in both hedonic and eudemonic aspects leads to the maximum level of well-being or flourishing. Therefore, combined feelings of accomplishment, which are higher-order (eudemonic) experiences, and feelings of pleasure, which are lower-order (hedonic) experiences, differentiate the concept of higher levels of well-being from the concept of the mere absence of suffering. When we experience personal achievement, meaningful creative contribution, altruistic experiences, these will not only count as eudemonic experiences but also provide hedonic pleasure.

Evaluating the flourishing levels of individuals is important because findings prove that flourishing is essential for societies and organizations [15]. Just as accounting is used to understand the financial health of organizations and countries, we are seeing more interest in taking measurements of well-being to understand their emotional health. Policy makers are becoming more interested in developing policies that will enhance the well-being of societies in a more balanced way. The World Health Organization (WHO), the European Public Health Association (EUPHA) and the European Commission (EC) have emphasized the importance of linking planning and health instead of treating them as separate domains [16].

Studies show that flourishing also brings benefits to the community in terms of improved public health [15,17].

VanderWeele and VanderWeele et al. indicate that flourishing is not limited to improved psychological well-being but also includes every facet of an individual's life [18,19]. Therefore, different areas of flourishing have been studied. Feeling happy and fulfilled, psychological and physical health, desires and ambitions, personality and honor, and social interactions can be listed as the different areas of flourishing. Furthermore, economic stability is also an important element in preserving flourishing.

Deci and Ryan (1985) suggest that in order to experience well-being, the basic psychological needs of competence, relatedness and autonomy must be met, as specified by the self-determination theory [8].

2.1.2. Implicit Person Theories

Carol Dweck, a well-known writer in the field of motivation, popularized the concept of "mindset" to demonstrate that the general beliefs that we have about whether people's characteristics are stable or malleable—our lay theories—will influence our attitudes and behaviors [20]. Dweck (1986) proposed that mindsets can be classified as fixed and growth [21]. People who have fixed mindsets believe that people's personal traits, such as knowledge, inventiveness and ability, are foreordained and stable characteristics [22]. Individuals with fixed mindsets accept that if a person is insufficient in some way, their situation will remain unchanged. On the other hand, people who have growth mindset trust that people's fundamental capacities can continue to improve through hard work and commitment. They believe that these natural traits are the initial stages for achieving accomplishments through learning, hard work and endurance. These assumptions or beliefs are also referred to as the implicit person theory (IPT), a particular presumption about the adaptability of a person's qualities that affect his or her conduct [21–23].

Dweck and her colleagues have focused on implicit person theories [24,25]. A person who possesses a fixed "implicit person theory"—also called entity theorist—will have a fixed outlook about people and trust that people's capacities are based on their fundamental abilities and are stable [20]. This leads them to think that these capacities are the reason for their level of success or failure. Such individuals are more likely to believe that their outcomes are due to their unchanging dispositional capacities and ignore situational factors [26].

2.1.3. Self-Determination Theory

Self-determination theory (SDT) is a comprehensive theory of motivation that encompasses several sub-theories. A distinction is made between autonomous motivation—feeling tempted to do something because we find it interesting or perceive it as our own wish—versus controlled motivation—feeling that something must be done because of some pressure or to satisfy someone else. However, SDT does not treat controlled and autonomous motivation as dichotomous, but accepts that they represent the theoretical maximum points of a continuum. As the level of autonomy increases, the type of motivation changes from controlled to autonomous.

SDT encompasses the Basic Psychological Needs Theory, which states that autonomy competence, relatedness and psychological needs must be met [8]. Thus, women ecotourism entrepreneurs need autonomy and freedom to decide and act independently, the competence to perform effectively and deal with financial, operational and managerial issues, and relatedness to find support from their contacts.

The cognitive evaluation theory, as a sub-theory of SDT, argues that the context may be supportive or controlling. A controlling context would use external conditional rewards or penalties, which for individuals already performing the task and getting intrinsic rewards from the task itself would mean a loss of autonomy. For example, in a non-profit organization where people were presumably engaged in their tasks due to the alignment of their personal values and goals with the organization, a loss of autonomy and intrinsic motivation was experienced after the introduction of merit pay systems [9]. For entrepreneurs that went into business with a desire to use their creativity and innovation, an environment with too many external conditions can lead to frustration. Women ecotourism entrepreneurs will experience this when they are operating under pressure from society to conform to certain norms that restrict their autonomy, competence and relatedness.

The causality orientation theory is also a sub-theory of SDT and focuses on the individual differences of general orientation in different people. Those with an autonomy orientation have a higher need for autonomy and those with a control orientation will be more comfortable with externally imposed deadlines and clear rules.

According to the self-determination theory, individuals from all societies have an essential psychological need for autonomy, capability and relatedness. It is argued that if these requirements are bolstered by social settings, flourishing is enhanced [8–10]. When the social context supports autonomy, and the individual has an autonomy orientation, this will increase motivation [9]. Furthermore, at a social level, Putnam [27,28] and Helliwel et al. [29] argue that the well-being of societies is also dependent on the social capital of individuals. Conversely, if the environment is controlling and the individual has an autonomy orientation, this may result in a loss of motivation. If the cultural context and other external environmental factors put restrictions and limitations on those necessities, the level of flourishing will decrease.

2.1.4. Women's Entrepreneurship and Ecotourism in Northern Cyprus

The inflexible roles and responsibilities of women that are imposed by society and cultural norms inherited from past generations should not be overlooked when discussing the position of women in work life. Women and men are exposed to certain gender restrictions from their birth to their death.

A UN Report on women shows that 70% of the global population who suffer from low living conditions are women. Although women work more than men, only 10% of world income goes to women, and they own less than 1% of the world's total assets [30]. Moreover, the number of uneducated women around the world is much higher than the number of uneducated men due to the inequalities that women face in society [28]. This is what encourages researchers to investigate ways to improve women's lives by searching for ways in which they can become involved in the workforce and take part in the world economy. As is widely known, if women change, the whole environment around them changes.

Women entrepreneurs, who are the focus of our research, contribute to the general economy of their country through their newly established businesses. Their willingness to achieve long-term success in the tourism industry affects the economy in a positive way. Worldwide, an increased number of women have started to participate in entrepreneurial exercises for money-related reasons as well as for psychological and social empowerment reasons. Most of these women entrepreneurs, however, also expect to have a balanced family life while engaging in their business activities [31,32].

According to prior research, women are more likely to be engaged in entrepreneurship that is directed at social and environmental problems [33]. Evidence confirms that necessity-based motivation factors are more common among female business entrepreneurs than among male business entrepreneurs. Various studies conducted in the USA, for instance, have demonstrated that female business entrepreneurs tend to be less affected than their male counterparts by the motivation to be more powerful, richer and to be their own boss. Rather, women tend to be inspired by earning an income in order to improve their standard of living [34].

In developing countries, studies have revealed that, for women, necessity motivation has a greater effect compared to opportunity motivation [35]. In developing countries, there is an increasing rise in the number of female entrepreneurs who conduct economic activities. The researchers mention that these women contribute to the general economy with their generous commitments. Heyzer [36] pointed out that those women who take part in the economy as small business owners have a significant effect on strengthening and improving women's living standards.

One of the routes through which women can be integrated into economic and social life is tourism [2]. With the development of tourism, numerous work opportunities for women have led them to employment and entrepreneurship. In addition, tourism gives them the freedom to earn their own money and be economically independent, which also enhances their social condition. Tourism is an important, employment-stimulating sector which is thriving around the world. It is estimated by the World Tourism Organization that approximately 96.7 million individuals are employed in the tourism sector; if indirect occupations are added to this amount, the sum is approximately 254 million employees [37,38]. This energetic industry is the principal source of national income, job creation and private sector growth in numerous nations.

In recent years, ecotourism has emerged as a means of long-term, sustainable community development [39]. Done properly, community-based ecotourism (CBET) should add to the natural preservation of wildlife and the environment and provide job opportunities for the community to obtain income [40]. To accomplish sustainable development in tourism, women should be encouraged to take part in tourism activities [3]. Excluding some special studies [38], gender has not been the main focus of research in ecotourism. However, there are many aspects of the gender perspective in ecotourism, as it is an important vehicle for women's entrepreneurship, especially in rural areas.

Knowing the importance of supporting women's entrepreneurship for its economic, social and psychological benefits, in our research, we chose women entrepreneurs who were involved in ecotourism activities in Northern Cyprus as our study population.

2.1.5. Cyprus as a Frozen Conflict Area

Cyprus is categorized and accepted as being a frozen conflict state, as there has been an ongoing political conflict between the recognized Republic of Cyprus and the unrecognized Turkish Republic of Northern Cyprus. The negotiations have continued for more than 40 years. In the meantime, Turkish Cypriots continue to live in an unrecognized country, faced with the consequences of a frozen conflict. Although the political problems thwart the possibility of a solution, people try to build a life where they satisfy their needs and try to achieve their goals. Like anywhere else, some choose to become entrepreneurs. In particular, women who live in rural areas, where job opportunities are limited, want to feel independent and empowered through entrepreneurship.

95% of the private sector in Northern Cyprus, consist of small- to medium-size businesses [41]. Furthermore, 80% of these businesses are sole proprietorship or family businesses [42]. According to a study, the appeal of working in the government sector and the limited availability of information, coupled with political and economic barriers, diminish the push factors for entrepreneurship as a career alternative [42]. However, the amount of women entrepreneurs in Northern Cyprus can be considered high according to the EU standards [43]. Although the push factors are not strong, people—mainly women who cannot find a governmental job—are pulled into entrepreneurship. They do so to be more social and to earn their own money, in order to become self-sufficient [43].

At that point, ecotourism plays an important role in empowering those women entrepreneurs, as Cyprus offers historical and natural beauty to tourists. However, tourism activities are limited and very difficult due to the state of frozen conflict. Economic and political embargoes, such as the lack of direct flights and being excluded from international organizations, cause problems and limit the opportunities. These limitations and uncertainty put psychological constraints on entrepreneurs. Those who have a growth mindset believe in change and believe they can achieve their goals, but also know and see the reality of the country they live in. This awareness leads them to feel less flourished and constrained.

In addition to the above-mentioned economic and political constraints, as Purrini [44] mentioned, women who live in these conflict zones, particularly in the rural regions, should be empowered, as they cannot take part of the decision making process. Women entrepreneurs should be supported and encouraged with training and financial support because the lack of capitalis a further major obstacle they face [45].

Due to the frozen conflict and its political consequences, Northern Cyprus has been mainly supported and influenced by Turkey since 1974. Therefore, Turkish culture and traditions have spread to the area. In the Gender Gap Report (2020) published by the World Economic Forum, Turkey is ranked 130 out of 153 countries, as shown in Table 1 [46]. This shows a clear gender inequality in the country and hence in Northern Cyprus as well. In 2016 and 2017, a study was conducted in Cyprus by the "Security Dialog Initiative", which is a non-governmental organization, together with the Gender Score Cyprus Project, implementing the Social Cohesion and Reconciliation (SCORE) index to determine the state of gender inequality in Northern Cyprus. The findings confirmed that Turkish Cypriot society is affected by a traditional culture where toxic masculinity is endorsed. According to this study, husbands' disciplinary actions toward their wives are backed by society. Also, society reduces the role of women to parenthood. The study shows that Turkish Cypriot women cannot freely express themselves in society; they feel that they are disadvantaged with regard to sharing family wealth, and they present lower levels of economic and political independence [47].

Table 1. Gender Gap in Turkey according to the Global Gap Index Report 2020.

Dimensions	Rank
Economic Participation and Opportunity	136/153
Educational Attainment	113/153
Health and Survival	64/153
Political Empowerment	109/153
Global Gender Gap Index	130/153

Powerful traditional gender roles lead society to expect women to be responsible for household duties and childcare. As a result of this work overload, women have very limited or no time to invest in themselves to improve their skills, have a hobby or join society and become involved in political activities. In addition to these findings, the most dramatic outcome of the study is that there is neither an awareness of gender inequality nor an understanding of the concept of gender equality. Both men and women accept gender inequality situations as norms and do not attempt to make any changes [47].

2.2. Hypotheses Development

2.2.1. Mindset and Flourishing

Previous studies have demonstrated the links between personality traits, well-being and flourishing [48]. Helliwell [49] found a direct connection between identity and well-being. Individuals with higher self-respect appear to be less inclined to experience despair. Hmieleski and Sheppard [50] argued that women entrepreneurs who are creative experience higher degrees of well-being and start-up business success. However, the self-determination theory says that individuals from all societies have an essential psychological need for autonomy, capability and relatedness. If these needs are bolstered by social settings, flourishing is enhanced. On the other hand, if the cultural context and other external environmental factors put restrictions and blockages on these needs, the level of flourishing declines [8–10].

Our research was conducted in Northern Cyprus, where gender inequality and frozen conflict play an important role, since these factors place restrictions on women. Therefore, we anticipate a negative relationship between growth mindset and the level of flourishing as a result of these restrictions. When women entrepreneurs believe in themselves and want to take actions for their lives, but are restricted as a result of these external factors, their flourishing level will be lessened compared to that of women who may already be convinced that change is not possible and accept their fate.

Therefore, based on the self-determination theory, we expect to see a negative impact of growth mindset on flourishing. We expect that people with growth mindset will think they can change things and achieve the things they want. However, in the context of Northern Cyprus, where they cannot make a change and achieve their goals due to the contextual limitations they face, they will be more frustrated and will experience less flourishing. Therefore, we developed our first hypothesis as follows:

Hypothesis 1 (H1). *Growth mindset has a negative relationship with flourishing.*

2.2.2. Psychological Empowerment, Growth Mindset and Flourishing

Elias and Ferguson [51]. define empowerment as the right of people to make individual choices, make their decisions on their own and have dignity. Researchers argue that the process of empowerment aims to enable individuals to obtain more power to become more self-reliant and self-confident people, to create their own way of living and, therefore, to become part of the process of social change [52].

According to Spreitzer [53] (p. 1443), "psychological empowerment refers to the intrinsic task motivation that results in feelings of competence, impact, task meaningfulness and self-determination related to the work-role". Empowering circumstances which provide the prospects for being independent pose a challenge, enhance accountability and make people appreciate what they have. In exchange, such appreciation leads to a sense of significance, proficiency, self-determination and power [54].

In the tourism context, when the inhabitants experience psychological empowerment they feel "pride" and "self-esteem", as they feel unique and think they have significant abilities and products to give to tourists [55]. Studies indicate that when citizens are not only involved but also empowered, their impact becomes much greater and leads to more sustainable efforts [56–58]. makes the distinction between mere involvement and empowerment and argues that empowerment is the "top end of the participation ladder where members of a community are active agents of change and they have the ability to find solutions to their problems, make decisions, implement actions and evaluate their solutions"[56] (p. 631). Community-based ecotourism where citizens are actively empowered socially, politically and psychologically is a key element of sustainable tourism [58].

Under normal circumstances, the relationship between the growth mindset and flourishing is expected to be positive [49]. However, people with a growth mindset who are restricted and thus disappointed by the conditions of the country they live in, when they repeatedly experience that in spite of their enthusiasm and efforts they cannot introduce the change that they believe could have been possible, and feel unappreciated, will not see themselves as valuable and useful [8]. Among the individuals with a higher level of growth mindset who believe that people and situations are not fixed but changeable, the constraints will lead to a feeling of unfulfilled potential.

However, we believe that women with higher levels of growth mindset will indeed experience greater flourishing if they are psychologically empowered through tourism. If there are community-based tourism activities in the regions where they live and if they are involved in, and empowered by, these sustainable tourism activities, they will feel useful and experience meaning in what they do [56]. Often, community-based tourism is supported by training and development and educational activities that contribute to empowerment. When women feel proud of themselves as they receive positive feedback from the tourists who appreciate their products, services and environment, they feel more competent, empowered to make decisions, useful and effective in their family and their community [58]. Women with a growth mindset who do not perceive or experience psychological empowerment know that they are capable of doing the things they want but, as a result of environmental pressures and obstacles, cannot. They cannot offer the services and products they want to offer freely to tourists when they are blocked by the people around them, such as their husband, father or neighbors, or restricted by the dominant norms of their community. Women with a growth mindset will feel even worse if they are accused of neglecting the household chores that they are expected to perform and have to ask permission to their husbands [8].

Based on the self-determination theory, we expect that maintaining women's empowerment will enhance their level of self-determination and lead to an increase in their subjective well-being. We believe that this relationship will be particularly stronger among the women entrepreneurs who have higher levels of growth mindset. Therefore, we expect to find a moderation effect of psychological empowerment that reverses the negative relationship between growth mindset and flourishing. As a result of this expectation, we developed our second hypothesis as follows:

Hypothesis 2 (H2). *Psychological empowerment interacts with the relationship between growth mindset and flourishing.*

3. Method

3.1. Model of the Study

This research applied a cross-sectional survey and regression analysis to assess how psychological empowerment through tourism interacts with the relationship between growth mindset and the level of flourishing of women entrepreneurs living in rural regions of Northern Cyprus.

Figure 1 shows the conceptual model and the hypotheses of this study. This model tests the effect of growth mindset on the flourishing of women entrepreneurs who live in rural parts of Northern Cyprus and engage in ecotourism activities (Hypothesis 1). The study also tested whether psychological empowerment through tourism interacts with the relationship between self-growth mindset and flourishing (Hypothesis 2).

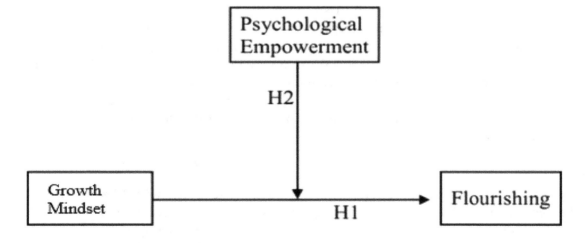

Figure 1. Conceptual Model.

3.2. Measures

To measure flourishing, the Turkish version of the Flourishing Scale, which has been adapted by Telef [59], was used in our study. To assess the psychological empowerment and growth mindsets of women entrepreneurs, the original scales were translated into Turkish and then translated back into English by two professional translators. They were compared with the original scales in order to check that the meanings of the items had been correctly translated into Turkish and would not be misinterpreted by the respondents. This process was performed according to the suggestions of Perrewé et al. [60]. Before distributing the questionnaires, a pilot study was completed to test that the questionnaires worked correctly. While preparing and distributing the questionnaires, the suggestions of Podsakoff, MacKenzie, Lee and Podsakoff [61] were applied to protect our study from common method bias.

3.2.1. Growth Mindset

Growth mindset was assessed with the 8-item implicit person theory created by Levy and Dweck [62]. This scale has 4 items associated with fixed mindset, like "As much as I hate to admit it, you can't teach an old dog new tricks. People can't really change their deepest attributes", and 4 items associated with growth mindset, like "People can always substantially change the kind of person they are". Respondents were asked to rate the items using a 6-point scale ranging from 1 (strongly disagree) and 6 (strongly agree). The previous research demonstrated the alpha coefficient of this scale to be 0.94, which shows the strong internal consistency of the scale [62]. We found the alpha coefficient of this scale to be 0.89 in our study.

3.2.2. Flourishing Scale

This scale consists of 8 items that evaluate respondents' perceived success in major segments of their lives, for example their self-esteem, how competent they feel or if they think they have a purpose in life. Initially, this scale was named the "Psychological Well-being Scale", but it was later changed to the "Flourishing Scale" to represent the content of the scale more accurately. The scale provides a single psychological well-being score [63]. The respondents were asked to rate answers on a 7-point Likert scale where 1 represents "strongly disagree" and 7 represents "strongly agree". One item, for example, reads: "I lead a purposeful and meaningful life." The scale's reliability has been demonstrated [63]. The Turkish version of the scale also had reliable results, with an alpha coefficient of 0.80 [59]. When we applied this scale in our study, we found a, alpha coefficient of 0.83.

3.2.3. Psychological Empowerment

Resident Empowerment through Tourism Scale (RETS) was used to assess the psychological empowerment of women entrepreneurs engaging in ecotourism activities, as it is a reliable and valid measurement tool that assesses residents' perceptions of empowerment [64]. The scale has 3 sections, to assess the psychological, political and social empowerment of residents through tourism. We have used the 5 items in the psychological empowerment subscale, consisting of statements such as "Tourism in . . . reminds me that I have a unique culture to share with visitors." or "Tourism in . . . makes me proud to be a . . . resident." The value of the alpha coefficient was 0.92 for this scale, which represents a strong construct reliability.

3.3. Questionnaire Administration

Following the suggestion of Hinkin [65], we applied a pilot study with 12 women entrepreneurs to test the items on a small scale before applying the survey on a larger scale. First, after the pilot study, to evaluate the substance and legitimacy of the scale items, some phrasings was corrected, as some of the words were found to be reasonably confusing, as suggested by DeVellis [66]. Essential modifications were made, and equivocal words were reworded.

Exploratory factor analysis (EFA) was applied using Varimax Rotation in IBM SPSS Statistics program to find conceptually incompatible items with a correlation threshold of 0.40, as suggested by Kim and Mueller [67]. The analyses revealed 3 factors that cumulatively explain 62% of the deviation, with eigenvalues above 1. The consistency of the items in the instruments used in the study was checked with the threshold Cronbach's alpha [68] of 0.70. One item from the flourishing scale had a loading below 0.50 and was eliminated, as recommended by Hair, Anderson, Tatham, Black and DeVellis [66,69].

Confirmatory factor analysis (CFA), as indicated by Hinkin [65], was used to assess the goodness of fit of the model and the items used in the model. The high loadings in the CFA demonstrate that the study has construct validity. Average Variance Extracted (AVE) and Composite Reliability (CR) were also used to ensure the internal consistency and illustrate the convergent and discriminant validity of the study.

3.4. Participants and Procedure

Context Population and Sampling

The purposive sample method was used. A list of sample populations was obtained from the Businesswomen Association of Northern Cyprus. The list consisted of 305 women entrepreneurs who were involved in ecotourism activities, such as traditional handcrafting and producing traditional food. The population also included boutique hotel or guesthouse owners and small restaurant owners who specialize in traditional foods. These women live in rural areas, mainly in small towns within five main regions of Northern Cyprus. Most of them were housewives before they became entrepreneurs. In each region, there is a mentor who helps these women in their operations. Generally, the mentors are the leaders of local women's associations or, in some regions, mayors who are taking on the responsibility of leading ecotourism activities in their region and providing support to women entrepreneurs. We visited these towns to meet these women in person. The list we used was not particularly applicable, as most of the women were no longer engaged in these activities, and some of them were unreachable. Therefore, we found a woman entrepreneur from each town and through her, using the snowball technique, reached out to other women. We contacted 200 women and asked them to complete the questionnaire. Data were collected in the period between April and June 2018 by visiting the women and in their respective locations. Questionnaires were distributed to those women entrepreneurs, and we kindly requested that they complete these questionnaires after we explained to them our research purposes and how we maintained the confidentiality of our research. We asked them to complete the questionnaires, which consisted of four sections, including a demographic information section. Our aim was to gather information on self-growth mindsets, women's psychological empowerment through tourism and women's flourishing.

Figure 2 shows the locations where the data was collected, and Table 2 presents the demographic profiles of the respondents. The sample consisted of 200 women respondents from 15 villages located in rural parts of Northern Cyprus. Only 6 of them, representing 3% of the population, were younger than 25. This means that young women are less involved in the ecotourism sector in Northern Cyprus. Only 18 (9%) of them had undergraduate degrees, and 15 (7.5%) were postgraduate degree holders. This information shows that women with university education are less likely to be engaged in ecotourism entrepreneurship activities in rural areas.

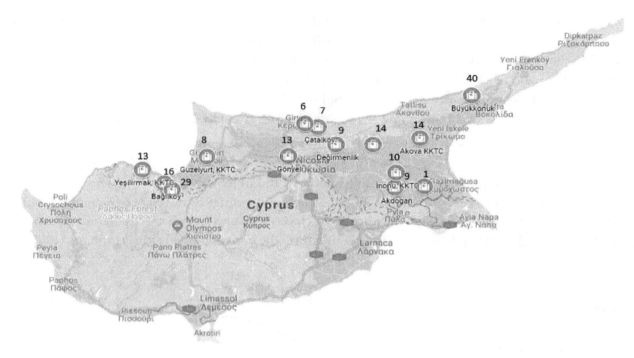

Figure 2. Number of Ecotourism Entrepreneurs Participating in the Study by Region.

Table 2. Respondents' profile ($n = 200$).

Age	N	%	Years of Experience	N	%	Education	N	%	No. of Children	N	%	Marital Status	N	%
<25	6	3	<1 year	14	7	Primary School Diploma	49	24.5	0	20	10	Single	17	8.5
25–34	37	18.5	1–3 years	32	16	Secondary School Diploma	43	21.5	1	25	12.5	In a relationship	3	1.5
35–44	40	20	4–6 years	42	21	High School Diploma	75	37.5	2	93	46.5	Married	156	78
>44	117	58.5	>6 years	112	55.5	Bachelor's Degree	18	9	3	52	26	Divorced	4	2
						Postgraduate Degree	15	7.5	>3	10	5	Separated	1	0.5
												Widowed	19	9.5
Total	200	100	Total	200	100	Total	200	100	Total	200	100	Total	200	100

4. Results

We applied confirmatory factor analyses using the AMOS software to examine the goodness of fit of our study model. The findings are illustrated in Table 3. The fit indicators show figures that are accepted as good fit indications according to the thresholds shown in Table 3.

All items show high loadings in their underlying variables. Table 3 shows that the Cronbach's alpha figures are greater than the threshold of 0.70 [68] and that CRs are greater than the accepted level of 0.70 [70]. Average Variance Extracted (AVE) figures are also greater than the cut-off figure of 0.50 [69].

The figures obtained from the analyses, which are shown in Tables 3 and 4, show proof of convergent and discriminant validity. The potential risk of common method bias was handled utilizing an analytical methodology. Harman's single-factor test explained 32.25% of the variance; therefore, the possible danger of common method bias appears to have been reduced [61].

Table 3. Goodness of fit of the model.

N = 200	Cut-Off Points
$\chi^2 = 759$	
df = 199, p = 000	
GFI = 0.863	1 = maximum fit (Tanaka & Huba, 1985)
NFI = 0.861	1 = maximum fit (Bentler & Bonett, 1980)
CFI = 0.91	1 = maximum fit (McDonald & Marsh, 1990)
RMSEA = 0.087	<0.08 = good fit (Browne & Cudeck, 1993)
C_{MIN}/df = 2.523	>1 and <5 = good fit (Marsh & Hocevar, 1985)
VIF = 1.010	< 3 = good fit (Hair et al., 2018)

Notes: GFI: Goodness of fit indices, NFI: Normed fit index, CFI: Comparative Fit Index, RMSEA: Root Mean Square Error of Approximation, C_{MIN}/df, relative $\chi2$.

Table 4. Means, SD and correlations of the study variables.

Variables	1	2	3	Mean	SD	CR	α	AVE
1. Flourishing	-			6.22	0.82	0.88	0.833	0.51
2. Psychological Empowerment	0.381 **	-		4.53	0.75	0.93	0.919	0.71
3. Growth Mindset	−0.223 **	−0.143 *	-	2.42	1.18	0.91	0.894	0.57

Notes: Composite scores for each variable were computed by averaging the respective item scores. * Correlations are significant at the 0.05 level. ** Correlations are significant at the 0.01 level.

Table 4 shows the means, standard deviations and correlation estimates of the variables used in our study. As hypothesized, growth mindset and the level of flourishing of women entrepreneurs are negatively related (r = −0.223, p < 0.01). This result provides support for Hypothesis 1.

Table 5 shows that Hypothesis 2, which anticipated that psychological empowerment would moderate the relationship between growth mindset and flourishing, is supported, as we can see a significant level of interaction terms (β = 0.260, p < 0.01).

Table 5. Flourishing as predicted by Growth Mindset and Psychological Empowerment.

Variables	Step 1	Step 2
	$\beta(t)$	$\beta(t)$
Growth Mindset	−0.171 (−2.620) **	−0.156 (−2.523)
Psychological Empowerment	0.357 (5.449) **	0.235 (3.542) **
Interaction term	-	0.260 (4.996) **
F	20.754	23.838
R^2	0.174	0.267
ΔR^2	-	0.093 **

Note: Interaction terms = Growth mindset x Psychological empowerment level ** Significant at the 0.01 level (2-tailed).

Therefore, complete support was reached. The research outcome approved the model of interest, as all hypothesized relationships were supported. Figure 3 shows the interaction effect of psychological empowerment in the relationship between growth mindset and flourishing.

As clearly seen in Figure 3, this study proves that when the psychological empowerment is low, women entrepreneurs' level of flourishing declines when their growth mindset level increases. When we enter a low value of empowerment at 1 standard deviation below its mean, the estimated beta for mindset in predicting flourishing is negative (−0.27), whereas when we enter a high value of empowerment at 1 standard deviation above its mean value, the estimated beta for mindset in predicting flourishing is positive (0.15). This can be explained by the negative impact of gender inequality and the frozen conflict conditions in Cyprus. Women entrepreneurs are negatively affected when they believe that they can change and improve their skills, but also that they will not accomplish their dreams due to the limitations they face in their community. However, when we add psychological empowerment to this relationship, the negative result is reversed to a positive one, which shows that if we empower women entrepreneurs psychologically through tourism, they will feel strong and empowered, and this will change the relationship between growth mindset and flourishing. When the women are psychologically empowered, their growth mindset will lead to a more fulfilled, happier life, although there are many constraints that they still have to face.

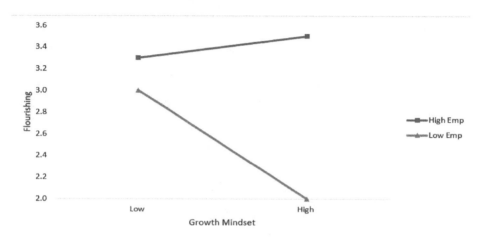

Figure 3. Slopes showing how Growth Mindset influences Flourishing differently under high and low Psychological Empowerment conditions.

5. Discussion and Conclusions

In the relatively unfavorable entrepreneurial ecosystem and restrictive social context of Northern Cyprus, empowerment through ecotourism activities can enable especially women with a growth mindset to experience higher levels of well-being. Psychologically empowering growth-mindset women entrepreneurs improves their autonomy and self-belief, which leads them to flourish. This will not only benefit the women who become ecotourism entrepreneurs but also society and the economy overall. There will be a positive impact on the GDP through an increased female employment rate, and the knowledge, skills and capabilities that women gain will contribute to the overall well-being of society. Furthermore, a UNESCO (2019) [71] report shows that empowering women has significant benefits for the environment and argues that when women have a larger role in governance in society, the sensitivity to the social and environmental impacts of policies increases.

However, we note that the impact of empowerment through tourism is less felt by women who have a lower growth mindset or fixed mindset. Those with a fixed mindset are likely to believe that characteristics are generally stable and impossible to change; therefore, they may not be so concerned or motivated in the first place to introduce change in themselves and their communities. Thus, they may be less likely to utilize the opportunities introduced by empowerment, and their level of well-being does not change as much as that of women with a high growth mindset, who feel more confident to pursue their dreams and create change in their lives by taking action.

Many scholars and practitioners also believe that it is possible to increase the growth mindset through interventions [7]. Especially in the field of education, there are many applications and recommendations on how teachers can develop a growth mindset amongst their students. For example, the use of a metaphor such as "the brain is similar to a muscle that needs to be exercised through learning and grows stronger and smarter as a result." This metaphor is reinforced by the teachers and replaces any belief that our talents, abilities and capacity is fixed and there is nothing we can do about it. Similarly, Dweck [20] argues that this can be extended to leadership and management, where managers can develop cultures where people believe in their own and other people's ability to change and develop. These cultures would value trial and error as part of the process of development and not penalize individuals for taking the initiative to try something new, even if it does not always succeed.

The mindset literature has generally advocated the value of growth mindset. Our study reveals that growth mindset without empowerment will not lead to flourishing. Thus, we contribute to the mindset literature and theories by showing how empowerment is a critical factor that can enable those with growth mindset to achieve higher levels of flourishing.

5.1. Practical Implications of This Study

We believe that if women change, their surroundings will change as well. From this perspective, this study proves that the key to happiness for women is to become psychologically empowered, and shows that ecotourism can be used as a means to create positive change in women's lives. Governmental and non-governmental organizations should support microfinance opportunities for rural development in such a way as to support women's empowerment and well-being. Additionally, the study clearly illustrates that the authorities should provide training programs to support women who live in rural areas of Northern Cyprus, to teach them new skills and to empower them. As the study demonstrates, higher levels of empowerment will enable the increased flourishing and well-being of women entrepreneurs. International organizations such as the United Nations and the European Union, which are already active in Northern Cyprus to help the community to develop and to reach a political solution in Cyprus, should also further support ecotourism and enhance their activities to help local NGOs and potential women entrepreneurs, who can be included in ecotourism. Moreover, as suggested by Sdino and Magoni, shared housing associated with ecotourism can be introduced for these women in order to help them earn their own money and contribute to ecotourism [72].

The programs to empower women ecotourism entrepreneurs should not only offer support by delivering know-how or helping to eliminate barriers but also include interventions to increase growth mindset. However, some findings show that the results of such interventions may be temporary [7]. Therefore programs to develop growth mindset must be systematic. Conscious efforts for the empowerment of women entrepreneurs are also needed to develop supportive environments where peer norms encourage challenge seeking and adaptive attitudes.

The findings of this study can be used by governmental, non-governmental and international organizations to design new programs and organize capacity-building activities such as training programs, workshops and field trips at the grassroots level with current and potential women entrepreneurs.

5.2. Limitations and Future Research

A qualitative study should be conducted to gain deeper insights related to our findings. Additionally, the scope of our study included only women entrepreneurs in Northern Cyprus, and future studies may replicate this study in other geographical regions to see how cultural and other contextual factors affect the relationship between growth mindset, psychological empowerment and the flourishing of women entrepreneurs.

Author Contributions: Conceptualization, M.E. and C.T.; methodology, M.E. and C.T.; investigation, M.E.; formal analysis, C.T. and M.E.; writing and original draft preparation, M.E. and C.T.; writing, review and editing, C.T. and M.E.; visualization, M.E. and C.T.; supervision, C.T. All authors have read and agreed to the published version of the manuscript.

References

1.   Gunsoy, E.; Hannam, K. Festivals, community development and sustainable tourism in the Karpaz region of Northern Cyprus. *J. Policy Res. Tour. Leis. Events* **2013**, *5*, 81–94. [CrossRef]
2.   Goeldner, C.R.; Ritchie, J.R.B. *Tourism: Principles, Practices, Philosophies*; John Wiley & Sons: Hoboken, NJ, USA, 2009.

3. Shokouhi, A.K.; Khoshfar, G.; Karimi, L. The Role of Tourism in Rural Women's Empowerment, Case Study: Village Ziarat City of Gorgan, Planning and Development of Tourism, the First Year. *Geogr. Plan. Space J.* **2013**, *3*, 151–179.
4. Thompson, B.S.; Gillen, J.; Friess, D.A. Challenging the principles of ecotourism: Insights from entrepreneurs on environmental and economic sustainability in Langkawi, Malaysia. *J. Sustain. Tour.* **2018**, *26*, 257–276. [CrossRef]
5. Howell, A.J. Implicit theories of personal and social attributes: Fundamental mindsets for a science of wellbeing. *Int. J. Wellbeing* **2016**, *6*, 113–130. [CrossRef]
6. Brown, K.W.; Ryan, R.M. The benefits of being present: Mindfulness and its role in psychological well-being. *J. Pers. Soc. Psychol.* **2003**, *84*, 822–848. [CrossRef] [PubMed]
7. Yeager, D.S.; Hanselman, P.; Walton, G.M.; Murray, J.S.; Crosnoe, R.; Muller, C.; Tipton, E.; Schneider, B.; Hulleman, C.S.; Hinojosa, C.P.; et al. A national experiment reveals where a growth mindset improves achievement. *Nature* **2019**, *573*, 364–369. [CrossRef] [PubMed]
8. Deci, E.L.; Ryan, R.M. *Intrinsic Motivation and Self-Determination in Human Behavior*; Plenum: New York, NY, USA, 1985.
9. Gagne, M.; Deci, E.L. Self-determination theory and work motivation. *J. Organ. Behav.* **2005**, *26*, 331–362. [CrossRef]
10. Ryan, R.M.; Deci, E.L. Self-determination theory and the facilitation of intrinsic motivation, social development, and well-being. *Am. Psychol.* **2000**, *55*, 68. [CrossRef]
11. Huppert, F.A. A new approach to reducing disorder and improving well-being. *Perspect. Psychol. Sci.* **2009**, *4*, 108–111. [CrossRef]
12. Keyes, C.L. The mental health continuum: From languishing to flourishing in life. *J. Health Soc. Behav.* **2002**, *43*, 207–222. [CrossRef]
13. Ryff, C.D.; Singer, B. The Contours of Positive Human Health. *Psychol. Inq.* **1998**, *9*, 1–28. [CrossRef]
14. Huta, V.; Ryan, R.M. Pursuing pleasure or virtue: The differential and overlapping well-being benefits of hedonic and eudaimonic motives. *J. Happiness Stud.* **2010**, *11*, 735–762. [CrossRef]
15. Howell, A.J. Flourishing: Achievement-related correlates of students' well-being. *J. Posit. Psychol.* **2009**, *4*, 1–13. [CrossRef]
16. Fehr, R.; Capolongo, S. Healing environment and urban health. *Epidemiol. Prev.* **2016**, *40*, 151–152. [CrossRef]
17. Keyes, C.L. Flourishing. In *The Corsini Encyclopedia of Psychology*; Weiner, I.B., Craighead, W.E., Eds.; John Wiley & Sons: Hoboken, NJ, USA, 2010.
18. Vanderweele, T.J. On the promotion of human flourishing. *Proc. Natl. Acad. Sci. USA* **2017**, *114*, 8148–8156. [CrossRef]
19. VanderWeele, T.J.; McNeely, E.; Koh, H.K. Reimagining Health—Flourishing. *JAMA* **2019**, *321*, 1667. [CrossRef]
20. Dweck, B.C.S. Ingredients of a Winning Mindset. In *Mindset: The New Psychology of Success*; Ballentine: New York, NY, USA, 2006; pp. 1–7.
21. Dweck, C.S. Motivational processes affecting learning. *Am. Psychol.* **1986**, *41*, 1040. [CrossRef]
22. Kam, C.; Risavy, S.D.; Perunovic, E.; Plant, L. Do subordinates formulate an impression of their manager's implicit person theory? *Appl. Psychol.* **2014**, *63*, 267–299. [CrossRef]
23. Heslin, P.A.; VandeWalle, D. Performance appraisal procedural justice: The role of a manager's implicit person theory. *J. Manag.* **2011**, *37*, 1694–1718. [CrossRef]
24. Dweck, C.S.; Leggett, E.L. A social-cognitive approach to motivation and personality. *Psychol. Rev.* **1988**, *95*, 256. [CrossRef]
25. Diveck, C.S.; Molden, D.C. *Self-Theories: Their Impact on Competence Motivation and Acquisition*; Eliot, A.J., Dweck, C.S., Eds.; APA: Washington, DC, USA, 2005.
26. Levontin, L.; Halperin, E.; Dweck, C.S. Implicit theories block negative attributions about a longstanding adversary: The case of Israelis and Arabs. *J. Exp. Soc. Psychol.* **2013**, *49*, 670–675. [CrossRef]
27. Putnam, R.D. *Bowling Alone: The Collapse and Revival of American Community*; Simon and Schuster: New York, NY, USA, 2000.
28. Bansal, S.P.; Kumar, J. Ecotourism for Community Development: A Stakeholder's Perspective in Great Himalayan National Park. In *Creating a Sustainable Ecology Using Technology-Driven Solutions*; IGI Global: Hershey, PA, USA, 2013.

29. Helliwell, J.F.; Barrington-Leigh, C.; Harris, A.; Huang, H. International Evidence on the Social Context of Well-Being. In *International Differences in Well-Being*; Oxford University Press: Oxford, UK, 2010; pp. 291–327.

30. UN Women Annual Report 2017–2018. Available online: https://annualreport.unwomen.org/en/2018 (accessed on 1 February 2019).

31. Li, Y.; Zhang, L.; Gao, Y.; Huang, Z.; Cui, L.; Liu, S.; Fang, Y.; Ren, G.; Fornacca, D.; Xiao, W. Ecotourism in China, misuse or genuine development? *An analysis based on map browser results. Sustainability* **2019**, *11*, 1–15. [CrossRef]

32. Itani, H.; Sidani, Y.M.; Baalbaki, I. United Arab Emirates female entrepreneurs: Motivations and frustrations. *Equal. Divers. Incl.* **2011**, *30*. [CrossRef]

33. Hechavarria, D.M.; Ingram, A.; Justo, R.; Terjesen, S. Are women more likely to pursue social and environmental entrepreneurship? In *Global Women's Entrepreneurship Research: Diverse Settings, Questions and Approaches*; Edward Elgar Publishing: Cheltenham, UK, 2012.

34. Kelley, D.J.; Brush, C.G.; Greene, G.P.; Litovsky, Y. *Report: Women Entrepreneurs Worldwide*; Babson College and the Global Entrepreneurship Research Association (GERA): London, UK, 2010.

35. Carter, S.L.; Anderson, S.; Shaw, E. *Women's Business Ownership: A Review of the Academic, Popular and Internet Literature*; University of Strathclyde: Glasgow, UK, 2001.

36. Heyzer, N. Smart development: Gender equality key to achieving the MDGs. In *Proceedings of the 61st Session of the UN General Assembly, Second Committee, Agenda Item 58, New York, NY, USA, 2 November 2006*; UN: New York, NY, USA, 2006.

37. World Tourism Organization. *2017 Annual Report*; UNWTO: Madrid, Spain, 2018.

38. Reimer, J.K.; Walter, P. How do you know it when you see it? Community-based ecotourism in the Cardamom Mountains of southwestern Cambodia. *Tour. Manag.* **2013**, *34*, 122–132. [CrossRef]

39. Scheyvens, R. Exploring the Tourism-Poverty Nexus. *Curr. Issues Tour.* **2007**, *10*, 231–254. [CrossRef]

40. Butler, R.; Hinch, T. *Tourism and Indigenous Peoples: Issues and Implications*; Butterworth-Heinemann: London, UK, 2007.

41. Tanova, C. Firm size and recruitment: Staffing practices in small and large organisations in north Cyprus. *Career Dev. Int.* **2003**, *8*, 107–114. [CrossRef]

42. Güven Lisaniler, F. Challenges in SME development: North Cyprus. In *Workshop on Investment and Finance in North Cyprus*; Oxford University: Oxford, UK, 2004.

43. Howells, K.; Krivokapic-Skoko, B. Constraints on Female Entrepreneurship in Northern Cyprus. *Kadin/Woman* **2000**, *8*, 29–58.

44. Purrini, M.K. Economic Empowerment of Rural Women through Enterprise Development in Post-Conflict Settings. Expert Group Meeting "Enabling rural women's economic empowerment: Institutions, opportunities and participation". In Proceedings of the Kosovo Women's Business Association, Gjakove, Kosovo, 20–23 September 2011.

45. Ramadani, V.; Rexhepi, G.; Abazi-Alili, H.; Beqiri, B.; Thaçi, A. A look at female entrepreneurship in Kosovo: An exploratory study. *J. Enterp. Communities* **2015**, *9*, 277–294. [CrossRef]

46. Global Gender Gap Report 2020. Available online: http://www3.weforum.org/docs/WEF_GGGR_2020.pdf (accessed on 1 February 2019).

47. Project, G.S.C. The Score For Peace. 2018. Available online: https://scoreforpeace.org/files/publication/pub_file//PB_GenderCy17_TCcPolicyBriefWeb_30052018_ID.pdf (accessed on 1 March 2019).

48. DeNeve, K.M.; Cooper, H. The happy personality: A meta-analysis of 137 personality traits and subjective well-being. *Psychol. Bull.* **1998**, *124*, 197–229. [CrossRef]

49. Helliwell, J.F. Well-Being, Social Capital and Public Policy: What's New? *Econ. J.* **2006**, *116*, C34–C45. [CrossRef]

50. Hmieleski, K.M.; Sheppard, L.D. The Yin and Yang of entrepreneurship: Gender differences in the importance of communal and agentic characteristics for entrepreneurs' subjective well-being and performance. *J. Bus. Ventur.* **2019**, *34*, 709–730. [CrossRef]

51. Elias, J.; Ferguson, L. The gender dimensions of New Labour's international development policy. In *New Labour and Women: Engendering Policy and Politics*; Annesley, C., Gains, F., Rummery, K., Eds.; Policy Press: Bristol, UK, 2007; pp. 211–228.

52. Bystydzienski, J. *Women Transforming Politics: Worldwide Strategies for Empowerment*; Indiana University Press: Bloomington, IN, USA, 1992.

53.   Spreitzer, G.M. Psychological empowerment in the workplace: Dimensions, measurement, and validation. *Acad. Manag. J.* **1995**, *38*, 1442–1465.

54.   Liden, R.C.; Wayne, S.J.; Sparrowe, R.T. An examination of the mediating role of psychological empowerment on the relations between the job, interpersonal relationships, and work outcomes. *J. Appl. Psychol.* **2000**, *85*, 407–416. [CrossRef] [PubMed]

55.   Di Castri, F. Sustainable tourism in small islands: Local empowerment as the key factor. *Int. J. Island Aff.* **2004**, *13*, 49–55.

56.   Cole, S. Information and empowerment: The keys to achieving sustainable tourism. *J. Sustain. Tour.* **2006**, *14*, 629–644. [CrossRef]

57.   Petric, L. Empowerment of communities for sustainable tourism development: Case of Croatia. *Tour. Int. Discip. J.* **2007**, *55*, 431–443.

58.   Scheyvens, R. Ecotourism and the empowerment of local communities. *Tour. Manag.* **1999**, *20*, 245–249. [CrossRef]

59.   Telef, B.B. The validity and reliability of the Turkish version of the psychological well-being. In Proceedings of the 11th National Congress of Counseling and Guidance, Selcuk-Izmir, Turkey, 3–5 October 2001.

60.   Perrewé, P.L.; Hochwarter, W.A.; Rossi, A.M.; Wallace, A.; Maignan, I.; Castro, S.L.; Ralston, D.A.; Westman, M.; Vollmer, G.; Tang, M.; et al. Are work stress relationships universal? A nine-region examination of role stressors, general self-efficacy, and burnout. *J. Int. Manag.* **2002**, *8*, 163–187. [CrossRef]

61.   Podsakoff, P.M.; MacKenzie, S.B.; Lee, J.-Y.; Podsakoff, N.P. Common method biases in behavioral research: A critical review of the literature and recommended remedies. *J. Appl. Psychol.* **2003**, *88*, 879–903. [CrossRef]

62.   Levy, S.R.; Stroessner, S.J.; Dweck, C.S. Stereotype formation and endorsement: The role of implicit theories. *J. Pers. Soc. Psychol.* **1998**, *74*, 1421–1436. [CrossRef]

63.   Chem, I.; The, M.; Financial, A. R(0.86). *Chart* **2003**, *81*, 2001–2004.

64.   Boley, B.B.; McGehee, N.G. Measuring empowerment: Developing and validating the Resident Empowerment through Tourism Scale (RETS). *Tour. Manag.* **2014**, *45*, 85–94. [CrossRef]

65.   Hinkin, T.R. A Brief Tutorial on the Development of Measures for Use in Survey Questionnaires. *Organ. Res. Methods* **1998**, *1*, 104–121. [CrossRef]

66.   DeVellis, R.F. *Scale Development: Theory and Applications*; Sage Publications Inc.: Thousand Oaks, CA, USA, 2012.

67.   Kim, J.; Mueller, C.W. *Introduction to Factor Analysis: What It Is and how to Do It*; Sage Publications: Beverly Hills, CA, USA, 1978.

68.   Nunnally, J.C.; Bernstein, I.H. The assessment of reliability. In *Psychometric Theory*; McGraw Hill: New York, NY, USA, 1994.

69.   Hair, J.F.; Black, W.C.; Babin, B.J.; Anderson, R.E.; Tatham, R.L. *Multivariate Data Analysis*; Prentice-Hall: Upper Saddle River, NJ, USA, 2006.

70.   Hair, J.F.; Anderson, R.E.; Tatham, R.L.; Black, W.C. *Multivariate Data Analysis*; Prentice-Hall: Upper Saddle River, NJ, USA, 1998.

71.   Global Education Monitoring Report 2019: Migration, Displacement and Education: Building Bridges, Not Walls. Available online: https://en.unesco.org/gem-report/infographics/2019-gem-report-migration-displacement-and-education-building-bridges-not-walls (accessed on 1 March 2019).

72.   Sdino, L.; Magoni, S. The Sharing Economy and Real Estate Market: The Phenomenon of Shared Houses. In Proceedings of the International Conference on Smart and Sustainable Planning for Cities and Regions, Bolzano, Italy, 22–24 March 2018; pp. 241–251.

9

Entrepreneurship and Innovation in Soccer: Web of Science Bibliometric Analysis

Paloma Escamilla-Fajardo [1], Juan Manuel Núñez-Pomar [1,*], Vanessa Ratten [2] and Josep Crespo [1]

[1] Department of Physical Education and Sport, Faculty of Physical Activity and Sport Sciences, University of Valencia, Gascó Oliag 3, 46010 Valencia, Spain; paloma.escamilla@uv.es (P.E.-F.); josep.crespo@uv.es (J.C.)

[2] La Trobe Business, La Trobe University, Plenty Rd & Kingsbury Dr, Bundoora VIC, Melbourne 3086, Australia; V.Ratten@latrobe.edu.au

* Correspondence: juan.m.nunez@uv.es

Abstract: According to the existing literature, there is growing interest in the sports industry by individuals involved in entrepreneurship and innovation. However, no bibliometric analyses on the importance of and interest that these individuals have in the football industry have been conducted. A total of 220 articles and reviews retrieved from Thomson Reuters Web of Science (Core Collection™) between 1997 and 2019 were analysed. These articles were published in 169 different journals by 609 authors from 340 different institutions in 46 countries. The following basic bibliometric analyses and co-occurrence networks were carried out: co-authorship and co-words. As a result, four clusters that summarise the following four different thematic areas were found: (1) football, entrepreneurship and social development, (2) football, innovation and management, (3) football, efficiency and new technology, and (4) football, injuries and innovation in rehabilitation. A thematic analysis of the four clusters found was carried out. Finally, practical implications and future lines of research were presented.

Keywords: soccer; football; innovation; entrepreneurship; bibliometric analysis; performance

---

1. Introduction

Globalisation, increasing competitiveness and the emergence of new sports disciplines have forced sports organisations to develop innovative ideas [1]. "Innovation represents new ideas and changes to sport organisations, coaching, sports events, performance and new competitive advantages" [1] (p. 292). The sports sector is considered a competitive market [2], so it is necessary to reinvent itself to differentiate itself from other sports providers [3] and achieve social and economic sustainability. The common objective of any type of sports organisation is to attain a market positioning and achieve the sustainability of its organisation. Nowadays, due to the dynamic and competitive market, innovative and proactive strategies are necessary. In this context, innovation is related to the management, production and marketing of products or services [4] and can provide vital solutions on the way to improve performance and sustainability [5]. A sports organisation, by its nature, in addition to being characterised by the pursuit of economic and social performance, needs to achieve sporting performance [6]. By idiosyncrasy, professional and non-professional sports clubs try to carry out strategies that improve their sports performance. In this context, innovation and the implementation of new technologies play an important role in football.

Similarly, in this dynamic environment, entrepreneurship is a vehicle to develop economic efficiency [7] and achieve the necessary economic sustainability [8]. According to Ratten [4] (p. 58), "Entrepreneurship is an integral part of sports management and creates a competitive advantage for people and organisations involved in sport". Sports entrepreneurship has attracted the attention of academics and professionals in recent years due to its importance in a strong competition context, however, "is still in its infancy" [9]. Entrepreneurship and innovation play significant roles in sports development [10]. Although innovation is a factor in entrepreneurship, it has been widely considered on an individual level in the field of sport [11–13].

Mediatisation and big data have helped to position football as the king of sports. Today, football moves large masses of fans and money, so it is necessary to take an active position from the entrepreneurial perspective in order to not lose the attention of the fans [13]. During the 1980s, business-oriented entrepreneurs appeared in football clubs [14]. It was from there that football went from being a sport discipline to professionalizing organisations through specialised training and skills, complexity and exclusivity [15]. In this context, entrepreneurship and innovation are perfect allies to improve the identity of the sports organisation and the players, in order to maximise the overall performance.

The role of sports has been widely considered from an entrepreneurial perspective [16] due to its growing importance in different spheres of today's society. However, although soccer is considered one of the most practised and followed sports worldwide [17], it is still in the early stages of its study from an entrepreneurial perspective. Currently, football is the sport with the largest amount of participation, repercussions and income generated worldwide, with influence not only in the sports aspect but also in the social, economic and even cultural aspects. According to Louzada, Moiorano and Ara [18], approximately 270 million people (including officials and referees) are actively involved in football, leading to a stratospheric economic and social impact. However, this popular game seems to have no limit in terms of influence, as one of the main objectives reported by FIFA [19] is that by 2026, more than 60% of the world's population will participate in the game to some extent.

Due to this degree of importance, football, referred to in this study as either football or soccer, encompasses several independent factors that act in a coordinated manner toward the same outcome. Soccer involves a large number of people and organisations and is considered a highly competitive sector. Hence, innovative strategies and an entrepreneurial attitude are vital to attain a competitive advantage and achieve the sustainability that organisations desire after a crisis like the one that occurred years ago. Nevertheless, football can be approached from two different perspectives: professional football and non-professional football. It is undeniable that sports, in general, have special characteristics. These characteristics, together with new technologies and globalisation, have helped make football a well-known sport worldwide. Because of this popularity, football has traditionally been widely used for different educational and social purposes. These social objectives include the formalisation and development of important social difficulties, such as fights against racism [20] and anti-Semitism [21], facilitation of the process of inclusion of refugees in another country [22] and vulnerable groups of expatriates [23], or the empowerment of the female collective [24]. These objectives are only examples of the social power of this sport worldwide.

On the other hand, professional football involves important leagues, tournaments and events that attract masses of individuals worldwide [25]. A clear example of this type of event is the 2018 FIFA World Cup in Russia, in which more than 3,030,000 tickets were sold and on average, 98% of the seats in the 12 Russian stadiums were filled [26]. It is also important to note the large number of fans who follow football, which is currently a mass phenomenon, even in countries where soccer is not the most popular sport [27]. In addition, the number of fans is continuously increasing, as reflected in the data on the latest football world championships; the number of fans increased from 5.2 million for the 2014 FIFA World Cup in Brazil to a total of 7.7 million for the 2018 FIFA World Cup in Russia [26]. As expected, "professional sport is indeed a hyper-competitive environment, which produces constant pressures on organisations to discover and exploit new opportunities to survive, grow, and win competitions" [28] (p. 70). This competitiveness may be one of the reasons why football must involve constant change and innovation. One of the most recent important technological innovations implemented is the *video assistant referee* (VAR), which uses real-time tracking data to make instant decisions at a later time. This technology was created and implemented to increase competitiveness in professional competitions. Similarly, electronic performance and tracking systems (EPTS) have been introduced recently.

However, despite the importance of football currently and the important technological innovations and entrepreneurial aspects that must be developed to maintain the current levels of competitiveness and sustainability and interest of the society, there are no studies that have investigated the origin and evolution of innovation and entrepreneurship in football from an academic perspective. Thus, this study has two main objectives: (i) to identify and analyse the evolution of articles related to entrepreneurship and innovation in football and (ii) to study the thematic areas related to the search carried out. To that end, a bibliometric analysis will be conducted. Bibliometrics, as it is now known, originated in the early 20th century. However, although bibliometric studies have evolved, they essentially involve analysing existing bibliographic material [29] and representing it in an explanatory and graphical way. Bibliometric analysis has two important uses: performance analysis of study area and science mapping [30]. In this way, the visions of the most important authors, journals, institutions, countries and publications are represented, taking into account the frequency of appearance and the number of citations received. This method is considered an instrument for priority analysis in different fields of science [31]. However, in order to provide a complementary qualitative perspective, this study will be complemented by a thematic analysis of the four clusters found.

Finally, the structure of the present study after the introduction section is as follows: the data collection and methods (Section 2), results and discussion (Section 3), conclusions, limitations and future lines of research (Section 4), acknowledgements and bibliographical references.

2. Materials and Methods

All data analysed in this article were retrieved on 31 December 2019 from the Thomson Reuters Web of Science database (WoS), specifically from the Web of Science Core Collection™, the main component covering a wide range of high-impact journals and high-quality articles that were previously reviewed by experts in the fields of study [32]. For the search, the terms football*, soccer*, innovate* and entrepreneur* were used in the topic search field, without limitations on the publication year or language of the documents. The previous terms have been used since innovation is the most recognised dimension of entrepreneurship [4], thus thinking that we would include the largest number of interesting documents in the search collection. Terms entered in the topic field are searched in the titles, abstracts, keywords (provided by the authors) and KeyWords Plus® (index terms automatically generated from the titles of articles cited by the Web of Science). Moreover, Boolean operators (AND-OR) were used to optimise the search for related documents.

Therefore, in the search field topic, the following terms were entered [(football* OR soccer*) and (innovate* OR entrepreneur*)]. In the first stage, 435 results met the predetermined search criteria. However, a criterion for the type of document was established. Only articles and reviews were considered in this study; therefore, five book chapters, three early access articles, 90 proceeding papers, six editorial materials, three meeting abstracts and a book review were excluded. Therefore, the total number of articles and reviews included in this study was 345, 323 articles and 22 reviews, which were published between 1993 and 2019.

However, because the word "football" can refer to different sports, the abstracts of the 345 documents were analysed. Afterward, 47 articles and three reviews were excluded because they referred to American football, the National Football League (NFL) and the National Collegiate Athletic Association (NCAA); 20 articles were excluded because they referred to Australian football; two articles were excluded because they referred to Gaelic football, and; 41 articles and 12 reviews that were not related to football (soccer) or innovation and entrepreneurship were excluded. They had only been added by KeyWords Plus, but the terms used for our search did not appear throughout the text or they included the search terms in the abstract, but were not related to the area of study. In the end, a total of 220 related articles and reviews were analysed. For analysis, the data were downloaded in plain text with the complete record and references cited.

To perform a bibliometric analysis, there must be a set of selected nodes and connections [33]. In this case, the nodes were the published articles, authors, citations and keywords, and the relationships between the nodes were the connections. Connections can also occur between words or authors; hence, co-word and co-authorship analyses were performed. The 220 records were downloaded as plain text files for use in HisCite (Software LLC, New York, NY, USA, version 10.12). However, the data were previously reviewed to eliminate duplicate data, review incomplete data, and aggregate the articles with authors, countries, journals, and institutions that referred to the same content but had been reported differently. First, basic bibliometric analyses were carried out to identify the authors, countries, journals and institutions with the largest number of articles and citations. In this study, qualitative indexes were considered: global citation score (GCS) and local citation score (LCS) [34]. GCS includes the number of citations the document has received in the Web of Science Core Collection, and, LCS is related to the number of citations that a document (always included in our search) has been cited by other different documents within the same collection [35].

Second, the co-occurrence networks between the authors and keywords were analysed by a similarity visualisation perspective (VOS) and the algorithm provided by VOSviewer [36]. This software was used to analyse and represent the existing relationships and networks between the authors and keywords.

Figure 1 shows the methodology followed, which involved 5 steps: (step 1) the keywords related to football/soccer, entrepreneurship and innovation were identified. Afterward, the search was defined, (step 2) 435 results were found, and after the analysis, 220 articles were finally included. (step 3) The articles were categorised by year, author, number of citations, journal, country and institution. (step 4) The co-authorship, co-citation and co-word maps were created. (step 5) The content on the networks was analysed, and the results were obtained.

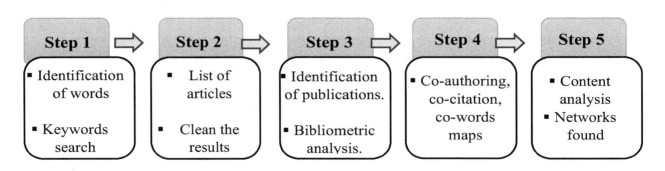

Figure 1. The bibliometric analysis process.

3. Results and Discussion

In the present study, after the data retrieved were organised, a total of 220 articles published in 169 different journals between 1997 and 2019 were analysed. Considering the results and as shown in Figure 2, an increasing trend can be observed from 2015 to the present; 65.45% (n = 144) of the total articles were published in the last five years (2015–2019). In fact, from 1997 to 2010, only 35 articles (15.90%) had been published, but since then, an increasing trend in the number of publications has been observed (Figure 2). However, the number of articles is extremely low (average of 10 articles published per year since 1997), so it can be considered a "niche" study area [37]. The change in the number of articles took place in 2011, with an increase from four articles in 2010 to 13 articles in 2011. This increase may be due to the impact of the global economic crisis that forced academics and professionals to analyse innovative strategies and develop entrepreneurial attitudes to maintain the sustainability of their organisations.

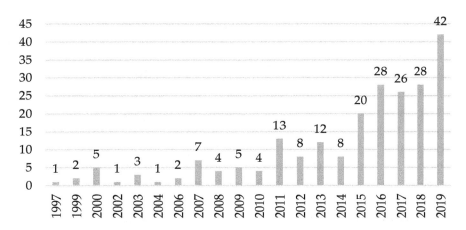

Figure 2. Number of articles published per year (1997–2019).

The results suggest that football is a subject that has aroused the interest of academics and professionals in recent years, although it is not possible to state unequivocally whether this trend will continue in the coming years. However, according to Price's law [38], the process of research involves four phases: (i) pioneers begin to publish on a field of research, (ii) there is exponential growth since many academics are attracted to the subject of study, (iii) there is a consolidation of knowledge and research related to the subject, and (iv) there is a decrease in the number of publications. Considering the above process, it can be considered that football is currently at a point of interest for academics and professionals, so the number of related publications is constantly growing compared to previous years. The data obtained confirm that the growing interest over recent years towards entrepreneurship and innovation in the sports industry [16] is also reflected in one of the most important sports in the world, football/soccer [17,28].

3.1. Analysis of the Authors by the Number of Publications and Number of Citations

Considering the 220 articles analysed in this study, there were a total of 609 authors from 46 countries who belonged to 340 different institutions. Table 1 shows the authors with the highest number of published articles on entrepreneurship and innovation in football/soccer. The order followed in Table 1 was (i) the highest number of publications to identify the productivity of the author in the analysed field of study and (ii) the highest number of citations, which is frequently used to analyse the impact of the papers [39] and the researchers.

Table 1. Authors with the highest number of publications in the search (≥2).

Author	Affiliation	No.	LCS	GCS	GCS/No.
Esson, J	Loughborough University (UK)	3	6	54	18
Lemmink, K	University of Groningen (Netherlands)	2	1	160	80
Jones, GA	Digital Imaging Research Centre (UK)	2	1	55	27.50
Orwell, J	Digital Imaging Research Centre (UK)	2	1	55	27.50
Ren, J	Northwestern Polytechnic University (China)	2	1	55	27.50
Xu, M	Xi'an Jiaotong Liverpool University (China)	2	1	55	27.50

No.: number of articles; LCS: local citations score; GCS: global citations score.

Therefore, the most important author was identified to be James Esson, who has three articles and a total of 54 citations in WoS (GCS). This author has published only these three articles, which are related to a common theme: the influence of football on the development and migration of the Ghanaian population. Second, Koen Lemmink has published two articles with a total of 160 citations in WoS. This author analysed the tactical performance of football teams using positioning data. Finally, Graeme A. Jones has published two articles in the same field of study as the last author. However, despite the fact that some authors are more productive than others, there is no clear "reference author(s)", so it can be considered a fragmented area of study.

However, the most important authors considering the number of citations are shown in Table 2 and partially coincide with the authors with the highest number of publications related to entrepreneurship and innovation in football. The most cited authors are Benoît Demil and Xavier Lecocq [40], for their article "Business Model Evolution: In Search of Dynamic Consistency", which presents an innovative business model and its evolution based on the Arsenal FC. The authors shown in Table 2 were determined to be the most relevant authors in the search carried out because they have a large number of citations [40]; however, Peters, Kraker, Lex, Gumpenberger and Gorraiz [41] stated that much of the information collected in the existing literature is not cited in a rigorous manner.

Table 2. Authors with the highest number of citations (≥156).

Author	Affiliation	No.	LCS	GCS	GCS/No.
Lecocq, X	University of Lille (France)	1	0	430	430
Demil, B	University of Lille (France)	1	0	430	430
Lemmink, K	University of Groningen (Netherlands)	2	2	160	80
Pongsakornrungsilp, S	Walailak University	1	0	120	120
Schroeder, J.E.	Rochester Institute of Technology (USA)	1	0	120	120

No.: number of articles; LCS: local citations score; GCS: global citations score.

Taking into account the countries of authors, the UK is the country with the highest number of articles published (n = 50), with 521 GCS, followed by the USA (39) with 486 GCS, and Germany (23) with 226 citations. A total of 50.90% (n = 112) of the articles analysed in this paper were published in the UK, USA and Germany (Table 3). This result is understandable because the most important football leagues are located in the most productive countries in terms of the number of publications: UK (English Premier League), USA (Major League Soccer), Germany (Bundesliga), Italy (Serie A) and Spain (LaLiga).

Table 3. Primary countries in which the authors conducted research (≥8).

Country	No. Art	LCS	GCS	GCS/No.	%
UK	50	11	521	10.42	22.62
USA	39	2	486	12.46	17.65
Germany	23	0	226	9.83	10.41
Italy	20	0	98	4.90	9.05
Australia	15	3	110	7.33	6.79
Spain	13	1	17	1.31	5.88
China Republic	12	1	88	7.33	5.43
Switzerland	10	0	57	5.70	4.52
Portugal	10	1	93	9.30	4.52
France	10	1	481	48.10	4.52

No.: number of articles; LCS: local citations score; GCS: global citations score.

Of the 220 articles, 87.27% (192) were written in English, eight were in Spanish (3.64%), and five were in Russian (2.27%). This result is consistent with the results obtained in previous studies, as English is known to be the most frequently used language in WoS academic publications.

3.2. Analysis of the Main Journals and Publications

The journals that have published the most articles on entrepreneurship and innovation in football/soccer include "Sport, Business and Management: An International Journal (SBM)", with six articles, "European Sport Management Quarterly", with five articles, and "International Journal of the History of Sport", with five articles. However, when we took into account the total number of citations received, the most important journal was found to be *"British Journal of Sports Medicine"*, with 111 citations in WoS and four articles published (Table 4).

Table 4. Main journals (≥3 articles).

Journal	No.	LCS	GCS	SJR	HI
Sport, Business and Management: an International Journal (SBM)	6	1	17	0.28	12
European Sport Management Quarterly	5	0	45	1.28	24
International Journal of the History of Sport	5	1	3	0.35	17
British Journal of Sports Medicine	4	0	111	4.14	141
International Journal of Sport Policy and Politics	3	1	8	0.76	22
Journal of Organizational Change Management	3	1	38	0.60	62
Managing Sport and Leisure	3	0	8	0.29	29
Sustainability	3	0	5	0.55	53
PLoS ONE	3	0	7	1.1	268

No.: number of articles; LCS: local citations score; GCS: global citations score; SJR: Scimago Journal Rank: HI: h-index.

However, when we considered the number of citations received in the publications analysed in this study, we found that *"Long Range Planning"* had 430 citations in WoS (GCS) for a published article, *"Organisation Studies"* had 156 citations GCS for a published article, and *"Marketing Theory"* had 120 citations for a published article (Table 5).

Table 5. Most cited journals (≥107 citations).

Journal	No.	LCS	GCS	IF *	HI *
Long Range Planning	1	0	430	2.04	89
Organization Studies	1	0	156	2.36	130
Marketing Theory	1	0	120	1.52	55
British Journal of Sports Medicine	4	0	111	4.14	141
European Journal of Sport Science	1	1	107	1.17	41

[1] No.: number of articles; LCS: local citations score; GCS: global citations score; IF: impact factor; HI: h-index; * = extracted from Scimago Journal Rank (SJR).

Table 6 shows the papers in our search collection that receive the most citations in WoS (GCS). The most cited article to date was that published by Demil and Lecocq [40], which analysed a business model that valued sustainability and interactions between the activity components of an English football club (Arsenal FC); it had received a total of 430 citations in WoS by the day the search was performed. The second highest-ranked article in terms of the number of citations was published by Pongsakornrungsilp and Schroeder [42], which received 120 citations; in that study, the authors studied the role of online football fans and related communities in co-creating value. Finally, the third highest-ranked article is published by Frencken et al. [43] which analysed the position of the players on the field and predicted their performance.

On the other hand, the number of articles that have been cited within the documents included in the search carried out is 9091, that is, an average of 41.32 references were included in each article analysed in the present study. The most-referenced article in our search collection was the book published by Yin [44], with a frequency of 8, the second most-referenced was the article published by Harvey [45], with a frequency of 7, and the third most-referenced was the one published by Ratten [4], which provides novel information on the theory of sports entrepreneurship in sport management (Table 7).

Table 6. Most cited articles by external papers (≥35 citations).

Article	Year	Authors	Journal	LCS	GCS
Business Model Evolution: In Search of Dynamic Consistency	2010	Demil, B. Lecocq, X.	*Long Range Planning*	0	430
Understanding value co-creation in a co-consuming brand community	2011	Pongsakornrungsilp, S. Schroeder, J.E.	*Marketing Theory*	0	120
Oscillations of centroid position and surface area of soccer teams in small-sided games	2011	Frencken, W. Lemmink, K. Delleman, N. Visscher, C.	*European Journal of Sport Science*	1	107
Current Approaches to Tactical Performance Analyses in Soccer Using Position Data	2017	Memmert, D. Lemmink, K. Sampaio, J.	*Sports Medicine*	1	53
A body and a dream at a vital conjuncture: Ghanaian youth, uncertainty and the allure of football	2011	Esson, J.	*Geoforum*	3	35

LCS: local citations score; GCS: global citations score.

Table 7. Most referenced articles in our search collection (≥5).

Article	Year	Authors	Journal	*f*	∑C
Case study research: Design and methods	2003	Yin, R	Book	8	568
The roots of geographical change: 1973 to the present	1989	Harvey, D.	*Geografiska Annaler: Series B, Human Geography*	7	7
Sport-based entrepreneurship: towards a new theory of entrepreneurship and sport management	2011	Ratten, V.	*International Entrepreneurship and Management Journal*	6	205
Supporters, followers, fans, and flaneurs: A taxonomy of spectator identities in football	2002	Giulianotti, R.	*Journal of Sport & Social Issues*	6	825
Building theories from case study research	1989	Eisenhardt, K.M.	*Academy of Management Review*	5	55.121
Football Academies and the Migration of African Football Labor to Europe	2007	Darby, P. Akindes, G. Kirwin, M.	*Journal of Sport and Social Issues*	5	219
The English football industry: profit, performance and industrial structure	1997	Szymanski, S. Smith, R.	*International Review of Applied Economics*	5	350

f: frequency, ∑C: citations in Google Scholar.

3.3. Co-Occurrence Analysis

Co-occurrence analyses provide information about the relationship or interaction between two nodes. Each node can be a publication, an author or a keyword. In this study, co-authorship and co-words were analysed.

3.3.1. Co-Authorship Analysis

A large number of co-authored publications indicate a close relationship between authors within the same field of study, which may encourage collaboration in future research [46]. However, in the present study, the average number of authors for each publication analysed was 2.77 (609/220). It can be concluded that there is collaborative research in entrepreneurship and innovation in football, but the level of collaboration is not extensive, as shown in Figure 3.

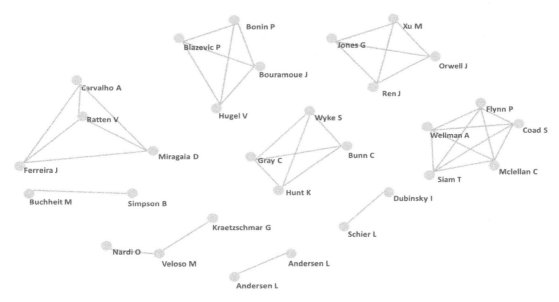

Figure 3. Co-authorship networks (≥2).

The minimum criterion established for representation is two co-authors. The five largest networks of co-authors included (i) Jones, G., Ren, J., Xu, M. and Orwell, J., who published articles related to the thematic area "performance and efficiency", and (ii) Bouramoue, J., Bonnin, P., Hugel, V. and Blazevic, P., who also published articles in the thematic area "performance and efficiency". The following network of co-authors, including (iii) Carvalho, A., Ratten, V., Miragaia, D. and Ferreira, J., published in the thematic area "innovation and management". (iv) Flynn, P., Wellman, A., Slam, T. and Mclellan, C. published articles in the thematic area "performance and efficiency", (v) another network of co-authorship with Wyke, S., Gray. C., Hunt, K. and Bunn, C. of whom published in the area of "performance and efficiency", (vi) there was a network between Dubinsky, I. and Schler, L., who published in the thematic area "entrepreneurship and migration policy", (vii) another network between Simpson, B. and Buchheit, M. published articles in the thematic area "performance and efficiency", (viii) Veloso, M., who has a network of co-authorship with Nardi, D. and (v) another network of co-authorship with Kraetzschmar, G., both of whom published in the area of "performance and efficiency", (ix) Dubinsky, I. and Schier, L published in the thematic area "entrepreneurship and migration policy", and finally, (x) Andersen L. and Andersen, L. published articles related to "injuries and rehabilitation"

3.3.2. Co-Word Analysis

Keywords have a fundamental role in the field of research since they can be a tool by which the evolution of a specific area of knowledge can be identified [47]. In the present study, a total of 1.092 keywords (keywords set by the authors and the keywords set by ISI WoS) were identified, of which 73.08% (798) were repeated only once, while only 292 (26.92%) co-occurred, i.e., they appeared more than once. Co-word analysis is "a content analysis technique that uses the words in documents to establish relationships and build a conceptual structure of the domain" [33] and it means that the concepts are closely related. Figure 4 reflects the main co-occurrence relationships present in the analysed articles.

In Table 8, the most cited keywords are listed; the most cited keyword was football/soccer (GCS = 756), followed by business (GCS = 461), evolution (GCS = 440) and consistency (GCS = 430) (Table 8). The criteria to select the keywords in Table 8 was, a frequency of appearance in the search collection equal or superior to 10 times for the most frequent keywords, and global citations in WoS (GCS) equal or superior to 140 citations for most cited keywords. The words football/soccer were considered as one word since they referred to the same sport discipline (F = 102; LCS = 12; GCS = 756). In the same way, in sport* all the variants were included, such as sporting, sports or sport (F = 51; LCS = 4; GCS =

327) and in innovate* were included innovative or innovation (F = 19; LCS = 1; GCS = 140). However, the keywords that receive more citations vary slightly from the most frequently used keywords.

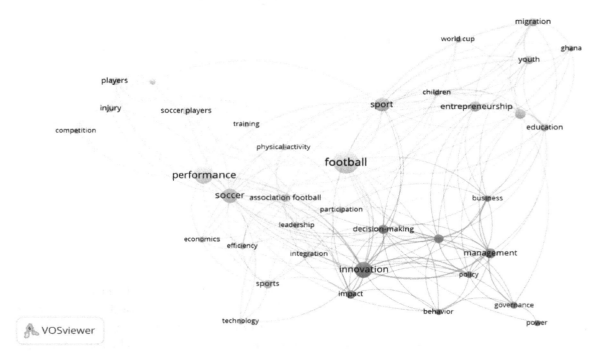

Figure 4. Co-word network.

Table 8. Most frequent keywords.

Most Frequent Keywords (≥10)				Most Cited Keywords (≥140)			
Keyword	***f***	**LCS**	**GCS**	**Keyword**	***f***	**LCS**	**GCS**
Football/Soccer	102	12	756	*Football/Soccer*	102	12	756
*Sport**	51	4	327	*Business*	10	1	461
*Innovat**	19	1	140	*Evolution*	4	0	440
*Entrepreneur**	14	5	226	*Consistency*	1	0	430
Professional	13	0	50	*Dynamic*	1	0	430
Elite	13	1	73	*Sport**	51	4	327
Development	12	4	83	*Entrepreneur**	14	5	226
Business	10	1	461	*Institutional*	2	0	165
Performance	10	1	77	*Innovat**	19	1	140

sport + sports; *f*: frequency; LCS: local citation score; GCS: global citations score.

Currently, with advanced analysis software such as VOSviewer, keywords can be identified, studied and represented in a systematic way. To show a co-word network, a map was created based on bibliographic data. To standardize the association values of the keywords, the "association strength" was applied [48], while the "Visualization of Similarities" (VOS) technique was used to position each term on the map in a graphic way [36]. Finally, to detect the different clusters, the VOSviewer algorithm gives the option to include different resolution parameters. In our case, we determined finally 37 keywords that were selected and the total strength of the co-occurrence links with other keywords was calculated.

After this analysis, four different clusters were differentiated by colours (blue, yellow, green and red). Figure 4 shows the graphical representation of the co-occurrence of keywords or co-words. This describes in a generalised way the structure of the knowledge or concepts that exist in the previous literature [49]. The analysis of the terms is represented by circles of different sizes and colours. The size of the circles represents the frequency of appearance of a specific term; that is, the larger the circle is, the larger the number of occurrences in the titles and abstracts of the analysed publications [50]. The colours of the circles correspond to the different clusters found in the search. The distance between the circles (keywords) provides relevant information about their relationship; the shorter the distance between the circles is, the stronger the relationship. This relationship is determined by the number of occurrences in which the terms appear together in the titles and abstracts [51].

Thematic analysis was conducted considering the terms that appear in the total of keywords, i.e., the keywords set by the authors and the keywords set by ISI WoS. The criterion of inclusion was an occurrence frequency of ≥ 4 times. Finally, a total of 37 terms were used in this study. The software VosViewer found four different clusters according to the thematic area and differentiated by four different colours:

- Blue cluster—"Football, entrepreneurship and social development"; the following keywords stand out: Sport, entrepreneurship, migration, education and politics. This cluster is composed of nine terms and related to the importance of football in the politics of less developed countries (e.g., Ghana) and its relationship with migration, policy and education, which was analysed from an entrepreneurial perspective.
- Red cluster—"Football, innovation and management": Composed of 10 terms; the following keywords stand out: innovation, management, organisations and football. This cluster relates to innovation policies and the impact on the management of soccer-related sports organisations.
- Green cluster—"Football, Performance and efficiency": Formed by 10 terms, which relate to the introduction of new technologies and innovations to improve the performance and efficiency of athletes and organisations.
- Yellow cluster—"Football, Innovation in injury treatment and rehabilitation": Composed of eight terms, which refer to the study and implementation of innovations and new technologies to treat injuries of professional and non-professional football players in order to improve their overall performance.

Cluster 1—Blue: Football, Entrepreneurship and Social Development

In general, this cluster aggregates papers related to the social function of sport, with football as a central element of contributions to social development. Even so, we can observe two approaches: on the one hand, we find studies that analyse football as a means of educating and developing people [52–55] through entrepreneurs who developed educational initiatives in the form of schools or academies [56,57]. Innovative football-based programmes can promote ethical and civic values while improving the health and well-being of participants [54,58–60]. On the other hand, we find papers related to social development through football in less-developed countries and its innovations in those communities, such as Ghana [61–64] or South Africa [65]. Similarly, there can be connection and learning between countries through football [66,67], encouraging entrepreneurship among the population and a possible path to success.

Sport is an important agent of social change and development because of its democratic, educational and inclusive nature [68]. This is why it is considered a vital element in modern and developed societies [69], however, due to globalisation and the mediatisation of information in today's society, the influence of sport, and in particular football, has reached every corner of the planet. Football has worldwide media coverage and generates a huge amount of money, and this can be exposed in the less developed countries as a future opportunity that would ensure personal economic sustainability [70]. One of the most cited articles in this cluster is the paper published by [61], which relates the possible causes of the increase of professional football players in West Africa. Football is used as a lens to expand opportunities and general development for young people. Consolidating a career in football is seen as a source of income, but also to demonstrate masculinity. The article discusses that professional football players are "entrepreneurs of self". Moreover, the aspirations and "self-starter" aspects that lead people with fewer resources and chances of success to a career in football were also identified.

The football industry in Ghana is notable for exporting young Ghanaian footballers to foreign leagues, and the author with the largest number of publications in our research collection, James Esson, conducts a case study to understand the causes and consequences of this entrepreneurial business [63]. According to Poli, Ravenel and Besson [71], 46.7% of professional football players in the top five football leagues are expatriates. This percentage is very high and strengthens the importance of this cluster in the search carried out. This area of knowledge involves the ability of football to motivate and inspire people from different regions of the world [61]. In addition, it is closely related to the institutional logic that surrounds different multi-sport sports organisations, among which football stands out as a key sport [72].

"Football has become a bridge between communities, and a vehicle for mobilising national and transnational solidarities that cut across deep-seated ethnic divides" [56]. In the existing literature in our search collection, a collaboration between countries with football as both a means and an end has been a topic of interest for academics and professionals in recent years [67]. One country can learn from another in different facets in which it excels, with football in Ghana, for example, is an outstanding activity to show the world [67]. In the same way, British entrepreneurs (players and coaches) were of significant importance in spreading the word about football around the world, as studied by Smith [73] in his study. Football has important entrepreneurial activities associated with it, such as major events, associations, sports clubs, etc. The big football events could help the development of slums that need more innovative strategies to improve economic activity and sustainability [65,74]. Similarly, thanks to the help of entrepreneurs, very important teams and events have been created at a national level [75].

On the other hand, in the context of the development of underdeveloped societies, is the creation of academies and organisations such as the Mandela Soccer Academy, aspiring the imaginations and hopes of entrepreneurs and promoting the development of young people in the country [57]. The above authors, included in our search collection, analyse the social and developmental role of innovative football academies in underdeveloped countries such as Ghana. Through football, young people and adults can find a path to success and sustainability, both in their home countries and in countries to which they migrate [64]. However, it is not only important to develop people in their own countries but to achieve equal treatment and inclusion with immigrants when they migrate to other countries. Football, supported by the changing behavior of whites towards blacks, has facilitated the desegregation process of professional football teams [53]. This paper reviews the role of African Americans in professional football and suggests avenues for future research.

This area of knowledge is attracting the attention of academics, governments and professionals, as entrepreneurship in sports is a vital aspect of success [4]. Sport plays a major role in government policies, and social enterprises related to football can be included in social innovation policies. Reid [76], an article within our search collection, analyses the efforts and innovative strategies made by football social enterprises and their social impact on a deprived community. In the same way, the impact of football is so significant that it has been used as the main activity in innovative social programmes developed by organisations and governments to improve the health of African citizens [58], raise concerns about gender equality [54] or approach ethnic issues [21,55]. Moreover, football has been used as a vehicle for mental health interventions [77] or develop sexual health education [52] from an entrepreneurial approach. For example, innovative activities to achieve social goals, such as midnight football in disadvantaged slums, are carried out within these government sports initiatives to promote social change [78], or innovative football-related programmes have been developed at universities, having a significant social impact on students [79]. Similarly, Gray et al. [80] developed a programme called Football Fans in Training (FFIT) to achieve a reduction in obesity through an innovative sports programme using club facilities. In this way, the participants, generally sedentary, felt an added motivation by having a close relationship with their favourite football club. This innovative program achieved good results so it was implemented and studied in South Africa [58]. However, this area of study must continue to develop entrepreneurial initiatives to combat existing discrimination in football [59,60].

Cluster 2—Red: Football, Innovation and Management

In cluster 2, represented by the colour red, there are also 10 keywords. This cluster includes papers related to innovation and entrepreneurship in the management of sports organisations (usually football clubs) and major football events. The studies that conform to our cluster can be divided into two different areas: (i) innovation in sports organisation management, and (ii) entrepreneurship in sports events.

The development of pay-TV and the increase in the cost of the domain to offer football matches in free access could have been a determining factor in the dizzying increase of professionalisation in the football sector and its growing commercialisation [81] until sport became a business. Similarly, changes related to the signing of image rights and television contracts, the participation of capitalist entrepreneurs in football projects and the construction of football stadiums, have transformed the management of football into a business today. In our search, the most cited article analyses the concept of "business model evolution" taking as a case study a professional football team of the English Premier League. This concept can be used as a tool to develop changes and innovations in the organisation towards a business model [40]. The initiatives and strategies adopted by football clubs have been analysed due to the great importance that football has at an economic, sportive and social level in our society [72], and in the way that their football players have been defined as superstars and are at the top end of the market value distribution. In our search, authors like Hoeber and Hoeber [82] stand out, they analyse the innovations developed by community sports organisations (CSOs) (among them soccer clubs) and classify them according to their form, type and magnitude. This study improves knowledge about entrepreneurship and innovation in small nonprofit sports clubs.

In the same vein, Schuhmacher and Kuester [83] collected ideas from users who participated in an "idea contest" to improve new online services for football clubs. "An idea contest is an invitation by a firm to the general public or a targeted group to submit contributions to a specific topic within a given timeline" [83] (p. 428). The authors show that lead user analysis increases the potential for creating useful and attractive innovations for the organisation. Just as the opinion of users/members is important, so also the opinion of football fans is vital. Pereira et al. [84] proposed a theoretical model in which fans of football clubs throughout Brazil would express their perception of innovation and their intention to renew the annuity. This study provides information to club managers about the variables that influence the perception and behaviour of their fans.

Various authors have studied the role of fans of specific football teams on important marketing and management variables of the organisation. Pongsakornrungsilp and Schroeder [42] analyse the role of fans of specific football teams on the creation of value through their consumption practices, while Sotelo Gonzalez [85] analyses the Spanish professional football league from the innovative perspective of social media. In the same vein, Vimieiro [86] examines and discusses the importance of communication material and production projects run by football fans in Brazil. Fans create stories and news through various formats that manage to promote an innovative and close approach that brings added social value to the football industry.

However, due to the growing economic, sporting and social impact of professional football leagues, several authors have analysed the changes and innovations that have taken place in English football in recent years [87], leading to the creation of the English Premier League (EPL), "the most lucrative worldwide" [88] (p. 136). The process followed by sponsors to improve the new service development (NSD) of two EPL teams has also been studied. EPL has been studied from different perspectives, Olson et al. [89] analyse the structure, strategy and culture of football clubs competing in EPL. The authors analyse the innovation orientation within the organisational behaviour of sports clubs, providing information relevant to the entrepreneurial and sports environment. On the other hand, Buraimo, Forrest, and Simmons [90] present an innovative model that estimates attendance at EFL matches through quantitative variables.

Sport entrepreneurship is an important factor for sports organisations. Along these lines, Radaelli et al. [28] carry out a longitudinal analysis with sports directors of Italian Serie A football clubs to find out the impact of adopting an entrepreneurial attitude as opposed to not adopting it. Along the same lines, Cohen and Peachey [91] examine the impact of a sport-for-development initiative and motivations towards becoming a social entrepreneur in Street Soccer USA. However, the overall performance of sports clubs and their sustainability is a common concern and goal for all of them. In this line, Miragaia et al. [92] analysed the influence of different variables on sports performance in European professional football clubs from a sustainable entrepreneurial approach, in the same way that Garcia et al. [93] evaluated the impact that marketing innovations could have on the income of football clubs, providing valuable information regarding economic performance. Finally, important aspects for football clubs have also been addressed, such as the analysis of an innovative and specific construction system for the pitch [94]. However, innovation and entrepreneurship in football is still in its infancy and several authors are analysing future changes and trends in professional football [95].

Another broad area of study within this cluster is that of large football events and stadiums, as these are generally related to important socio-cultural and economic opportunities for the host cities or countries [96]. This author analyses the "urban entrepreneurship" and security aspects of the European Football Championships 2008 in the eight host cities of Austria and Switzerland (Euro 2008), as well as a way of sustaining the urban entrepreneurial strategy realised in UEFA European Championship (Euro 2012). However, for an event to take place, the host city or cities must first be selected. In this context, Müller [97] analyses the important process known as "event seizure" of the 2018 World Cup in Russia. At a time when the hosts have been questioned, Ludvigsen [98] analyses the "multiple host format" by providing an innovative strategy to address the organisational and security implications.

In relation to major events, a large area of study emerges: football stadiums. In recent years, considerable efforts have been made to learn about innovative techniques and enterprising management models to achieve maximum profitability and make the most of their resources. Various authors have analysed innovative techniques in relation to structural aspects of football stadiums such as the roof [99,100] and even to transform the football stadium into a pro-environmental stadium design through innovations and initiatives developed by entrepreneurs, owners and investors [101]. However, this type of event and the construction or remodeling of stadiums involves the movement of large amounts of money, hence Eick [102] studied the shadows that exist after the celebration of the FIFA World Cup in Germany 2006, providing first a description of the "neo-communitarian entrepreneur" of the 20th century.

Cluster 3—Green: Football, Efficiency and New Technology.

In cluster 3, represented by the colour green, there are 10 keywords, such as soccer, football, technology, efficiency and sports. However, it should be noted that it is very close to the term performance because of its close relationship in terms of content. This cluster includes papers related to the analysis of technique and tactics during training and competitions through innovations or new technologies to achieve maximum efficiency.

Football sports clubs are characterised by their sporting objective, which is considered an idiosyncratic feature of competitive sports clubs, compared to other organisations in other sectors of activity. Hence, exploring new processes or materials to achieve greater efficiency has been the subject of study for many academics and professionals. However, this interest has increased in recent decades due to the extensive professionalisation of football sports clubs and their growing economic, sporting and social impact. In this context, player tracking has become one of the most developed aspects in the control of the load in football, so that seeking innovations and implementing them can have considerable improvements in the final efficiency of the player, the team, and, consequently, the football club [103]. In their study, the previous authors discuss the limitations of some traditional methods and present powerful innovative variables that can always be used from a cost/benefit approach. In the same line, other studies study the position of the player or the ball itself through innovative and proactive materials and processes. The most cited article in this cluster, investigates the positions of players on the field to know the flow of attack and defense in professional football for men. To do so, they used an innovative player tracking system that provides important information, mainly about goal plays, and that can be implemented by other football clubs to improve their performance and sustainability [43]. Memmert, Lemmink, and Sampaio [104] offer in their paper an overview of position data in soccer, based on two professional soccer clubs, in addition to providing new ways to develop this important technique. One of the studies that has provided an entrepreneurial vision in training is that of Yang [105], in which he explores the innovative applications of the computer virtual reality technology in football, explaining practical cases and providing new information for the field of education.

However, to achieve high performance and improve the competitiveness of the team, planned, controlled and proactive training is necessary. Training can be very varied in physical demands, technique, tactics, etc, and these, in turn, are different from competitive matches. Therefore, Abbott, Brickley, and Smeeton [106] analyse the position of the players through a novel global positioning system (GPS) during training sessions of different physical demands and their comparison with the real competition. Similarly, Szwarc et al. [107] analyse goalkeeper information by proposing two innovative instruments in the sector: the goalkeeper's activity index (GAI) and an analysis of 5-min periods performed with a video tracking system, while Murgia et al. [108] analyse the effectiveness of perceptive training on goalkeeper skills by innovatively including a training protocol in which goalkeepers schedule training sessions on their own. Van Maarseveen, Oudejans, and Savelsbergh [109] explore the skills of talented female soccer players through two innovative methods of analysis and behavioural gaze data.

In addition to developing the skills of players individually and also as a team, another important aspect in the world of professional football is to detect talent. In this sense, Maanijou and Mirroshandel [17] introduce an innovative system of talent detection in football players. This entrepreneurial approach processes information available on the Internet through classification algorithms. This could help coaches, physical trainers and managers to categorise football players according to their ranking. This experimental research was carried out with the Persian first division league and obtained good results, which can be cautiously extrapolated to other international football leagues in the future. Similarly, Diquigiovanni and Scarpa [110] developed an innovative hierarchical grouping method to divide participants according to their playing style and predict team performance. This study was conducted with the Italian Serie A teams.

However, in addition to the players, the ball is one of the characteristics of football compared to other sports. In this context, several authors have analysed the trajectory and behaviour of the ball through innovative techniques and state-of-the-art cameras [111–114]. The valuable information provided by the above authors improves the knowledge of football, but can also be used from an entrepreneurial lens in the sports ball market.

However, it is not only footballers, coaches, managers and trainers who are important: referees also play a key role. In this context, Kolbinger and Link [115] presents the initiative developed in recent years for referees to use spray to improve compliance with the rules. However, in order to enforce the rules, decision making is fundamental in this collective, hence Samuel et al. [116] analyse a new and successful decision-making simulator for soccer referees that could become a potential training method for referees. Finally, in this cluster appear the soccer robot systems. Yoshida [117] introduced an innovative design approach of autonomous soccer robots designed to play in the RoboCup League. In the article he discusses different types of robots as a new system used in system life concept.

Cluster 4—Yellow: Football, Injuries and Innovation in Rehabilitation

In this cluster, represented by the colour yellow, there are eight keywords; the following keywords are considered the most important: soccer player, injury, performance and competition. This area of study is most related to injuries and recovery in soccer players, specifically those involved in professional soccer. It should be noted that the word soccer is closely related to word performance.

"The marketing of elite sport consequently produces extreme performance pressures on clubs, teams, managers, coaches, trainers, sports associations and athletes, especially those at the highest levels in their sports. One of the consequences is a conspicuous high rate of injury" [88] (p. 136). In this context, prevention is the best way to reduce the number of injuries, and therefore implementing new techniques and innovations can help improve both prevention and treatment, and has attracted the attention of academics and practitioners in recent years. There is currently a great deal of pressure on professionals and researchers to innovate and achieve the fastest and most effective treatments to treat professional football players' injuries, and thereby return them to peak performance. In this line, Faulkner et al. [88] analyse conventional therapies and access to innovative techniques in professional football and cycling.

The application of artificial intelligence (AI) has opened up an innovative and useful perspective in the prediction and treatment of injuries. Pares et al. [118] examine the effectiveness of Physium, an innovative device that could be used to prevent the risk of injury in football players at risk of injury according to the Saló Darder (SD) test. This research was totally innovative in the field of player injury prevention and recovery. For their part, Claudino et al. [119] conducted a systematic review of studies encompassing 11 techniques or methods that included the use of AI in the risk of injury in team sports, including football, providing practical implications for sports entrepreneurs. Sousa, Cabri, and Donaghy [120] conducted a detailed review to provide novel information on sports physiotherapy, with football as one of the most common sports to be studied. Twenty-seven percent of the documents analysed included innovative approaches that can improve understanding of the area of study, giving rise to novel practical implications.

But what factors can influence injuries? In this context, Contrò et al. [121] analysed the phenotype of professional football players to determine whether it influenced injuries and performance in a novel way. This cluster also included articles that analysed forms of injury prevention such as masks [122] or innovative operating and treatment techniques for more frequent injuries in football, such as pubalgia [123] or vestibular dysfunction after impact on the head [124].

Finally, several authors analysed new techniques and surgical procedures for football injuries, such as Contreras-Muñoz et al. [125] or Mithoefer et al. [126]. The latter authors investigated the evolution and results derived from new changes and innovations related to autologous chondrocyte implantation (ACI), a technique used in football and analysed in this article in football players.

4. Conclusions, Limitations and Future Lines of Research

The results of this study partly help us understand the current state and evolution of entrepreneurship and innovation in football. This information is important because it provides an overview of the publications, authors, countries, institutions and journals with the highest number of publications and the highest number of citations according to an analysis of a total of 220 articles. In addition, perhaps one of the greatest contributions is the identification of the thematic areas in which research related to innovation and entrepreneurship in football is developed. This allows, on the one hand, to identify the topics and areas of interest for researchers and academics, and on the other hand, to point out future lines of research in the perspective of the development and state of each of the clusters mentioned. The thematic areas addressed by each of them converge on a common theme, which is none other than the entrepreneurial ecosystem known as football, but they differ profoundly in the subject matter from which they are approached: from an approach to social development in which football can even function as a social elevator, to a technical-health or sports performance perspective, as well as a cluster related to innovation in sports management.

This variety shows how around a successful activity with a high social and economic impact, a high academic interest is developed from multiple fields. This high interest also has another, less friendly side: there are important gaps in the existing bibliography, most of the articles found are of a transversal nature and do not follow up the sample to analyse the evolution of performance measures, and the collaboration networks found among the authors are few and far between, which makes it difficult to establish a coherent connection. Despite this, entrepreneurship and innovation in football continue to develop, showing an upward trend in growth, as evidenced by the evolution of the number of publications.

The study may have limitations that should be discussed. The search was carried out in Web of Science, as this database is widely used for academic searches and has been used in previous studies [32,50], but valuable information may have been missed in our study. Nevertheless, we ensured that the quality and impact of the publications are high. In the same way, a qualitative analysis was performed to determine whether to include or exclude articles in the study; this process may have involved biases, but it increased the credibility of the study results by excluding articles referring to American football, Australian football and Gaelic football and including only those referring to football/soccer.

In a bibliometric analysis, the information is analysed quantitatively; therefore, important qualitative information is not interpreted [49]. In future research, it is proposed that a qualitative study of the search results is conducted so that valuable information for academics and professionals can be obtained. This type of study may provide detailed information on the gaps in the existing literature. The area of sports, specifically football, from an entrepreneurial and innovative perspective, is still in its infancy, so it is important to focus attention on its theoretical and empirical development.

Author Contributions: Conceptualization, J.M.N.-P. and V.R.; methodology, P.E.-F.; software, J.M.N.-P.; formal analysis, J.M.N.-P.; investigation, J.C.; writing—original draft preparation, V.R.; supervision, P.E.-F.; project administration, V.R.; funding acquisition, J.C. All authors have read and agreed to the published version of the manuscript.

References

1. Tjønndal, A. Sport innovation: Developing a typology. *Eur.J. Sport Soc.* **2017**, *14*, 291–310. [CrossRef]
2. Ratten, V. Developing a theory of sport-based entrepreneurship. *J. Manag. Org.* **2010**, *16*, 557–565. [CrossRef]
3. Vos, S.; Breesch, D.; Scheerder, J. Undeclared work in non-profit sports clubs: A mixed method approach for assessing the size and motives. *VOLUNTAS: Int. J. Vol. Nonpr. Org.* **2012**, *23*, 846–869. [CrossRef]
4. Ratten, V. Sport-based entrepreneurship: Towards a new theory of entrepreneurship and sport management. *Int. Entrepr. Manag. J.* **2011**, *7*, 57–69. [CrossRef]
5. Ringuet-Riot, C.J.; Hahn, A.; James, D.A. A structured approach for technology innovation in sport. *Sports Technol.* **2013**, *6*, 137–149. [CrossRef]
6. Ratten, V. Sport entrepreneurship: Challenges and directions for future research. *Int. J. Entrep. Vent.* **2012**, *4*, 65–76. [CrossRef]
7. Ball, S. The importance of entrepreneurship to hospitality, leisure, sport and tourism. *Hosp. Leis. Sport Tour. Netw.* **2005**, *1*, 1–14.
8. Henry, C.; Hill, F.; Leitch, C.M. *Education and Training for Aspiring Entrepreneurs: The Issue of Effectiveness*, 1st ed.; Aldershot, Ashgate Publishing: New York, NY, USA, 2003.
9. Pellegrini, M.M.; Rialti, R.; Marzi, G.; Caputo, A. Sport entrepreneurship: A synthesis of existing literature and future perspectives. *Int. Entrep. Manag. J.* **2020**, *4*, 1–32. [CrossRef]
10. Ratten, V.; Ferreira, J.J. *Sport Entrepreneurship and Innovation*, 1st ed.; Taylor & Francis: New York, NY, USA, 2016.
11. Forslund, M. Innovation in soccer clubs–the case of Sweden. *Soccer Soc.* **2017**, *18*, 374–395. [CrossRef]
12. Winand, M.; Scheerder, J.; Vos, S.; Zintz, T. Do non-profit sport organisations innovate? Types and preferences of service innovation within regional sport federations. *Innovation* **2016**, *18*, 289–308. [CrossRef]
13. Giulianotti, R. Supporters, followers, fans, and flaneurs: A taxonomy of spectator identities in football. *J. Sport Soc. Issue* **2002**, *26*, 25–46. [CrossRef]
14. Leach, S.; Szymanski, S. Making money out of football. *Scot. J. Polit. Econ.* **2015**, *62*, 25–50. [CrossRef]

15. Dowling, M.; Edwards, J.; Washington, M. Understanding the concept of professionalisation in sport management research. *Sport Manag. Rev.* **2014**, *17*, 520–529. [CrossRef]

16. Ratten, V. Sport entrepreneurial ecosystems and knowledge spillovers. *Knowl. Manag. Res. Pract.* **2019**, *20*, 1–10. [CrossRef]

17. Maanijou, R.; Mirroshandel, S.A. Introducing an expert system for prediction of soccer player ranking using ensemble learning. *Neural Comp. Appl.* **2019**, *31*, 1–18. [CrossRef]

18. Louzada, F.; Maiorano, A.C.; Ara, A. iSports: A web-oriented expert system for talent identification in soccer'. *Exp. Syst. Appl.* **2016**, *44*, 400–412. [CrossRef]

19. Fédération Internationale de Football Association (FIFA). Activity Report 2017. The Year in Review. Available online: https://img.fifa.com/image/upload/qxjpyt3niwbipbca0vmm.pdf (accessed on 15 February 2020).

20. Dixon, K.; Lowes, J.; Gibbons, T. Show Racism the Red Card: Potential barriers to the effective implementation of the anti-racist message. *Soccer Soc.* **2016**, *17*, 140–154. [CrossRef]

21. Poulton, E. Tackling antisemitism within English football: A critical analysis of policies and campaigns using a multiple streams approach. *Int. J. Sport Policy Polit.* **2019**, *10*, 1–23. [CrossRef]

22. McDonald, B.; Spaaij, R.; Dukic, D. Moments of social inclusion: Asylum seekers, football and solidarity. *Sport Soc.* **2019**, *22*, 935–949. [CrossRef]

23. van Bakel, M.; Salzbrenner, S. Going abroad to play: Motivations, challenges, and support of sports expatriates'. *Thund. Int. Bus. Rev.* **2019**, *61*, 505–517. [CrossRef]

24. Majumdar, B. Forwards and backwards: Women's soccer in twentieth-century India. *Soccer Soc.* **2003**, *4*, 80–94. [CrossRef]

25. Vico, R.P.; Uvinha, R.R.; Gustavo, N. Sports mega-events in the perception of the local community: The case of Itaquera region in São Paulo at the 2014 FIFA World Cup Brazil. *Soccer Soc.* **2019**, *20*, 810–823. [CrossRef]

26. Fédération Internationale de Football Association (FIFA). Activity Report 2018. Available online: https://resources.fifa.com/image/upload/yjibhdqzfwwz5onqszo0.pdf (accessed on 15 February 2020).

27. Gerke, M. For club and country? The impact of the international game on US soccer supporters from the 1994 World Cup to the present. *Soccer Soc.* **2019**, *20*, 770–779. [CrossRef]

28. Radaelli, G.; Dell'Era, C.; Frattini, F.; Messeni Petruzzelli, A. Entrepreneurship and human capital in professional sport: A longitudinal analysis of the Italian soccer league. *Entrep. Theor. Pract.* **2018**, *42*, 70–93. [CrossRef]

29. Donthu, N.; Kumar, S.; Pattnaik, D. Forty-five years of Journal of Business Research: A bibliometric analysis. *J. Bus. Res.* **2020**, *10*, 1–14. [CrossRef]

30. Cobo, M.J.; López-Herrera, A.G.; Herrera-Viedma, E.; Herrera, F. Science mapping software tools: Review, analysis, and cooperative study among tools. *J. Am. Soc. Inf. Sci. Technol.* **2011**, *62*, 1382–1402. [CrossRef]

31. Giménez-Espert, M.C.; Prado-Gascó, V.J. Bibliometric analysis of six nursing journals from the Web of Science, 2012–2017'. *J. Adv. Nurs.* **2019**, *75*, 543–554. [CrossRef]

32. Skute, I. Opening the black box of academic entrepreneurship: A bibliometric analysis. *Scientometrics* **2019**, *24*, 1–29. [CrossRef]

33. Zupic, I.; Čater, T. Bibliometric methods in management and organization. *Org. Res. Meth.* **2015**, *18*, 429–472. [CrossRef]

34. Shen, L.; Xiong, B.; Li, W.; Lan, F.; Evans, R.; Zhang, W. Visualizing collaboration characteristics and topic burst on international mobile health research: Bibliometric analysis. *JMIR Health Health* **2018**, *6*, 135–147. [CrossRef]

35. Garfield, E.; Pudovkin, A.I.; Istomin, V.S. Mapping the output of topical searches in the Web of Knowledge and the case of Watson-Crick. *Inf. Technol. Libr.* **2003**, *22*, 183–188.

36. van Eck, N.; Waltman, L. Software survey: VOSviewer, a computer program for bibliometric mapping. *Scientometric* **2009**, *84*, 523–538. [CrossRef] [PubMed]

37. Bramwell, B.; Lane, B. From niche to general relevance? Sustainable tourism, research and the role of tourism journals. *J. Tour. Stud.* **2005**, *16*, 52–71.

38. Price, D.J.S. *Little Science, Big Science*; Columbia University Press: New York, NY, USA, 1963.

39. Havemann, F.; Larsen, B. Bibliometric indicators of young authors in astrophysics: Can later stars be predicted? *Scientometrics* **2015**, *102*, 1413–1434. [CrossRef]

40. Demil, B.; Lecocq, X. Business model evolution: In search of dynamic consistency. *Long Rang. Plan.* **2010**, *43*, 227–246. [CrossRef]

41. Peters, I.; Kraker, P.; Lex, E.; Gumpenberger, C.; Gorraiz, J. Research data explored: Citations versus altmetrics. In Proceedings of the 15th international conference on scientometrics and informetrics, Istanbul, Turkey, 29 June–3 July 2015.

42. Pongsakornrungsilp, S.; Schroeder, J.E. Understanding value co-creation in a co-consuming brand community. *Mark. Theory* **2011**, *11*, 303–324. [CrossRef]

43. Frencken, W.; Lemmink, K.; Delleman, N.; Visscher, C. Oscillations of centroid position and surface area of soccer teams in small-sided games. *Eur. J. Sport Sci.* **2011**, *11*, 215–223. [CrossRef]

44. Yin, R. *Case Study Research: Design and Methods*; Sage Publications: Thousand Oaks, CA, USA, 2003.

45. Harvey, D. The roots of geographical change: 1973 to the present. *Geograf. Annal. Ser. B Hum. Geogr.* **1989**, *71*, 1–3. [CrossRef]

46. Wang, B.; Pan, S.Y.; Ke, R.Y.; Wang, K.; Wei, Y.M. An overview of climate change vulnerability: A bibliometric analysis based on Web of Science database. *Nat. Hazards* **2014**, *74*, 1649–1666. [CrossRef]

47. Barki, H.; Rivard, S.; Talbot, J. A keyword classification scheme for IS research literature: An update. *Mis Q.* **1993**, *12*, 209–226. [CrossRef]

48. Van Eck, N.J.; Waltman, L. VOS: A new method for visualizing similarities between objects. In *Advances in Data Analysis*, 2nd ed.; Springer: Berlin, Germany, 2007; Volume 2, pp. 299–306.

49. Cheng, F.F.; Huang, Y.W.; Yu, H.C.; Wu, C.S. Mapping knowledge structure by keyword co-occurrence and social network analysis: Evidence from Library Hi Tech between 2006 and 2017. *Libr. Hi-Tech* **2018**, *36*, 636–650. [CrossRef]

50. Van Nunen, K.; Li, J.; Reniers, G.; Ponnet, K. Bibliometric analysis of safety culture research. *Saf. Sci.* **2018**, *108*, 248–258. [CrossRef]

51. Rodrigues, S.P.; Van Eck, N.J.; Waltman, L.; Jansen, F.W. Mapping patient safety: A large-scale literature review using bibliometric visualisation techniques. *BMJ Open* **2014**, *4*, 1–8. [CrossRef] [PubMed]

52. Kaplan, K.C.; Lewis, J.; Gebrian, B.; Theall, K. Soccer and sexual health education: A promising approach for reducing adolescent births in Haiti. *Rev. Panam. Salud Públ.* **2005**, *37*, 316–323.

53. Lomax, M.E. The African American experience in professional football. *J. Soc. Hist.* **1999**, *33*, 163–178. [CrossRef]

54. Rodríguez, R.; Miraflores, G.A. gender equality proposal in Physical Education: Adaptations of football rules. *RETOS-Nuev. Tend. Educ. Fis. Dep. Recre.* **2018**, *33*, 293–297.

55. Zhou, Q.; Wang, D. Ethics and Morality of Football Players and Evaluation of Football Education Teaching Model in Colleges. *Euphrosyne-Rev. Filol. Clas.* **2018**, *46*, 39–48.

56. Dubinsky, I.; Schler, L. The Mandela Soccer Academy: Historical and Contemporary Intersections between Ghana, Lebanon, and the West. *Int. J. Hist. Sport.* **2016**, *33*, 1730–1747. [CrossRef]

57. Dubinsky, I.; Schler, L. Goal dreams: Conflicting development imaginaries in Ghanaian football academies. *J. Mod. Afr. Stud.* **2019**, *57*, 247–272. [CrossRef]

58. Draper, C.E.; Tomaz, S.A.; Zihindula, G.; Bunn, C.; Gray, C.M.; Hunt, K.; Micklesfield, L.K.; Wyke, S. Development, feasibility, acceptability and potential effectiveness of a healthy lifestyle programme delivered in churches in urban and rural South Africa. *PLoS ONE* **2019**, *14*, e0219787. [CrossRef]

59. Kerr, C. An industry test for ethnic discrimination in major league soccer. *Appl. Econ. Lett.* **2019**, *26*, 1358–1363. [CrossRef]

60. Lawrence, S.; Davis, C. Fans for diversity? A Critical Race Theory analysis of Black, Asian and Minority Ethnic (BAME) supporters' experiences of football fandom. *Int. J. Sport Policy Polit.* **2019**, *11*, 701–713. [CrossRef]

61. Esson, J. A body and a dream at a vital conjuncture: Ghanaian youth, uncertainty and the allure of football. *Geoforum* **2013**, *47*, 84–92. [CrossRef]

62. Esson, J. Escape to victory: Development, youth entrepreneurship and the migration of Ghanaian footballers. *Geoforum* **2015**, *64*, 47–55. [CrossRef]

63. Esson, J. *Football as a Vehicle for Development: Lessons from Male Ghanaian Youth*, 1st ed.; Springer: Berlin, Germany, 2016.

64. Paller, J.W. Informal institutions and personal rule in urban Ghana. *Afr. Stud. Rev.* **2014**, *57*, 123–142. [CrossRef]

65. Fleischer, M.; Fuhrmann, M.; Haferburg, C.; Krüger, F. "Festivalisation" of Urban Governance in South African Cities: Framing the Urban Social Sustainability of Mega-Event Driven Development from Below. *Sustainability* **2013**, *5*, 5225–5248. [CrossRef]

66. David, M.; Millward, P. Football's Coming Home? Digital reterritorialization, contradictions in the transnational coverage of sport and the sociology of alternative football broadcasts. *Br. J. Soc.* **2012**, *63*, 349–369. [CrossRef]

67. Khoo-Dzisi, A. Re-Framing Ghana-Korea People to People Solidarity. *Afr. Asian Stud.* **2019**, *18*, 153–187. [CrossRef]

68. Coalter, F. *A Wider Social Role for Sport: Who's Keeping the Score*, 1st ed.; Routledge: New York, NY, USA, 2007.

69. Eime, R.M.; Young, J.A.; Harvey, J.T.; Charity, M.J.; Payne, W.R. A systematic review of the psychological and social benefits of participation in sport for children and adolescents: Informing development of a conceptual model of health through sport. *Int. J. Behav. Nutr. Phys. Act.* **2013**, *10*, 98–117. [CrossRef]

70. Poli, R. Understanding globalization through football: The new international division of labour, migratory channels and transnational trade circuits. *Int. Rev. Soc. Sport.* **2010**, *45*, 491–506. [CrossRef]

71. Poli, R.; Ravenel, L.; Besson, R. Foreign players in football teams. *CIES Foot Obser. Mont. Rep.* **2016**, *12*, 1–9.

72. Skirstad, B.; Chelladurai, P. For 'love' and money: A sports club's innovative response to multiple logics. *J. Sport Manag.* **2011**, *25*, 339–353. [CrossRef]

73. Smith, G. The influence of overseas coaching and management on the occupational subculture of English professional soccer: Views from the dugout. *Soccer Soc.* **2019**, *20*, 61–85. [CrossRef]

74. Rego-Fagerlande, S.M. Big sports events in Rio de Janeiro: Their effects on the slums. *Bitác. Urb. Territ.* **2018**, *28*, 143–151.

75. Rocha, L.G.B.S.P. Los empresarios, la patria y el balón: Nacionalismo, organización empresarial y financiamiento del equipo de fútbol brasileño de 1970. *Estud. Hist.* **2019**, *32*, 655–674. [CrossRef]

76. Reid, G. A fairytale narrative for community sport? Exploring the politics of sport social enterprise. *Int. J. Sport Policy Polit.* **2017**, *9*, 597–611. [CrossRef]

77. Pringle, A. The growing role of football as a vehicle for interventions in mental health care. *J. Psych. Ment. Health Nurs.* **2009**, *16*, 553–557. [CrossRef]

78. Ekholm, D.; Dahlstedt, M. Rationalities of goodwill: On the promotion of philanthropy through sports-based interventions in Sweden. *Manag. Sport Leis.* **2018**, *23*, 336–349. [CrossRef]

79. Yu, H.-B. Research on the Reform and Development of the Football Courses in Universities. *Agro Food Ind. Hi-Tech* **2018**, *28*, 3304–3307.

80. Gray, C.M.; Wyke, S.; Zhang, R.; Anderson, A.S.; Barry, S.; Boyer, N.; Brennan, G.; Briggs, A.; Bunn, C.; Donnachie, C. Long-term weight loss trajectories following participation in a randomised controlled trial of a weight management programme for men delivered through professional football clubs: A longitudinal cohort study and economic evaluation. *Int. J. Behav. Nutr. Phys. Act.* **2018**, *15*, 60–76. [CrossRef]

81. Beech, J.G.; Beech, J.; Chadwick, S. *The Business of Sport Management*, 1st ed.; Pearson Education: London, UK, 2004; pp. 1–452.

82. Hoeber, L.; Hoeber, O. Determinants of an innovation process: A case study of technological innovation in a community sport organization. *J. Sport Manag.* **2012**, *26*, 213–223. [CrossRef]

83. Schuhmacher, M.C.; Kuester, S. Identification of lead user characteristics driving the quality of service innovation ideas. *Creat. Innov. Manag.* **2012**, *21*, 427–442. [CrossRef]

84. Pereira, M.J.R.; Moura, L.R.C.; Souki, G.Q.; Cunha, N.R. da S. Proposition and test of an explanatory model of innovation perception and it's consequences. *Rev. Brasil. Mark.* **2020**, *18*, 25–50. [CrossRef]

85. Sotelo Gonzalez, J. Sport and Social Media: Spain's" Primera Division" football league case. *Hist. Comun. Soc.* **2012**, *17*, 217–230.

86. Vimieiro, A.C. The digital productivity of football supporters: Formats, motivations and styles. *Convergence* **2018**, *24*, 374–390. [CrossRef]

87. King, A. New directors, customers, and fans: The transformation of English football in the 1990s. *Soc. Sport J.* **1997**, *14*, 224–240. [CrossRef]

88. Faulkner, A.; McNamee, M.; Coveney, C.; Gabe, J. Where biomedicalisation and magic meet: Therapeutic innovations of elite sports injury in British professional football and cycling. *Soc. Sci. Med.* **2017**, *178*, 136–143. [CrossRef]

89. Olson, E.M.; Duray, R.; Cooper, C.; Olson, K.M. Strategy, structure, and culture within the English Premier League. *Sport Bus. Manag. An. Int. J.* **2016**, *6*, 55–75. [CrossRef]
90. Buraimo, B.; Forrest, D.; Simmons, R. Insights for clubs from modelling match attendance in football. *J. Oper. Res.Soc.* **2009**, *60*, 147–155. [CrossRef]
91. Cohen, A.; Peachey, J.W. The making of a social entrepreneur: From participant to cause champion within a sport-for-development context. *Sport Manag. Rev.* **2015**, *18*, 111–125. [CrossRef]
92. Miragaia, D.; Ferreira, J.; Carvalho, A.; Ratten, V. Interactions between financial efficiency and sports performance. *J. Entrep. Public Policy* **2019**, *8*, 84–102. [CrossRef]
93. Garcia, S.F.A.; Louzada, R.; Galli, L.L.; Barbosa, A.L. Impact of marketing innovations in football clubs revenues: The case of Corinthians. *PODIUM: Sport Leis. Tour. Rev.* **2015**, *4*, 48–61. [CrossRef]
94. Lulli, F.; Volterrani, M.; Magni, S.; Armeni, R. An innovative hybrid natural–artificial sports pitch construction system. *Proc. Inst. Mech. Eng. Part P J. Sport. Eng. Technol.* **2011**, *225*, 171–175. [CrossRef]
95. Merkel, S.; Schmidt, S.L.; Schreyer, D. The future of professional football. *Sport Bus. Manag. An. Int. J.* **2016**, *6*, 295–319. [CrossRef]
96. Klauser, F.R. Interpretative flexibility of the event-city: Security, branding and urban entrepreneurialism at the European Football Championships 2008. *Int. J. Urban Reg. Res.* **2012**, *36*, 1039–1052. [CrossRef]
97. Müller, M. How mega-events capture their hosts: Event seizure and the World Cup 2018 in Russia. *Urban Geogr.* **2017**, *38*, 1113–1132. [CrossRef]
98. Ludvigsen, J.A. "Continent-wide" sports spectacles: The "multiple host format" of Euro 2020 and United 2026 and its implications. *J. Conv. Event Tour.* **2019**, *20*, 163–181. [CrossRef]
99. Diord, S.; Magalhães, F.; Cunha, Á.; Caetano, E.; Martins, N. Automated modal tracking in a football stadium suspension roof for detection of structural changes. *Struct. Contr. Health Monit.* **2017**, *24*, 1–19. [CrossRef]
100. Schmieder, M. Translucent roof system for the Essen football stadium. *STAHLBAU* **2013**, *82*, 801–804. [CrossRef]
101. Kellison, T.B.; Hong, S. The adoption and diffusion of pro-environmental stadium design. *Eur. Sport Manag. Quart.* **2015**, *15*, 249–269. [CrossRef]
102. Eick, V. Lack of legacy? Shadows of surveillance after the 2006 FIFA World Cup in Germany. *Urban Stud.* **2011**, *48*, 3329–3345. [CrossRef]
103. Buchheit, M.; Simpson, B.M. Player-tracking technology: Half-full or half-empty glass? *Int. J. Sports Phys. Perform.* **2017**, *12*, S2–S35. [CrossRef]
104. Memmert, D.; Lemmink, K.A.; Sampaio, J. Current approaches to tactical performance analyses in soccer using position data. *Sports Med.* **2017**, *47*, 1–10. [CrossRef] [PubMed]
105. Yang, Y. The innovation of college physical training based on computer virtual reality technology. *J. Discret. Math. Sci. Cryptogr.* **2018**, *21*, 1275–1280. [CrossRef]
106. Abbott, W.; Brickley, G.; Smeeton, N.J. Positional differences in GPS outputs and perceived exertion during soccer training games and competition. *J. Strenght Condit. Res.* **2018**, *32*, 3222–3231. [CrossRef] [PubMed]
107. Szwarc, A.; Jaszczur-Nowicki, J.; Aschenbrenner, P.; Zasada, M.; Padulo, J.; Lipinska, P. Motion analysis of elite Polish soccer goalkeepers throughout a season. *Biol. Sport* **2019**, *36*, 357–371. [CrossRef]
108. Murgia, M.; Sors, F.; Muroni, A.F.; Santoro, I.; Prpic, V.; Galmonte, A.; Agostini, T. Using perceptual home-training to improve anticipation skills of soccer goalkeepers. *Psych. Sport Exerc.* **2014**, *15*, 642–648. [CrossRef]
109. Van Maarseveen, M.J.; Oudejans, R.R.; Savelsbergh, G.J. Pattern recall skills of talented soccer players: Two new methods applied. *Hum. Mov. Sci.* **2015**, *41*, 59–75. [CrossRef]
110. Diquigiovanni, J.; Scarpa, B. Analysis of association football playing styles: An innovative method to cluster networks. *Stat. Model.* **2019**, *19*, 28–54. [CrossRef]
111. Ren, J.; Orwell, J.; Jones, G.A.; Xu, M. Real-time modeling of 3-d soccer ball trajectories from multiple fixed cameras. *IEEE Trans. Circ. Syst. Video Technol.* **2008**, *18*, 350–362.
112. Ren, J.; Orwell, J.; Jones, G.A.; Xu, M. Tracking the soccer ball using multiple fixed cameras. *Comp. Vis. Imag. Underst.* **2009**, *113*, 633–642. [CrossRef]
113. Ronkainen, J.; Harland, A. Laser tracking system for sports ball trajectory measurement. *Proc. Inst. Mech. Eng. Part P J. Sport. Eng. Technol.* **2010**, *224*, 219–228. [CrossRef]
114. Mazzeo, P.L.; Spagnolo, P.; Leo, M.; De Marco, T.; Distante, C. Ball detection in soccer images using isophote's curvature and discriminative features. *Patt. Anal. Appl.* **2016**, *19*, 709–718. [CrossRef]

115. Kolbinger, O.; Link, D. The use of vanishing spray reduces the extent of rule violations in soccer. *SpringerPlus* **2016**, *5*, 1572. [CrossRef] [PubMed]

116. Samuel, R.D.; Galily, Y.; Guy, O.; Sharoni, E.; Tenenbaum, G. A decision-making simulator for soccer referees. *Int. J. Sports Sci. Coach.* **2019**, *14*, 480–489. [CrossRef]

117. Yoshida, K. Challenge: Concept of system life and its application to robotics. *Robot. Auton. Syst.* **2010**, *58*, 833–839. [CrossRef]

118. Pares, J.; Taboada, C.; Temporal, D.; Carré, C. Physium in risk reduction of injuries in elite indoor football players: A pilot study. *J. Sport Health Res.* **2016**, *8*, 223–230.

119. Claudino, J.G.; de Oliveira Capanema, D.; de Souza, T.V.; Serrão, J.C.; Pereira, A.C.M.; Nassis, G.P. Current approaches to the use of artificial intelligence for injury risk assessment and performance prediction in team sports: A systematic review. *Sports Med. Open* **2019**, *5*, 28–41. [CrossRef]

120. Sousa, J.P.; Cabri, J.; Donaghy, M. Case research in sports physiotherapy: A review of studies. *Phys. Therap. Sport* **2007**, *8*, 197–206. [CrossRef]

121. Contrò, V.; Schiera, G.; Abbruzzo, A.; Bianco, A.; Amato, A.; Sacco, A.; Macchiarella, A.; Palma, A.; Proia, P. An innovative way to highlight the power of each polymorphism on elite athletes phenotype expression. *Eur. J. Transl. Myolog.* **2018**, *28*, 1–18. [CrossRef]

122. Cascone, P.; Petrucci, B.; Ramieri, V.; TitoMatteo, M. Security hi-tech individual extra-light device mask: A new protection for [soccer] players. *J. Cranio-Fac. Surg.* **2008**, *19*, 772–776. [CrossRef] [PubMed]

123. Gaudino, F.; Weber, M.A. Osteitis pubis oder Symphysitis pubis. *Der Radiologe* **2019**, *59*, 218–223. [CrossRef] [PubMed]

124. Hwang, S.; Ma, L.; Kawata, K.; Tierney, R.; Jeka, J.J. Vestibular dysfunction after subconcussive head impact. *J. Neurotrauma* **2017**, *34*, 8–15. [CrossRef] [PubMed]

125. Contreras-Muñoz, P.; Fernández-Martín, A.; Torrella, R.; Serres, X.; De la Varga, M.; Viscor, G.; Järvinen, T.A.H.; Martínez-Ibáñez, V.; Peiró, J.L.; Rodas, G. A new surgical model of skeletal muscle injuries in rats reproduces human sports lesions. *Int. J. Sports Med.* **2016**, *37*, 183–190. [CrossRef] [PubMed]

126. Mithoefer, K.; Peterson, L.; Saris, D.B.; Mandelbaum, B.R. Evolution and current role of autologous chondrocyte implantation for treatment of articular cartilage defects in the football (soccer) player. *Cartilage* **2012**, *3*, 31–36. [CrossRef] [PubMed]

10

Cultural Antecedents of Green Entrepreneurship in Saudi Arabia: An Institutional Approach

Wafa Alwakid [1,2,*], Sebastian Aparicio [3,4] and David Urbano [5]

[1] Department of Business, Universitat Autònoma de Barcelona, Edifici B Campus UAB, Bellaterra (Cerdanyola del Vallès), 08193 Barcelona, Spain

[2] Department of Business Administration, Jouf University, Al Jouf 75471, Saudi Arabia

[3] Durham University Business School, Durham University, Mill Hill Lane, Durham DH1 3LB, UK; sebastian.aparicio@durham.ac.uk

[4] Fundación ECSIM, Medellin, Colombia

[5] Department of Business and Centre for Entrepreneurship and Social Innovation Research (CREIS), Universitat Autònoma de Barcelona, Edifici B Campus UAB, Bellaterra (Cerdanyola del Vallès), 08193 Barcelona, Spain; david.urbano@uab.cat

* Correspondence: wafanaif.alwakid@e-campus.uab.cat

Abstract: Recent decades have brought cultural changes toward the increase of environmentally-friendly initiatives such as green entrepreneurship. Some countries are failing to develop environmental initiatives, whereas others are transitioning and advancing toward this new trend. In particular, Saudi Arabia has initiated efforts toward becoming an ecologically-friendly society. Motivated by this, we explore whether cultural characteristics are associated with green entrepreneurship in Saudi Arabia. Institutional economics is adopted to frame our hypotheses and analysis. The hypothesized relationships were empirically tested in a sample of 84 observations from 21 cities during the period 2015–2018. Data were collected from reports by the Saudi General Authority and analyzed through regression models. The main results show that cultural characteristics, such as environmental actions, environmental consciousness, and temporal orientation, increase the level of green entrepreneurial activity across cities in Saudi Arabia. The findings of this study contribute to existing knowledge on green entrepreneurship, as well as to the discussion of implications for policy and practice related to environmentally-friendly productive activities.

Keywords: green entrepreneurship; sustainable entrepreneurial activity; culture; institutional approach; developing countries; Saudi Arabia

1. Introduction

Research on sustainable entrepreneurship has considerably grown in recent decades, which has enabled scholars to link entrepreneurship and sustainable development [1]. Ultimately, researchers have utilized the term "sustainable entrepreneurship", along with added expressions such as "green entrepreneurship" or "environmental entrepreneurship" [2–5]. Although there are slight differences among these terms, in general, this type of entrepreneurial activity is seen as part of a new global societal trend in an era where the focus on green policies is stronger than ever. Furthermore, green-related entrepreneurship has become an important subfield of entrepreneurship research [2]. Such societal challenges bring a need for better knowledge of both the antecedents and consequences antecedents of green entrepreneurial activity. In this paper, we consider green entrepreneurship, in line with an intensified call for conducting business in a "greener" way. A preoccupation with green entrepreneurial activity has thus arisen [6–8], boosted by a culture of green entrepreneurship that shapes new breeds of entrepreneurs [9] and contributes to molding social norms that support this "greenism" [10].

In this study, it is suggested that the socio-cultural norms that enhance green entrepreneurial activity in Saudi Arabia offer the opportunity to observe the early roots of post-material culture [11]. In Saudi Arabia, cultural identity is the feeling of belonging to a group and is part of a person's self-concept and self-awareness. This relates to generations, nationality, religion, race, language, social class, region, or any social group that has its own unique culture [11]. In this way, cultural identity is not only a distinctive feature of the individual, but of a similar group of people who share the same views [12]. Likewise, culture plays a direct and vital role in achieving the three strategic pillars of Saudi Arabia's 2030 vision, which are: (1) building a prosperous economy, (2) building a vibrant society, and (3) building a homeland [13]. One of the main objectives tangential to these three pillars involves increasing environmentally-friendly activities, including green entrepreneurship. However, there is a lack of evidence that enables us to gain a full understanding of whether different cultural characteristics are helpful in accomplishing this sustainable production objective.

From an institutional economics point of view [14,15], the role of formal (particularly economic regulations) and informal institutions (particularly culture) in sustainability has been discussed [16]. Meek et al. [17] and Urbano et al. [18] also discussed how informal institutional factors may explain more differing types of entrepreneurial activities, including green entrepreneurship, than formal institutions. In this sense, according to Adler [19] and Andries and Stephan [20], there are institutional factors characterized by cultural differences in environmental activities and actions. Encouraging an environmental consciousness that embraces these aspects is one way to expand sustainability [21,22]. It is also vital to comprehend how entrepreneurship accounts for social values, beliefs, and culture, which change over time and space [23,24]. In this regard, organizational processes have a temporal dimension, often implicit and without discourse, that clearly characterizes the entrepreneurial process [25]. It is still unknown, however, whether these three institutional factors as cultural characteristics (i.e., environmental actions, environmental consciousness, and temporal orientation) directly explain green entrepreneurship [9,17,22] in developing countries such as Saudi Arabia.

Thus, in this study, institutional economics [14,15] is used to enhance our comprehension of cultural influences (i.e., informal institutions) on green entrepreneurship in Saudi Arabian cities. Drawing on this, it is suggested that national culture affects environmentally-friendly policies [16]. In particular, we analyze the influence of three cultural factors on green entrepreneurship: (1) environmental actions, (2) environmental consciousness, and (3) temporal orientation. To test the suggested hypotheses, we rely on balanced panel data, with a sample of 84 observations during the 2015–2018 period. After testing the fixed-effects models for 21 cities in Saudi Arabia, we find that the three assessed cultural factors positively explain green entrepreneurial activity across cities in Saudi Arabia.

While the field of green entrepreneurship is relatively new and empirical documentation has started to make a contribution to existing knowledge, there is still no consensus on defining this term [10,22,26,27]. With this in mind, our contribution to the literature is twofold. Firstly, many scholars have studied the influence of informal institutions and values on the intentions and actions of entrepreneurs [17]. Scholars have assessed different informal factors in their studies, but this paper reveals a further connection between informal institutional factors, particularly cultural ones, and green entrepreneurship. Secondly, being both an oil producer and a new member of a consortium that focuses on the environmental consequences of economic activities, Saudi Arabia is an excellent case study of this subject, and scholars and practitioners may find these results useful for learning and decision making. Furthermore, the relationship between (informal) institutions and green entrepreneurship offers a fertile means of explanation that can contribute to policy-making. Knowledge of the consequences of green entrepreneurial practices may allow for forecasting the long- and short-term changes in society, and also for understanding which types of incentives could be provided in order to direct social and sustainable development [21]. A significant set of green-aware companies would be expected to change and encourage others to adopt green entrepreneurship.

After this brief Introduction, Section 2 contextualizes the case of Saudi Arabia, and Section 3 introduces the conceptual foundations for the literature analysis and hypothesis development.

In Section 4, the methodology and data are explained, and then, the findings are presented and assessed in Section 5. Finally, Section 6 focuses on the conclusions, implications and limitations for potential research avenues.

2. Green Entrepreneurship in Saudi Arabia

Previous academic work indicated a positive correlation between entrepreneurship and economic expansion [18]. Furthermore, entrepreneurship encourages the economy to improve through creative methods [28]. In general, the more active the entrepreneurship is, the more positive the influence on economic growth will be [18,28]. In addition, the actions of entrepreneurship are deemed an indication of the vital determinants concerning localized economic progression [29]. Indeed, policy-makers expect that entrepreneurship has a positive influence on the country's wealth and employment [29]. Likewise, several scholars have argued that when institutions are not properly working, the influence of entrepreneurship might be negative [29].

Indeed, this is the case of developing countries [29]. Accordingly, Saudi Arabia is enjoying an emerging global economic boost, relying at present on oil, but with ambitious strategies to diversify the economy away from these natural resources and toward the promotion of entrepreneurial expansion [30]. Currently, Saudi Arabia is living through a significant social and economic renaissance by guiding itself confidently toward a lucrative future, as well as creating a diversified and sustainable financial backbone by attracting knowledge-based investors [31]. As it grows, a corporate business has forwarded strategies, heralding the requirement to monitor entrepreneurship closely.

Due to worldwide affiliation toward the economy as the basis of supporting the state's competitive prowess, through close attention to youth creativity, the Saudi government has actively supported entrepreneurship to establish a competitive and sustainable Saudi nation [31]. Within Saudi Arabia, there are many obstacles and constraints that entrepreneurs must face, including the non-existence of an independent regulatory strategy and framework for the responsible progression of enterprises. This is considered to be one of the most significant challenges facing entrepreneurship. In addition, Saudi Arabia's involvement with the World Trade Organization concluded with several failed endeavors, unable to compete with international initiatives and resources [31]. Despite this, the Saudi government envisions a tendency toward green entrepreneurship among the younger generation [32]. Hence, Saudi Arabia has encouraged its youth to enhance free business through the offer of scholarships, examples being the Fastest 100 Growing Companies Award, the Prince Salman Award for Entrepreneurship, and the Most Competitive Youth Award [33]. This level of encouragement and innovative progression clearly motivates entrepreneurs to pursue green activities [33].

According to the 2019 Global Entrepreneurship Monitor report, almost 76.3% of the adult population in Saudi Arabia believes that the country offers better opportunities to start a business [34]. Part of this success can be attributed to the use of green entrepreneurship, which has allowed businesses to appreciate that there are environmental, economic, and social factors in running their businesses. Therefore, these businesses attempt to seek innovative solutions to the way in which products and services are procured and consumed. Similarly, Saudi Arabia has scaled-up its business operation models, which can assist in greening the Saudi Arabian economy. Saudi Vision 2030 believes that the Saudi Arabian economy should offer opportunities that can stimulate the economy, while at the same time generating revenues for other sectors [35].

The result is that businesses operate in an environment that is safe and healthy, which is important for the survival of any business and guarantees a competitive advantage over others. Entrepreneurship requires that a business discovers new ideas that can be used to make the business flourish over time. Through this, new business ideas are created while the businesses experience exponential growth. With regard to innovation, Saudi Arabia now has policies that mean to help entrepreneurs, while at the same time stimulate growth for a competitive edge [36]. In order to support innovation and entrepreneurship, the country uses Saudi Arabia Vision 2030 as a mechanism to encourage a national culture that ultimately promotes the growth of enterprises, as they play a critical role in the economy.

3. Literature Review

To comprehend the possible mechanisms behind the relationship between culture and green entrepreneurship, we used institutional economics [14,15]. It is suggested that institutions involve the deeper aspects of social strata, acting as authoritative guidelines and curbs in behavior [14,15]. North [14,15] classified institutions as formal (i.e., constitutions, contracts, common law, government policy) and informal (i.e., attitudes, values, norms, beliefs, or in broader terms, the culture of a society). Generally, institutions can be viewed as rules within society, shaping human interaction [14] (p. 3). Despite the lack of formal sanctions, they are pervasive and direct behaviors. Formal institutions can change quickly, yet informal ones are slower to change [37]. The institutional economics framework offered by North [14,15] may contribute to our understanding of how culture affects productive activities such as green entrepreneurship. Although there have been a number of studies analyzing formal institutions as initial steps toward entrepreneurial activity (see Bjørnskov and Foss [38], Urbano et al. [18], and Zhai et al. [39] for thorough literature reviews), it has been argued that informal institutions are more influential within society [18,40,41]. An additional conclusion relates to interactions between formal and informal institutions, with many regulations potentially working better depending on the cultural values of society [42]. Informal institutions limit the influence of formal bodies and vice versa [43].

Similar ideas, particularly focused on culture, have explored green entrepreneurship [17,18]. Although there is not a consensus about what green entrepreneurial activity means [44] (see Appendix A for different definitions), we adopt the approach offered by Gast et al. [10], who defined this sort of activity as "the process of identifying, evaluating and seizing entrepreneurial opportunities that minimize a venture's impact on the natural environment and therefore create benefits for society as a whole and for local communities" [10] (p. 46). This is similar to the work of Silajdžić et al. [45] (p. 377), who suggested that green entrepreneurs "are those who start businesses based on the principle of sustainability with strong underlying green values and who sell green products or services", and also Yi [46] (p. 4), who suggested that green entrepreneurship is "a kind of social activity that aims at protecting and preserving the natural environment". Hence, green entrepreneurship is characterized by some basic features of entrepreneurial activity coupled with giving priority to the skills and initiative of the entrepreneurial seeking success through the social or environment innovations for sustainability [1].

Culture may be seen as heavily influential when pursuing sustainability [47] (p. 236). Several studies view culture as a significant variable in sustainability-related actions [48–51]. For instance, cultural habits play a vital role in assessing variation within corporate social responsibility (CSR) [52]. Similarly, regarding consumer views of corporate responsibility, studies advocate global culture-related differences [53,54]. Some scholars that have examined the relationship between the rate of green entrepreneurship and culture have provided a deeper understanding of how culture is defined in international and inter-cultural business management research [55,56]. Having a socially supportive culture affects the level of national entrepreneurship and its quality. In this paper, we focused on green entrepreneurship and its association with culture, through cultural habits as proxies of informal institutions, as Stephan et al. [54] suggested. Although there might be other important institutional factors affecting sustainable development, including green entrepreneurship [16,18], cultural aspects observed through actions, consciousness, and temporal orientation reflect what societies think and do to support entrepreneurship and other productive activities in the pursuit of sustainability [17].

Hence, the main cultural dimensions that we examined are environmental actions, environmental consciousness, and temporal orientation, which might have an association with green entrepreneurship. In regard to the latter (i.e., temporal orientation), it is suggested that long-term economic development reflects shared values and beliefs (i.e., informal), as well as laws and bureaucracy (i.e., formal institutions) that regulate human interactions [15]. This is due to cultural norms forcing limitations on formal institutional development [36]. The sedentary nature of cultural change also presents obstacles for extreme institutional change [56]. People thus observe dominant practices (e.g., in green entrepreneurship) and reflect them through their own values, attitudes, and behaviors. There is no doubt that total entrepreneurial activity acts as a catalyst for economic growth [23,41], so those values, attitudes, and behaviors are transferred from entrepreneurs to society. The mechanisms are quite simple: institutions boost entrepreneurship, as they create the context for economic growth and other developmental outcomes [18]. From this point of view, the environmental actions focused on entrepreneurship can shed light on the processes that are common in a green approach to economic activity. Green entrepreneurs are a different type of entrepreneur [9]. Instead of building their life on profit-making, they are also concerned about social justice [9] (p. 828). Personal motivation and a forward-thinking approach to sustainability are also important characteristics of entrepreneurs [9] (pp. 837–840).

In general, green entrepreneurship plays a rising role in the protection of the environment [46]. Based on this idea, Ndubisi and Nair [57] suggested that there is a need for companies to adopt a green approach. This is embedded in a culture of reflexive development, where concern about environmental issues and the need for sustainability become the societal norm. This creates another link between existing institutions and environmental consciousness, which consists of the propensity to encounter examples of green entrepreneurship in the immediate area, as well as values reflected by entrepreneurs. It is important to contextualize the situation of green entrepreneurs [58], which is consistent with theories of post-modernization and reflexive modernization [11]. People become aware (or conscious) of the side-effects of technology and try to control them. This is exactly the case with environmental consciousness for green entrepreneurs, who tend to live in relative abundance and develop a culture of concern about the quality of the environment and sustainability. They are active both in the existing businesses that pursue a process of greening, but also as part of new businesses that become green as soon as they are set up [27].

The institutional perspective [14,15] enables us to understand the reasons why governments encourage all members in society to support sustainability initiatives actively such as green entrepreneurship [59]. Such a culture created is visible through social norms and policies that foster green entrepreneurial activity. Indeed, companies that promote green measures are even more visible for societies: they are easier to notice and create an institutional framework that individuals can observe and internalize. Evidence for this interpretation is found in a number of studies, such as Thang et al. [60], Papadopoulos et al. [61], Silajdžić et al. [45], and Karimi and Nabavi [62], which demonstrated relationships between social and structural interventions and subsequent attempts by organizations to engage in "greening" of their entrepreneurial activities. These studies showed different attempts of introducing green entrepreneurial practices in Vietnam [60], Greece and Cyprus [61], Bosnia and Herzegovina [45], and Tehran [62]. All these countries were engaged in a period of economic and social change, which required involvement and intervention with wider stakeholders.

Interpreting an institutional change entails that culture can be applied at various levels [56]. When considered at the aggregate level, one may observe cultural descriptive norms and practices, whereas at the individual level, cultural values trigger attitudes and behaviors focused on the environment. Policies that promote green entrepreneurship and corresponding green behaviors are based on a culture of caring for others, combined with promoting performance, as demonstrated or hypothesized by various scholars [16,22,27,63]. Several authors [9,19,64,65] have also noted such key cultural dimensions, which need further attention. Hence, in this paper, we focused on environmental actions, environmental consciousness, and temporal orientation.

It is worth noticing that embracing sustainability does not automatically lead to practicing it [44]. Cultural values may precede practices since they dictate behavior [66]. There are cultural differences regarding the initial mode of activity; some cultures emphasize action and outcomes [19], and in developing countries, environmental actions are of prime importance [21]. Green entrepreneurs run businesses to achieve dual environmental and business objectives to ensure their sectors are more sustainable [67,68]. For those wishing to be greener in their businesses, there is a disparity between self-principle customers' interests, affecting public behavior [22]. Their motivation to act is initiated by the desire to prevent and solve specific environmental issues or to alter their sectors; hence, wider alternatives and more environmentally-friendly practices become normalized [69]. Where businesses previously placed priority on cost-saving, environmental benefits may be of only minor concern, suggesting that a global, mainstream view of green principles is in its infancy. Consumers are partially motivated by sustainability itself, but are also motivated by simultaneously occurring underlying and/or societal sustainability issues [70]. Evans and Abrahamse [71] forwarded the argument that appealing to these underlying issues may expand sustainability commitment. While saving money may attract individuals to sustainable habits, it may have limited influence if wider consumption practices continue [22]. We thus suggest the hypothesis that:

Hypothesis 1 (H1). *Environmental actions are positively associated with green entrepreneurship in Saudi Arabia.*

There has recently been increasing environmental consciousness or interest in protecting the environment around the world [21]. Indeed, environmental awareness has recently increased in society at every level [17]; however, there are differences in cultures, and people's relationships differ regarding the natural environment [17]. In some cultures, individuals have complete control over their environment, while others live in environmental harmony and view people and nature as one. In yet other cultures, individuals are controlled by the environment, accepting the power it conveys [19]. Entrepreneurship and wealth/economic growth are closely linked, hence heavily promoted and encouraged in the modern world [41]. The environmental consciousness also leads green entrepreneurship to affect green innovation and social-environmental responsibility [72]. Recently, with increased interest in environmental and social issues, entrepreneurship conjoins the objectives of sustainable development and the accumulation of wealth [73,74].

This consciousness may be observed across age groups. However, there is increasing evidence from different cultural contexts showing that the younger generations (treated as a proxy for those of typically undergraduate age) are especially interested in environmental conscientiousness, actively seeking educational opportunities that support green entrepreneurship and/or sustainability initiatives. For example, Soomro et al. [32] and Yi [46] provided evidence about the positive association between environmental consciousness through education and its subsequent intent to engage young people in green entrepreneurial activities. These studies were carried out in Pakistan and China, respectively, indicating a broader global awareness of environmental conscientiousness and pointing toward the potential wider generalizability of this particular study on the basis of transferable concepts in rapidly developing economies. Similarly, evidence from Serbia also found that the social desirability for environmental education is translated into economic and environmental practice [75].

Environmental consciousness is related to the social image, which supports individuals to become green entrepreneurs and take care of the environment [76,77]. In emerging markets, there is a sensitivity to environmental issues and an effort to combine them with green entrepreneurship [77]. Furthermore, in developing countries, the need to produce environmentally-friendly and ecological resources has swayed entrepreneurs to give careful consideration to environmental issues in their objectives [21]. Entrepreneurs are now motivated to consider environmental issues to meet their social responsibility, so the exploration of green entrepreneurship extends research through non-financial desires [78]. Green entrepreneurs negotiate disparity between business activities, environmental mission statements, and wider contexts relating to sustainable and growth-focused economies [22]. As such, entrepreneurs interested in sustainability, as influencers, prioritize environmental issues over profits where possible, being conscious of the optimal effort to reduce damages to the environment. They may present a win-win situation for both economic growth and the environment and may meet their own personal goals. These entrepreneurs gradually enhance the environment and educate a wide audience on benefits related to environmental protection through products and services [27]. Green entrepreneurs are labeled as novel entrepreneurial investors, aiming to integrate environmental awareness with business advancement through holistic measures; a unique logical approach as compared to conventional entrepreneurs [74]. Indeed, the commitment to the environment displayed by green entrepreneurs enhances their reputation compared to other entrepreneurs [64]. On this basis, we propose that:

Hypothesis 2 (H2). *Environmental consciousness is positively associated with green entrepreneurship in Saudi Arabia.*

Our final cultural factor deals with temporal orientation, utilized in the literature to evaluate cognitive involvement throughout history, the present, and into the future [79,80]. There are cultural differences regarding an individual's temporal orientation, that is to say orientation to the past, present, or future [25]. In past-oriented cultures, tradition is central to the wisdom of societal life [25], whereas future-oriented societies disregard the past and focus entirely on the future, resulting in an extensive long-term timeline [81]. In contrast, present-oriented cultures have a limited timeline, focusing on short-term gains [25]. This concept is vital, since it influences the manner in which individuals incorporate their perceptions of past experiences, present situations, and future objectives into their opinions, cognitions, and the way they behave [82]. For example, several authors have discovered that a present time perspective focuses less on future strategic processes than other differing cultures [81,83]. Individuals embedded in a present time perspective focus predominantly on the present, perceiving that future planning is futile, unlike those with a future time perspective [79]. Green entrepreneurs offer clear solutions regarding social transformation [84], creating long-term outcomes and an enhanced positive future.

Time itself is a factor that may help us to understand changing attitudes toward entrepreneurship [85]. For instance, organizational processes involve temporal dimensions that are implicit with no discourse, and temporal issues clearly and accurately describe the entrepreneurial process [25]. Past experiences and comprehension of previous activity are the basis on which present actions are taken, moving forward to future wealth gain. These temporal dimensions are carried out over many levels within entrepreneurial campaigns [25]. Entrepreneurs and the individuals working alongside them act in the present to ensure future gains [25]. Some of the characteristics of entrepreneurs derive from personal experiences and history, including temporal orientation (past, present, or future), along with the future time-based perspective, choosing deadlines, taking advantage of evolving opportunities, perceiving and anticipating problems and phase development concerns, as well as aims and ambitions for the future. This interpretation was observed in both Grinevich et al. [68] and Yi [46], who demonstrated the importance of both temporal and conceptual interpretations of green entrepreneurship is relative to prevailing circumstances. To a lesser extent, the earlier work of Papadopoulos et al. [61] supported this interpretation, although it was acknowledged that the main concerns of entrepreneurs were responding to government initiatives related to green entrepreneurship, which were still limited at that time. These are critical issues that need careful consideration for successful entrepreneurship [25]. At the industry or environmental level, time figures into the entrepreneurship equation on the basis of a quick response; the enhanced pace of technology results in obsolete software slowing down the process, leading to possible critical blockages in terms of meeting the demands of customers, suppliers, stockholders, and venture backers [25].

At the country level, there is an enhanced realization in entrepreneurial research that economic activity can be better comprehended within temporal, historical, spatial, institutional, and social contexts since they give individuals an enhanced opportunity to invest and set distinct boundaries for future activities [86]. A vital aspect of the social sustainability endeavor is that it emphasizes the business-based long-term benefits that society expects [87]. This is due to the fact that one of the objectives of sustainability is that of inter-generational equity [88]. The requirements of today's generations must not limit or compromise future generations [89]. It follows that in the future, society needs to be more aware of long-term impacts. Drawing on this idea, there is evidence on the effect of green entrepreneurship on the organization's financial performance [72,77], which involves future planning. Furthermore, utilizing the green logic alongside the social and economic aspects in a flexible manner constitutes temporal adjustments [59]. Companies within these future-oriented cultures may well involve themselves in social sustainability practices, contributing to social justice, enhanced social recognition, and trust with and between stakeholders and society [89]. Based on these ideas, the following hypothesis is suggested:

Hypothesis 3 (H3). *Temporal orientation is positively associated with green entrepreneurship in Saudi Arabia.*

4. Methodology

4.1. Data and Variables

Extensive literature has prioritized the identification of major factors contributing to cultural differences. The concept behind this view is that human societies endure the same problems, for which there are many proposed solutions, and where each culture within society makes a choice. This suggests that societies may be classified in accordance with major cultural dimensions [90], which may in turn explain green entrepreneurial activities [17]. In order to understand this relationship, we used variables and data from a number of different sources, which are explained below.

4.1.1. Dependent Variable

For the dependent variable, we measured green entrepreneurship according to the Organisation for Economic Co-operation and Development (OECD) [91], which defines this particular type of entrepreneurial activity as an environmental commitment. This definition is also consistent with the conceptual foundation we adopted thanks to Gast et al. [10]. According to Kraus et al. [92], sustainability studies have focused mainly on issues involving the environment, which is an important issue in Saudi Arabia [13]. The information for our dependent variable came from annual reports (General Authority for Meteorology and Environmental Protection). This variable showed the percentage of small- and medium-sized enterprises (SMEs) that were environmentally friendly out of the total number of SMEs in the city. This variable was in line with Miska and Schiffinger's [59] focus on corporate sustainability practices and performance orientation practices as factors affecting green entrepreneurship. We note that there may be some methodological critique of using a dependent variable throughout a percentage [93], but in line with Liu and Xin [94], it was considered appropriate in the conditions of this study because the dependent variable was standardized.

4.1.2. Independent Variables

Environmental actions, which consisted of motivation for action and emphasize the value of the activity, were the independent variables. The motivation ratio was the development and growth of environmental capabilities. The value of the environmental actions was the percentage of the accomplished goals of the defined environmental measures in each city. According to Kraus et al. [92], environmental activities carried out are not only due to environmental awareness, but to meet legal regulations, minimize costs, and link to a community's sense of sustainability. In addition, green entrepreneurs show environmental actions by achieving dual environmental and business objectives and by wishing to transform sectors to become more sustainable [67,68]. The information for these variables came from annual reports (General Authority for Statistics in Saudi Arabia—Knowledge statistics) (see Table 1). The framing of mainstream and set "green" issues revealed evidence of the tensions and politics present when creating a green economy. Gibbs and O'Neill [22] presented a novel and interpretive concept, with the evolving issue of "being" and "becoming" a green entrepreneur, rather than the fixed categories presented in previous literature.

Table 1. Description of the variables.

	Variable	Description	Source
Dependent variable	Green entrepreneurship	This variable shows the percentage of the number of SMEs that are environmentally friendly out of the total number of SMEs in the city. Green entrepreneurship can be measured as environmental commitment [91]. The variable was standardized.	Annual reports of the General Authority for Statistics in Saudi Arabia.
Independent variables	Environmental actions	The percentage of accomplished goals of the defined environmental measures in each city. The ratio involves the development and growth of environmental capabilities by the local government. There are environmental actions in achieving both environmental and business goals [67,68]. The variable was standardized.	Annual reports of the General Authority for Statistics in Saudi Arabia.
	Environmental consciousness	The percentage of the maintenance of natural resources. This variable considers the reduction/control in the use of natural resources relative to outputs, by living in balance with natural forces [12]. The variable was standardized.	
	Time orientation	The percentage of public and private organizations that have adopted environmental measures in each city. As entrepreneurship needs to compete by taking advantage of fast-changing market conditions [94], this variable takes into consideration the speed at which organizations embrace environmental initiatives. The variable was standardized.	
Control variables	Annual growth rate	The value of a city's recourses for the agricultural sector. The variable was standardized.	Annual reports of the General Authority for Statistics in Saudi Arabia.
	The population of each city	The population of the area. The variable was standardized.	
	Size of the city	The size of the city in squared kilometers (km^2). The variable was standardized.	
	Education	The percentage of people who have a tertiary education in each city. The variable was standardized.	

General Authority for Statistics in Saudi Arabia.

We considered environmental consciousness as the percentage of the maintenance of the natural resource, e.g., prudent use of water. The rate considered the reduction/control in the use of natural resources relative to outputs, by living in balance with natural forces [12]. Kirkwood and Walton [78] considered the environmental consciousness of green entrepreneurs as involving the manner in which they conduct their businesses while keeping to their environmental commitment. Hence, environmental preferences may allow for benefits exceeding simple cost-savings, since customers forge deals with entrepreneurship that are associated with a positive image and are recognized as "modern" [92]. The data for this variable came from annual reports (General Authority for Statistics in Saudi Arabia—Knowledge statistics). Kirkwood and Walton [78] studied the motivations and the key green aspects of entrepreneurs interested in sustainability issues, as well as the degree of the greening of the organization, so our variable could be comparable and useful and could build on the existing literature.

In temporal orientation, the percentage of public and private organizations that have adopted environmental measures in each city was considered. The information for this variable came from annual reports, which showed the speed at which organizations embrace environmental initiatives (General Authority for Statistics in Saudi Arabia—Knowledge statistics). Shipp et al. [82] examined the average percentage of temporal orientation. Entrepreneurs operating in such environments often need to compete by taking advantage of the fast-changing market conditions in terms of creating novel products or services, thus satisfying the requirements of emerging environmental needs [95].

4.1.3. Control Variables

We included other variables in our models to control for additional factors that might partly explain green entrepreneurship. The annual agricultural growth rate represents the value of a country's resources, which becomes increasingly sensitive to competitive forces in world markets. Environmental issues are also sensitive to world markets, as they shape the potential for economic growth by conditioning survival. In Saudi Arabia, unsustainable use of resources is an important issue, triggered mainly by the inadequacy of natural resources [13]. This challenges the sustainability of green entrepreneurship and requires many resources that depend on the annual growth rate of the agricultural sector [13]. The data used for this were from the annual reports of General Authority for Statistics in Saudi Arabia. The annual growth rate took into consideration the average value of the city's recourses that each city produced yearly in the agricultural sector. We also controlled for the population of the city, as green entrepreneurship is aimed at minimizing threats to environmental resources, such as increased population rate [95,96].

One approach suggested for sustainability is a reduction in population growth [97]. Saudi Arabia is one of the world's most populous countries, growing from 4 million in 1960 to more than 33 million in 2018 [12]. The data here came from the annual reports of the General Authority for Statistics in Saudi Arabia, and the value of this control variable was the population in each area. The size of the city was also included as a control variable, as it may affect the number and quantity of environmental resources; a larger city is more likely to have access to more environmental resources than a smaller city [13]. We also controlled for the level of education; culture may be affected by the level of education, which may be needed for sustainable developmental objectives at all levels and social arenas, to transform society by re-classifying and updating education and to aid individuals in developing the skills and values required for sustainable development [98]. In addition, extant literature showed a significant and positive influence of education and sustainability orientation on green entrepreneurship inclination [32]. Furthermore, there was research suggesting that education had a positive correlation with entrepreneurial activity [99], and this variable was measured as a percentage of people with tertiary educational levels in each city. Both independent and control variables were also standardized. A summary of the variables we used in this study is presented in Table 1.

4.2. Method and Model

Fixed effects (FE) models were used to test whether environmental actions (*EA*), environmental consciousness (*EC*), and temporal orientation (*TO*) affect green entrepreneurship. In this regard, Equation (1) shows our main specification, which is estimated through linear regression:

$$LnGE_{it} = \alpha + \beta_1 LnEA_{it} + \beta_2 LnEC_{it} + \beta_3 LnTO_{it} + \phi_k LnCV_{k,it} + \varepsilon_{it} \tag{1}$$

where GE_{it} is green entrepreneurship in city i at time t; EA_{it} represents the vector of environmental actions across city i and time t; EC_{it} denotes environmental consciousness; TO_{it} is temporal orientation; ϕ_k represents the estimators for the k control variables (CV_{it}—population, size of the city, annual growth rate of agriculture, and education); and ε_{it} is the error term that captures those variables that might affect green entrepreneurship, but were unknown in this study. All variables were transformed into natural logarithms for a direct interpretation [41].

A city-level analysis enhances the more detailed exploration of entrepreneurship trends, both within and between states, as these can vary significantly [100]. In addition, since different cities may increase the level and regularity of observations, this may lead to having a higher level of confirmed and verified results. Considering different cities in an array of locations allowed us to evaluate any significant influence, while the panel data technique allowed us to observe time effects using a cross-regional approach [101]. Panel data are also better able to measure and identify effects not detectable simply in pure cross-section or pure time series data [101]. In this study, we focused only on the fixed effects, since utilizing the full fixed model and carrying out the selection on the random effects within it resulted in additional noise, stemming from unnecessary fixed effects [101].

As noted, the advantages of this methodology in this study included that we were able to obtain a sample from Saudi Arabia with a regular time series. We also found that our final dataset contained a representative sample of this homogeneous group. Our completed sample consisted of panel data with 84 observations and 21 cities during the period spanning from 2015 to 2018.

5. Results

The statistics for the non-standardized variables in the study are presented in Table 2. Green entrepreneurship varied from 20.42 to 77.65%, with an average of 45.73%. Environmental actions ranged from 39.89 to 76.33%, with an average of 51.62% (standard deviation (SD) = 7.27%); environmental consciousness ranged from 34.52 to 86.53% (M = 56.56%, SD = 10.77%); and temporal orientation varied from 37.92 to 86.00% (M = 59.21%, SD = 10.89%). Pearson's correlation was run to assess the relationship between green entrepreneurship and environmental actions, environmental consciousness, as well as temporal orientation. The test revealed that some of the variables had significant positive relationships and some insignificant relationships. For example, environmental actions had no correlation with environmental consciousness (r = 0.131), although there was a small correlation between green entrepreneurship and environmental actions (r = −0.024) and temporal orientation (r = −0.008). Furthermore, there existed a correlation between green entrepreneurship and temporal orientation (r = 0.216), as well as between green entrepreneurship and environmental consciousness (r = −0.014). Lastly, there was a moderate correlation between environmental consciousness and temporal orientation (r = 0.182). Table 2 shows that the three cultural diminutions were statistically correlated with green entrepreneurship; thus, the correlations met our initial expectations.

Table 2. Descriptive statistics and correlation matrix.

	Variable	N	Mean	Std. Dev.	Min	Max	VIF	1
1	Green entrepreneurship	84	45.736	12.780	20.42	77.65		1
2	Environmental actions	84	51.620	7.272	39.89	76.33	1.120	−0.024
3	Environmental consciousness	84	56.595	10.778	34.52	86.53	1.410	−0.014
4	Temporal orientation	84	59.209	10.888	37.92	86.00	1.230	0.036
5	Population of the area	84	1983	2399	4761	8597	2.070	0.249 *
6	Size of the city	84	1230	1188	1200	5400	1.910	0.278 *
7	Annual growth rate	84	3.921	0.600	3.01	5.84	1.070	0.336 *
8	Education	84	62.177	7.123	47.85	81.45	1.150	0.653

			2	3	4	5	6	7
2	Environmental actions	84	1					
3	Environmental consciousness	84	0.131	1				
4	Temporal orientation	84	−0.008	0.182	1			
5	Population of the area	84	0.187	0.295 *	−0.256 *	1		
6	Size of the city	84	0.216 *	−0.079	−0.294 *	0.601 *	1	
7	Annual growth rate	84	−0.111	0.114	0.057	−0.086	−0.000	1
8	Education	84	−0.081	0.101	−0.247 *	0.224 *	0.222 *	0.060

* $p < 0.10$. Note: N, number of observations; Std. Dev., standard deviation; VIF, variance inflation factor.

Multicollinearity analysis was conducted prior to conducting the regression analysis, to check whether there were any problems due to linear combinations. A common technique, used to test for multicollinearity among the predictor variables in this study, is the variance inflation factor (VIF). Values above 0.90 were suggestive of a multicollinearity problem [102]. A VIF value in excess of 10 is also concerning [103]. In our case, we found an average VIF value equal to 1.42. This implied that multicollinearity was not a problematic issue or a concern for this study. We acknowledge that in smaller samples such as ours, there may be some methodological concerns with respect to collinearity, especially noted in the variable of education. However, given the pre-existing knowledge of the role of education in these conditions [98,99] and that a potential collinearity is not harmful enough [104,105], we considered all independent and control variables relevant to support the internal consistency of our findings and analysis.

Table 3 illustrates all of the linear regression models, and only the controlled variables were included in Model 1, which was a starting point in predicting green entrepreneurship with demographic and economic variables. The other three models were then set, each with only one predictor representing each hypothesis. The first regressed green entrepreneurship on environmental actions (Model 2). The second considered the influence of environmental consciousness on green entrepreneurial activity (Model 3), whilst the third regressed green entrepreneurship on temporal orientation (Model 4). The control variables were then added to the three models, with one independent variable representing all hypotheses (Models 5, 6, and 7). Finally, an additional Model 8 was explored, which included all predictors (i.e., independent variables and controls). Throughout this empirical strategy, we tested whether differing linear combinations created different results or whether a robust specification was found otherwise. In addition, for robustness purposes, a new set of models without the control variable education was performed. Appendix B shows that the results for the main variables remained similar as compared to Table 3.

Table 3. Regression analysis (DV = green entrepreneurship).

	1	2	3	4	5	6	7	8
Environmental actions		0.215 *			0.265 **			0.282 **
		(0.113)			(0.111)			(0.115)
Environmental consciousness			0.274 **			0.292 **		0.305 ***
			(0.109)			(0.107)		(0.102)
Temporal orientation				0.275 *			0.244	0.342 **
				(0.147)			(0.160)	(0.132)
The population of the area	−0.056 ***				−0.075 ***	−0.065 ***	−0.052 ***	−0.080 ***
	(0.008)				(0.012)	(0.008)	(0.009)	(0.012)
Size of the city	0.000				0.000	0.000	0.000	0.000
	(0.001)				(0.001)	(0.001)	(0.001)	(0.001)
Annual growth rate	0.246 **				0.268 **	0.250 **	0.197	0.204 *
	(0.116)				(0.110)	(0.112)	(0.129)	(0.106)
Education	0.080				0.096	0.092	0.113	0.156 **
	(0.094)				(0.089)	(0.080)	(0.093)	(0.061)
Constant	0.564 *	0.813 ***	0.784 ***	0.773 ***	−0.039	0.046	0.177	−1.162 **
	(0.294)	(0.221)	(0.179)	(0.247)	(0.348)	(0.303)	(0.398)	(0.517)
Observations	84	84	84	84	84	84	84	84
R^2 within	0.081	0.054	0.076	0.055	0.16	0.166	0.121	0.31
R^2 between	0.000	0.016	0.005	0.003	0.006	0.004	0.002	0.016
R^2 overall	0.002	0.001	0.000	0.000	0.000	0.000	0.000	0.001

$* p < 0.10$, $** p < 0.05$, $*** p < 0.01$. Robust standard errors in parentheses. DV: Dependent variable.

Testing the hypothesis suggested a positive association between environmental actions and green entrepreneurship in different regions of Saudi Arabia, as stated in Hypothesis 1. We found that culture, such as environmental actions, had a positive influence on green entrepreneurship. Green entrepreneurs have to enhance the value of green entrepreneurship by balancing running a business with sustainability ideals [67]. A further variable employed to understand green entrepreneurship was that of environmental consciousness. Hypothesis 2 states that environmental consciousness is positively associated with green entrepreneurship in Saudi Arabia. We found that environmental consciousness was positively related to green entrepreneurship. The same positivity of influence was noticeable for the second hypothesis, but overall, the influence of environmental consciousness was not contrary to expectations, being positive. Green entrepreneurs could incrementally enhance the environment through their own businesses, and with their products and services, they are potentially able to educate a wide audience regarding many advantages in environmental protection [64]. Hypothesis 3, which suggested that temporal orientation was positively associated with green entrepreneurship in Saudi Arabia, was also fully supported. Individuals focus their attention on temporal orientation (past/present/future) and clarify responses to implicit and explicit temporal orientation [82]. Temporal orientation had a significantly positive influence on green entrepreneurial measures within Saudi Arabia.

6. Discussion and Conclusions

At the present time, there is limited knowledge about the association between culture and green entrepreneurship with specific reference to Saudi Arabia. In particular, our study examined the influence of cultural factors (i.e., environmental actions, environmental consciousness, and temporal orientation) on green entrepreneurial activity in Saudi Arabia. We found that there was a positive relationship between culture and green entrepreneurship, which varied across regions. Our results might encourage entrepreneurs to adopt a green approach that aims to develop an entrepreneurial activity that solves environmental problems. This could mean that culture has had a strong influence on environmental commitment in Saudi Arabia to solve environmental issues.

We also found that environmental actions increased the level of green entrepreneurial activity in Saudi Arabia. Cultural practices act as an improved indication of sustainability endeavors [16]. Actions and motivations derive from the need to approach environmental issues, resulting in alternative and enhanced environmentally-friendly products and practices that are widely disseminated [69]. Additionally, we discovered that environmental consciousness had a positive influence on green entrepreneurship, given that green entrepreneurs have to consider the balance between business and environmental approaches [22]. Green entrepreneurs were thus identified as novel entrepreneurial players, in search of ways to fuse environmental awareness and business acumen in a holistic way [74]. Indeed, it is their overall objective regarding the sanctity of the environment that separates them from other entrepreneurs [64]. The main influence of temporal orientation on green entrepreneurship was also found to be positive and significant. The strategies of many successful entrepreneurs often involve time-based origins [25].

6.1. Implications for Theory

Green entrepreneurs are emotionally engaged by building a strong bond with society. Green entrepreneurs can also be cognitively engaged in understanding the clear mission and purpose of a new business by receiving information and appropriate feedback from social needs. If green entrepreneurs have a strong bond with society, then they feel that they are valued by local and national entities; thus, their opinions and actions may be taken into consideration to propose solutions for sustainable development processes [21]. This allows entrepreneurs to develop an emotional engagement that helps their venture to succeed in its sustainable goals by understanding contextualized societal culture. An important implication for the analysis of informal institutions [14,15], particularly for culture as an antecedent of green entrepreneurial activity, was found in this study. For example, the cultural dimensions of green entrepreneurship, in its three forms, are beneficial for more sustainable business activity in harmony with the environment. This may be the first step toward a more environmentally-friendly-focused society, leading to the conservation of resources for future generations.

Green entrepreneurship is a novel field of research, which needs further exploration regarding the role of entrepreneurial activity as a means for sustaining the environment and ecosystems, whilst forwarding both economic and non-economic gains for investors and society in general [73]. Research into informal institutions needs a theory-based consultation regarding the notion of such institutions being vital for certain outcomes in green entrepreneurship. Our findings present a more generalized perspective by illustrating the fact that informal institutions (culture) also ensure added general consensus, reinforcing the influence on green entrepreneurship (e.g., environmental actions, environmental consciousness, and temporal orientation). In this sense, further theoretical understanding may better guide scholars studying Saudi Arabia to further advance the comprehension of culture as the awareness of society toward sustainability. It may also serve to encourage the advertising of results related to sustainability in order to increase legitimacy and support from the entire population, as well as from entrepreneurs.

6.2. Implications for Practice

We focused on different cities in different regions of the Kingdom of Saudi Arabia. Government and private individuals are both key instigators of entrepreneurial actions. It is hence vital that entrepreneurs enhance their understanding of how these approaches are determined and shaped. Consideration of uncertain influences on business-based sustainability strategy, such as the cultural characteristics evaluated in this study, may well be of benefit to entrepreneurs in assessing, more appropriately, the significance of the informal institutional application of pressure on both corporate and strategic activities. As our findings illustrated, cultural influence on sustainability may apply to many cities sharing similar cultures, rather than being limited to individual ones. By achieving the formation of productive clusters, entrepreneurs that operate on an intra-city basis may benefit from such an approach. Our study offers insight to aid entrepreneurs in coping with the challenges of strategically balancing sustainability practices as international ventures with the expectation to be local between cities that have common shared cultural values and corporate sustainability.

Future entrepreneurs may be interested in finding and applying environmentally-friendly solutions for green market needs, and market needs overall. Their contribution to social development can also effectively create enhanced opportunities in green entrepreneurship. In doing so, they not only contribute to their own careers, but also to the employment of others.

6.3. Limitations and Future Research

In spite of these strengths, there are other limitations to this study. Firstly, as the present paper explored the relationship between culture and green entrepreneurship, represented by environmental commitment in Saudi Arabia, it would be beneficial to consider other cultural dimensions that may affect green entrepreneurial activity [17]. For example, it would be supportive to consider variables at the city level, such as crime rates, air pollution, unofficial companies, etc. Secondly, we used secondary data for the 2015–2018 period; subsequent studies should focus on a wider time span to achieve long-term analyses, in which dynamic effects may also illustrate the different or similar responses of entrepreneurship when institutional factors change in developing countries [106]. Thirdly, future research may extend the analysis to cross-country comparisons, such as examining other regions in the Arab Gulf. Fourthly, there are no global databases for green entrepreneurship, so future research could experiment with various proxies for green entrepreneurship and could determine whether the results remain stable across variables and techniques. We are aware that a lack of data sources poses a challenge to overcome, particularly when attempting to conduct cross-country comparisons, due to the limited number of indicators and the differences in measurements across countries [107]. Further efforts are needed to create homogenous information concerning green entrepreneurship, as well as its antecedents and those consequences beyond economic terms [108]. Future research should improve the quality and scope of the indicators, for both dependent, as well as independent variables, which may increase reliability and the ability to analyze causal relationships in a cross-sectional setting [18].

Author Contributions: Writing—original draft, W.A.; Writing—review & editing, S.A. and D.U. All authors have read and agreed to the published version of the manuscript.

Acknowledgments: The authors acknowledge the anonymous Editor and reviewers for valuable comments and suggestions. In addition, Wafa Alwakid acknowledges Jouf University for financial support for Ph.D. studies. Sebastian Aparicio acknowledges Durham University Business School for constant support. Additionally, Sebastian acknowledges COLCIENCIAS Ph.D. programme (617/2013), as well as Sapiencia-Enlaza Mundos (Municipio de Medellín) for financial support during Ph.D. studies. Finally, David Urbano acknowledges the financial support from project ECO2017-87885-P (Spanish Ministry of Economy & Competitiveness), 2017-SGR-1056 (Economy & Knowledge Department, Catalan Government) and ICREA under ICREA Academia programme.

Appendix A

Table A1. Definitions of green entrepreneurship and related concepts.

	Labels	Definitions	Citations
1	Green entrepreneurial activity	"The process of identifying, evaluating and seizing entrepreneurial opportunities that minimize a venture's impact on the natural environment and therefore create benefits for society as a whole and for local communities"	[10]
2	Green entrepreneurship	[Green entrepreneurs engage in ...] "a kind of social activity that aims at protecting and preserving the natural environment"	[46]
3	Environmental orientation	"The recognition by managers of the importance of environmental issues facing their firms by mainstreaming green product strategies"	[61]
4	Green logic	"Part of a complex institutional environment, facing a sharing platform, alongside the social and economic logic"	[68]
5	Green entrepreneurs	"Those who start businesses based on the principle of sustainability with strong underlying green values and who sell green products or services"	[45]

Appendix B

Table A2. Regression for green entrepreneurship without the control variable education.

	1	2	3	4	5	6	7	8
Environmental actions		0.215 * (0.113)			0.259 ** (0.115)			0.270 ** (0.118)
Environmental consciousness			0.274 ** (0.109)			0.288 ** (0.107)		0.296 ** (0.106)
Temporal orientation				0.275 * (0.147)			0.219 (0.156)	0.304 ** (0.136)
The population of the area	−0.058 *** (0.008)				−0.076 *** (0.012)	−0.067 *** (0.008)	−0.055 *** (0.009)	−0.082 *** (0.012)
Size of the city	0.000 (0.000)				0.000 (0.000)	0.000 (0.000)	0.000 (0.000)	0.000 (0.000)
Annual growth rate	0.248 * (0.121)				0.269 ** (0.116)	0.252 ** (0.117)	0.204 (0.135)	0.214 * (0.116)
Constant	0.732 *** (0.231)	0.813 *** (0.221)	0.784 *** (0.179)	0.773 *** (0.247)	0.175 (0.360)	0.246 (0.277)	0.449 (0.292)	−0.741 (0.487)
Observations	84	84	84	84	84	84	84	84
R^2 within	0.074	0.054	0.076	0.055	0.149	0.157	0.107	0.284
R^2 between	0.000	0.016	0.005	0.003	0.006	0.004	0.002	0.016
R^2 overall	0.001	0.001	0.000	0.000	0.000	0.000	0.000	0.002

* $p < 0.10$, ** $p < 0.05$, *** $p < 0.01$. Robust standard errors in parentheses.

References

1. Schaltegger, S.; Wagner, M. Types of Sustainable Entrepreneurship and Conditions for Sustainability Innovation: From the Administration of a Technical Challenge to the Management of an Entrepreneurial Opportunity. In *Sustainable Innovation and Entrepreneurship*; Edward Elgar: Cheltenham, UK, 2008; pp. 27–40.

2. Dixon, S.E.; Clifford, A. Ecopreneurship—A New Approach to Managing the Triple Bottom Line. *J. Organ. Chang. Manag.* **2007**, *20*, 326–345. [CrossRef]

3. Krueger, N.F. Sustainable Entrepreneurship: Broadening the Definition of Opportunity. In Proceedings of the 19th National Conference of United States Association for Small Business and Entrepreneurship Small Business and Entrepreneurship, California, LA, USA, 13–16 January 2005; pp. 13–16.

4. Schlange, L.E. What Drives Sustainable Entrepreneurs? *3rd Appl. Bus. Entrep. Assoc. Int. (ABEAI) Conf.* **2006**, *24*, 16–20.

5. Chick, A. *Green Entrepreneurship: A Sustainable Development Challenge*; Sage: Thousand Oaks, CA, USA, 2008.

6. Gliedt, T.; Parker, P. Green Community Entrepreneurship: Creative Destruction in the Social Economy. *Int. J. Soc. Econ.* **2007**, *34*, 538–553. [CrossRef]

7. Harini, V.; Meenakshi, D.T. Green Entrepreneurship Alternative (Business) Solution to Save Environment. *Asia Pac. J. Manag. Entrep. Res.* **2012**, *1*, 79.

8. Linnanen, L. An Insiders Experiences with Environmental Entrepreneurship. *Greener Manag. Int.* **2005**, *2002*, 71–80. [CrossRef]

9. Allen, J.C.; Malin, S. Green Entrepreneurship: A Method for Managing Natural Resources? *Soc. Nat. Resour.* **2008**, *21*, 828–844. [CrossRef]

10. Gast, J.; Gundolf, K.; Cesinger, B. Doing Business in a Green Way: A Systematic Review of the Ecological Sustainability Entrepreneurship Literature and Future Research Directions. *J. Clean Prod.* **2017**, *147*, 44–56. [CrossRef]

11. Inglehart, R.F. *Cultural Evolution*; Cambridge University Press: Cambridge, UK, 2018.

12. General Organization for Statistics. The Total Population. 2019. Available online: https://www.stats.gov.sa/en/indicators/1 (accessed on 25 November 2019).

13. Mewa (Ministry of Environment Water & Agriculture). Sustainable Development. 2019. Available online: https://www.mewa.gov.sa/en/Ministry/initiatives/SustainableDevelopment/Pages/default.aspx (accessed on 29 January 2020).

14. North, D.C. *Institutions, Institutional Change and Economic Performance*; Cambridge University Press: Cambridge, UK, 1990.

15. North, D.C. *Understanding the Process of Economic Change*; Princeton University Press: Princeton, NJ, USA, 2005.

16. Roy, A.; Goll, I. Predictors of Various Facets of Sustainability of Nations: The Role of Cultural and Economic Factors. *Int. Bus. Rev.* **2014**, *23*, 849–861. [CrossRef]

17. Meek, W.R.; Pacheco, D.F.; York, J.G. The Impact of Social Norms on Entrepreneurial Action: Evidence from the Environmental Entrepreneurship Context. *J. Bus. Ventur.* **2010**, *25*, 493–509. [CrossRef]

18. Urbano, D.; Audrestch, D.; Aparicio, S. Twenty-Five Years of Research on Institutions Entreprenurship and Economic Growth: What Has Been Learned? *Small Bus. Econ.* **2019**, *1*, 21–49. [CrossRef]

19. Adler, N.J. Cross-Cultural Management Research: The Ostrich and the Trend. *Acad. Manag. Rev.* **1983**, *8*, 226.

20. Andries, P.; Stephan, U. Environmental Innovation and Firm Performance: How Firm Size and Motives Matter. *Sustainability* **2019**, *11*, 3585. [CrossRef]

21. Lotfi, M.; Yousefi, A.; Jafari, S. The Effect of Emerging Green Market on Green Entrepreneurship and Sustainable Development in Knowledge-Based Companies. *Sustainability* **2018**, *10*, 2308. [CrossRef]

22. Gibbs, D.; O'Neill, K. Building a Green Economy? Sustainability Transitions in the UK Building Sector. *Geoforum* **2014**, *59*, 133–141. [CrossRef]

23. Audretsch, D.B.; Keilbach, M. Resolving the Knowledge Paradox: Knowledge-Spillover Entrepreneurship and Economic Growth. *Res. Policy* **2008**, *37*, 1697–1705. [CrossRef]

24. Boumal, W.J.; Strom, R.J. Entrepreneurship and economic growth. *Strateg. Entrep. J.* **2007**, *17*, 233–237. [CrossRef]

25. Bird, B.J.; West, G.P. Time and Entrepreneurship. *Entrep. Theory Pract.* **1998**, *22*, 5–9. [CrossRef]

26. Gevrenova, T. Nature and Characteristics of Green Entrepreneurship. *Trakia J. Sci.* **2017**, *13* (Suppl. 2), 321–323. [CrossRef]

27. Schaper, M. Understanding the Green Entrepreneur. *J. Enterprising Cult.* **2016**, *12*, 27–40.

28. Saberi, M.; Hamdan, A. The moderating role of governmental support in the relationship between entrepreneurship and economic growth. *J. Entrep. Emerg. Econ.* **2019**, *11*, 200–216. [CrossRef]

29. Dvouletý, O.; Gordievskaya, A.; Procházka, D. Investigating the relationship between entrepreneurship and regional development: Case of developing countries. *J. Glob. Entrep. Res.* **2018**, *8*, 16. [CrossRef]

30. McAdam, M.; Crowley, C.; Harrison, R. The Emancipatory Potential of Female Digital Entrepreneurship: Institutional Voids in Saudi Arabia. *Acad. Manag. Proc.* **2018**, *1*, 10255. [CrossRef]

31. Alessa, A.; Alajmi, S. The development of Saudi Arabian Entrepreneurship and Knowledge society. *Int. J. Manag. Excell.* **2017**, *9*, 1155. [CrossRef]

32. Soomro, B.; Ghumro, I.; Shah, N. Green entrepreneurship inclination among the younger generation: An avenue towards a green economy. *Sustain. Dev.* **2019**, *10*, 1002. [CrossRef]
33. Zaydane, Amro Alaa' Entrepreneurship: The driving force of national economies, Gulf Arab Academy for Studies. *Manama Branch Bahrain* **2011**, *3*, 9.
34. Ashri, O. On The Fast Track: Saudi Arabia's Entrepreneurship Ecosystem. Available online: https://www.entrepreneur.com/article/336766 (accessed on 1 May 2020).
35. Thompson, M. 'Saudi Vision 2030': A viable response to youth aspirations and concerns? *Asian Aff.* **2017**, *48*, 205–221. [CrossRef]
36. Ahamad Nalband, N.; Alkelabi, S.; Awad Jaber, D. Innovation Practices in Saudi Arabian Businesses. *Int. J. Bus. Manag.* **2016**, *11*, 136. [CrossRef]
37. Williamson, O.E. The New Institutional Economics: Taking Stock, Looking Ahead. *J. Econ. Lit.* **2000**, *38*, 595–613. [CrossRef]
38. Bjørnskov, C.; Foss, N.J. Institutions, Entrepreneurship, and Economic Growth: What Do We Know? And What Do We Still Need to Know? *Acad. Manag. Perspect.* **2016**, *30*, 292–315. [CrossRef]
39. Zhai, Q.; Su, J.; Ye, M.; Xu, Y. How Do Institutions Relate to Entrepreneurship: An Integrative Model. *Entrep. Res. J.* **2018**, *9*. [CrossRef]
40. Su, Z. The Co-Evolution of Institutions and Entrepreneurship. *Asia Pac. J. Manag.* **2020**. [CrossRef]
41. Urbano, D.; Aparicio, S. Entrepreneurship Capital Types and Economic Growth: International Evidence. *Technol. Forecast Soc.* **2016**, *102*, 34–44. [CrossRef]
42. Thornton, P.H.; Ribeiro-Soriano, D.; Urbano, D. Socio-Cultural Factors and Entrepreneurial Activity. *Int. Small Bus. J.* **2011**, *29*, 105–118. [CrossRef]
43. Urbano, D.; Audrestch, D.; Aparicio, S. Institutional Factors, Opportunity Entrepreneurship and Economic Growth: Panel Data Evidence. *Technol. Forecast Soc.* **2016**, *102*, 45–61.
44. Melay, I.; Kraus, S. Green entrepreneurship: Definitions of related concepts. *Int. J. Strateg. Manag.* **2012**, *12*, 1–13.
45. Silajdžić, I.; Kurtagić, S.; Vučijak, B. Green entrepreneurship in transition economies: A case study of Bosnia and Herzegovina. *J. Clean. Prod.* **2015**, *88*, 376–384. [CrossRef]
46. Yi, G. From green entrepreneurial intentions to green entrepreneurial behaviors: The role of university entrepreneurial support and external institutional support. *Int. Entrep. Manag. J.* **2020**, 1–17. [CrossRef]
47. Caprar, D.V.; Neville, B.A. "Norming" and "Conforming": Integrating Cultural and Institutional Explanations for Sustainability Adoption in Business. *J. Bus. Ethics.* **2012**, *110*, 231–245. [CrossRef]
48. Haxhi, I.; Ees, H.V. Explaining Diversity in the Worldwide Diffusion of Codes of Good Governance. *J. Int. Bus. Stud.* **2009**, *41*, 710–726. [CrossRef]
49. Ringov, D.; Zollo, M. The Impact of National Culture on Corporate Social Performance. *Corp. Gov. Int. J. Bus. Soc.* **2007**, *7*, 476–485. [CrossRef]
50. Waldman, D.A.; de Luque, M.S.; Washburn, N.; Adetoun, B.; Barrasa, A. Cultural and Leadership Predictors of Corporate Social Responsibility Values of Top Management: A GLOBE Study of 15 Countries. *J. Int. Bus. Stud.* **2006**, 823–837. [CrossRef]
51. Ioannou, I.; Serafeim, G. What Drives Corporate Social Performance? The Role of Nation-Level Institutions. *J. Int. Bus. Stud.* **2012**, *43*, 834–864. [CrossRef]
52. Szőcs, I.; Schlegelmilch, B.B.; Rusch, T.; Shamma, H.M. Linking Cause Assessment, Corporate Philanthropy, and Corporate Reputation. *J. Acad. Mark. Sci.* **2016**, *44*, 376–396. [CrossRef]
53. Williams, G.A.; Zinkin, J. The Effect of Culture on Consumers Willingness to Punish Irresponsible/Corporate Behaviour: Applying Hofstedes Typology to the Punishment Aspect of Corporate Social Responsibility. *Bus. Ethics Eur. Rev.* **2008**, *17*, 210–226. [CrossRef]
54. Stephan, U.; Uhlaner, L.M. Performance-Based vs Socially Supportive Culture: A Cross-National Study of Descriptive Norms and Entrepreneurship. *J. Int. Bus. Stud.* **2010**, *41*, 1347–1364. [CrossRef]
55. Grinevich, V.; Huber, F.; Karataş-Özkan, M.; Yavuz, Ç. Green entrepreneurship in the sharing economy: Utilising multiplicity of institutional logics. *Small Bus. Econ.* **2019**, *52*, 859–876. [CrossRef]
56. Roland, G. Understanding Institutional Change: Fast-Moving and Slow-Moving Institutions. *Stud. Comp. Int. Dev.* **2004**, *38*, 109–131. [CrossRef]
57. Ndumbisi, N.O.; Nair, S.R. Green Entrepreneurship (GE) and Green Value Added (GVA): A Conceptual Framework. *Int. J. Entrep.* **2009**, *13*, 21–34.

58. Gibbs, D. Sustainability Entrepreneurs, Ecopreneurs and the Development of a Sustainable Economy. *Greener Manag. Int.* **2006**, *6*, 63–78. [CrossRef]

59. Parboteeah, K.P.; Addae, H.M.; Cullen, J.B. Propensity to Support Sustainability Initiatives: A Cross-National Model. *J. Bus. Ethics* **2012**, *105*, 403–413. [CrossRef]

60. Thang, N.N.; Quang, T.; Son, N.H. The knowledge creation and green entrepreneurship-A study of two Vietnamese green firms. *Asian Acad. Manag. J.* **2013**, *2*, 21.

61. Papadopoulos, I.; Karagouni, G.; Trigkas, M.; Beltsiou, Z. Mainstreaming green product strategies. *Euromed J. Bus.* **2014**, *9*, 293–317. [CrossRef]

62. Karimi, R.; Nabavi Chashmi, S. Designing Green Entrepreneurship Model in Sustainable Development Consistent with the Performance of Tehran Industrial Towns. *J. Bus. Bus. Mark.* **2019**, *26*, 95–102. [CrossRef]

63. Miska, C.; Szőcs, I.; Schiffinger, M. Culture's Effects on Corporate Sustainability Practices: A Multi-Domain and Multi-Level View. *J. World Bus.* **2018**, *53*, 263–279. [CrossRef]

64. Kluckhohn, C. *Values and Value-orientations in the Theory of Action: An Exploration in Definition and Classification Toward a General Theory of Action*; Harvard University Press: Cambridge, MA, USA, 1951.

65. Kluckhohn, F.R.; Strodtbeck, F.L. *Variations in Value Orientations*; Kluckhohn, F.R., Strodtbeck, F.L., Eds.; Row, Peterson: Evanston, IL, USA, 1961.

66. Anbari, F.T.; Khilkhanova, E.V.; Romanova, M.V.; Umpleby, S.A. Cross Cultural Differences and Their Implications for Managing International Projects. Available online: http://www.gwu.edu/~{}umpleby/recent_papers/2003_cross_cultural_differences_managi_international_projects_anbari_khilkhanova_romanova_umpleby.htm (accessed on 30 January 2020).

67. Egri, C.P.; Khilji, S.E.; Ralston, D.A.; Palmer, I.; Girson, I.; Milton, L.; Richards, M.; Ramburuth, P.; Mockaitis, A. Do Anglo Countries Still Form a Values Cluster? Evidence of the Complexity of Value Change. *J. World Bus.* **2012**, *47*, 267–276. [CrossRef]

68. Jolink, A.; Niesten, E. Sustainable Development and Business Models of Entrepreneurs in the Organic Food Industry. *Bus. Strateg. Environ.* **2013**, *24*, 386–401. [CrossRef]

69. Schaltegger, S. A Framework for Ecopreneurship. *Greener Manag. Int.* **2002**, *2002*, 45–58. [CrossRef]

70. Gibbs, D. Industrial Ecology and Eco-Industrial Development-The UK's National Industrial Symbiosis Programme (NISP). In *Environmental Informatics and Industrial Environmental Protection: Concepts, Methods and Tools: EnviroInfo 2009*; Wohlgemuth, V., Page, B., Voigt, K., Eds.; University of Applied Sciences: Berlin, Germany, 2009; Volume 2, pp. 245–251.

71. Evans, D.; Abrahamse, W. Beyond Rhetoric: The Possibilities of and for 'Sustainable Lifestyles'. *Environ. Polit.* **2009**, *18*, 486–502. [CrossRef]

72. Acs, Z.J.; Estrin, S.; Mickiewicz, T.; Szerb, L. Entrepreneurship, Institutional Economics, and Economic Growth: An Ecosystem Perspective. *Small Bus. Econ.* **2018**, *51*, 501–514. [CrossRef]

73. Pacheco, D.F.; Dean, T.J.; Payne, D.S. Escaping the Green Prison: Entrepreneurship and the Creation of Opportunities for Sustainable Development. *J. Bus. Ventur.* **2010**, *25*, 464–480. [CrossRef]

74. Tilley, F.; Parrish, B.D. From Poles to Wholes: Facilitating an Integrated Approach to Green entrepreneurship. *World Rev. Entrep. Manag. Sustain. Dev.* **2006**, *2*, 281.

75. Radović-Marković, M.; Živanović, B. Fostering Green Entrepreneurship and Women's Empowerment through Education and Banks' Investments in Tourism: Evidence from Serbia. *Sustainability* **2019**, *11*, 6826. [CrossRef]

76. Rodgers, C. Green entrepreneurship in SMEs: A Case Study Analysis. *Corp. Soc. Responsib. Environ. Manag.* **2010**, *17*, 125–132. [CrossRef]

77. Thompson, N.; Kiefer, K.; York, J.G. Distinctions Not Dichotomies: Exploring Social, Sustainable, and Environmental Entrepreneurship. In *Social and Sustainable Entrepreneurship*; Lumpkin, G.T., Katz, J.A., Eds.; Emerald Group Publishing Limited: Bingley, UK, 2011; Volume 13, pp. 201–229.

78. Kirkwood, J.; Walton, S. How Green Is Green? Ecopreneurs Balancing Environmental Concerns and Business Goals. *Australas J. Environ. Manag.* **2014**, *21*, 37–51. [CrossRef]

79. Zimbardo, P.G.; Boyd, J.N. Putting Time in Perspective: A Valid, Reliable Individual-Differences Metric. *J. Pers. Soc. Psychol.* **1999**, *77*, 1271–1288. [CrossRef]

80. Zimbardo, P.G.; Keough, K.A.; Boyd, J.N. Present Time Perspective as a Predictor of Risky Driving. *Pers. Indiv. Differ.* **1997**, *23*, 1007–1023. [CrossRef]

81. West, G.P.; Meyer, G.D. Temporal Dimensions of Opportunistic Change in Technology-Based Ventures. *Entrep. Theory Pract.* **1998**, *22*, 31–52. [CrossRef]

82. Shipp, A.J.; Edwards, J.R.; Lambert, L.S. Conceptualization and Measurement of Temporal Focus: The Subjective Experience of the Past, Present, and Future. *Organ. Behav. Hum. Dec.* **2009**, *110*, 1–22. [CrossRef]

83. Bird, B.J. The Operation of Intentions in Time: The Emergence of the New Venture. *Entrep. Theory Pract.* **1992**, *17*, 11–20. [CrossRef]

84. Isaak, R. *Green Logic: Ecopreneurship, Theory and Ethics*; Greenleaf Publishing: Sheffield, UK, 1998.

85. Lévesque, M.; Stephan, U. It's Time We Talk About Time in Entrepreneurship. *Entrep. Theory Pract.* **2019**, in press. [CrossRef]

86. Welter, F. Contextualizing Entrepreneurship-Conceptual Challenges and Ways Forward. *Entrep. Theory Pract.* **2011**, *35*, 165–184. [CrossRef]

87. Schwartz, M.S.; Carroll, A.B. Integrating and Unifying Competing and Complementary Frameworks. *Bus. Soc.* **2008**, *47*, 148–186. [CrossRef]

88. Bansal, P.; Song, H.-C. Similar But Not the Same: Differentiating Corporate Sustainability from Corporate Responsibility. *Acad. Manag. Ann.* **2016**, *11*, 105–149. [CrossRef]

89. Bansal, P.; Desjardins, M.R. Business Sustainability: It Is about Time. *Strateg. Organ.* **2014**, *12*, 70–78. [CrossRef]

90. Klasing, M.J. Cultural Dimensions, Collective Values and Their Importance for Institutions. *J. Comp. Econ.* **2013**, *41*, 447–467. [CrossRef]

91. OECD. Entrepreneurship at a Glance. 2011. Available online: https://www.oecdilibrary.org/docserver/97892640977114en.pdf?expires=1558955662andid=idandaccname=guestandchecksum=142B4BCD48043481BBF787B4DB078A9 (accessed on 29 January 2020).

92. Kraus, P.; Stokes, P.; Cooper, S.; Liu, Y.; Moore, N.; Britzelmaier, B.; Tarba, S. Cultural Antecedents of Sustainability and Regional Economic Development—A Study of SME 'Mittelstand' Firms in Baden-Württemberg (Germany). *Entrep. Region. Dev.* **2020**, 1–25. [CrossRef]

93. Papke, L.; Wooldridge, J. Panel data methods for fractional response variables with an application to test pass rates. *J. Econom.* **2008**, *145*, 121–133. [CrossRef]

94. Liu, W.; Xin, J. Modeling fractional outcomes with SAS. *SAS Support Resour.* **2014**, *1*, 1304.

95. Zahra, S.A. Governance, Ownership, and Corporate Entrepreneurship: The Moderating Impact of Industry Technological Opportunities. *Acad. Manag. Ann.* **1996**, *39*, 1713–1735.

96. Uslu, Y.D.; Hancıoğlu, Y.; Demir, E. Applicability to Green Entrepreneurship in Turkey: A Situation Analysis. *Proc. Soc. Behav.* **2015**, *195*, 1238–1245. [CrossRef]

97. Audretsch, D.; Belitski, M.; Desai, S. National Business Regulations and City Entrepreneurship in Europe: A Multilevel Nested Analysis. *Entrep. Theory Pract.* **2018**, *43*, 1148–1165. [CrossRef]

98. Zahedi, A.; Otterpohl, R. Towards Sustainable Development by Creation of Green Social Entrepreneurs Communities. *Proc. Cirp.* **2015**, *26*, 196–201. [CrossRef]

99. Moe.gov.sa. Kingdom of Saudi Arabia—Ministry of Education. 2019. Available online: https://www.moe.gov.sa/en/Pages/StatisticalInformation (accessed on 29 January 2020).

100. Estrin, S.; Mickiewicz, T.; Stephan, U. Entrepreneurship, Social Capital, and Institutions: Social and Commercial Entrepreneurship Across Nations. *Entrep. Theory Pract.* **2013**, *37*, 479–504. [CrossRef]

101. Baltagi, B.H. *Econometric Analysis of Panel Data. A Companion to Econometric Analysis of Panel Data*; John Wiley & Sons Inc: Chichester, UK, 2009.

102. Bondell, H.D.; Krishna, A.; Ghosh, S.K. Joint Variable Selection for Fixed and Random Effects in Linear Mixed-Effects Models. *Biometrics* **2010**, *66*, 1069–1077. [CrossRef] [PubMed]

103. Hair, J.F. *Multivariate Data Analysis: A Global Perspective*; Pearson: Upper Saddle River, NJ, USA, 2010.

104. Myers, R. *Classical and Modern Regression with Applications*, 2nd ed.; Duxbury: Boston, MA, USA, 1990.

105. Mason, C.; Perreault, W. Collinearity, Power, and Interpretation of Multiple Regression Analysis. *J. Mark. Res.* **1991**, *28*, 268–280. [CrossRef]

106. Urbano, D.; Audretsch, D.; Aparicio, S.; Noguera, M. Does Entrepreneurial Activity Matter for Economic Growth in Developing Countries? The Role of the Institutional Environment. *Int. Entrep. Manag. J.* **2019**, in press. [CrossRef]

107. Schillo, R.S.; Persaud, A.; Jin, M. Entrepreneurial Readiness in the Context of National Systems of Entrepreneurship. *Small Bus. Econ.* **2016**, *46*, 619–637. [CrossRef]

108. Aparicio, S.; Audretsch, D.; Urbano, D. Does entrepreneurship matter for inclusive growth? The role of social progress orientation. *Entrep. Res. J.* **2020**, in press. [CrossRef]

11

College Students' Entrepreneurial Mindset: Educational Experiences Override Gender and Major

Eunju Jung [1],* **and Yongjin Lee** [2],*

[1]   Graduate School of Education, Sejong University, Seoul 05006, Korea
[2]   Department of Liberal Arts, Hansei University, Gunpo, Gyeonggi-do 15852, Korea
*   Correspondence: doduli@sejong.ac.kr (E.J.); eduist@hansei.ac.kr (Y.L.)

Abstract: Entrepreneurship education has been popularly adopted in higher education contexts. Although evidence-based implementations of such education are widely acknowledged as beneficial, valid assessments of it are sparse. One possible outcome of entrepreneurship education is a change in students' entrepreneurial mindset, which can be measured by the recently validated College Students' Entrepreneurial Mindset Scale (CS-EMS). However, this scale awaits evidence regarding measurement invariance. This study aims to (1) examine measurement invariance of the CS-EMS; (2) compare the latent and observed means across groups based on gender, major, and educational experiences; and (3) investigate the conditional effects of the three grouping variables. Using data from 317 Korean college students' survey responses, we conducted sequential tests of factorial invariance and latent mean comparisons using multiple-group confirmatory factor analysis. Additionally, the conditional effects of the gender, major, and educational experiences were tested by structural equation modeling. The results indicate that strict invariance held for the groups compared by either gender or educational experiences, while scalar invariance held between the engineering and non-engineering groups. While the male, engineering, and educational experience groups generally scored higher on both the latent and observed sub-scales, the results of the conditional effects of grouping variables indicated that educational experiences mattered most. One practical implication for the educators is that the CS-EMS is a promising assessment tool for addressing the effectiveness of entrepreneurship education, especially when the targeted educational goals are any of its sub-constructs.

Keywords: entrepreneurial mindset; college students; gender; engineering; educational experience; measurement invariance; latent mean comparisons

1. Introduction

Since the Harvard Business School's pioneering entrepreneurship class was offered in 1947, entrepreneurial education has been expanded to diverse disciplines in higher education [1–4]. In addition, entrepreneurship education has gained global popularity among both undergraduate and graduate students [1,5]. It is also highly valued in Korea, and such courses are not uncommon in higher education curricula in diverse disciplines [6–9]. The wide dissemination of entrepreneurship education can be attributed to its expected beneficial outcomes, such as improved skills, knowledge, and attitudes related to venture creation [10], increased self-employment and ability to launch start-ups [10,11], and eventually economic growth [12]. Yet, the expected benefits are not limited to the realm of business, management, and the economy, especially in the context of higher education. The scope of entrepreneurship education has been extended to embrace broader educational goals for college students, such as improved career self-efficacy, career adaptability, project-management skills, self-regulation, and intrapreneurship in certain professional fields after graduation [13]. Due to the increasing volatility and uncertainty in job market and various career fields, college students today face more challenges than their counterparts in the past [14]. They are more likely to encounter a shortage of stable life-long careers, more project-based short-term jobs, and jobs replaced by artificial intelligence (AI). As a result, they might need more career adaptability to allow them to pursue multiple different career paths. For them, an entrepreneurial mindset, which might enhance their career adaptability, would be a valuable asset in today's era of uncertainty and fluctuation in the workplace [14].

Participating in the broadening of entrepreneurship education, Korean universities have provided diverse educational programs ranging from short-term, intensive, experiential, and extracurricular programs [13], to formal classes lasting one semester [15]. The educational goals range from the promotion of creativity to teamwork, communication skills, product development, and opportunity identification [13]. In addition, an enhanced entrepreneurial mindset was expected in most of the programs. However, the effectiveness of entrepreneurship education has not been thoroughly studied; to date, educational effectiveness has been measured by only one or a couple of entrepreneurial intention questions in many studies (e.g., [16–19]).

This can be mainly attributed to the lack of quality-assured assessment tools to measure various aspects of educational outcomes in higher education settings. Among the available measurement instruments, the Builder Profile [20] and the Global University Entrepreneurial Spirit Students' Survey (GUESSS [21]) had little evidence of reliability and validity. Although the Individual Entrepreneurial Orientation (IEO) [22,23] and the Entrepreneurial Mindset Profile (EMP) [24] thoroughly examined reliability of and evidence for multiple validity issues (e.g., construct validity, criterion-related validity, predictive validity, etc.), their measurement invariance has never been investigated.

The College Students' Entrepreneurial Mindset Scale (CS-EMS) [25], a recently developed and validated assessment, is promising for systematic measurement of the sub-constructs of *innovativeness*, *need for achievement*, *risk-taking*, *autonomy*, and *proactiveness*, which are the mindsets that are targeted for improvement across a wide spectrum of entrepreneurship classes. Yet, the measurement invariance of the CS-EMS across gender, major, and educational experiences has never been examined, and it is unknown which grouping variable has the most influence on the sub-scales of the CS-EMS.

To fill the void in the literature on entrepreneurship in higher education, this study was designed to pursue the following three goals. First, we tested four increasingly stringent measurement invariance models (i.e., configural, metric, scalar, and strict invariance models) of the CS-EMS across gender, major, and experience groups using the multi-group confirmatory factor analysis (MG-CFA) framework. Second, we examined the latent and observed mean differences in the sub-scales of the CS-EMS across the studied groups only if scalar invariance had been established. Third, we investigated the conditional effects of the three grouping variables (i.e., *gender*, *major*, and *experience*) using the structural equation modeling framework.

We expect that the findings of the current study will be able to guide educators when they use assessment tools to compare groups. Specifically, entrepreneurship educators will learn that cross-group comparisons based on observed or latent means should be preceded by a measurement invariance test [26–29]. In addition, the findings from the cross-group mean comparisons reveal the compared groups' current status regarding the entrepreneurial mindset, and educators might be able to design their entrepreneurship education programs with more emphasis on the areas that need improvement in particular gender [30–32], major [30,31], or experience groups [33,34]. Moreover, the findings based on the conditional effects of the grouping variables imply the necessity of entrepreneurship education for college students if educational experiences with entrepreneurship are found to be the factor with the most influence on the CS-EMS sub-scales. Last, but not least, we expect that the CS-EMS will serve as an important assessment tool for reliably and validly measuring the effects of entrepreneurship education in cases where the targeted educational objectives are related to any of the sub-constructs of the CS-EMS [35,36].

In the remainder of this manuscript, we first review the previous studies that are most relevant to the current study in terms of four themes: concepts of entrepreneurship and entrepreneurial mindset, currently available assessment tools and their limitations, measurement invariance, entrepreneurship education for college students, and issues related to gender or major differences. Next, we describe the characteristics of the participants, the CS-EMS instrument, and the analytic procedure, providing information on the materials and methods. Then, we illustrate the results of the current study for the measurement invariance test, cross-group mean comparisons, and conditional effects of the gender, major, and experience variables. Subsequently, we discuss the findings, implications, limitations, and suggestions for future studies, followed by the conclusions of the study.

2. Literature Review

2.1. Concepts of Entrepreneurship and Entrepreneurial Mindset

Researchers have defined entrepreneurship as a compound construct with various assets. Venkataraman [37,38] asserted that entrepreneurship refers to an activity that involves the discovery, evaluation, and exploitation of opportunities to introduce new goods and services, ways of organizing, processes, and raw materials [38]. Based on Miller and Friesen's work [39], the concepts of innovativeness, risk-taking, and proactiveness are commonly used to characterize and test entrepreneurship [40,41]. In addition to those three elements, Lumpkin and Dess [42] identified two more dimensions, autonomy and competitive aggressiveness, that are used to conceptualize entrepreneurial orientation. Entrepreneurial orientation has emerged as a key construct in the entrepreneurship literature. It has been viewed as a characteristic of organizations that can be measured by looking at the top management's entrepreneurial style, as evidenced by the firms' strategic decisions and operating management philosophy [43]. This concept of entrepreneurship focuses more on entrepreneurial behaviors, including seeking, identifying, grasping or creating opportunities, taking the initiative, solving problems, organizing and coordinating resources, networking effectively, combining things innovatively, taking calculated risks, and acting proactively in complex situations [44–46].

Entrepreneurship has been also defined as a mental attitude deeper than an intent to merely create a business. It requires application of energy and passion to create and implement new ideas and creative solutions [5]. Bosman and Fernhaber [47] describe the entrepreneurial mindset as an inclination toward entrepreneurial activities. A mindset is an individual's mental attitude or state that predetermines one's responses to and interpretations of a given situation [31]. An entrepreneurial mindset includes an individual's willingness to blend risk-taking, creativity, and innovation with the intention of creating value as well as an individual's ability to plan and manage projects in order to achieve objectives [47–49]. It relates to being dynamic, flexible, and self-regulating in an uncertain environment [44,45]. The entrepreneurial mindset develops over time and requires practice [47]. This supports individuals during daily life and makes employees more aware of the context of their work and better able to seize opportunities [47]. Thus, entrepreneurial-minded learning has received increased interest as a pedagogical approach within the higher education field [30,31].

When discussing entrepreneurship, the literature separates entrepreneurial mindsets from entrepreneurial behaviors [50]. Entrepreneurial mindsets refer to the abilities and general attitude of an individual, while entrepreneurial behaviors are made evident through the individual's actions. Both entrepreneurial mindsets and behaviors are valid concepts not only when dealing with business but also in all human activities [50]. Because entrepreneurship is not only about knowing facts but also a way of thinking and acting [46], recently, higher education programs have defined entrepreneurship broadly and included enterprising behaviors outside the business context [46,51–53].

2.2. Assessments for Entrepreneurial Mindsets

The literature has described several assessment instruments that are designed to measure an individual's entrepreneurial orientation and mindset. However, previous measures for entrepreneurial characteristics lack quality evidence, justifying the need for a validated measure of the entrepreneurial mindset. Some instances of instruments are reviewed as follows.

First, Badal and Struer [20] developed Builder Profile 10 to identify individual characteristics that are associated with building a successful business. The instruments include 30 items representing ten characteristics (determination, independence, confidence, delegator, risk, profitability, relationship, disruptor, knowledge, and selling). Evidence regarding its construct validity has never been examined, although its validity has been extensively investigated in relation to other variables. In addition, to our knowledge, it has never been validated for college students and has only been validated with high school and entrepreneur samples in the US.

Second, the Global University Entrepreneurial Spirit Students' Survey was developed in 2006 and designed to measure university students' perceptions of entrepreneurs (11 items) and their entrepreneurial competencies (seven items) in addition to entrepreneurial intentions. Although it has been widely used internationally until recently [21,54], its reliability and validity have never been tested.

Third, the Individual Entrepreneurial Orientation (IEO) scale, which has ten items, was developed by Bolton and his colleagues [22], and they found that the three correlated-factor structure was tenable based on validation with 1,100 university students. The three sub-factors were innovativeness, risk-taking, and proactiveness. Popov and colleagues [23] recently examined the construct validity of the IEO scale with Serbian college students and adults, and their results also supported the three correlated-factor structure of the ten items. However, neither study considered the measurement invariance of the IEO.

Fourth, the Entrepreneurial Mindset Profile (EMP) [24] was developed in 2015, and it was constituted of 14 dimensions with 72 items. Among the 14 dimensions, seven dimensions (i.e., independence, limited structure, non-conformity, risk acceptance, action orientation, passion, and need to achieve) represented traits of entrepreneurs, while the remaining seven dimensions (i.e., future focus, idea generation, execution, self-confidence, optimism, persistence, and interpersonal sensitivity) represented skills for entrepreneurs. They provided validity evidence based on the internal structure of the items and their relations to other variables. Although they compared the sub-scale scores of the EMP across gender, they did not consider measurement invariance before making a cross-group mean comparison.

2.3. Measurement Invariance

Measure invariance is an important issue, especially when a researcher wants to make cross-group comparisons using a measurement instrument consisting of multiple items that are assumed to have a smaller number of factors underlying them [27,28,55,56]. The core question in measurement invariance is whether the assessment or measurement in use operates in the same way across different groups based on either demographic characteristics (e.g., gender [57,58], nationality [57,59], language in use [55], etc.) or certain artifactual categorizations (e.g. experimental vs. treatment group [60,61]; pre- vs. post-measurement [62,63]; internet-based test vs. paper-and-pencil test [64]).

One of the most widely used methods to test measurement invariance is a multiple-group confirmatory factor analysis (MG-CFA) model which is a multi-group extension of a confirmatory factor analysis model [26–29,56,65]. Measurement invariance tested under the MG-CFA framework is also called factorial invariance, and it is well-known for its flexibility in examining every measurement parameter: factor loading (λ), intercept (τ), and unique variance (θ) [26,29,56]. The conventional way to test measurement invariance involves four sequential steps to evaluate increasingly constrained models – from configural invariance to strict invariance – across the studied groups [26–29]. Configural invariance indicates that the same factor structure holds between the groups while all measurement parameters are freely estimated for each group, which implies that the groups interpret a given set of items using equal conceptual grounding [37,55,66]. Once configural invariance is established, metric invariance is tested by imposing equality constraints on all factor loadings between the groups. Under the condition of metric invariance, the strength of the relationship between a factor and items belonging to the factor is equivalent across the groups [28,55,66]. Upon the established metric invariance, strict invariance is tested by equally constraining all sets of intercepts between groups. Scalar invariance can be interpreted as indicating that the origin of the item score is the same across the groups [27,28,55,67]. Finally, strict invariance is tested by adding equality constraints on the pair of unique variances between the groups upon the established scalar invariance model [68]. The status of strict invariance can be interpreted as indicating that the degree of errors is equivalent across groups [29]. Among the four measurement invariance conditions, the scalar invariance condition is necessary to compare the latent and observed means across groups [26,27,29], and thus, we drew the following hypotheses:

Hypothesis 1 (H1). *The CS-EMS presents at least scalar invariance across gender, major, and experience groups.*

Hypothesis 1a (H1a). *The CS-EMS presents at least scalar invariance between the male and female groups.*

Hypothesis 1b (H1b). *The CS-EMS presents at least scalar invariance between the engineering and non-engineering groups.*

Hypothesis 1c (H1c). *The CS-EMS presents at least scalar invariance between the experience and no-experience groups.*

2.4. Entrepreneurship Education for College Students

Entrepreneurship education mainly focuses on the development of certain beliefs, values, and attitudes, with the aim of causing individuals to consider entrepreneurship as an attractive and valid alternative to paid employment or unemployment [34,69]. Since the early 2000s, entrepreneurship education programs in higher education have grown rapidly and globally [1,2,5,70] in an effort to promote entrepreneurial outcomes [36]. The global interest in entrepreneurship education is a result of the association between entrepreneurship and economic growth, which has motivated policymakers to focus on cultivating and sustaining entrepreneurship [71]. Entrepreneurship education is a major approach to developing entrepreneurial intentions, mindsets, and behaviors [72]. However, the research on the impact of entrepreneurship education on entrepreneurial mindsets or intentions has yielded mixed results [1,35]. The literature has suggested that it is important to analyze the impact of entrepreneurship in gender-specific and pedagogy-specific manners [1]. In the following subsection, the studies on gender differences, major differences, and differences based on educational experiences in entrepreneurship are introduced.

2.4.1. Comparisons Based on Gender

Past research on gender differences in entrepreneurship has typically found that females are more conservative in entrepreneurial activities than males [73,74]. The image of the entrepreneur has traditionally been masculinized and rooted in masculine discourse [75]. Moreover, research has found that for women who work in gender incongruent occupations dominated by men, the experience of discrimination has a negative association with their well-being [76].

Research on the impact of entrepreneurship education on students' intention and mindset has reported gender-specific differences [77]. With students who have less exposure to entrepreneurship, the general effect of entrepreneurship education tends to be positive because participation in the programs usually increases their entrepreneurial intentions, attitudes, and self-efficacy [78]. Nowiński et al. [79] investigated whether entrepreneurial education contributes to the entrepreneurial intentions of university students in the Czech Republic, Hungary, Poland, and Slovakia. They indicated that although women generally have lower entrepreneurial intentions and display lower levels of entrepreneurial self-efficacy, they benefit from entrepreneurship education more than men do [79]. However, emerging literature shows that the relations between gender and the entrepreneurial mindset are more complex and multi-faceted. For example, Majumdar and Varadarajan [80] investigated the entrepreneurial mindset of women in the Arab world and suggested that the propensity for future entrepreneurship does not depend on gender; rather, it depends on factors like creativity, motivation, and awareness. An educational system that lacks a supportive environment and concrete initiatives can deeply affect female students, causing them to fear engaging in entrepreneurship [81]. Although efforts to promote an entrepreneurial mindset within society have increased, there has still been little attention on assessment and analysis of the entrepreneurial mindset amongst female students in the context of higher education. In addition, the results from the previous studies generally indicate that the females showed a lower level of entrepreneurial attitudes, intentions, and behaviors, thus we suggest the following hypotheses:

Hypothesis 2 (H2). *The male group scores higher on each of the five sub-constructs of the CS-EMS than the female group.*

Hypothesis 2a (H2a). *The male group scores higher on innovativeness than the female group.*

Hypothesis 2b (H2b). *The male group scores higher on need for achievement than the female group.*

Hypothesis 2c (H2c). *The male group scores higher on risk-taking than the female group.*

Hypothesis 2d (H2d). *The male group scores higher on autonomy than the female group.*

Hypothesis 2e (H2e). *The male group scores higher on proactiveness than the female group.*

2.4.2. Comparison Based on Major: Engineering vs. Non-Engineering

Specifically, engineering education institutes play an important role in entrepreneurial development [14]. Engineers often take positions in which entrepreneurship is highly valued because they work in areas in which technological development is moving very quickly. As entrepreneurship serves as an integral part of the economy, engineers need to develop an entrepreneurial mindset through authentic educational experiences [82]. Thus, engineering education institutes have been interested in developing an academic entrepreneurship education community through the development of engineering-specific entrepreneurship centers and programs [83].

In South Korea, there is strong pressure to develop entrepreneurship and innovation competencies in engineering education [14]. The industry has influenced the process to improve this part of engineering education, which in turn has prompted the government to consider entrepreneurship education to be crucial [14]. In the accreditation process for engineering education, universities should prove that their curricula, including capstone design courses, promote students' entrepreneurial mindset, and skills. Capstone design courses often guide students from the problem identification stage through prototyping, with a heavy focus on technological feasibility and an entrepreneurial mind. While the creation of engineering entrepreneurship programs seems to address the need for reforms in undergraduate engineering programs, such programs usually measure output metrics, such as enrollment and degrees, as opposed to evidence of the program's impact on each individual student's mindset [83]. To our knowledge, no study has directly compared the difference in entrepreneurial mindset among different majors. However, considering the efforts to promote students' entrepreneurial attitudes, intentions, and behaviors made by engineering disciplines we suggest the following hypotheses regarding major difference:

Hypothesis 3 (H3). *The engineering group scores higher on each of the five sub-constructs of the CS-EMS than the non-engineering group.*

Hypothesis 3a (H3a). *The engineering group scores higher on innovativeness than the non-engineering group.*

Hypothesis 3b (H3b). *The engineering group scores higher on need for achievement than the non-engineering group.*

Hypothesis 3c (H3c). *The engineering group scores higher on risk-taking than the non-engineering group.*

Hypothesis 3d (H3d). *The engineering group scores higher on autonomy than the non-engineering group.*

Hypothesis 3e (H3e). *The engineering group scores higher on proactiveness than the non-engineering group.*

2.4.3. Comparison Based on Educational Experiences in Entrepreneurship

Regarding the impact of entrepreneurship education, Bae and colleagues' meta-analytic review [36] found a significant correlation between entrepreneurship education and entrepreneurial intentions. They emphasized that it is important to consider the significant impact of moderators, such as the attributes of entrepreneurship education, differences between students, and cultural values, on entrepreneurial intentions. Most studies suggest a positive link between the educational program and students' entrepreneurial intentions, attitude, knowledge, and skills [84–87], but some articles report results that are not significant or negative. For example, Lanero, et al. [88] reported that there is no significant link between entrepreneurship education and entrepreneurial attitudes among Spanish students. Also, Mentoor and Friedrich [89] found a negative link between educational experiences and attitudes toward entrepreneurship among South African students. Indeed, there is still limited attention given to the impact of entrepreneurship education and the quality-assured assessment tools to measure various aspects of educational outcomes within the context of cross-cultural and academic majors [2]. Therefore, we aim to confirm the influence of educational experience in entrepreneurship with the validated assessment tool, and suggest the following hypotheses:

Hypothesis 4 (H4). *The group with educational experiences in entrepreneurship scores higher on each of the five sub-constructs of the CS-EMS than the group without such experiences.*

Hypothesis 4a (H4a). *The group with educational experiences in entrepreneurship scores higher on innovativeness than the group without such experiences.*

Hypothesis 4b (H4b). *The group with educational experiences in entrepreneurship scores higher on need for achievement than the group without such experiences.*

Hypothesis 4c (H4c). *The group with educational experiences in entrepreneurship scores higher on risk-taking than the group without such experiences.*

Hypothesis 4d (H4d). *The group with educational experiences in entrepreneurship scores higher on autonomy than the group without such experiences.*

Hypothesis 4e (H4e). *The group with educational experiences in entrepreneurship scores higher on proactiveness than the group without such experiences.*

The Hypotheses 2 through 4 deal with only marginal effects of gender, major, and educational experiences on entrepreneurship mindsets, and thus the actual effects of the variables might be confounded [90,91]. Therefore, it is imperative to investigate the conditional effects of gender, major, and educational experiences to separate out the unique contribution of each variable [90,91] on the entrepreneurship mindsets. Based on a great deal of evidences for the effect of entrepreneurship education on entrepreneurial attitude [78,92–94], intention [36,78,95–97], and behavior [98–101], we believe that the educational experiences in entrepreneurship would play the most crucial role in the college students' entrepreneurial mindset even after controlling for the effects of gender and major.

Hence, we also suggest the following hypotheses regarding the conditional effect of gender, major, and educational experiences:

Hypothesis 5 (H5). *Educational experience is the most influencing factor for the scores of the CS-EMS sub-constructs after controlling for gender and major.*

Hypothesis 5a (H5a). *Educational experience is the most influencing factor for innovativeness after controlling for gender and major.*

Hypothesis 5b (H5b). *Educational experience is the most influencing factor for need for achievement after controlling for gender and major.*

Hypothesis 5c (H5c). *Educational experience is the most influencing factor for risk-taking after controlling for gender and major.*

Hypothesis 5d (H5d). *Educational experience is the most influencing factor for autonomy after controlling for gender and major.*

Hypothesis 5e (H5e). *Educational experience is the most influencing factor for proactiveness after controlling for gender and major.*

3. Materials and Methods

3.1. Participants

We used the dataset that was collected for the initial validation of the CS-EMS [25]. At a large private university in Korea, they collected data via emails with an online survey link. A total of 317 students provided completed and valid responses. At the beginning of the online survey, the purpose of the study and the possible use of the data were presented. Only the data from participants who provided consent were analyzed in the current study. Table 1 shows the distribution of the participants' major, grade, and educational experience by gender. Of the 317 participants, 68.5% were males and 31.5% were females. The participants' majors included engineering (47.3%), economics (17.4%), liberal arts (13.9%), social sciences (13.2%), and sciences (8.2%). The majority of the participants was either juniors (28.7%) or seniors (35.7%), while 19.1% were freshmen and 16.6% were sophomores. Among the participants, 52.7% had at least one educational experience with entrepreneurship (e.g., formal classes, extracurricular activities at university, competitions out of university). It is important to be aware that the imbalanced gender representation was largely due to the large number of students from engineering majors (N = 150; 47.3%). Male students majoring in engineering (N = 123) represented 68.5% of the total number of male participants. In addition, 70 male participants majoring in engineering represented 57.4% of the male participants who had some educational experience in entrepreneurship.

3.2. Instrument

Jung and Lee [25] developed the CS-EMS with 19 items, and they investigated the evidence related to construct validity and predictive validity with regard to entrepreneurial intentions. Based on their results, the CS-EMS stipulated five sub-factors: *innovativeness, need for achievement, risk-taking, autonomy,* and *proactiveness.* In their study, each sub-factor was operationally defined as follows: (1) *innovativeness*: propensity to seek new opportunities and solutions; (2) *need for achievement*: propensity to achieve something quickly and well; (3) *risk-taking*: propensity to try something with either unclear expectations or the possibility of failure; (4) *autonomy*: propensity to act independently while being reluctant to rely on others; and (5) *proactiveness*: propensity to plan and act in advance. Table 2 presents the English-translated items of the Entrepreneurial Mindset Scale by sub-factor. Each of the items was measured with a 5-point Likert scale ranging from 1 (strongly disagree) to 5 (strongly agree). Sub-scale scores represent the average of the items under a sub-factor. Higher scores indicate a higher level of the entrepreneurial mindset sub-factor. Table 2 presents the mean, standard deviation, skewness, and kurtosis of each item. The range of item means was 2.85 (SD = 1.13; Item 14) to 4.12 (SD = 0.85; item 4), while the skewness and kurtosis values ranged from −0.85 to 0.28 and from −0.86 to 0.97, respectively.

Table 1. Participants' Characteristics.

Category	Male		Female		Total	
	N	%	N	%	N	%
Major						
Engineering	123	82.0	27	18.0	150	47.3
Science	18	69.2	8	30.8	26	8.2
Economics	32	58.2	23	41.8	55	17.4
Liberal Arts	29	51.8	27	48.2	44	13.9
Social Science	15	50.0	15	50.0	42	13.2
Grade [a]						
Freshman	36	60.0	24	40.0	60	19.1
Sophomore	25	48.1	27	51.9	52	16.6
Junior	66	73.3	24	26.7	90	28.7
Senior	87	77.7	25	22.3	112	35.7
Educational Experience in Entrepreneurship						
Yes	122	73.1	55	26.9	167	52.7
No	95	63.3	44	36.7	150	47.3
Total	217	68.5	100	3.2	317	100.0

Note. [a] Three of the respondents did not provided their grade.

Table 2. English-translated College Students' Entrepreneurial Mindset Scale.

#	Item	M [a]	SD [b]	Skew. [c]	Kurt. [d]
Innovativeness					
Item 1	I like to take on a new challenge.	3.65	0.91	−0.42	−0.36
Item 2	I try to work in a novel way.	3.47	0.98	−0.23	−0.59
Item 3	I am likely to accept new ideas.	3.99	0.81	−0.75	0.79
Item 4	I like imaginative ideas.	4.12	0.85	−0.85	0.52
Item 5	I try to look for new opportunities earlier than others.	3.74	0.90	−0.32	−0.39
Item 6	I persistently try to come up with outstanding ideas.	3.50	0.91	0.00	−0.56
Need for Achievement					
Item 7	I act aggressively to achieve a goal.	4.08	0.78	−0.78	0.97
Item 8	I am more passionate than others.	3.82	0.84	−0.33	−0.29
Item 9	I have a strong will to achieve something.	4.02	0.79	−0.61	0.32
Item 10	I persist in pushing forward necessary things against all odds.	4.09	0.76	−0.63	0.50
Risk-taking					
Item 11	I tend to push forward something with high expected value even with high risk.	3.57	1.00	−0.28	−0.66
Item 12	I tend to take risks for new opportunities.	3.43	1.00	−0.15	−0.65
Item 13	I tend to take challenges even when there is a risk of failure.	3.47	0.99	−0.26	−0.67
Autonomy					
Item 14	I am reluctant to receive outside aid.	2.85	1.13	0.28	−0.86
Item 15	I prefer solving problems independently.	3.42	1.04	−0.35	−0.52
Item 16	I prefer acting based on my own decision.	3.86	0.85	−0.73	0.58
Proactiveness					
Item 17	I proactively plan new things.	3.83	0.76	−0.43	0.05
Item 18	I plan and act in advance rather than waiting for something to be given.	3.72	0.88	−0.42	−0.18
Item 19	I tend to actively overcome hardships rather than attributing to the environment.	3.79	0.82	−0.42	−0.03

Note. [a] Mean; [b] standard deviation; [c] skewness; and [d] kurtosis.

Jung and Lee [25] found that the Cronbach's α of the whole scale was 0.94, while the Cronbach's αs for the *innovativeness, need for achievement, risk-taking, autonomy,* and *proactiveness* sub-scales were 0.88, 0.83, 0.88, 0.77, and 0.80, respectively. In their study, the correlated five-factor model was confirmed based on the results from both exploratory and confirmatory factor analyses. Predictive validity was evidenced by the significant correlations (range: 0.22~0.54) between each of the three start-up intention variables (weak and vague intention, moderate intention, and strong and firm intention) and four sub-factors (*innovativeness, need for achievement, risk-taking,* and *proactiveness*), except for autonomy. The autonomy sub-scale score had a statistically significant correlation (.11) only with strong and firm intention.

3.3. Analytic Procedure

Data analyses were conducted in four phases to fulfill the purposes of the study. In the first phase, we examined the factor structure of the CS-EMS with six groups of interest (i.e., male, female, engineering, non-engineering, educational experiences, no educational experiences) separately using confirmatory factor analysis (CFA). The major reason we selected CFA is that this method is built on theories rather than guided by data [102,103]. Since a correlated five-factor model had already been established by Jung and Lee [25], CFA was considered a more appropriate starting point than exploratory factor analysis (EFA). In addition, CFA is known for providing a more trustworthy solution than EFA for models with multiple factors [102], such as the one used in our study. Most importantly, CFA is a more powerful method to test every element of factorial invariance [28], whereas EFA is capable of testing only factor loading invariance [26].

As shown in Table 2 in the previous section, neither the skewness (range: −0.85~0.28) nor kurtosis (range: −0.86~0.97) of any item appeared to seriously violate the normality assumption of the CFA based on the criteria (skewness ≤ ±2; kurtosis ≤ ±7) suggested by Hair et al. [104] and Byrne [105]. Therefore, we used the maximum likelihood estimation method to evaluate the model [102]. The adequacy of the tested CFA models was evaluated using conventionally reported fit indices, such as the chi-square (χ^2) fit statistic at a 0.05 significance level, the root mean square of approximation (*RMSEA*), the comparative fit index (*CFI*), and the standardized root mean squared residual (*SRMR*). In some conditions with large samples and/or a complex model, χ^2 is too sensitive to retain an acceptable model [102]. Thus, we carefully examined model adequacy, referring to the other fit indices while considering the models acceptable with *RMSEA* ≤ 0.08, the *CFI* ≥ 0.90, and the *SRMR* ≤ 0.08 [102,106,107].

In the second phase, we tested H1. The four levels of factorial invariance (configural, metric, scalar, and strict invariance) were tested sequentially using a MG-CFA model. For example, the configural invariance model was compared with the metric invariance model based on the difference (Δ) in the model fit indices. The model with more invariance constraints is generally expected to have deteriorated fit statistics. A significant value of $\Delta\chi^2$ indicates that the model with more invariance constraints (e.g., the metric invariance model) is poorer than the model with fewer invariance constraints (e.g., the configural invariance model). Like χ^2, $\Delta\chi^2$ may overly reject acceptable models. Therefore, we consulted ΔRMSEA, ΔCFI, and ΔSRMR as well for the cases in which $\Delta\chi^2$ was statistically significant. We used the criteria for acceptable models in accordance with Chen's [108] recommendations. He suggested that a metric invariance model is acceptable when ΔRMSEA ≥ 0.010, ΔCFI ≥ −0.005, and ΔSRMR ≥ 0.025 and that either a scalar or strict invariance model is acceptable when ΔRMSEA ≥ 0.010, ΔCFI ≥ −0.005, and ΔSRMR ≥ 0.005, given a group size < 300.

In the third phase, we tested H2 through H4 by investigating the observed and latent sub-factor mean differences between every pair of compared groups when at least the scalar invariance condition is satisfied [27,55]. In the final phase, we simultaneously tested the effect of the gender, major, and educational experiences on the sub-factors of the CS-EMS using the structural equation modeling framework to test H5. While the observed mean difference between the groups was examined using *IBM SPSS 26*, the remaining analyses (i.e., confirmatory factor analysis, multiple-group confirmatory factor analysis, latent mean comparisons, structural equation modeling) were conducted using *MPlus8*.

4. Results

4.1. Confirmatory Factor Analysis

Before performing a measurement invariance test, we fitted the correlated five-factor model (Figure 1) to each of the six groups (i.e., male, female, engineering, non-engineering, educational experiences, and no educational experiences) separately. In Figure 1 λ_{ij}, τ_{ij}, δ_{ij}, and θ_{ij} represent the factor loading, intercept, unique factor score, and unique variance of the i_{th} factor's j_{th} item, respectively.

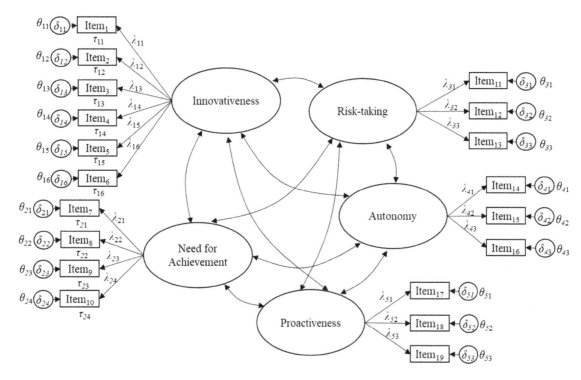

Figure 1. The correlated five-factor model of the Entrepreneurial Mindset Scale.

The results of the CFA analyses can be found in Table 3. The chi-square (χ^2) fit statistic for the CFA model was statistically significant for all groups, which means that the tested model does not fit the data. However, the limitation of the χ^2 fit statistic (i.e., it can easily reject a viable model when given a large sample [102]) allowed us to refer to alternative fit statistics, such as *RMSEA*, *CFI*, and *SRMR*. All the alternative fit statistics consistently indicated that the tested CFA model was tenable for all groups; for all *CFI* > 0.90 and *RMSEA* and *SRMR* < 0.08. Thus, the correlated five-factor model without any model modification served as the baseline model for sequential tests of factorial invariance, which were performed in the next analyses.

Table 3. Confirmatory Factor Analysis Results for Each of the Six Groups.

Sub-Groups	χ^2	df	p-Value	RMSEA	CFI	SRMR
Male	301.345	142	<0.000	0.072	0.920	0.062
Female	197.154	142	0.002	0.062	0.952	0.068
Engineering	267.909	142	<0.000	0.077	0.908	0.069
Non-Engineering	261.844	142	<0.000	0.071	0.934	0.058
Experience	280.792	142	<0.000	0.077	0.923	0.063
No experience	264.220	142	<0.000	0.076	0.913	0.065

Note. RMSEA: the root mean square of approximation; CFI: the comparative fit index; SRMR: the standardized root mean squared residual.

Table 4 presents the Cronbach's αs of the whole scale and each of the five sub-scales (*innovativeness, need for achievement, risk-taking, autonomy,* and *proactiveness*) for the six groups. The Cronbach's α of the whole scale ranged from 0.882 to 0.919 while those of the sub-scales ranged from 0.717 to 0.902 across the six groups. All of them appeared to be adequate [109,110].

Table 4. Cronbach's αs of the CS-EMS by Group.

Sub-Groups	Whole Scale	Innovative-Ness	Need for Achievement	Risk-Taking	Autonomy	Proactive-Ness
Male	0.891	0.863	0.813	0.883	0.717	0.803
Female	0.919	0.902	0.853	0.878	0.851	0.796
Engineering	0.886	0.864	0.799	0.866	0.743	0.821
Non-Engineering	0.914	0.886	0.850	0.896	0.793	0.789
Experience	0.916	0.881	0.860	0.897	0.729	0.796
No experience	0.882	0.874	0.789	0.858	0.809	0.793

4.2. Measurement Invariance Test

The results directly addressing Hypothesis 1 (H1: The CS-EMS presents at least scalar invariance across gender, major, and experience groups.) are presented in this section. The results of the hierarchical factorial invariance tests by gender, major, and educational experience are presented in Table 5. In addition to the overall model fit information for each invariance model, the chi-square difference test results and differences in *RMSEA, CFI,* and *SRMR* between a less restricted model and a more restricted model are presented. One thing we should address here is that we used the method that does not require a reference variable [26,29,56] to be appointed for identifying the metric and scalar invariance models.

Table 5. Factorial Invariance Test results across Gender, Major, and Educational Experiences.

	χ^2	df	RMSEA	CFI	SRMR	$\Delta\chi^2$	Δdf	ΔRMSEA	ΔCFI	ΔSRMR
Gender										
Configural	498.499 **	284	0.069	0.932	0.064					
Metric	521.084 **	298	0.069	0.929	0.073	22.585	14	0.000	−0.003	0.009
Scalar	531.878 **	312	0.067	0.930	0.073	10.794	14	−0.002 [a]	0.001	0.000
Strict	565.710 **	331	0.067	0.925	0.078	33.832 *	19	0.000	−0.005	0.005
Major										
Configural	529.752 **	284	0.074	0.923	0.063					
Metric	543.050 **	298	0.072	0.923	0.070	13.298	14	−0.002 [a]	0.000	0.007
Scalar	559.411 **	312	0.071	0.923	0.072	16.361	14	−0.001 [a]	0.000	0.002
Strict	587.722 **	331	0.070	0.920	0.081	28.311	19	−0.001 [a]	−0.003	0.009
Educational Experience										
Configural	545.012 **	284	0.070	0.918	0.064					
Metric	552.262 **	298	0.073	0.920	0.067	7.250	14	0.003	0.002	0.003
Scalar	574.837 **	312	0.073	0.918	0.069	22.575	14	0.000	−0.002	0.002
Strict	600.762 **	331	0.072	0.915	0.076	25.925	19	−0.001 [a]	−0.003	0.007

Note. * $p < 0.05$; ** $p < 0.01$; RMSEA: the root mean square of approximation; CFI: the comparative fit index; SRMR: the standardized root mean squared residual; Δ represents a difference test for each statistic between less restricted model (e.g., configural invariance model) and more restricted model (e.g., metric invariance model); [a] In these cases, the changes in the *RMSEA* were not expected (i.e., an increase in values).

4.2.1. Configural Invariance Model

The configural invariance model holds across gender ($\chi^2 = 529.752$, $df = 284$, $p < 0.001$; $RMSEA = 0.074$; $CFI = 0.923$; $SRMR = 0.063$), major ($\chi^2 = 498.499$, $df = 284$, $p < 0.001$; $RMSEA = 0.069$; $CFI = 0.932$; $SRMR = 0.064$), and educational experience ($\chi^2 = 545.012$, $df = 284$, $p < 0.001$; $RMSEA = 0.070$; $CFI = 0.918$; $SRMR = 0.064$) based on the same criteria for the CFA.

4.2.2. Metric Invariance Model

Metric invariance holds for every comparison based on the non-significant chi-square difference tests between the configural invariance model and metric invariance model (gender: $\Delta\chi^2 = 13.298$, $df = 14$, $p = 0.503$; major: $\Delta\chi^2 = 22.585$, $df = 14$, $p = 0.067$; educational experience: $\Delta\chi^2 = 7.250$, $df = 14$, $p = 0.925$). Based on the Chen's [108] recommendation for the metric invariance test with samples sizes less than 300 ($\Delta RMSEA \geq 0.010$, $\Delta CFI \geq -0.005$, $\Delta SRMR \geq 0.025$), the differences in $RMSEA$, CFI, and $SRMR$ (gender: $\Delta RMSEA = 0.000$, $\Delta CFI = -0.003$, $\Delta SRMR = 0.009$; major: $\Delta RMSEA = -0.002$, $\Delta CFI = 0.000$, $\Delta SRMR = 0.007$; educational experience: $\Delta RMSEA = 0.003$, $\Delta CFI = 0.002$, $\Delta SRMR = 0.003$) also supported metric invariance across the gender, major, and educational experience groups.

4.2.3. Scalar Invariance Model

After imposing invariant intercept constraints, the chi-square difference tests between the metric invariance model and scalar invariance model were not statistically significant for all comparisons (gender: $\Delta\chi^2 = 16.361$, $df = 14$, $p = 0.292$; major: $\Delta\chi^2 = 10.794$, $df = 14$, $p = 0.702$; educational experience: $\Delta\chi^2 = 22.575$, $df = 14$, $p = 0.068$). There were no outstanding changes in $RMSEA$, CFI, and $SRMR$ (gender: $\Delta RMSEA = -0.001$, $\Delta CFI = 0.000$, $\Delta SRMR = 0.002$; major: $\Delta RMSEA = -0.002$, $\Delta CFI = 0.001$, $\Delta SRMR = 0.000$; educational experience: $\Delta RMSEA = 0.000$, $\Delta CFI = -0.002$, $\Delta SRMR = 0.002$) based on Chen's [108] criteria for the scalar invariance test with samples of less than 300 ($\Delta RMSEA \geq 0.010$, $\Delta CFI \geq -0.005$, $\Delta SRMR \geq 0.005$). Hence, the results confirmed Hypothesis 1a (H1a: The CS-EMS presents at least scalar invariance between the male and female groups.), Hypothesis 1b (H1b: The CS-EMS presents at least scalar invariance between the engineering and non-engineering groups.), and Hypothesis 1c (H1c: The CS-EMS presents at least scalar invariance between the experience and no-experience groups.).

4.2.4. Strict Invariance Model

The chi-square difference tests between the scalar invariance model and strict invariance model were not significant across the pairs based on either major or educational experiences (major: $\Delta\chi^2 = 28.311$, $df = 19$, $p = 0.078$; educational experience: $\Delta\chi^2 = 25.925$, $df = 19$, $p = 0.132$). Based on Chen's [108] suggestions for strict invariance tests with samples of less than 300 ($\Delta RMSEA \geq 0.010$, $\Delta CFI \geq -0.005$, $\Delta SRMR \geq 0.005$), the changes in the other fit indices were negligible (major: $\Delta RMSEA = -0.001$, $\Delta CFI = -0.003$; educational experience: $\Delta RMSEA = -0.001$, $\Delta CFI = -0.003$, $\Delta SRMR = 0.007$) except for $SRMR$ (major: $\Delta SRMR = 0.009$; educational experiences: $\Delta SRMR = 0.007$). For the gender comparison, the chi-square difference test results indicated that the strict invariance model was significantly worse than the scalar invariance model. In addition, changes in the two other fit indices ($\Delta CFI = -0.005$; $\Delta SRMR = 0.005$) indicated that the strict invariance model was worse than the scalar invariance model. However, we did not pursue partial strict invariance since scalar invariance is a sufficient condition for latent and observed mean comparisons [26,29]. We provide the measurement parameter estimates (λ_{ij}, τ_{ij}, and θ_{ij}) of the final confirmed factorial invariance model by gender, major, and educational experience in Appendix A (Tables A1–A3).

4.3. Comparison of Latent and Observed Means

In this section, we present the results that are directly related to Hypothesis 2 (H2: The male group scores higher on each of the five sub-constructs of the CS-EMS than the female group.), Hypothesis 3 (H3: The engineering group scores higher on each of the five sub-constructs of the CS-EMS than the non-engineering group.), and Hypothesis 4 (H4: The group with educational experiences in entrepreneurship scores higher on each of the five sub-constructs of the CS-EMS than the group without such experiences.). The latent means were tested between every set of the compared groups under the finally confirmed factorial invariance model using a MG-CFA. For the groups based on major (engineering vs. non-engineering) and educational experience (with educational experiences in entrepreneurship vs. without educational experiences in entrepreneurship), the latent means were compared using the strict invariance model. To compare the latent means between males and females, the scalar invariance model was used. For each comparison, non-engineering students, females, and the students without educational experiences in entrepreneurship served reference groups with a fixed latent mean score of zero. Table 6 shows the estimated sub-scale latent and observed means of the groups by gender, major, and educational experience.

Table 6. Factorial Invariance Test results across Gender, Major, and Educational Experience Groups.

		Gender		Major		Educational Experience	
		Male M (SE)	**Female** M (SD)	**Eng.** M (SE)	**Non-Eng.** M (SD)	**Yes** M (SE)	**No** M (SD)
Innovativeness	ξ_i	0.44 (0.15) **	0.00 (0.00)	0.37 (0.11) **	0.00 (0.00)	0.42 (0.13) **	0.00 (0.00)
	O_i	3.83 (0.66) **	3.57 (0.77)	3.89 (0.63) **	3.62 (0.75)	3.86 (0.71) **	3.61 (0.68)
Need for Achievement	ξ_i	0.22 (0.15) *	0.00 (0.00)	0.17 (0.11) **	0.00 (0.00)	0.21 (0.13) **	0.00 (0.00)
	O_i	4.04 (0.60) *	3.92 (0.73)	4.06 (0.60) *	3.95 (0.68)	4.06 (0.68) **	3.94 (0.61)
Risk-taking	ξ_i	0.33 (0.13) **	0.00 (0.00)	0.28 (0.12) **	0.00 (0.00)	0.44 (0.13) **	0.00 (0.00)
	O_i	3.58 (0.90) **	3.29 (0.87)	3.63 (0.87) **	3.36 (0.91)	3.66 (0.90) **	3.30 (0.85)
Autonomy	ξ_i	0.05 (0.15) *	0.00 (0.00)	−0.09 (0.12) *	0.00 (0.00)	−0.13 (0.11) **	0.00 (0.00)
	O_i	3.37 (0.79) *	3.39 (0.96)	3.37 (0.82) *	3.37 (0.87)	3.33 (0.81) **	3.44 (0.89)
Proactiveness	ξ_i	0.40 (0.16) *	0.00 (0.00)	0.14 (0.12) *	0.00 (0.00)	0.52 (0.13) **	0.00 (0.00)
	O_i	3.85 (0.64) **	3.62 (0.78)	3.82 (0.67) *	3.85 (0.71)	3.93 (0.67) **	3.61 (0.68)

Note. ξ_i: Estimated latent mean; O_i: observed mean; M: mean; SE: standard error of the estimated mean; SD: standard deviation; * $p < 0.05$; ** $p < 0.01$.

4.3.1. Comparison Based on Gender

Among the five sub-scales, the male group had significantly higher latent means on the *innovativeness* ($M = 0.44$, $SE = 0.15$), *risk-taking* ($M = 0.33$, $SE = 0.13$), and *proactiveness* ($M = 0.40$, $SE = 0.16$) sub-scales than the female group, which confirmed Hypothesis 2a (H2a: The male group scores higher on innovativeness than the female group.), Hypothesis 2c (H2c: The male group scores higher on risk-taking than the female group.), and Hypothesis 2e (H2e: The male group scores higher on proactiveness than the female group.). The latent means of two sub-scales (*need for achievement* and *autonomy*) did not differ across the groups, and thus Hypothesis 2b (H2b: The male group scores higher on need for achievement than the female group.) and Hypothesis 2d (H2d: The male group scores higher on autonomy than the female group.) were rejected. Regarding the sub-scales' observed means, the male group scored higher on the *innovativeness* ($M = 3.83$, $SD = 0.66$), *risk-taking* ($M = 3.58$, $SD = 0.90$), and *proactiveness* ($M = 3.85$, $SD = 0.64$) sub-scales than the female group. The effect sizes (Cohen's d, 1988) for the observed mean scores of *innovativeness*, *risk-taking*, and *proactiveness* were 0.38, 0.33, and 0.34, respectively, which indicate small to medium effects (Cohen, 1988).

4.3.2. Comparison Based on Major

The engineering major group had significantly higher latent means for the *innovativeness* (M = 0.37, SE = 0.11) and *risk-taking* ($M = 0.28$, $SE = 0.12$) sub-scale compared to the non-engineering major group, which supported Hypothesis 3a (H3a: The engineering group scores higher on innovativeness than the non-engineering group.) and Hypothesis 3e (H3e: The engineering group scores higher on proactiveness than the non-engineering group.). Yet, the two groups did not differ in the latent means of the *need for achievement, autonomy,* and *proactiveness* sub-scales, and thus we rejected Hypothesis 3b (H3b: The engineering group scores higher on need for achievement than the non-engineering group.), Hypothesis 3c (H3c: The engineering group scores higher on risk-taking than the non-engineering group.), and Hypothesis 3d (H3d: The engineering group scores higher on autonomy than the non-engineering group.). The same pattern of significant differences could be found in the observed sub-scale mean comparisons. The engineering major group had higher observed sub-scale mean scores for both *innovativeness* ($M = 3.89$, $SD = 0.63$) and *risk-taking* ($M = 3.62$, $SD = 0.75$) compared to the non-engineering major group. The Cohen's *d* effect sizes for the *innovativeness* and *risk-taking* sub-scales were 0.39 and 0.29, respectively, which indicate small (0.02) to medium effects (0.05) according to Cohen (1988).

4.3.3. Comparison Based on Educational Experiences in Entrepreneurship

The group with educational experiences in entrepreneurship scored substantially higher on the *innovativeness* ($M = 0.42, SE = 0.13$), *risk-taking* ($M = 0.44, SE = 0.13$), and *proactiveness* ($M = 0.52, SE = 0.13$) sub-scales than the group without such experiences, which confirmed Hypothesis 4a (H4a: The group with educational experiences in entrepreneurship scores higher on each of the five sub-constructs of the CS-EMS than the group without such experiences.), Hypothesis 4c (H4c: The group with educational experiences in entrepreneurship scores higher on risk-taking than the group without such experiences.), and Hypothesis 4e (H4e: The group with educational experiences in entrepreneurship scores higher on proactiveness than the group without such experiences.). The remaining sub-scales, *need for achievement* and *autonomy*, did not differ across the groups, and thus we rejected Hypothesis 4b (H4b: The group with educational experiences in entrepreneurship scores higher on need for achievement than the group without such experiences.) and Hypothesis 4d (H4d: The group with educational experiences in entrepreneurship scores higher on autonomy than the group without such experiences.). For the observed sub-scale scores, the group with educational experiences in entrepreneurship scored higher on the *innovativeness* ($M = 3.86, SD = 0.71$), *risk-taking* ($M = 3.66, SD = 0.90$), and *proactiveness* ($M = 3.93, SD = 0.67$) sub-scales than the group without educational experiences. The effect sizes for the observed mean scores of the *innovativeness*, *risk-taking*, and *proactiveness* sub-scales were 0.37, 0.41, and 0.48, respectively, which indicate small to medium effects (Cohen, 1988).

4.4. Structural Equation Modeling: Tests of Conditional Group Effects on Each Sub-Scale

This section addresses Hypothesis 5 (H5: Educational experience is the most influencing factor for the scores of the CS-EMS sub-constructs after controlling for gender and major.) directly. In the previous phase, we tested the sub-scales' latent means across each pair of groups without considering the effect of the other groups. Thus, we investigated the conditional effect of the group on the latent scores of the CS-EMS sub-scales by including all three grouping variables as independent variables in the model under the structural equation modeling framework (Figure 2). By doing so, the effect of the overrepresentation of male participants majoring in engineering can be controlled, and we can single out the effects of each of the three variables.

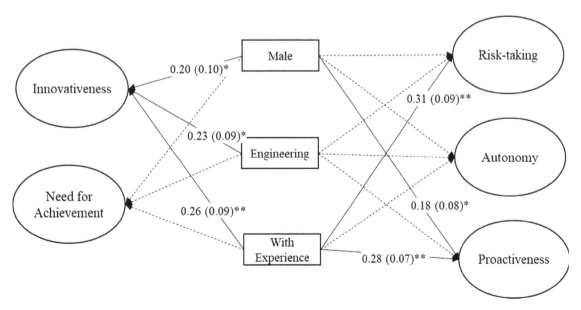

Figure 2. Tests of the Grouping Variable Effects on the Entrepreneurial Mindset Sub-scales.

4.4.1. Innovativeness

In the simple latent and observed mean comparisons, the *innovativeness* sub-scale scores significantly differed across all comparison pairs. Even after controlling for the remaining variables, each of the three grouping variables (gender, major, and experience) had a significant effect on the *innovativeness* sub-scale score. To interpret the estimated effect, the male group's *innovativeness* score was 0.20 higher than the female group when the effect of the major and experience variables was considered. The engineering major group's *innovativeness* score was 0.23 higher than the non-engineering major group when controlling for the effect of major and gender. The group with educational experiences in entrepreneurship scored 0.26 higher on the *innovativeness* sub-scale than the group without educational experiences when the effects of major and gender were accounted for. To sum up the results, we considered Hypothesis 5a (H5a: Educational experience is the most influencing factor for *innovativeness* after controlling for gender and major.) to be supported.

4.4.2. Need for Achievement

Similarly, in the results for the simple latent and observed mean comparisons, none of the three grouping variables (*gender, major,* and *experience*) had a significant effect on the score of the *need for achievement* sub-scale. Thus, we rejected Hypothesis 5b (H5b: Educational experience is the most influencing factor for *need for achievement* after controlling for gender and major.).

4.4.3. Risk-Taking

Whereas the *risk-taking* sub-scale scores significantly differed across all pairs of comparison in the simple latent and observed mean difference tests, only experience had a significant effect on the *risk-taking* sub-scale. That is, the score for the *risk-taking* sub-scale was 0.31 higher for the group with educational experiences in entrepreneurship than the group without such experiences after controlling for the effects of gender and major. Interestingly, the effects of *gender* and *major* disappeared when the other grouping variables were considered. Hence, the result confirmed Hypothesis 5c (H5c: Educational experience is the most influencing factor for *risk-taking* after controlling for gender and major.).

4.4.4. Autonomy

None of the three grouping variables (*gender, major,* and *experience*) had a significant effect on the *need for achievement* sub-scale score, which was consistent with the results of the simple latent and observed mean comparisons. Therefore, we rejected Hypothesis 5d (H5d: Educational experience is the most influencing factor for *autonomy* after controlling for gender and major.).

4.4.5. Proactiveness

In the simple latent and observed mean comparisons, the *proactiveness* sub-scale scores significantly differed across groups based on either gender or educational experiences. A similar pattern was found through a structural equation modeling analysis. The same two grouping variables (gender and experience) had a significant effect on the *proactiveness* sub-scale scores. Specifically, the male group's *proactiveness* score was 0.18 higher than that of the female group after controlling for the effect of major and experience, while the group with educational experiences in entrepreneurship scored 0.28 higher on the *proactiveness* sub-scale than the group without such experiences when the effects of major and gender was considered. Hence, Hypothesis 5e (H5e: Educational experience is the most influencing factor for *proactiveness* after controlling for gender and major.) was confirmed by the result.

To briefly summarize the results of the current study by the hypotheses, we present Table 7. Table 7 provides the information on whether each of the hypotheses was confirmed or not.

Table 7. Summary of the Study Results based on the Research Hypotheses.

Hypothesis	Result
H1: The CS-EMS presents at least scalar invariance across gender, major, and experience groups.	
H1a: The CS-EMS presents at least scalar invariance between the male and female groups.	Confirmed
H1b: The CS-EMS presents at least scalar invariance between the engineering and non-engineering groups.	Confirmed
H1c: The CS-EMS presents at least scalar invariance between the experience and no-experience groups.	Confirmed
H2: The male group scores higher on each of the five sub-constructs of the CS-EMS than the female group.	
H2a: The male group scores higher on innovativeness than the female group.	Confirmed
H2b: The male group scores higher on need for achievement than the female group.	Rejected
H2c: The male group scores higher on risk-taking than the female group.	Confirmed
H2d: The male group scores higher on autonomy than the female group.	Rejected
H2e: The male group scores higher on proactiveness than the female group.	Confirmed
H3: The engineering group scores higher on each of the five sub-constructs of the CS-EMS than the non-engineering group.	
H3a: The engineering group scores higher on innovativeness than the non-engineering group.	Confirmed
H3b: The engineering group scores higher on need for achievement than the non-engineering group.	Rejected
H3c: The engineering group scores higher on risk-taking than the non-engineering group.	Rejected
H3d: The engineering group scores higher on autonomy than the non-engineering group.	Rejected
H3e: The engineering group scores higher on proactiveness than the non-engineering group.	Confirmed
H4: The group with educational experiences in entrepreneurship scores higher on each of the five sub-constructs of the CS-EMS than the group without such experiences.	
H4a: The group with educational experiences in entrepreneurship scores higher on innovativeness than the group without such experiences.	Confirmed
H4b: The group with educational experiences in entrepreneurship scores higher on need for achievement than the group without such experiences.	Rejected
H4c: The group with educational experiences in entrepreneurship scores higher on risk-taking than the group without such experiences.	Confirmed
H4d: The group with educational experiences in entrepreneurship scores higher on autonomy than the group without such experiences.	Rejected
H4e: The group with educational experiences in entrepreneurship scores higher on proactiveness than the group without such experiences.	Confirmed
H5: Educational experience is the most influencing factor for the scores of the CS-EMS sub-constructs after controlling for gender and major.	
H5a: Educational experience is the most influencing factor for innovativeness after controlling for gender and major.	Confirmed
H5b: Educational experience is the most influencing factor for need for achievement after controlling for gender and major.	Rejected
H5c: Educational experience is the most influencing factor for risk-taking after controlling for gender and major.	Confirmed
H5d: Educational experience is the most influencing factor for autonomy after controlling for gender and major.	Rejected
H5e: Educational experience is the most influencing factor for proactiveness after controlling for gender and major.	Confirmed

5. Discussion

5.1. Findings and Implications

We began this study with the motivation to contribute to the literature on entrepreneurship in higher education by investigating the untouched topic of measurement invariance of the CS-EMS, which is required for cross-group mean comparisons [26–29,55]. To do so, we focused on comparing the groups of participants by gender, major (engineering vs. non-engineering), or educational experiences in entrepreneurship. In this section, we summarized the findings based on the outline of the analytic procedures and results: (1) confirmatory factor analysis, (2) measurement invariance tests, (3) cross-group latent and observed mean comparisons, and (4) examination of the conditional effects of the grouping variables, while discussing the implications of each finding.

First, we found that the correlated five factor model [25] was viable for all six groups (male, female, engineering, non-engineering, educational experience, and no educational experience). This finding was not consistent with previous studies [22,23,111], in which only three sub-factors (*innovativeness*, *risk-taking*, and *proactiveness*) were included. Instead, our findings are more closely aligned with the study of Lumpkin and Dess [42], in which they introduced five traits (*innovativeness*, *risk-taking*, *proactiveness*, *autonomy*, and *competitive aggressiveness*) related to entrepreneurial orientation at the organizational level. Given the inconsistency in the structure of individual-level entrepreneurial propensity/ orientation/ mindset, our findings might encourage future research to validate the factor structure of the CS-EMS in different countries or different educational contexts. We provided the English-translated items of the CS-EMS in the hope of observing further investigations related to the structural validity of the CS-EMS.

Secondly, we found that the strict invariance model was tenable across both pairs of groups for major and educational experience. To put it another way, all levels (factor loadings, intercepts, and unique variances) of the measurement property operated in the same way between the male and female groups as well as between the group with educational experiences in entrepreneurship and the group without such experiences. Yet, only scalar invariance was retained between the male and female groups, which means that the extent of the unique variance – the approximation of measurement errors – was not equivalent between the groups. Because the required condition (i.e., at least scalar invariance) for comparing latent and observed group means was met, we did not pursue partial strict invariance [26,29,55]. In some studies, measurement invariance of entrepreneurial attitude and intention was tested across only gender. For example, measurement invariance of entrepreneurial intention held between males and females [74,112]. In addition, measurement invariance of entrepreneurial attitude was also established between males and females. To our knowledge, this study is the first to investigate measurement invariance of the entrepreneurial mindset not only between the gender groups but also between groups based on major and educational experience. As a result, we contribute to entrepreneurship literature by reporting evidence of measurement invariance across plausible groups of interest in the context of higher education.

Third, we tested the latent means for each comparison based upon the established measurement invariance model. We also examined the observed mean differences between each set of the compared groups. The pattern of significant difference was consistent between the latent and observed mean comparisons. Male students had generally higher scores on the CS-EMS sub-scales except for *need for achievement* and *autonomy*, compared to the female students. This finding is consistent with formal studies in which male participants scored higher on other entrepreneurship-related variables, such as entrepreneurial orientation [113,114], intention [79,112], and attitude [112]. However, some inconsistent results on the gender difference also exist [115,116]. The gender difference found in the current study raises the old but persistent question, "Is it innate or socially constructed?" Since our study used the term "gender" as analogous to biological sex, future research should thoroughly investigate whether the gender difference in the CS-EMS is given or constructed, following the example of Goktan and Gupta's [113] study by including the concepts of both biological sex and gender (masculinity vs. femininity). In the comparison by major, the engineering-major group scored higher on the *innovativeness* and *risk-taking* sub-scales. Unfortunately, we could not find any study that directly compares the entrepreneurial orientation or mindset between engineering majors and non-engineering majors. Therefore, it is not possible to discuss the finding in relation to the results of other studies. Instead, one plausible explanation might be that engineering is a field in which males are dominant in most countries [117,118] and, due to the effects of gendered stereotypes, the male participants might have higher self-efficacy and more positive self-reflection than the female participants in our study. Regarding educational experiences in entrepreneurship, the students with experiences showed higher scores on the *innovativeness, risk-taking*, and *proactiveness* sub-scales than the students without such experiences. This finding implies that two sub-scales (*need for achievement* and *autonomy*) might not be the outcomes of entrepreneurship education, while the other three sub-scales (*innovativeness, risk-taking*, and *proactiveness*) might be. Even though the five correlated-factor model was sustained for the CS-EMS, the *need for achievement* and *autonomy* sub-scales might not measure educational impact effectively. In addition, those sub-scales were found to not be closely related to the entrepreneurial intention variables described by Jung and Lee [25]. Yet, those sub-factors might positively predict other career-related variables (e.g., career adaptability). Further research is needed to investigate this matter. Thus, we are very reluctant to claim that these two sub-scales are not useful.

Finally, as far as the conditional effects of the grouping variables are concerned, only three sub-scales (*innovativeness, risk-taking*, and *proactiveness*) of the CS-EMS were influenced by at least one of the grouping variables, whereas the *need for achievement* and *autonomy* sub-scales were not influenced by any of those variables. Among the three grouping variables, the educational experience variable appeared to have the most influence on the *innovativeness, risk-taking*, and *proactiveness* sub-scales, as the largest difference between the two groups was observed for these three sub-scales. This finding suggests that the factor with the most influence on the entrepreneurial mindset is educational experiences in entrepreneurship, and the effect of gender and major might be confounded after students have educational experiences. However, our speculation might not be appropriate for making causal inferences within this study. We will revisit this issue when discussing the limitations of the study.

5.2. Limitations and Suggestions for Future Studies

Despite its values and contributions, the current study is not free from limitations. The first limitation is related to generalizability. Since we collected data at only one university, which is one of the top colleges in Korea, the results of the current study might not be applicable to other contexts, such as colleges located in other places domestically or globally. To address this limitation, more replication studies should comprehensively discuss the generalizability issue regarding the structural validity and measurement invariance of the CS-EMS. In particular, cross-cultural measurement invariance tests between different countries could be added to the future research agenda. The second limitation is related to the nature of the self-reported assessment tool. Because the CS-EMS measures the extent of the entrepreneurial mindset based on self-reports, some sort of bias (e.g., distribution leaning toward socially desirable values or insincere responses [1]) might have confounded the actual status of the participants' entrepreneurial mindset. Hence, educators or researchers should carefully interpret the scores from the CS-EMS while collecting more evidence regarding educational impact using multiple assessments (e.g., peer evaluation, portfolios, project products). The third limitation is that we cannot make any inferences regarding the causal relationship between the participants' educational experiences and the level of their entrepreneurial mindset. Our data were cross-sectionally collected survey data, and the *experience* variable was made based on heterogeneous past educational experiences, including semester-length formal entrepreneurship classes, extracurricular activities with varying hours, out-of-college competitions to conceive plausible business ideas, and so on. Thus, future research should incorporate an experimental design that can validly measure the actual impact of entrepreneurship education using the CS-EMS. If the design includes pre-and post-measurement, longitudinal measurement invariance should be tested [28,119] before proceeding to latent or observed mean comparisons between the pre- and post-scores. However, future researchers should be aware that measurement invariance needs a sufficient amount of data [120–122].

6. Conclusions

Given the limited evidence regarding the quality of the currently available assessment tools, the CS-EMS would be more useful than the other tools [20–24] for the educators who want to validly measure the educational outcomes or design their own entrepreneurship guided by the current status of the college students' entrepreneurial mindset. In an earlier study, the validity of CS-EMS had been supported by the evidence grounded on structural validity (the five correlated-factor structure) and predictive validity with entrepreneurial intention [25]. The current study provided evidence of measurement invariance, which indicates validity based on the use of assessment results [123], and it legitimately uses CS-EMS scores to compare different groups. Based on the satisfied conditions (scalar or strict invariance) for the cross-group mean comparison, the simple between-group comparisons revealed that the male engineering majors with educational experience generally scored higher on the CS-EMS subscales than their counterparts. As far as the major variable is concerned, the engineering students scored higher on innovativeness compared to the non-engineering students, which might be due to the majors' technology orientation. Regarding the difference based on gender, educators should be aware that female students showed a lower level of innovativeness and proactiveness than the male students. To cultivate the development of sustainable entrepreneurship among female students, universities may invigorate female support programs in entrepreneurial education [124].

Furthermore, we found that educational experience in entrepreneurship is the factor with the most influence on the three sub-scales (*innovativeness*, *risk-taking*, and *proactiveness*) which have been acknowledged to be the core characteristics of entrepreneurial individuals [22,23]. That finding also implies that the CS-EMS has potential as an assessment to efficiently measure the effectiveness of the entrepreneurial education targeting the sub-construct of the CS-EMS. Our finding supports former studies stating that entrepreneurship education is an important factor for building an entrepreneurial mindset [125]. Entrepreneurially-oriented educational programs might enable students to obtain the attitudes needed to gain practical experience and have a positive impact on students' entrepreneurial intentions [32,124]. However, to confirm the causal relationship between educational experiences and the entrepreneurial mindset, further studies with an experimental design are required to gain causal evidence. As a final remark, we would like to gladly introduce the CM-EMS items for future researchers in other countries, and we hope for future studies that perform cross-cultural comparisons using the CS-EMS.

Author Contributions: Conceptualization, E.J. and Y.L.; methodology, E.J.; formal analysis, E.J.; writing—original draft preparation, E.J. and Y.L.; writing—revision and editing, E.J. and Y.L.; validation, Y.L. All authors have read and agreed to the published version of the manuscript.

Appendix A

Table A1. Parameter Estimates of the Scalar Invariance Model: Groups based on Gender.

| Item | Factor Loading (λ_{ij}) | | Intercept (τ_{ij}) | | Residual Variances ($\theta_{ij}{}^G$) | | | |
| | | | | | Male | | Female | |
	Estimate	S.E.	Estimate	S.E.	Estimate	S.E.	Estimate	S.E.
Innovativeness								
Item 1	0.69	(0.05)	3.75	(0.06)	0.28	(0.03)	0.26	(0.05)
Item 2	0.75	(0.05)	3.57	(0.06)	0.31	(0.04)	0.25	(0.05)
Item 3	0.54	(0.04)	4.07	(0.05)	0.29	(0.03)	0.33	(0.05)
Item 4	0.49	(0.04)	4.19	(0.05)	0.43	(0.04)	0.48	(0.07)
Item 5	0.61	(0.05)	3.82	(0.05)	0.36	(0.04)	0.40	(0.06)
Item 6	0.60	(0.05)	3.59	(0.06)	0.42	(0.05)	0.35	(0.06)
Need for Achievement								
Item 7	0.54	(0.04)	4.12	(0.05)	0.27	(0.03)	0.26	(0.05)
Item 8	0.58	(0.05)	3.86	(0.05)	0.28	(0.04)	0.41	(0.07)
Item 9	0.58	(0.04)	4.06	(0.05)	0.23	(0.03)	0.22	(0.05)
Item 10	0.48	(0.04)	4.12	(0.05)	0.29	(0.03)	0.33	(0.06)
Risk-taking								
Item 11	0.82	(0.05)	3.66	(0.07)	0.36	(0.04)	0.27	(0.05)
Item 12	0.92	(0.05)	3.53	(0.07)	0.15	(0.03)	0.16	(0.07)
Item 13	0.81	(0.05)	3.55	(0.06)	0.30	(0.04)	0.38	(0.07)
Autonomy								
Item 14	0.73	(0.06)	2.87	(0.07)	0.66	(0.08)	0.60	(0.11)
Item 15	0.87	(0.06)	3.43	(0.07)	0.23	(0.07)	0.08	(0.09)
Item 16	0.49	(0.05)	3.87	(0.05)	0.47	(0.05)	0.41	(0.07)
Proactiveness								
Item 17	0.55	(0.04)	3.89	(0.05)	0.19	(0.03)	0.33	(0.06)
Item 18	0.63	(0.05)	3.80	(0.06)	0.31	(0.04)	0.29	(0.06)
Item 19	0.55	(0.04)	3.87	(0.05)	0.23	(0.03)	0.47	(0.08)

Note. Each item and its number correspond to those in Table 2.

Table A2. Parameter Estimates of the Scalar Invariance Model: Groups based on Major

| Item | Factor Loading (λ_{ij}) | | Intercept (τ_{ij}) | | Residual Variances (θ_{ij}) | |
	Estimate	S.E.	Estimate	S.E.	Estimate	S.E.
Innovativeness						
Item1	0.79	(0.06)	3.52	(0.07)	0.28	(0.03)
Item 2	0.87	(0.06)	3.32	(0.08)	0.29	(0.03)
Item 3	0.63	(0.05)	3.88	(0.06)	0.30	(0.03)
Item 4	0.57	(0.05)	4.02	(0.06)	0.45	(0.04)
Item 5	0.70	(0.06)	3.61	(0.07)	0.37	(0.03)
Item 6	0.71	(0.06)	3.38	(0.07)	0.39	(0.04)
Need for Achievement						
Item 7	0.62	(0.05)	4.03	(0.06)	0.27	(0.03)
Item 8	0.67	(0.05)	3.77	(0.06)	0.31	(0.03)
Item 9	0.67	(0.05)	3.97	(0.06)	0.24	(0.03)
Item 10	0.55	(0.05)	4.05	(0.05)	0.31	(0.03)
Risk-taking						
Item 11	0.81	(0.06)	3.47	(0.07)	0.33	(0.03)
Item 12	0.92	(0.06)	3.31	(0.08)	0.15	(0.03)
Item 13	0.81	(0.06)	3.36	(0.07)	0.33	(0.03)

Table A2. *Cont.*

Item	Factor Loading (λ_{ij})		Intercept (τ_{ij})		Residual Variances (θ_{ij})	
	Estimate	S.E.	Estimate	S.E.	Estimate	S.E.
Autonomy						
Item 14	0.81	(0.07)	2.89	(0.08)	0.64	(0.07)
Item 15	0.98	(0.07)	3.46	(0.08)	0.17	(0.07)
Item 16	0.53	(0.06)	3.89	(0.06)	0.46	(0.04)
Proactiveness						
Item 17	0.61	(0.05)	3.79	(0.06)	0.23	(0.03)
Item 18	0.70	(0.06)	3.67	(0.07)	0.31	(0.03)
Item 19	0.61	(0.05)	3.76	(0.06)	0.31	(0.03)

Note. Each item and its number correspond to those in Table 2.

Table A3. Parameter Estimates of the Scalar Invariance Model: Groups based on Educational Experiences.

Item	Factor Loading (λ_{ij})		Intercept (τ_{ij})		Residual Variances (θ_{ij})	
	Estimate	S.E.	Estimate	S.E.	Estimate	S.E.
Innovativeness						
Item 1	0.70	(0.05)	3.50	(0.07)	0.27	(0.03)
Item 2	0.77	(0.06)	3.30	(0.07)	0.29	(0.03)
Item 3	0.56	(0.05)	3.87	(0.06)	0.30	(0.03)
Item 4	0.50	(0.05)	4.01	(0.06)	0.45	(0.04)
Item 5	0.62	(0.05)	3.60	(0.06)	0.38	(0.03)
Item 6	0.62	(0.05)	3.37	(0.06)	0.39	(0.04)
Need for Achievement						
Item 7	0.55	(0.05)	4.02	(0.06)	0.27	(0.03)
Item 8	0.58	(0.05)	3.76	(0.06)	0.31	(0.03)
Item 9	0.58	(0.05)	3.96	(0.06)	0.23	(0.03)
Item 10	0.48	(0.05)	4.04	(0.05)	0.31	(0.03)
Risk-taking						
Item 11	0.77	(0.06)	3.40	(0.07)	0.33	(0.03)
Item 12	0.87	(0.06)	3.23	(0.08)	0.16	(0.03)
Item 13	0.77	(0.06)	3.29	(0.07)	0.33	(0.03)
Autonomy						
Item 14	0.84	(0.08)	2.91	(0.08)	0.63	(0.06)
Item 15	0.99	(0.07)	3.49	(0.09)	0.19	(0.06)
Item 16	0.54	(0.06)	3.90	(0.06)	0.45	(0.04)
Proactiveness						
Item 17	0.57	(0.05)	3.67	(0.06)	0.24	(0.03)
Item 18	0.66	(0.06)	3.54	(0.07)	0.30	(0.03)
Item 19	0.58	(0.05)	3.64	(0.06)	0.31	(0.03)

Note. Each item and its number correspond to those in Table 2.

References

1. Nabi, G.; Liñán, F.; Fayolle, A.; Krueger, N.; Walmsley, A. The impact of entrepreneurship education in higher education: A systematic review and research agenda. *Acad. Manag. Learn. Educ.* **2017**, *16*, 277–299. [CrossRef]

2. Huang-Saad, A.Y.; Morton, C.S.; Libarkin, J.C. Entrepreneurship Assessment in Higher Education: A Research Review for Engineering Education Researchers. *J. Eng. Educ* **2018**, *107*, 263–290. [CrossRef]

3. Katz, J.A. Fully mature but not fully legitimate: A different perspective on the state of entrepreneurship education. *J. Small Bus. Manag.* **2008**, *46*, 550–566. [CrossRef]

4. Daniel, T.A.; Kent, C.A. An assessment of youth entrepreneurship programs in the United States. *J. Priv. Enterp.* **2005**, *20*, 126–147.

5. Kuratko, D.F. The emergence of entrepreneurship education: Development, trends, and challenges. *Entrep. Theory Pract.* **2005**, *29*, 577–597. [CrossRef]

6. Mok, Y.; Choi, M. A Study on Curriculum Design for Entrepreneurship Education in Udergraduate School. *J. Korea Acad.-Ind. Coop. Soc.* **2010**, *11*, 320–334.

7. Kim, S.; Ko, H.; Lee, Y. A Study of Entrepreneurship Education of University in Science and Engineering for Visualization of Technology-based Startup. *J. Eng. Educ. Res.* **2015**, *18*, 3–7.

8. Kim, J. The Effect of Entrepreneurship on Entrepreneurial Intention: Focusing on Mediating Effects of Fear on Business. *Asia-Pac. J. Bus. Ventur.* **2018**, *13*, 73–82.

9. Gupta, V.K.; Guo, C.; Canever, M.; Yim, H.R.; Sraw, G.K.; Liu, M. Institutional environment for entrepreneurship in rapidly emerging major economies: The case of Brazil, China, India, and Korea. *Int. Entrep. Manag. J.* **2014**, *10*, 367–384. [CrossRef]

10. Greene, F.J.; Saridakis, G. The role of higher education skills and support in graduate self-employment. *Stud. High. Educ* **2008**, *33*, 653–672. [CrossRef]

11. Rideout, E.C.; Gray, D.O. Does Entrepreneurship Education Really Work? A Review and Methodological Critique of the Empirical Literature on the Effects of University-Based Entrepreneurship Education. *J. Small Bus. Manag.* **2013**, *51*, 329–351. [CrossRef]

12. Global Entrepreneurship Monitor. Available online: http://entreprenorskapsforum.se/wp-content/uploads/2010/02/GEM-Global-Report_2007.pdf (accessed on 7 October 2020).

13. Duval-Couetil, N.; Shartrand, A.; Reed, T. The Role of Entrepreneurship Program Models and Experiential Activities on Engineering Student Outcomes. *Adv. Eng. Educ.* **2016**, *5*, n1.

14. Gumaelius, L.; Lee, Y.; Morimura, K.; Kolmos, A. The Role of Entrepreneurial Skills in Engineering Education: A Case Study Performed in Denmark, Japan, Korea and Sweden. In Proceedings of the 45th Annual Conference of the European Society for Engineering Education, SEFI 2017, Azores, Portugal, 18–21 September 2017; European Society for Engineering Education (SEFI): Terceira Island, Azores, Portugal, 2017; pp. 593–602.

15. Kim, Y.S.; Seong, S.K. On the Contents and Pedagogy of Entrepreneurship Education: A Way of Modular Education based on the HAKS Model. *J. Bus. Educ.* **2015**, *29*, 1–30.

16. Kim, M.; Eom, W. Research Trends on Entrepreneurship Education in Korea. *Glob. Creat. Lead.* **2019**, *9*, 1–20.

17. Yang, J. Effect of Entrepreneurial Education on Entrepreneurial Intention of University Students: Focused on mediating effect of self-efficacy and Entrepreneurial motivation. *Asia-Pac. J. Bus. Ventur. Entrep.* **2014**, *9*, 65–77.

18. Kim, T. Entrepreneurship Education and Entrepreneurial Intention—Fear to Start-up and Start-up Communities in Class. *Asia-Pac. J. Bus. Ventur. Entrep.* **2019**, *14*, 95–104.

19. Yu, J.S.; Suh, C.S.; Yu, Y.H.; Kim, Y.S. University Students' Starts-up Intention and Its Antecedents: Focusing on Entrepreneurship Education for Freshman Orientation. *Asia-Pac. J. Bus. Ventur. Entrep.* **2016**, *11*, 91–104.

20. Builder Profile 10 Methodology Report. Available online: https://www.gallup.com/builder/227249/bp10-methodology-report-pdf-item.aspx (accessed on 7 October 2020).

21. Student Entrepreneurship 2016: Insights from 50 Countries. 2016. Available online: https://boris.unibe.ch/89857/ (accessed on 8 October 2020).

22. Bolton, D.L.; Lane, M.D. Individual entrepreneurial orientation: Development of a measurement instrument. *Educ. + Train.* **2012**, *54*, 219–233. [CrossRef]

23. Popov, B.; Varga, S.; Jelić, D.; Dinić, B. Psychometric evaluation of the Serbian adaptation of the individual entrepreneurial orientation scale. *Educ. + Train.* **2019**, *61*, 65–78. [CrossRef]

24. Davis, M.H.; Hall, J.A.; Mayer, P.S. Developing a new measure of entrepreneurial mindset: Reliability, validity, and implications for practitioners. *Consult. Psychol. J. Pract. Res.* **2016**, *68*, 21. [CrossRef]

25. Jung, E.; Lee, Y. Development and Validation of Indicators to Measure Entrepreneurship Mindset and Competency Scales for College Students. *Korea Educ. Rev.* **2019**, *25*, 259–287. [CrossRef]

26. Jung, E.; Yoon, M. Comparisons of three empirical methods for partial factorial invariance: Forward, backward, and factor-ratio tests. *Struct. Equ. Model. A Multidiscip. J.* **2016**, *23*, 567–584. [CrossRef]

27. Steenkamp, J.-B.E.; Baumgartner, H. Assessing measurement invariance in cross-national consumer research. *J. Consum. Res.* **1998**, *25*, 78–90. [CrossRef]

28. Vandenberg, R.J.; Lance, C.E. A review and synthesis of the measurement invariance literature: Suggestions, practices, and recommendations for organizational research. *Organ. Res. Methods* **2000**, *3*, 4–70. [CrossRef]

29. Jung, E.; Yoon, M. Two-step approach to partial factorial invariance: Selecting a reference variable and identifying the source of noninvariance. *Struct. Equ. Model. A Multidiscip. J.* **2017**, *24*, 65–79. [CrossRef]
30. Morton, C.S.; Huang-Saad, A.; Libarkin, J. Entrepreneurship Education for Women in Engineering: A Systematic Re-view of Entrepreneurship Assessment Literature with a Focus on Gender. In Proceedings of the American Society for Engineering Education Annual Conference & Exposition. ASEE Annual Conference Proceedings, New Orleans, LA, USA, 26–29 June 2016.
31. Kim, S.Y.; Lim, S.; Jang, J.Y.; Kang, J.; Park, M.J.; Park, H.K. Entrepreneurship Perception and Needs Analysis of Entrepreneurship Education for Female Engineering Students Using an Importance-Performance Analysis. *J. Eng. Educ. Res.* **2017**, *20*, 43–51.
32. Westhead, P.; Solesvik, M.Z. Entrepreneurship education and entrepreneurial intention: Do female students benefit? *Int Small Bus. J.* **2016**, *34*, 979–1003. [CrossRef]
33. Rauch, A.; Hulsink, W. Putting entrepreneurship education where the intention to act lies: An investigation into the impact of entrepreneurship education on entrepreneurial behavior. *Acad. Manag. Learn. Educ.* **2015**, *14*, 187–204. [CrossRef]
34. Raposo, M.; Do Paço, A. Entrepreneurship education: Relationship between education and entrepreneurial activity. *Psicothema* **2011**, *23*, 453–457.
35. Martin, B.C.; McNally, J.J.; Kay, M.J. Examining the formation of human capital in entrepreneurship: A meta-analysis of entrepreneurship education outcomes. *J. Bus. Ventur.* **2013**, *28*, 211–224. [CrossRef]
36. Bae, T.J.; Qian, S.; Miao, C.; Fiet, J.O. The relationship between entrepreneurship education and entrepreneurial intentions: A meta–analytic review. *Entrep. Theory Pract.* **2014**, *38*, 217–254. [CrossRef]
37. Venkataraman, S. The distinctive domain of entrepreneurship research. In *Seminal Ideas for the Next Twenty-Five Years of Advances*; Emerald Publishing Limited: Bingly, UK, 1997; pp. 5–20.
38. Shane, S.; Venkataraman, S. The promise of entrepreneurship as a field of research. *Acad. Manag. Rev.* **2000**, *25*, 217–226. [CrossRef]
39. Miller, D.; Friesen, P.H. Innovation in conservative and entrepreneurial firms: Two models of strategic momentum. *Strateg. Manag. J.* **1982**, *3*, 1–25. [CrossRef]
40. Stevenson, H.H.; Jarillo, J.C. A paradigm of entrepreneurship: Entrepreneurial management. In *Entrepreneurship*; Springer: Berlin/Heidelberg, Germany, 2007; pp. 155–170.
41. Kreiser, P.M.; Marino, L.D.; Weaver, K.M. Assessing the psychometric properties of the entrepreneurial orientation scale: A multi-country analysis. *Entrep. Theory Pract.* **2002**, *26*, 71–93. [CrossRef]
42. Lumpkin, G.T.; Dess, G.G. Clarifying the entrepreneurial orientation construct and linking it to performance. *Acad. Manag. Rev.* **1996**, *21*, 135–172. [CrossRef]
43. Miller, D. The correlates of entrepreneurship in three types of firms. *Manag. Sci.* **1983**, *29*, 770–791. [CrossRef]
44. Ilozor, B.; Sarki, A.; Hodd, M.; Heinonen, J.; Poikkijoki, S.A. An entrepreneurial-directed approach to entrepreneurship education: Mission impossible? *J. Manag. Dev.* **2006**, *25*, 80–94.
45. Haynie, J.M.; Shepherd, D.; Mosakowski, E.; Earley, P.C. A situated metacognitive model of the entrepreneurial mindset. *J. Bus. Ventur.* **2010**, *25*, 217–229. [CrossRef]
46. Gibb, A.A. Enterprise culture and education: Understanding enterprise education and its links with small business, entrepreneurship and wider educational goals. *Int. Small Bus. J.* **1993**, *11*, 11–34. [CrossRef]
47. Bosman, L.; Fernhaber, S. SpringerLink. In *Teaching the Entrepreneurial Mindset to Engineers*; Springer: Berlin/Heidelberg, Germany, 2018.
48. Commission of the European Communities. *Euro-barometer*; Commission of the European Communities: Brussels, Belgium, 2006.
49. Office for Official Publications of the European Communities. *Green Paper Entrepreneurship in Europe*; Official Publications of the European Communities: Brussels, Belgium, 2003.
50. Mäkimurto-Koivumaa, S.; Belt, P. About, for, in or through entrepreneurship in engineering education. *Eur. J. Eng. Educ.* **2016**, *41*, 512–529. [CrossRef]
51. Rae, D. Understanding entrepreneurial learning: A question of how? *Int. J. Entrep. Behav. Res.* **2000**, *6*, 145–159. [CrossRef]
52. Kirby, D.A. Entrepreneurship education: Can business schools meet the challenge? *Educ. + Train.* **2004**, *46*, 510–519. [CrossRef]
53. Seikkula-Leino, J. Implementing entrepreneurship education through curriculum reform. In Proceedings of the ICSB World Conference Proceedings, Halifax, NS, Canada, 22–25 June 2008; p. 1.

54. Díaz-Casero, J.C.; Fernández-Portillo, A.; Sánchez-Escobedo, M.-C.; Hernández-Mogollón, R. The influence of university context on entrepreneurial intentions. In *Entrepreneurial Universities*; Springer: Berlin/Heidelberg, Germany, 2017; pp. 65–81.

55. Schmitt, N.; Kuljanin, G. Measurement invariance: Review of practice and implications. *Hum. Resour. Manag. Rev.* **2008**, *18*, 210–222. [CrossRef]

56. Yoon, M.; Millsap, R.E. Detecting violations of factorial invariance using data-based specification searches: A Monte Carlo study. *Struct. Equ. Model. A Multidiscip. J.* **2007**, *14*, 435–463. [CrossRef]

57. Piña-Watson, B.; Castillo, L.G.; Jung, E.; Ojeda, L.; Castillo-Reyes, R. The Marianismo Beliefs Scale: Validation with Mexican American Adolescent Girls and Boys. *J. Lat. /O Psychol.* **2014**, *2*, 113.

58. Levant, R.F.; Hall, R.J.; Rankin, T.J. Male Role Norms Inventory–Short Form (MRNI-SF): Development, confirmatory factor analytic investigation of structure, and measurement invariance across gender. *J. Couns. Psychol.* **2013**, *60*, 228. [CrossRef]

59. Castillo, L.G.; Cano, M.A.; Yoon, M.; Jung, E.; Brown, E.J.; Zamboanga, B.L.; Kim, S.Y.; Schwartz, S.J.; Huynh, Q.-L.; Weisskirch, R.S. Factor structure and factorial invariance of the Multidimensional Acculturative Stress Inventory. *Psychol. Assess.* **2015**, *27*, 915. [CrossRef]

60. Agala, C.B.; Fried, B.J.; Thomas, J.C.; Reynolds, H.W.; Lich, K.H.; Whetten, K.; Zimmer, C.; Morrissey, J.P. Reliability, validity and measurement invariance of the Simplified Medication Adherence Questionnaire (SMAQ) among HIV-positive women in Ethiopia: A quasi-experimental study. *BMC Public Health* **2020**, *20*, 1–16. [CrossRef]

61. Meganck, R.; Vanheule, S.; Desmet, M. Factorial validity and measurement invariance of the 20-item Toronto Alexithymia Scale in clinical and nonclinical samples. *Assessment* **2008**, *15*, 36–47. [CrossRef]

62. Spurk, D.; Abele, A.E.; Volmer, J. The career satisfaction scale: Longitudinal measurement invariance and latent growth analysis. *J. Occup. Organ. Psych.* **2011**, *84*, 315–326. [CrossRef]

63. Maltese, A.; Harsh, J.; Jung, E. Evaluating undergraduate research experiences—Development of a self-report tool. *Educ. Sci.* **2017**, *7*, 87. [CrossRef]

64. Meade, A.W.; Michels, L.C.; Lautenschlager, G.J. Are Internet and paper-and-pencil personality tests truly comparable? An experimental design measurement invariance study. *Organ. Res. Methods* **2007**, *10*, 322–345. [CrossRef]

65. Johnson, E.C.; Meade, A.W.; DuVernet, A.M. The Role of Referent Indicators in Tests of Measurement Invariance. *Struct. Equ. Model.* **2009**, *16*, 642–657. [CrossRef]

66. Horn, J.L.; McArdle, J.J. A practical and theoretical guide to measurement invariance in aging research. *Exp. Aging Res.* **1992**, *18*, 117–144. [CrossRef] [PubMed]

67. Meredith, W. Measurement invariance, factor analysis and factorial invariance. *Psychometrika* **1993**, *58*, 525–543. [CrossRef]

68. Widaman, K.F.; Reise, S.P. Exploring the measurement invariance of psychological instruments: Applications in the substance use domain. In *The Science of Prevention: Methodological Advances from Alcohol and Substance Abuse Research*; Bryant, K.J., Windle, M., West, S.G., Eds.; American Psychological Association: Washington, DC, USA, 1997; pp. 281–324. [CrossRef]

69. Holmgren, C.; From, J.; Olofsson, A.; Karlsson, H.; Snyder, K.; Sundtröm, U. Entrepreneurship education: Salvation or damnation? *Int. J. Entrep.* **2004**, *8*, 55.

70. Solomon, G. An examination of entrepreneurship education in the United States. *J. Small Bus. Enterp. Dev.* **2007**, *14*, 168–182. [CrossRef]

71. Global Entrepreneurship Monitor Gem 2001 Summary Report. Available online: https://www.aidaf-ey.unibocconi.it/wps/allegatiCTP/Paul%20reynolds%201.pdf (accessed on 8 October 2020).

72. Pauceanu, A.M.; Alpenidze, O.; Edu, T.; Zaharia, R.M. What determinants influence students to start their own business? empirical evidence from United Arab Emirates Universities. *Sustainability* **2019**, *11*, 92. [CrossRef]

73. Schlaegel, C.; Koenig, M. Determinants of entrepreneurial intent: A meta–analytic test and integration of competing models. *Entrep. Theory Pract.* **2014**, *38*, 291–332. [CrossRef]

74. Maes, J.; Leroy, H.; Sels, L. Gender differences in entrepreneurial intentions: A TPB multi-group analysis at factor and indicator level. *Eur. Manag. J.* **2014**, *32*, 784–794. [CrossRef]

75.   Ahl, H. Why research on women entrepreneurs needs new directions. *Entrep. Theory Pract.* **2006**, *30*, 595–621. [CrossRef]

76.   Zampetakis, L.A.; Bakatsaki, M.; Kafetsios, K.; Moustakis, V.S. Sex differences in entrepreneurs' business growth intentions: An identity approach. *J. Innov. Entrep.* **2016**, *5*, 29. [CrossRef]

77.   Joensuu, S.; Viljamaa, A.; Varamäki, E.; Tornikoski, E. Development of entrepreneurial intention in higher education and the effect of gender-a latent growth curve analysis. *Educ. + Train.* **2013**, *55*, 781–803. [CrossRef]

78.   Fayolle, A.; Gailly, B. The impact of entrepreneurship education on entrepreneurial attitudes and intention: Hysteresis and persistence. *J. Small Bus. Manag.* **2015**, *53*, 75–93. [CrossRef]

79.   Nowiński, W.; Haddoud, M.Y.; Lančarič, D.; Egerová, D.; Czeglédi, C. The impact of entrepreneurship education, entrepreneurial self-efficacy and gender on entrepreneurial intentions of university students in the Visegrad countries. *Stud. High. Educ.* **2019**, *44*, 361–379. [CrossRef]

80.   Majumdar, S.; Varadarajan, D. Students' attitude towards entrepreneurship: Does gender matter in the UAE? *Foresight* **2013**, *15*, 278–293. [CrossRef]

81.   Mehtap, S.; Pellegrini, M.M.; Caputo, A.; Welsh, D.H. Entrepreneurial intentions of young women in the Arab world. *Int. J. Entrep. Behav. Res.* **2017**, *23*, 880–902. [CrossRef]

82.   Bosman, L.; Fernhaber, S. Applying authentic learning through cultivation of the entrepreneurial mindset in the engineering classroom. *Educ. Sci.* **2019**, *9*, 7. [CrossRef]

83.   Gilmartin, S.K.; Shartrand, A.; Chen, H.L.; Estrada, C.; Sheppard, S. Investigating entrepreneurship program models in undergraduate engineering education. *Int. J. Eng. Educ.* **2016**, *32*, 2048–2065.

84.   Burrows, K.; Wragg, N. Introducing enterprise–research into the practical aspects of introducing innovative enterprise schemes as extra curricula activities in higher education. *High. Educ. Ski. Work-Based Learn.* **2013**, *3*, 168–179. [CrossRef]

85.   Premand, P.; Brodmann, S.; Almeida, R.; Grun, R.; Barouni, M. Entrepreneurship education and entry into self-employment among university graduates. *World Dev.* **2016**, *77*, 311–327. [CrossRef]

86.   Boukamcha, F. Impact of training on entrepreneurial intention: An interactive cognitive perspective. *Eur. Bus. Rev.* **2015**, *27*, 593–616. [CrossRef]

87.   Chang, J.Y.C.; Benamraoui, A.; Rieple, A. Stimulating learning about social entrepreneurship through income generation projects. *Int. J. Entrep. Behav. Res.* **2014**, *20*, 417–437. [CrossRef]

88.   Lanero, A.; Vázquez, J.L.; Gutiérrez, P.; García, M.P. The impact of entrepreneurship education in European universities: An intention-based approach analyzed in the Spanish area. *Int. Rev. Public Nonprofit Mark.* **2011**, *8*, 111–130. [CrossRef]

89.   Mentoor, E.R.; Friedrich, C. Is entrepreneurial education at South African universities successful? An empirical example. *Ind. High. Educ.* **2007**, *21*, 221–232. [CrossRef]

90.   Austin, P.C.; Manca, A.; Zwarenstein, M.; Juurlink, D.N.; Stanbrook, M.B. Covariate adjustment in RCTs results in increased power to detect conditional effects compared with the power to detect unadjusted or marginal effects. *J. Clin. Epidemiol.* **2010**, *63*, 1392. [CrossRef]

91.   Lee, Y.; Nelder, J.A. Conditional and marginal models: Another view. *Stat. Sci.* **2004**, *19*, 219–238. [CrossRef]

92.   Duval-Couetil, N.; Reed-Rhoads, T.; Haghighi, S. Engineering students and entrepreneurship education: Involvement, attitudes and outcomes. *Int. J. Eng. Educ.* **2012**, *28*, 425.

93.   Stamboulis, Y.; Barlas, A. Entrepreneurship education impact on student attitudes. *Int. J. Manag. Educ.* **2014**, *12*, 365–373. [CrossRef]

94.   Johansen, V.; Schanke, T.; Clausen, T.H. Entrepreneurship education and pupils' attitudes towards entrepreneurs. *Entrep.-Born Made Educ.* **2012**, *7*, 113–126. [CrossRef]

95.   Küttim, M.; Kallaste, M.; Venesaar, U.; Kiis, A. Entrepreneurship education at university level and students' entrepreneurial intentions. *Procedia-Soc. Behav. Sci.* **2014**, *110*, 658–668.

96.   Vodă, A.I.; Florea, N. Impact of personality traits and entrepreneurship education on entrepreneurial intentions of business and engineering students. *Sustainability* **2019**, *11*, 1192.

97.   Shah, I.A.; Amjed, S.; Jaboob, S. The moderating role of entrepreneurship education in shaping entrepreneurial intentions. *J. Econ. Struct.* **2020**, *9*, 1–15. [CrossRef]

98.   Dou, X.; Zhu, X.; Zhang, J.Q.; Wang, J. Outcomes of entrepreneurship education in China: A customer experience management perspective. *J. Bus. Res.* **2019**, *103*, 338–347. [CrossRef]

99.   Welsh, D.H.; Tullar, W.L.; Nemati, H. Entrepreneurship education: Process, method, or both? *J. Innov. Knowl.* **2016** *1*, 125–132. [CrossRef]

100. Asghar, M.Z.; Hakkarainen, P.S.; Nada, N. An analysis of the relationship between the components of entrepreneurship education and the antecedents of theory of planned behavior. *Pak. J. Commer. Soc. Sci. (Pjcss)* **2016**, *10*, 45–68.

101. Kim, J.; Jeon, B.H. The effects of university entrepreneurship education on innovation behavior: Focusing on moderating effect of team-based learning. *Asia-Pac. J. Bus. Ventur. Entrep.* **2017**, *12*, 99–109.

102. Brown, T.A. *Confirmatory Factor Analysis for Applied Research*; Guilford Press: New Yor, NY, USA, 2015.

103. Raykov, T.; Marcoulides, G.A. *Introduction to Psychometric Theory*; Routledge: New York, NY, USA, 2011.

104. Hair, J.; Black, W.; Babin, B.; Anderson, R. *Multivariate Data Analysis*, 7th ed.; Pearson Prentice Hall: Upper Saddle River, NJ, USA, 2009.

105. Byrne, B.M. *Structural Equation Modeling with AMOS Basic Concepts, Applications, and Programming (Multivariate Applications Series)*; Routledge: New York, NY, USA, 2010.

106. Hu, L.; Bentler, P.M. Cutoff criteria for fit indexes in covariance structure analysis: Conventional criteria versus new alternatives. *Struct. Equ. Model. A Multidiscip. J.* **1999**, *6*, 1–55. [CrossRef]

107. Barrett, P. Structural equation modelling: Adjudging model fit. *Personal. Individ. Differ.* **2007**, *42*, 815–824. [CrossRef]

108. Chen, F.F. Sensitivity of goodness of fit indexes to lack of measurement invariance. *Struct. Equ. Model.* **2007**, *14*, 464–504. [CrossRef]

109. Davidshofer, K.; Murphy, C.O. *Psychological Testing: Principles and Applications*; Pearson/Prentice Hall: Upper Saddle River, NJ, USA, 2005.

110. Nunally, J.C.; Bernstein, I.H. *Psychometric Theory*; McGraw-Hill: New York, NY, USA, 1978.

111. Bolton, D.L. Individual entrepreneurial orientation: Further investigation of a measurement instrument. *Acad. Entrep. J.* **2012**, *18*, 91.

112. Zampetakis, L.A.; Bakatsaki, M.; Litos, C.; Kafetsios, K.G.; Moustakis, V. Gender-based differential item functioning in the application of the theory of planned behavior for the study of entrepreneurial intentions. *Front. Psychol.* **2017**, *8*, 451. [CrossRef] [PubMed]

113. Goktan, A.B.; Gupta, V.K. Sex, gender, and individual entrepreneurial orientation: Evidence from four countries. *Int. Entrep. Manag. J.* **2015**, *11*, 95–112. [CrossRef]

114. Fellnhofer, K.; Puumalainen, K.; Sjögrén, H. Entrepreneurial orientation and performance–are sexes equal? *Int. J. Entrep. Behav. Res.* **2016**, *22*, 346–374. [CrossRef]

115. Marques, C.S.; Santos, G.; Galvão, A.; Mascarenhas, C.; Justino, E. Entrepreneurship education, gender and family background as antecedents on the entrepreneurial orientation of university students. *Int. J. Innov. Sci.* **2018**, *10*, 58–70. [CrossRef]

116. Palalic, R.; Ramadani, V.; Dana, L.P. Entrepreneurship in Bosnia and Herzegovina: Focus on gender. *Eur. Bus. Rev.* **2017**, *29*, 476–496. [CrossRef]

117. Beraud, A. A European research on women and Engineering Education (2001–2002). *Eur. J. Eng. Educ.* **2003**, *28*, 435–451. [CrossRef]

118. Zengin-Arslan, B. Women in engineering education in Turkey: Understanding the gendered distribution. *Int. J. Eng. Educ.* **2002**, *18*, 400–408.

119. Kim, E.S.; Willson, V.L. Testing measurement invariance across groups in longitudinal data: Multigroup second-order latent growth model. *Struct. Equ. Model. A Multidiscip. J.* **2014**, *21*, 566–576. [CrossRef]

120. Cheung, G.W.; Rensvold, R.B. Evaluating goodness-of-fit indexes for testing measurement invariance. *Struct. Equ. Model.* **2002**, *9*, 233–255. [CrossRef]

121. Meade, A.W.; Bauer, D.J. Power and precision in confirmatory factor analytic tests of measurement invariance. *Struct. Equ. Model. A Multidiscip. J.* **2007**, *14*, 611–635. [CrossRef]

122. Meade, A.W.; Johnson, E.C.; Braddy, P.W. Power and sensitivity of alternative fit indices in tests of measurement invariance. *J. Appl. Psychol.* **2008**, *93*, 568. [CrossRef] [PubMed]

123. American Educational Research Association; American Psychological Association; National Council on Measurement in Education; Joint Committee on Standards for Educational, & Psychological Testing. *Standards for Educational and Psychological Testing*; American Educational Research Association: Washington, DC, USA, 1999.

124. Butkouskaya, V.; Romagosa, F.; Noguera, M. Obstacles to Sustainable Entrepreneurship Amongst Tourism Students: A Gender Comparison. *Sustainability* **2020**, *12*, 1812. [CrossRef]

125. Saeed, S.; Yousafzai, S.Y.; Yani-De-Soriano, M.; Muffatto, M. The role of perceived university support in the formation of students' entrepreneurial intention. *J. Small Bus. Manag.* **2015**, *53*, 1127–1145. [CrossRef]

12

The Effects of Rural and Urban Areas on Time Allocated to Self-Employment: Differences between Men and Women

Nicholas Litsardopoulos [1,*], **George Saridakis** [2] **and Chris Hand** [1]

[1]   Kingston Business School, Kingston University London, Kingston Hill KT2 7LB, UK; c.hand@kingston.ac.uk
[2]   Kent Business School, University of Kent, Canterbury CT2 7FS, UK; g.saridakis@kent.ac.uk
*   Correspondence: n.litsardopoulos@kingston.ac.uk

Abstract: This study investigates the association of the rural–urban divide and the time individuals allocate to self-employment. The empirical analysis uses fixed effects modelling on data from the UK Household Longitudinal Survey over the period 2009–2019. The study identifies significant differences in the time men and women allocate to self-employment between rural and urban areas according to their career age group. While men and women tend to allocate more time to self-employment in their senior career age when residents of urban areas, the time they allocate to self-employment between rural and urban areas in early- and mid-career age differs markedly. More importantly, we find that significant differences exist not only between residents of rural and urban areas, but also between residents of these areas and in-migrants to these areas. We find a significant positive effect on the time senior career age women who migrate to rural areas allocate to self-employment. In contrast, we find that early career men who move from rural to urban areas allocate significantly more time to self-employment. The results reveal the existence of complex dynamics between gender and age, which affect the allocation of time to self-employment between rural and urban areas.

Keywords: time in self-employment; gender; regional development; rural and urban areas; age; UK

1. Introduction

The development of the modern city as a centre for work has transformed the landscape of business opportunities for both the wage- and the self-employed [1–3]. The process of urbanism is strongly associated with economic growth that often dictates *what* the economy will produce, *how* will it produce, *where* will it produce, and for *whom* [4,5]. The study of urbanism and how *the city* has become a focus for socioeconomic pursuit dates to Wirth's 1938 publication of "Urbanism as a way of life" [6]. The city has become an engine of economic growth, and the location where venture capitalists and firms cluster [4]. A 2011 McKinsey report indicates that the top 600 urban centres (ranked by GDP) generate half the world's GDP [2]. Evidence from the United States suggests that venture capital-backed start-ups in digital industries are highly concentrated in dense urban areas (e.g., Lower Manhattan and downtown San Francisco) [3]. However, urbanisation and the idea of *the city* as an economic growth centre has also received criticism over the years [7–10]. A recent study by the Massachusetts Institute of Technology (MIT) Task Force on the Work of the Future explores the occupational changes in urban employment and incomes for the period 1980–2020, indicating that middle income jobs are fast disappearing from thriving cities such as New York and San Francisco [10]. The study shows that whereas the socioeconomic status of highly educated workers has improved during the past decade, that of non-highly educated workers has deteriorated.

The fast growth of urban economies has resulted in a continuous movement of young and well-educated people from rural areas to large cities [10–12]. In the UK, the Greater London area accounts for almost a third of the economy in England and Wales [13]. Such vibrant local economies are attractive for start-ups and offer greater opportunities for entrepreneurs. Moreover, major urban areas, such as London, account for the largest share of start-ups and creation of jobs, as well as a large share of the national economy [2,13,14]. However, with start-up costs being much higher in major cities (i.e., office, storage, personnel, etc.), it will be harder to break even in an urban area than a rural area, and failure will be considerably more costly. Most start-ups will not survive beyond their fifth year in business, while many do not survive even their first year [15–17]. Moreover, the hazard rate is likely higher in urban than rural areas [18]. Wirth argues that "On the whole, the city discourages an economic life in which the individual in time of crisis has a basis of subsistence to fall back upon, and it discourages self-employment" [6] (pp. 21–22). He explains that this is because while income is on average higher in the city than in the countryside, homeownership is rare and housing accommodation expenses are higher in the cities, absorbing as a result a large share of the earned income. Moreover, the rising cost of urban living (e.g., housing) has eroded the real earnings of city workers, pushing many workers away from major cities [10].

Urban areas offer a larger variety of jobs and possibilities for higher gross earnings compared to rural areas [14], which attracts large numbers of individuals from rural areas to major cities in pursuit of better employment opportunities and higher incomes. However, an increasing number of people also move out of major cities and into rural areas [14,19]. Urban areas offer several advantages in terms of access to goods and services compared to rural areas, but the greater noise and air pollution of urban areas, as well as the higher cost of living, can have a negative effect on individual life satisfaction and overall quality of life [5,20,21]. During the years leading to the 2008 financial crisis, there was an increase in the movement of people from urban to rural areas in the UK, which also continued during the recovery years [22,23]. While it is not uncommon for people to move out of major cities when jobs become scarce during financial downturns, data analysed by Champion [24] for the UK Government's Foresight Future of Cities Project indicate that the 2008 financial crisis had a profound impact on within-UK migration patterns, with no recovery of urban migration rates having been observed by 2011.

People who move to rural areas will often commute to cities in close proximity for work [25], which suggests the reason for moving to a rural area was not primarily for employment reasons. Nevertheless, people who move to rural areas might also seek to become self-employed [26]. A study on college graduates in the United States found that graduates who were residents of rural areas were more likely to be self-employed rather than wage-employees compared to the graduates residents of urban areas [27]. Several differences between urban and rural areas, such as differences in life satisfaction and the likelihood of self-employment, have already been investigated. In this paper, we argue that self-employment can offer a sustainable source of income to individuals in rural areas and the means to promoting sustainable regional economic development. However, it is unclear if individuals switch their employment when they move from a rural to an urban area (and vice versa) or if they continue their previous wage- or self-employment at the new location. Additionally, while there is research on the different drivers of self-employment for men and women [28–30], less is known about whether the effect of location on self-employment is the same for men and women, or if there are differences.

To answer these questions, our research uses data from the UK Household Longitudinal Survey (UKHLS) over the period 2009–2019. We employ fixed effect modelling to control for unobserved heterogeneity and examine subsamples of men and women. Since time-invariant variables are automatically omitted in the fixed effects model, any changes in the response variable must be due to variation in other than the fixed characteristics [31–33]. The rich data of UKHLS allow us to capture the effect of the rural–urban divide, while controlling for individual characteristics, such as educational achievement and socioeconomic class.

The paper follows the following structure. Section 2 reviews the literature and derives the hypotheses to be tested. Section 3 describes the data used in this paper and the empirical model.

Section 4 presents the empirical results and discussion. Section 5 offers a discussion of the results and directions for future research. Lastly, Section 6 concludes the paper.

2. Literature Review

Urban districts account for 86 percent of the business economy in England and Wales, and for 78 percent in Scotland [13]. The world's top 10 leading areas of venture capital investment are major cities that in 2010, accounted for 52 percent of the world venture capital investment, but just 1.4 percent of world's population [3]. Major cities such as San Francisco, New York, and London act as clusters of entrepreneurship, which attract a large share of venture capital investment. London also accounted for approximately 20 percent of UK's highest growth firms over the period 2005–2008 [34], which, not surprisingly, was the largest share of high-growth companies among UK regions. However, Wales and Northern Ireland also had an above average share of high growth firms, even though they are much smaller and peripheral regional economies compared to London [34]. Additionally, accessible rural areas have a high gross value added per worker, which is second only to that of major urban areas [13]. This suggests that rural areas in the periphery can sustain healthy local economies. Furthermore, the growing interest in rural areas is revealed in the statistics of newly constructed building prices. That is, villages, hamlets, and small towns that are identified as rural areas have seen a greater overall price growth of new dwellings compared to major cities [35]. While the overall rural population of England decreased by 0.2 percent over the period of 2011 to 2018, the population of Lower Super Output Areas (LSOAs) increased by 4.4 percent (LSOAs have an average population of 1500 people or 650 households. The 'Rural population and migration: Mid-year population 2018' report, notes that analyses using LSOAs may slightly underestimate the rural population).

The de-urbanisation that took place during the 2008 financial crisis may have originally pushed people away from cities since they could not support the cost of living associated with major cities (e.g., cost of housing). However, Champion [24] suggests that those who moved out of major cities, such as London, did not return later when the economy picked up. Rural in-migrants may have found that self-employment in rural areas offered a sustainable solution to income and standards of living. Williams and Shepherd [36] find that in the aftermath of an extreme event in rural Australia, individuals created business ventures as a means to overcome adversity, which not only created value for the entrepreneurs themselves, but also for their local communities. Mayer, Habersetzer, and Meili [37] argue that rural entrepreneurs who maintain links with urban centres can use the advantages of both areas (e.g., local knowledge) to their benefit and contribute to local sustainable development. Nevertheless, it has been observed that people often turn to self-employment out of necessity during economic crises when there are no wage-based sources of income, but when the economy recovers, those necessity-entrepreneurs tend to return to wage-employment once more [15,38,39]. However, self-employment has been continuously rising in the UK, even after the economy recovered from the 2008 economic crisis [22,23].

With the advancement of intercity connectivity (i.e., high-speed rail, highways, etc.) and the increasingly reduced costs associated with the transportation of goods, logistics, and accounting, it would be plausible to assume that individuals who wish to pursue their entrepreneurial aspirations could do so without the need to live in a major city [26,37,40]. Evidence from the United States suggests that growth in rural self-employment is fostered by the relative proximity of rural areas to smaller metropolitan areas, but generally hampered by their proximity to larger metropolitan areas [41]. Rural areas in the UK have seen, in recent years, the restructuring of traditional rural industries and the development of local community enterprises, as well as rural small and medium enterprises (SMEs) [40,42]. Audretsch and Feldman [4] suggest that when start-ups are supported by networks, they enjoy a high degree of stability and also that cooperation of firms within a network can reduce the size-inherent disadvantages of small firms and so improve their viability. With the emergence of a myriad online platforms that connect businesses with other businesses and customers, the contemporary entrepreneur may have a new network available to them, which enables them to operate their business without being physically present in the city.

In a study of long distance commuting in rural England, Champion, Coombes, and Brown [25] find that almost 35 percent of rural residents travel to work at distances of less than 5 km, another 17 percent travel to work at distances of at least 20 km, while approximately 11 percent of rural residents work from home. They also find that approximately 20 percent of recent movers to rural areas commute at least 20 km for their work, compared with only 12 percent of longer-term rural residents. The study notes some differences between residents and recent movers, but it also reveals that a large share of rural area residents works locally. Champion, Coombes, and Brown [25] note that the rationale for local work using the limit of 5 km, is because no settlement in rural England has a diameter larger than 5 km. Moreover, the study indicates that the reason for moving into a rural area is not primarily to move closer to the workplace. This may have to do with decisions related to quality of life away from problems of atmospheric pollution, noise, and traffic congestion that are often associated with cities [5,21,43]. It may also relate to the inflated home prices in major cities that force people to move to rural areas where they may find more affordable accommodation [20,44]. Ryan-Collins' [20,44] research on homeownership, housing rents, and the increased cost of living in a big city, argues that local authorities have gradually withdrawn from offering affordable housing in the UK that has resulted in inflated house prices, which in major cities (e.g., London, Manchester) can be over 7 times the median income. Stockdale's [43] findings support the argument of rural in-migration due to rising urban costs and pollution, indicating that 62 percent of in-migrants in rural England continue to commute to their workplace at distances greater than 20 km away (likely an urban centre) from their rural residence. These workers earn more than 25,000 GBP per annum, when 49 percent of those who work locally earn that income. The DEFRA [14] report also notes that people living in rural areas, but commute to work in urban areas, have seen a greater increase in median incomes compared to those who live and work in urban areas (i.e., 2.3 percent versus 1.4 percent, based on 2016–2017 median earnings). Nevertheless, it is still possible that at a later period, the rural area in-migrants may find wage-employment closer to home or start their own business locally [25].

The attractiveness of rural areas can also be seen in the higher reported life satisfaction of rural areas compared to urban areas [21]. Rural areas appear to attract professionals and individuals from managerial classes who seek to combine employment with higher quality-of-life and more affordable housing [43]. However, managerial experience has also been associated with the launch of new businesses [45], and evidence suggests that such individuals indeed start up new businesses in the rural areas they migrate to. For example, Findlay, Short, and Stockdale [46] find that only 7 percent of the people who had recently moved to a rural area of Scotland worked in the primary sector, with the majority of recent in-migrants being employed in the service sector. They also observe that many in-migrants, who are highly skilled professionals, either operate their own business or work as managers in other businesses. The presence of skilled professionals and other individuals from managerial classes in rural areas can act as a vehicle for knowledge transmission and spillovers from urban to rural areas [47], and also encourage the overall entrepreneurial activity of rural areas [4]. Rural in-migrants strengthen rural–urban links, which can contribute to the long-run sustainable economic development of rural areas [37].

Furthermore, a study of Scotland shows that 45 percent of in-migrants who establish a business within the rural area were employing others and had created on average 1.6 extra jobs [46]. Stockdale [43] also finds that self-employed in-migrants to rural areas bring their businesses with them, creating opportunities for local employment expansion. A common theme about the in-migrants that move to rural areas is that it was "part of their life goals in shifting to becoming self-employed" [43] (p. 125). In-migrants appear to bring with them elements from their urban life experience that not only diversify the rural economies but also affect conditions associated with the generation of employment [43,46]. The above findings suggest that the migration process actually creates jobs in rural areas and is a more complex phenomenon than a simple residential relocation of urban households [46]. Therefore, self-employment and rural economic development appear intertwined with the quality of life possible in rural areas [48].

It is reasonable to assume that not all self-employed in rural areas become self-employed due to pull factors such as opportunities for higher income [27], but many turn to self-employment due to push factors, including the lack of better alternatives in wage-employment [49,50]. However, it has also been suggested that rural areas attract individuals who were already self-employed [43]. Nevertheless, important differences may exist between residents of rural areas and in-migrants with regards to their allocation of time to self-employment. The number of registered businesses in rural areas is greater than in urban areas when accounting for their population [14], which suggests that rural-based businesses are smaller than urban-based ones. The DEFRA [14] report finds that the rural areas in England had 585 registered businesses per 10,000 population, when urban areas had 406. Nevertheless, businesses in urban areas of England employed approximately 28.9 million employees, compared to just above 3.5 million employees for the rural areas. Evidently, a large percentage of businesses in rural areas are businesses with only a few employees, or even self-employed professionals with no employees. There is also some evidence of a growing number of individuals living in rural areas who work from home [26]. Therefore, either due to pull or push factors, it is possible that individuals will tend to spend more time as self-employed rather than wage-employees in rural areas compared to urban areas.

Nevertheless, in-migrants of rural and urban areas might allocate differently their time to self-employment compared to those who reside in rural or urban areas [51]. The demographics of rural/urban areas suggest that individuals tend to live in major cities when younger and in rural areas when older. DEFRA [14] reports that approximately 55 percent of the individuals living in rural areas are aged above 45 years old compared to approximately 40 percent in urban areas. The self-employed tend to be in general older than wage-employees [52,53]. This is often associated with accumulation of experience and expertise that lead to specialisation and the ability to recognise entrepreneurial opportunities [52,54,55]. Hence, greater self-employment might be expected in rural areas based on the rural age profile. However, urban areas may offer better overall opportunities for either wage- or self-employment, depending on the career stage, age, and employment experience/expertise of individuals, due to greater business activity taking place in urban areas compared to rural areas [13,14,56].

There is also some evidence of differences between men and women in terms of rural self-employment. Champion, Coombes, and Brown [25] find that men who migrate to rural areas are more likely to commute more than 20 km for work than women, suggesting that that men who migrate to rural areas tend to maintain their previous jobs in the city whilst women will tend to find employment closer to home. The authors suggest that women tend to work locally because of gender roles associated with caring for family and home. It could be argued though, that more experienced women who migrate to rural areas will be more likely to become self-employed than others. Based on their experience, they are better able to spot opportunities and respond to them.

The above literature leads us to form three hypotheses: H1, H2α, and H2β. We express these hypotheses as:

H1: *Individuals who live in rural areas will have spent more time in self-employment than individuals who live in urban areas.*

H2α: *Older men who migrate from urban areas to rural areas are less likely to have spent more time in self-employment.*

H2β: *Older women who migrate from urban areas to rural areas are more likely to have spent more time in self-employment.*

3. Materials and Methods

3.1. Data

We used data from the UK Household Longitudinal Study (UKHLS), also known as the Understanding Society survey (for further information, see Knies, [57]). The Understanding Society survey is a well-established and widely used longitudinal dataset, based at the University of Essex and funded by the Economic and Social Research Council (ESRC). The Understanding Society survey collects data from every household member, aged 16 and above. The same household is surveyed in the same quarter each year, mainly from face-to-face interviews, with a small supplement of telephone interviews. Understanding Society covers approximately 40 thousand households (at wave 1). At the time of this study, there were data for nine waves publicly available. The analysis retained only the observation for participants who were either wage-employed or self-employed in waves 1–9, surveyed over the period 2009–2019. This way, we limited the effects from becoming self-employed out of necessity due to unemployment [58–60]. Any participants with missing values among the variables examined in the models were removed. The final sample contained 43,614 observations, of which 46.99 percent were men and 53.01 percent were women.

3.2. Model Specification

The data analysis used fixed effects (FE) modelling to examine the data, though a random effects (RE) model is also reported for comparative reasons. The FE estimator (also known as the within estimator) provides effect estimates of the time-varying factors. As such, the time-constant unobserved heterogeneity no longer presents a problem [31–33]. Formally, the FE model is expressed as:

$$y_{it} - \overline{y_i} = \beta(x_{it} - \overline{x}) + e_{it} - \overline{e}_i \tag{1}$$

The dependent variable for time in self-employment (tSEMP) is constructed as the share of time spent in self-employment to total time in employment (either wage-employment or self-employment). Following the empirical entrepreneurship literature, self-employment can be used as a proxy for en-trepreneurship, since entrepreneurs are typically individuals who have started and developed their own business enterprises [39,55,61,62]. Nevertheless, we are aware of the issues arising from this approach and we discuss them in Section 5.2 Limitations and further research. tSEMP is a continuous variable that denotes the ratio of time in self-employment to total employment time. tSEMP ranges from 0 to 1, where 0 indicates that no time at all was dedicated in self-employment and 1 indicates that all employment time was dedicated in self-employment. Using this approach to measure the employment experience of individuals offers a way to measure self-employment experience which captures the actual share of self-employment experi-ence at each wave. This way, the risk of recall bias occurring from asking respondents to recall infor-mation in retrospect is being limited [63–66]. The independent variable for Urban/Rural is derived from the Office for National Statistics Rural and Urban Classification of Output Areas 2001. The indicator assumes a value of (1) if the address falls within urban settlements with a population of 10,000 or more, or (0) otherwise. However, we expected the effect of residential location to differ for residents and for in-migrants. Following the definition of long-term migrant used by the UK Department for Environment, Food and Rural Affairs and the Of-fice for National Statistics, this study uses the term 'resident' for those who usually live in an area and have resided there for at least a year. To examine if and how residents and in-migrants differ, we first created two variables which captured, for those who moved, the time the respondents moved into a rural area or the time they moved into an urban area. We also created a variable which took the value of 1 if the respondent lived in an urban area throughout the period covered by our data. For movers, this was the period lived in an urban area after the urban migration took place. In our model, our reference category was rural area residence. This allowed us to capture the specific effect of rural and urban in-migration on the time spent in self-employment sepa-rately from the effect of rural and urban residence. We also created an age variable with three age groups, for early career age (up to 25 years of age), middle career age (over 25 and up to 45 years of age), and senior career age (over 45 years of age), using the age information from Department for Education [67] and DEFRA [14], which we used as a proxy for experience.

Other control variables included health status, part-time employment, education, marital status, the presence of children in the household and their age, and homeownership. Controls were also included for the five socioeconomic status categories (NS-SEC5), the industrial sector they were employed in, and the geographical region of the household. Following previous studies [68], homeownership was used as a proxy of individuals' financial standing as well as the combined gross personal monthly income from job/business, savings, and investments. 'Gross personal income' is by default calculated per month in the UKHLS, and therefore, it was transformed to per annum before it was combined with 'income from savings and investments' which is, by default, calculated per annum in the UKHLS. Table A1 in the Appendix A presents a descriptive summary of the variables used in the analysis.

4. Results

4.1. Descriptive Statistics

The majority of men and women are employed in salaried jobs, that is 82.22 percent of men and 91.05 percent of women, with a small share of them working as self-employed (i.e., 17.78 percent of men and 8.95 percent of women). In total, 76.79 percent of men and 74.79 percent of women are living in urban areas, whereas 23.21 percent of men and 25.21 percent of women are living in rural areas. The mean age of individuals living in rural areas is 47.1 years of age and 44.5 for those in urban areas (see the descriptive statistics in Table A1 in the Appendix A). In line with the literature, the age distribution indicates the expected negative skew for rural areas (see Table A2 in the Appendix A). Approximately 54.2 percent of the sample population living in rural areas are aged above 45 years, whereas the share of the sample population above the age of 45 is approximately 53.4 percent.

4.2. Empirical Analysis

The analysis offers some important insight in the effects of gender and age towards the time individuals spend in self-employment in urban and rural areas. Overall, the results indicate that age plays a dominant role in men's and women's allocation of time to self-employment. Table 1 presents the analysis results for the overall model and the separate model specifications for men and women.

Table 1. Rural–Urban areas and Time in Self-employment: Random and Fixed effects models.

	RE Mix-Gender	FE Mix-Gender	FE Men	FE Women
	I	II	III	IV
Urban Area Residence	−0.003	0.006 **	0.005	0.006 **
Urban migration	−0.013 ***	−0.007	−0.009	−0.005
Rural migration	−0.001	0.003	0.000	0.005
(Baseline: Rural Area Residence)				
Gender: woman	−0.061 ***	(omitted)	(omitted)	(omitted)
Career Age group				
Middle	0.007 ***	0.007 ***	0.005	0.010 ***
Senior	0.012 ***	0.010 ***	0.006	0.013 ***
(Baseline: Early career)				
Health status	0.000	0.000	−0.001	0.000
Part-time work	0.006 ***	0.004 ***	0.016 ***	0.001
Educational achievement				
High School	−0.014 *	0.005	0.005	0.005
+16 Education	−0.005	0.004	0.011	0.000
University	−0.011	−0.003	−0.012	0.002
Vocational Qualification	−0.012	−0.001	0.007	−0.005
(Baseline: Elementary school)				

Table 1. *Cont.*

	RE Mix-Gender	FE Mix-Gender	FE Men	FE Women
Marital status				
Married/Civil Partner	0.005 ***	0.005 ***	0.007 **	0.003
Divorced/Separated	0.007 ***	0.006 **	0.008 **	0.003
Widowed	0.002	−0.001	−0.024 **	0.005
(Baseline: Single/never married)				
Number of Children in HH				
Aged 0–4	−0.003 ***	−0.003 ***	−0.002	−0.003 ***
Aged 5–11	0.000	0.001	−0.002	0.004 ***
Aged 12–15	0.000	0.000	−0.001	0.001
(Baseline: No children)				
Socioeconomic class				
Management and professional	0.013 ***	0.012 ***	0.018 ***	0.008 ***
Intermediate	0.003	0.003 *	0.003	0.003
Small employer and own account	0.349 ***	0.318 ***	0.328 ***	0.300 ***
Lower supervisory and technical	−0.001	−0.001	−0.003	0.003
(Baseline: Routine and Semi-routine)				
Income from job/business and investments	0.000 ***	0.000 ***	0.000 ***	0.000
Homeownership	0.001	−0.001	−0.006 *	0.003 *
Industrial Sector				
Agriculture, forestry, and fishing	0.066 ***	0.026 **	0.054 ***	−0.002
Mining and quarrying	−0.001	0.000	0.001	(omitted)
Manufacturing	0.008 **	0.003	0.011	0.007
Electricity, gas, steam, and air conditioning	0.009	0.009	0.015	0.004
Water supply; sewerage, waste management, and remediation activities	−0.005	−0.009	0.011	−0.067 **
Construction	0.053 ***	0.035 ***	0.058 ***	0.006
Wholesale and retail trade; repair of motor vehicles and motorcycles	0.011 ***	0.004	0.022 ***	−0.007 *
Transportation and storage	0.023 ***	0.019 ***	0.034 ***	0.012 *
Accommodation and food service activities	0.022 ***	0.014 ***	0.033 ***	0.002
Information and communication	0.021 ***	0.010 *	0.020 **	0.009
Financial and insurance activities	0.008	0.000	0.019 *	−0.011 *
Real estate activities	0.041 ***	0.037 ***	0.041 ***	0.053 ***
Professional, scientific, and technical activities	0.041 ***	0.029 ***	0.041 ***	0.023 ***
Administrative and support service activities	0.026 ***	0.018 ***	0.040 ***	0.004
Education	0.017 ***	0.011 ***	0.048 ***	−0.005
Human health and social work activities	0.006 *	0.001	−0.031 ***	0.006 *
Arts, entertainment, and recreation	0.020 ***	0.001	0.017	−0.003
Other service activities	0.019 ***	0.005	0.002	0.006
Activities of households as employers	0.040 ***	0.044 ***	0.061 **	0.040 ***
Activities of extraterritorial organisations	0.006	0.002		−0.006
(Baseline: Public services)				
Region				
North East	−0.012	0.022 *	0.037 **	−0.002
North West	−0.031 ***	−0.030 ***	−0.034 **	−0.018
Yorkshire And The Humber	−0.016 **	0.012	0.040 ***	−0.013
East Midlands	0.011	0.049 ***	0.062 ***	0.037 ***
West Midlands	−0.019 **	0.009	0.004	0.009
East Of England	−0.028 ***	−0.025 ***	−0.016	−0.030 ***
South East	−0.014 **	−0.022 ***	−0.038 **	0.000
South West	−0.002	0.004	−0.005	0.016
Wales	−0.025 **	−0.014	−0.002	−0.032 *
Scotland	−0.044 ***	−0.048 ***	−0.035 *	−0.049 ***
Northern Ireland	−0.029 *	0.217 ***	(omitted)	0.238 ***
(Baseline: London)				
Constant	0.114 ***	0.059 ***	0.092 ***	0.031 **
Statistics				
χ^2	22,982.890			
F		365.760	176.490	210.150
R-sq: within	0.365	0.367	0.372	0.375
R-sq: between	0.623	0.498	0.585	0.418
R-sq: overall	0.588	0.476	0.553	0.405
Corr(u_i, Xb)	0 (assumed)	0.452	0.534	0.367
N	38385	38385	17460	20925

Note: * $p < 0.1$; ** $p < 0.05$; *** $p < 0.01$; we also tested the models restricting the sample to the labour force using the latest information from Gov.uk on Working, jobs, and pensions. The results of the restricted models are consistent with the original results and the conclusions remain unchanged.

The results in Table 1 for the RE model (Column I) show that urban area residence is not a significant explanatory variable of the time individuals allocate to self-employment. Urban migration, however, is a significant explanatory variable ($p < 0.01$). Urban migration has a significantly negative effect on the time individuals allocate to self-employment. This shows that compared to rural areas, individuals who migrate to urban areas spend, on average, less time in self-employment. The random effects model results include effects from time-invariant variables (e.g., gender) and any interaction effects correlated with it, which makes it difficult to gain further insights. Nevertheless, the negative effect is not unexpected considering that self-employment is a source of employment when the supply of salaried jobs is limited [69–71], and urban areas offer many more wage-employment opportunities compared to rural areas [2,14]. The FE model (Column II) suggests that urban area residence has a positive effect on the time individuals allocate to self-employment compared to rural area residence. However, the time-invariant control for gender is omitted, forcing other variables to absorb the gender effect, which likely is quite significant. A Hausman specification test (HT) comparing the RE and FE models (Columns I and II) indicates that the RE specification does not adequately model individual effects ($\chi^2 = 3843.32$; $p < 0.001$). Hence, the mixed results offer only limited support for Hypothesis 1, that "Individuals who live in rural areas will spend more time in self-employment than individuals who live in urban areas".

To examine the effects further, we estimate the FE model separately for men and women and present them in Columns III and IV of Table 1. We find that the urban residence effect is positively associated with time in self-employment for women, whereas for men, the effect is non-significant (perhaps suggesting that the greater opportunities for self-employment are counterbalanced by the availability of paid employment opportunities). Additionally, neither urban migration, nor rural migration appear to affect the time men and women allocate to self-employment. Furthermore, as might be expected, both middle and senior career age groups have a positive effect on time in self-employment for women ($p < 0.01$) [55,72,73]. However, age does not appear to have significant explanatory power for men.

To examine the effects further, we analyse the FE models of men and women and decompose the models by career age groups. The results overall indicate that there exist differences between in-migrants and residents of urban and rural areas. Table 2 presents the analysis results for the model specification separated by age group for men and women.

Table 2. Urban–Rural areas and Time in Self-Employment: Men and Women by Career Age group.

	Early Career Men (FE)	Middle Career Men (FE)	Senior Career Men (FE)	Early Career Women (FE)	Middle Career Women (FE)	Senior Career Women (FE)
	I	II	III	IV	V	VI
Urban Area Residence	0.058 ***	−0.004	0.041 ***	−0.0023	0.013 ***	0.018 ***
Urban migration	0.037 *	0.004	−0.028 **	−0.002	−0.006	0.003
Rural migration (Baseline: Rural Area Residence)	0.024	0.005	0.016	−0.005	0.008	0.018 **
Age	−0.000	0.000	0.001 ***	0.001 **	0.001 ***	0.000
Health status	0.003	−0.002	0.002 *	−0.001	0.000	0.000
Part-time work	−0.002	0.019 ***	0.001	−0.003	0.003 *	0.000
Homeownership	0.015	−0.009 **	0.011	−0.009 ***	0.004 *	0.011 ***
Constant	−0.054	0.072 **	0.065 *	−0.002	0.001	0.027
Statistics						
F	22.710	87.030	82.630	65.880	105.300	84.040
R-sq: within	0.748	0.381	0.358	0.878	0.395	0.313
R-sq: between	0.298	0.654	0.471	0.756	0.277	0.488
R-sq: overall	0.252	0.598	0.464	0.715	0.292	0.484
Corr(u_i, Xb)	0.127	0.591	0.418	0.172	0.182	0.491
N	438	8345	8677	565	9747	10613

Note: Other controls as in Table 1; * $p < 0.1$; ** $p < 0.05$; *** $p < 0.01$; We also test the models excluding the Age variable, and the results are similar.

The results indicate an overall greater allocation of time to self-employment for men and women who live in urban areas, particularly at older ages. This can be explained from the perspective of the greater business opportunity availability in urban areas, where individuals can utilise their accumulated employment experience, expertise, and wealth to start up their own business [54,55,73–75]. Nevertheless, there are several differences in the effect of urban and rural areas between men and women and across age groups.

The path men follow with regards to self-employment appears consistent with the self-employment and entrepreneurship literature. That is, urban area residence has a positive effect on the time younger and senior career age men allocate to self-employment. This is not surprising since cities offer young professionals entrepreneurship opportunities that may be limited in rural areas [2,14], allowing younger individuals to make career choices that often involve self-employment [55,76]. Additionally, older individuals also tend to turn to self-employment and start their own businesses after accumulating sufficient professional experience to make the transition [39,52,53,55]. Urban in-migrants also appear to allocate more time to self-employment rather than seek wage-employment when younger. Contrarily, urban in-migrant men in senior career ages allocate significantly less time to self-employment ($p < 0.05$).

Additionally, the linear age control for senior career men is also positively associated with time in self-employment ($p < 0.01$), offering further support that as men get older, they tend to allocate more time to self-employment. However, the results also show a difference between residents of urban areas and urban in-migrants. Specifically, senior age men who are in-migrants to urban areas spend significantly less time in self-employment, perhaps suggesting that much of the migration to urban areas is linked to wage-employment opportunities. Moreover, rural versus urban location does not appear to have a significant effect on the allocation of time to self-employment for middle career age men, which might indicate contrasting themes arising within this particular age group of men. The non-significant effects might be an indication that middle career age men have contrasting behaviours that cancel out each other. It is worth observing that the constant is also significant at $p < 0.05$ in this specification. Overall, the results do not indicate that men alter their allocation of time between wage- and self-employment due to migration in a rural or an urban area. Hence, we do not find support for Hypothesis 2α that "Older men who migrate from urban areas to rural areas are less likely to spend more time in self-employment".

Women who are urban area residents allocate more time to self-employment compared to women in rural areas when in middle or senior career ages. When younger, the urban versus rural location does not significantly affect the time women allocate to self-employment. However, the linear age variable in this group has a significant positive effect on the time spent in self-employment; something we did not observe for men. Women, similarly to men, tend to allocate more time to self-employment as they get older, but at the same time, the impact of age has a stronger effect at a comparatively earlier stage in life for women than men. Often, women use self-employment to balance work and family [73,77,78], which, combined with the business opportunities available in urban areas, might explain the positive effect of urban residence for mid-career ages. Furthermore, rural migration has a significant positive effect on time in self-employment for senior career age women. This is also something we did not observe for men. This is supportive of the literature that suggests women who move to rural areas tend to find employment closer to home [25], which suggests they are more likely to turn to self-employment. The results offer support for Hypothesis 2β that "Older women who migrate from urban areas to rural are more likely to spend more time in self-employment".

Moreover, some of the control variables also offer interesting insights considering the effects of the rural–urban divide and the effect of age we have analysed so far. Specifically, part-time employment has a significant and positive association with time in self-employment for both men and women in the middle career age groups ($p < 0.01$ and $p < 0.05$, respectively). Since this age group is typically when families are likely to be formed, the dual demands for work and family balance might influence the decision to turn to part-time employment [76,79–81]. The significant influence of part-time employment in this group might also be linked to the general rise in part-time self-employment in the aftermath of the 2008 economic crisis [22,82]. Health is also interesting, since it has a significant and positive effect only for men in the senior career age. Not surprisingly, this offers support for previous findings that older men choose self-employment for retirement reasons [72,76].

5. Discussion

5.1. Summary

This study examined the effects that living in a rural or urban area have on the time people allocate to self-employment. The empirical analysis used fixed effects modelling on rich panel data from the UKHLS over the period 2009–2019. The fixed effects model allowed us to control for unobserved heterogeneity, while the rich survey data enabled us to control for several individual characteristics, such as educational achievement, socioeconomic class, industrial sector of employment, marital status, and number of children, among others. Departing from previous analyses that use the typical binary wage- or self-employment variables and examine the transition to self-employment as an end in itself, our approach perceives the transition, to and from self-employment, as part of a continuous employment experience. Using this novel approach to measuring the time people spend in wage- and self-employment, the analysis shows that there exist important differences not only between rural and urban areas, but also differences between men and women. The gender differences between the time spent in self-employment in rural and urban areas become more pronounced when examined using separate age groups. Generally, the effects of rural and urban migration, as well as rural and urban residence, appear gendered and age group-specific. Our findings contribute towards the theoretical and methodological approach of examining self-employment and the rural–urban divide, as well as policy implications for rural development.

In line with the self-employment and entrepreneurship literature [2,39,52,53,76], we find that older individuals tend to veer towards self-employment as they get older. Urban areas are, in general, positively associated with time in self-employment across most age groups. This effect is likely associated with the greater business opportunities available in larger markets of cities, compared to the smaller markets of rural towns and villages [2,14]. Therefore, major cities in the UK evidently remain centres of entrepreneurial activity [1–3]. Urban residence is positively associated with the time young men and senior men allocate to self-employment. Migration to urban areas is also positively associated with time in self-employment for men. However, our results show that younger men differ from senior men in their motivation to enter self-employment. Younger men, who tend to be less risk averse than older men, are willing to try out several career options in their efforts to find a job that satisfies their needs, including self-employment [72,76]. It might also be the case that young career age men are not concerned with future family and parenting responsibilities, and therefore, are more prone to take risks [83]. Older men might turn to self-employment after having increased their financial and human capital from a career in wage-employment [54,55,73,84]. Nevertheless, our findings cast doubt that senior career age men who move to rural areas from urban areas turn to self-employment and set up local businesses, as conjectured by Champion, Coombes, and Brown [25]. If we extrapolate a bit further, the finding that senior career age men who move from rural to urban areas allocate significantly less time to self-employment (see Table 2, Column III), may suggest that these men had been pushed to self-employment when previously residing in rural areas.

Interestingly, young women living in urban areas do not appear to be as attracted into self-employment as young men do. While young women's age still has a positive effect on time in self-employment, neither their urban residence nor urban migration alter their allocation of time between wage- and self-employment. This could be associated with family and parenting obligations, which for women, typically comes at an earlier life-stage [56]. In relatively more gender-egalitarian societies, such as the UK, wage-employment may offer a level of security for working class young mothers, which may not be accessible in self-employment [56]. Instead, women allocate more time to self-employment at middle career ages and senior career ages. This difference in the self-employment attitudes of men and women at their early career age might be related to self-efficacy [85–87]. In this sense, younger women who live in urban areas might feel more uncertain than young men in choosing the riskier career path of self-employment. This changes quickly after they accumulate some employment experience [85,87], which might explain the significant and positive effect of urban area residence for women in their middle career age group. Nevertheless, this age group includes the age period when people tend to have children and from families (e.g., late 20s to early 40s). Since women typically bear the greatest burden of family responsibilities, they will be more likely to turn to self-employment and part-time work to balance work and family [56,88,89]. The results show that for this group of women, urban residence and part-time employment are positively associated with time in self-employment. Therefore, the positive association may be associated more with work and family factors, rather than attitudinal choices to specific employment type [89–92]. However, urban migration is not, which indicates that women in mid-career ages who migrate to urban areas do not significantly change their allocation of time to self-employment.

When looking at the senior career women, the results show that both urban residence and rural migration positively affect the allocation of time to self-employment. Women in this age group who live in urban areas might turn to self-employment due to age effects associated with human and financial capital, similarly to women in the mid-career age group [55,73,84]. The age effect though might not be the only reason that rural in-migrant women turn to self-employment. It may be the case that they bring new ideas from their experience in the city and start up their business there. Considering that rural in-migrant women do not travel far from home to work [25], this suggests they work locally in the rural area they live. Given the limited wage-employment opportunities of rural areas [14], there might not find suitable jobs for these in-migrant women, hence, they choose to become self-employed. However, their past experience from working in urban areas might still facilitate their entrepreneurial aspiration, regardless of initial motives [36,37,83].

5.2. Limitations and Further Research

Like any other study, our study has some limitations. In this analysis, we use self-employment as a proxy for entrepreneurship. While there are distinctions between the two concepts, there are also major overlapping themes between the two. For example, both entrepreneurs and self-employed are individuals who typically do not work for someone else's business but have started and developed their own business enterprises. In empirical studies that examine individual-level data and not firm-level data, and given the practical difficulties in identifying the entrepreneur, self-employment has been traditionally used as a proxy [93]. Another limitation is that our analysis does not directly control for opportunity or necessity entrepreneurship. Therefore, we cannot know with certainty if men and women were pulled or pushed into self-employment. However, as our sample was restricted to those continuously in wage- or self-employment, the results are more likely to capture the effects of *pull* rather than *push* factors. Investigating whether the urban or rural location impacts the emergence of necessity or opportunity entrepreneurial activity in each area would be a fruitful avenue for future research. Additionally, the UK is a developed country with mature welfare institutions, which further decreases the probability of entrepreneurial activity out of necessity [94]. Nevertheless, more research is needed to fully understand the push or pull factors of self-employment motivations of rural/urban residents and in-migrants. It must also be noted that regional heterogeneity can affect the differences between rural and urban areas, as it is evident from the results of the region control variable. These remain potentially important issues to address in future research on sustainable regional development.

6. Conclusions

The results show that there exist complex dynamics of gender and age, which affect the allocation of time to self-employment between rural and urban areas. Residents and in-migrants of rural/urban areas also exhibit differences in the time they allocate to self-employment based on their gender and career age group. The rural versus urban location appears to exert contrasting effects on men and women that need to be considered in entrepreneurship policy, as well as rural/urban development planning. Nevertheless, our findings show that overall, urban areas are positively associated with the time individuals allocate to self-employment and remain a magnet for young men with entrepreneurial intentions. These findings support those by Champion and Shepherd, [11] Dobbs et al., [2], ONS [13], and DEFRA [14]. Rural areas, on the contrary, are positively associated with the time senior career women allocate to self-employment, which may reveal links with age and social entrepreneurship [83]. However, limited internet connection and speed is still a factor that hinders rural entrepreneurship [95]. Improvements in communication and transportation infrastructure can minimise the distance between rural and urban areas, which allows entrepreneurs to conduct their business from rural areas without the need to live in a major city [40,41]. Self-employment might be driven by different reasons for young or senior men and women who live in rural or urban areas, but nevertheless, self-employment offers an opportunity to create jobs for the self-employed and others in the area they live [14,96].

Author Contributions: Formal analysis, N.L.; Investigation, N.L.; Methodology, N.L. and G.S.; Project administration, N.L.; Supervision, G.S. and C.H.; Writing—original draft, N.L.; Writing—review & editing, N.L., G.S. and C.H. All authors have read and agreed to the published version of the manuscript.

Appendix A

Table A1. Descriptive statistics.

Summary Statistics				
	Males		Females	
	Mean	Std. Dev.	Mean	Std. Dev.
Self-Emp. dummy	0.178	-	0.089	-
Wage-Emp. dummy	0.822	-	0.911	-
Part-Time Employment	0.074	-	0.352	-
Age	45.152	10.581	45.120	10.234
Self-Employees Age	49.846	10.679	48.771	10.800
Wage-Employees Age	44.137	10.282	44.761	10.106
Homeownership	0.838	-	0.823	-
Urban Area Residence	0.768	-	0.748	-
Health status	3.671	0.920	3.660	0.938
Income from job/business and investments	37,296.640	26,102.990	25,636.310	18,212.790
Marital status				
Single/Never Married	0.216	-	0.215	-
Married/Civil Partner	0.682	-	0.611	-
Divorced/Separated	0.095	-	0.155	-
Widowed	0.006	-	0.019	-
Number of Children in HH				
Aged 0–4	0.201	-	0.157	-
Aged 5–11	0.335	-	0.307	-
Aged 12–15	0.175	-	0.195	-
Educational achievement				
Elementary Education	0.094	-	0.081	-
High School	0.315	-	0.295	-
+16 Education	0.115	-	0.097	-
University	0.384	-	0.377	-
Vocational Qualification	0.091	-	0.150	-
Socioeconomic class				
Management and professional	0.512	-	0.500	-
Intermediate	0.100	-	0.176	-
Small employer and own account	0.127	-	0.063	-
Lower supervisory and technical	0.089	-	0.044	-
Routine and Semi-routine	0.172	-	0.217	-

Table A1. *Cont.*

Summary Statistics				
	Males		Females	
Industrial Sector				
Agriculture, forestry, and fishing	0.010	-	0.005	-
Mining and quarrying	0.003	-	0.001	-
Manufacturing	0.156	-	0.049	-
Electricity, gas, steam, and air conditioning	0.008	-	0.004	-
Water supply; sewerage, waste management, and remediation activities	0.007	-	0.003	-
Construction	0.095	-	0.012	-
Wholesale and retail trade; repair of motor vehicles and motorcycles	0.106	-	0.128	-
Transportation and storage	0.073	-	0.020	-
Accommodation and food service activities	0.017	-	0.025	-
Information and communication	0.073	-	0.016	-
Financial and insurance activities	0.041	-	0.033	-
Real estate activities	0.012	-	0.009	-
Professional, scientific, and technical activities	0.075	-	0.062	-
Administrative and support service activities	0.046	-	0.033	-
Public administration and defence; compulsory social security	0.087	-	0.086	-
Education	0.087	-	0.187	-
Human health and social work activities	0.069	-	0.271	-
Arts, entertainment, and recreation	0.015	-	0.020	-
Other service activities	0.017	-	0.034	-
Activities of households as employers	0.001	-	0.002	-
Activities of extraterritorial organisations	0.000	-	0.000	-
Region				
North East	0.043	-	0.047	-
North West	0.110	-	0.108	-
Yorkshire And The Humber	0.076	-	0.077	-
East Midlands	0.082	-	0.089	-
West Midlands	0.088	-	0.091	-
East Of England	0.102	-	0.100	-
London	0.101	-	0.082	-
South East	0.145	-	0.133	-
South West	0.109	-	0.111	-
Wales	0.038	-	0.043	-
Scotland	0.071	-	0.083	-
Northern Ireland	0.034	-	0.038	-
Total Observation	**17,460**		**20,925**	

Table A2. Age in Rural/Urban Areas: Skewness and Kurtosis.

Age	Rural Area	Urban Areas
Mean	47.082	44.509
Skewness	−0.092	−0.027
Kurtosis	2.708	2.538
Skewness/Kurtosis tests for Normality (95 Cl)		
Pr(Skewness)	0.000	0.060
Pr(Kurtosis)	0.000	0.000
Adj chi2(2)	51.980	-
Prob > chi2	0.000	0.000
Observations	9328	29,057

References

1. Feldman, M.P.; Audretsch, D.B. *Location, Location, Location: The Geography of Innovation and Knowledge Spillovers*; FS IV 96-28; WZB: Berlin, Germany, 1996.
2. Dobbs, R.; Smit, S.; Remes, J.; Manyika, J.; Roxburgh, C.; Restrepo, A. *Urban World: Mapping the Economic Power of Cities*; McKinsey Global Institute: San Francisco, CA, USA, 2001; Volume 62.
3. Adler, P.; Florida, R.; King, K.; Mellander, C. The city and high-tech startups: The spatial organization of Schumpeterian entrepreneurship. *Cities* **2019**, *87*, 121–130. [CrossRef]
4. Audretsch, D.B.; Feldman, M.P. Knowledge spillovers and the geography of innovation. In *Handbook of Regional and Urban Economics*; Henderson, V., Thisse, J.-F., Eds.; Elsevier: Amsterdam, The Netherlands, 2004; pp. 2713–2739. [CrossRef]
5. Knox, P.; Pinch, S. *Urban Social Geography: An Introduction*; Routledge: London, UK, 2014.
6. Wirth, L. Urbanism as a way of life. *Am. J. Sociol.* **1938**, *44*, 25–48. [CrossRef]
7. Molotch, H. The City as a Growth Machine: Toward a Political Economy of Place. *Am. J. Sociol.* **1976**, *82*, 309–332. [CrossRef]
8. Davis, M. *Planet of Slums*; Verso: New York, NY, USA, 2006.
9. Côté, J.E.; Levine, C.G. *Identity, Formation, Agency, and Culture: A Social Psychological Synthesis*; Psychology Press: London, UK, 2014.
10. Autor, D. *The Faltering Escalator of Urban Opportunity The Faltering Escalator of Urban*; MIT: Cambridge, MA, USA, 2020.
11. Champion, T.; Shepherd, J. Demographic change in rural England. In *The Ageing Countryside: The Growing Older Population of Rural England*; Age Concern Books: London, UK, 2006; pp. 29–50.
12. Public Health England. *Health and Wellbeing in Rural Areas*; Public Health England: London, UK, 2017.
13. ONS. *Exploring Labour Productivity in Rural and Urban Areas in Great Britain: 2014*; Office for National Statistic: Newport, UK, 2017.
14. DEFRA. *Statistical Digest of Rural England 2019*; Department for Environment, Food and Rural Affairs: London, UK, 2019.
15. Taylor, M.P. Survival of the Fittest? An Analysis of Self-Employment Duration in Britain. *Econ. J.* **1999**, *109*, 140–155. [CrossRef]
16. Saridakis, G.; Mole, K.; Storey, D.J. New small firm survival in England. *Empirica* **2008**, *35*, 25–39. [CrossRef]
17. Coad, A.; Frankish, J.; Roberts, R.G.; Storey, D.J. Growth paths and survival chances: An application of Gambler's Ruin theory. *J. Bus. Ventur.* **2013**, *28*, 615–632. [CrossRef]
18. Fritsch, M.; Brixy, U.; Falck, O. The Effect of Industry, Region, and Time on New Business Survival—A Multi-Dimensional Analysis. *Rev. Ind. Organ.* **2006**, *28*, 285–306. [CrossRef]
19. Saridakis, G.; Mendoza González, M.A.; Hand, C.; Muñoz Torres, R.I. Do regional self-employment rates converge in the UK? Empirical evidence using club-clustering algorithm. *Ann. Reg. Sci.* **2020**, *65*, 179–192. [CrossRef]
20. Ryan-Collins, J. *Rethinking the Economics of Land and Housing*, 1st ed.; Lloyd, T., MacFarlane, L., Eds.; Zed Books: London, UK, 2017.
21. Hand, C. Spatial influences on domains of life satisfaction in the UK. *Reg. Stud.* **2019**, *54*, 802–813. [CrossRef]
22. Wales, P.; Agyiri, A. *Trends in Self-Employment in the UK: 2001 to 2015*; ONS: London, UK, 2016.
23. ONS. *A01: Summary of Labour Market Statistics*; Office for National Statistics: Newport, UK, 2018.
24. Champion, T. *People in Cities: The Numbers*; Future of Cities, University of Newcastle: Callaghan, Australia, 2014.
25. Champion, T.; Coombes, M.; Brown, D.L. Migration and longer-distance commuting inac raaural England. *Reg. Stud.* **2009**, *43*, 1245–1259. [CrossRef]
26. Lowe, P.; Ward, N. Sustainable rural economies: Some lessons from the english experience. *Sustain. Dev.* **2007**, *15*, 307–317. [CrossRef]
27. Yu, L.; Artz, G.M. Does rural entrepreneurship pay? *Small Bus. Econ.* **2019**, *53*, 647–668. [CrossRef]
28. Clark, A.E. Job satisfaction and gender: Why are women so happy at work? *Lab. Econ.* **1997**, *4*, 341–372. [CrossRef]
29. Mallon, M.; Cohen, L. Time for a change? Women's accounts of the move from organizational careers to self-employment. *Br. J. Manag.* **2001**, *12*, 217–230. [CrossRef]

30. Bender, K.A.; Donohue, S.M.; Heywood, J.S. Job satisfaction and gender segregation. *Oxf. Econ. Pap.-New Ser.* **2005**, *57*, 479–496. [CrossRef]

31. Mátyás, L.; Sevestre, P. (Eds.) *The Econometrics of Panel Data: Fundamentals and Recent Developments in Theory and Practice*; Advanced Studies in Theoretical and Applied Econometrics; Springer: Berlin/Heidelberg, Germany, 2008; Volume 46. [CrossRef]

32. Wooldridge, J.M. *Econometric Analysis of Cross Section and Panel Data*; MIT Press: London, UK, 2010.

33. Andreß, H.-J.; Golsch, K.; Schmidt, A.W. *Applied Panel Data Analysis for Economic and Social Surveys*; Springer Science & Business Media: London, UK, 2013.

34. Anyadike-Danes, M.; Bonner, K.; Hart, M.; Mason, C. *Measuring Business Growth: High-Growth Irms and Their Contribution to Employment in the UK*; MBG/35; NESTA: London, UK, 2009. [CrossRef]

35. ONS. *Property Sales in Rural and Urban Areas of England and Wales: September 2011 to Year Ending September 2015*; ONS: Newport, UK, 2016.

36. Williams, T.A.; Shepherd, D.A. Victim entrepreneurs doing well by doing good: Venture creation and well-being in the aftermath of a resource shock. *J. Bus. Ventur.* **2016**, *31*, 365–387. [CrossRef]

37. Mayer, H.; Habersetzer, A.; Meili, R. Rural–Urban Linkages and Sustainable Regional Development: The Role of Entrepreneurs in Linking Peripheries and Centers. *Sustainability* **2016**, *8*, 745. [CrossRef]

38. Frankish, J.S.; Roberts, R.G.; Coad, A.; Storey, D.J. Is Entrepreneurship a Route Out of Deprivation? *Reg. Stud.* **2014**, *48*, 1090–1107. [CrossRef]

39. Saridakis, G.; Marlow, S.; Storey, D.J. Do different factors explain male and female self-employment rates? *J. Bus. Ventur.* **2014**, *29*, 345–362. [CrossRef]

40. Mahroum, S.; Atterton, J.; Ward, N.; Williams, A.M.; Naylor, R.; Hindle, R.; Rowe, F. *Rural Innovation*; IGI Global: London, UK, 2007. [CrossRef]

41. Tsvetkova, A.; Partridge, M.; Betz, M. Entrepreneurial and Employment Responses to Economic Conditions across the Rural-Urban Continuum. *Ann. Am. Acad. Polit. Soc. Sci.* **2017**, *672*, 83–102. [CrossRef]

42. Ward, N.; Atterton, J.H.; Kim, T.-Y.; Lowe, P.D.; Phillipson, J.; Thompson, N. *Universities, the Knowledge Economy and "Neo-Endogenous Rural Development"*; CRE Discussion Paper; Newcastle University: Newcastle upon Tyne, UK, 2005.

43. Stockdale, A. In-Migration and Its Impacts on the Rural Economy. In *The New Rural Economy: Change, Dynamism and Government Policy*; Hill, B., Ed.; Institute for Economic Affairs: London, UK, 2005.

44. Ryan-Collins, J. *Why Can't You Afford a Home?* John Wiley & Sons: Cambridge, UK, 2018.

45. Capelleras, J.-L.; Contin-Pilart, I.; Larraza-Kintana, M.; Martin-Sanchez, V. Population Density and Individual Human Capital Influences on Entrepreneurial Growth Aspirations. In *Academy of Management Proceedings*; Academy of Management: Briarcliff Manor, NY, USA, 2015; Volume 2015, p. 14319.

46. Findlay, A.M.; Short, D.; Stockdale, A. The labour-market impact of migration to rural areas. *Appl. Geogr.* **2000**, *20*, 333–348. [CrossRef]

47. Audretsch, D.B.; Thurik, R. *Linking Entrepreneurship to Growth*; OECD Publishing: Paris, France, 2001; p. 34. [CrossRef]

48. Abreu, M.; Oner, O.; Brouwer, A.; van Leeuwen, E. Well-being effects of self-employment: A spatial inquiry. *J. Bus. Ventur.* **2019**, *34*, 589–607. [CrossRef]

49. Schjoedt, L.; Shaver, K.G. Deciding on an entrepreneurial career: A test of the pull and push hypotheses using the panel study of entrepreneurial dynamics data. *Entrep. Theory Pract.* **2007**, *31*, 733–752. [CrossRef]

50. Faggio, G.; Silva, O. Self-employment and entrepreneurship in urban and rural labour markets. *J. Urban Econ.* **2014**, *84*, 67–85. [CrossRef]

51. Lowe, P.; Ward, N. England's Rural Futures: A Socio-Geographical Approach to Scenarios Analysis. *Reg. Stud.* **2009**, *43*, 1319–1332. [CrossRef]

52. Blanchflower, D.G.; Oswald, A.; Stutzer, A. Latent entrepreneurship across nations. *Eur. Econ. Rev.* **2001**, *45*, 680–691. [CrossRef]

53. Warr, P.; Inceoglu, I. Work Orientations, Well-Being and Job Content of Self-Employed and Employed Professionals. *Work Employ. Soc.* **2018**, *32*, 292–311. [CrossRef]

54. Smeaton, D. Self-Employed Workers: Calling the Shots or Hesitant Independents? A Consideration of the Trends. *Work Employ. Soc.* **2003**, *17*, 379–391. [CrossRef]

55. Henley, A. Entrepreneurial Aspiration and Transition into Self-Employment: Evidence from British Longitudinal Data. *Entrep. Reg. Dev.* **2007**, *19*, 253–280. [CrossRef]

56. Cheraghi, M.; Adsbøll Wickstrøm, K.; Klyver, K. Life-Course and Entry to Entrepreneurship: Embedded in Gender and Gender-Egalitarianism. *Entrep. Reg. Dev.* **2019**, *31*, 242–258. [CrossRef]

57. Knies, G. *Understanding Society: Waves 1-8, 2009–2017 and Harmonised British Household Panel Survey: Waves 1-18, 1991–2009, User Guide*; The Institute for Social and Economic Research: Colchester, UK, 2018.

58. McMullen, J.S.; Bagby, D.R.; Palich, L.E. Economic Freedom and the Motivation to Engage in Entrepreneurial Action. *Entrep. Theory Pract.* **2008**, *32*, 875–895. [CrossRef]

59. Kautonen, T.; Palmroos, J. The Impact of a Necessity-Based Start-up on Subsequent Entrepreneurial Satisfaction. *Int. Entrep. Manag. J.* **2010**, *6*, 285–300. [CrossRef]

60. Millán, J.M.; Hessels, J.; Thurik, R.; Aguado, R. Determinants of Job Satisfaction: A European Comparison of Self-Employed and Paid Employees. *Small Bus. Econ.* **2013**, *40*, 651–670. [CrossRef]

61. Blanchflower, D.G.; Oswald, A.J. What Makes an Entrepreneur? *J. Labor Econ.* **1998**, *16*, 26–60. [CrossRef]

62. Román, C.; Congregado, E.; Millán, J.M. Start-up Incentives: Entrepreneurship Policy or Active Labour Market Programme? *J. Bus. Ventur.* **2013**, *28*, 151–175. [CrossRef]

63. Paull, G. *Biases in the Reporting of Labour Market Dynamics*; IFS Working Papers; 02/10; IFS: London, UK, 2002.

64. Winter, S.G. Mistaken Perceptions: Cases and Consequences. *Br. J. Manag.* **2003**, *14*, 39–44. [CrossRef]

65. Cassar, G.; Craig, J. An Investigation of Hindsight Bias in Nascent Venture Activity. *J. Bus. Ventur.* **2009**, *24*, 149–164. [CrossRef]

66. Manzoni, A. In and out of Employment: Effects in Panel and Life-History Data. *Adv. Life Course Res.* **2012**, *17*, 11–24. [CrossRef]

67. Department for Education. *Post-16 Education: Highest Level of Achievement by Age 25 England*; Department for Education: London, UK, 2018.

68. Lofstrom, M.; Bates, T.; Parker, S.C. Why Are Some People More Likely to Become Small-Businesses Owners than Others: Entrepreneurship Entry and Industry-Specific Barriers. *J. Bus. Ventur.* **2014**, *29*, 232–251. [CrossRef]

69. Earle, J.S.; Sakova, Z. Business Start-Ups or Disguised Unemployment? Evidence on the Character of Self-Employment from Transition Economies. *Labour Econ.* **2000**, *7*, 575–601. [CrossRef]

70. Svaleryd, H. Self-Employment and the Local Business Cycle. *Small Bus. Econ.* **2015**, *44*, 55–70. [CrossRef]

71. Bosma, N.; Sternberg, R. Entrepreneurship as an Urban Event? Empirical Evidence from European Cities. *Entrep. Reg. Context* **2019**, *48*, 78–95. [CrossRef]

72. Blanchflower, D.G.; Mayer, B.D. *A Longitudinal Analysis of Young Entrepreneurs in Australia and in the United States*; NBER Working Paper; 3746; NBER: Cambridge, MA, USA, 1991.

73. Burke, A.E.; FitzRoy, F.R.; Nolan, M.A. Self-Employment Wealth and Job Creation: The Roles of Gender, Non-Pecuniary Motivation and Entrepreneurial Ability. *Small Bus. Econ.* **2002**, *19*, 255–270. [CrossRef]

74. Clark, A.E.; Oswald, A.J. Satisfaction and Comparison Income. *J. Public Econ.* **1996**, *61*, 359–381. [CrossRef]

75. Nanda, R. *Cost of External Finance and Selection into Entrepreneurship*; HBS Working Paper 08–047; Harvard Business School: Boston, MA, USA, 2008.

76. Georgellis, Y.; Wall, H.J. Gender Differences in Self-Employment. *Int. Rev. Appl. Econ.* **2005**, *19*, 321–342. [CrossRef]

77. Still, L.V.; Timms, W. Women's Business: The Flexible Alternative Workstyle for Women. *Women Manag. Rev.* **2000**, *15*, 272–283. [CrossRef]

78. Craig, L.; Powell, A.; Cortis, N. Self-Employment, Work-Family Time and the Gender Division of Labour. *Work Employ. Soc.* **2012**, *26*, 716–734. [CrossRef]

79. Ajayi-Obe, O.; Parker, S.C. The Changing Nature of Work among the Self-Employed in the 1990s: Evidence from Britain. *J. Lab. Res.* **2005**, *26*, 501–517. [CrossRef]

80. Keizer, R.; Dykstra, P.A.; Poortman, A.-R. The Transition to Parenthood and Well-Being: The Impact of Partner Status and Work Hour Transitions. *J. Fam. Psychol.* **2010**, *24*, 429–438. [CrossRef]

81. Zou, M. Gender, Work Orientations and Job Satisfaction. *Work Employ. Soc.* **2015**, *29*, 3–22. [CrossRef]

82. ONS. *Labour Market Overview, UK*; ONS: Newport, UK, 2020.

83. Jayawarna, D.; Rouse, J.; Kitching, J. Entrepreneur Motivations and Life Course. *Int. Small Bus. J.* **2013**, *31*, 34–56. [CrossRef]

84. Clark, A.E.; Oswald, A.; Warr, P. Is Job Satisfaction U-Shaped in Age? *J. Occup. Organ. Psychol.* **1996**, *69*, 57–81. [CrossRef]

85. Bandura, A. Exercise of Personal Agency through the Self-Efficacy Mechanism. In *Self-Efficacy: Thought Control of Action*; Schwarzer, R., Ed.; Hemisphere Publishing Corporation: Washington, DC, USA, 1992; pp. 3–38.

86. Bandura, A.; Barbaranelli, C.; Caprara, G.V.; Pastorelli, C. Self-Efficacy Beliefs as Shapers of Children's Aspirations and Career Trajectories. *Child Dev.* **2001**, *72*, 187–206. [CrossRef] [PubMed]

87. Wilson, F.; Kickul, J.; Marlino, D. Gender, Entrepreneurial Self-Efficacy, and Entrepreneurial Career Intentions: Implications for Entrepreneurship Education. *Entrep. Theory Pract.* **2007**, *31*, 387–406. [CrossRef]

88. Burton, M.D.; Sørensen, J.B.; Dobrev, S.D. A Careers Perspective on Entrepreneurship. *Entrep. Theory Pract.* **2016**, *40*, 237–247. [CrossRef]

89. Zhou, M. Motherhood, Employment, and the Dynamics of Women's Gender Attitudes. *Gend. Soc.* **2017**, *31*, 751–776. [CrossRef]

90. Goffee, R.; Scase, R. *Women in Charge: The Experience of Female Entrepreneurs*; Allen and Unwin Ltd.: London, UK, 1985.

91. Greene, F.J.; Han, L.; Marlow, S. Like Mother, Like Daughter? Analyzing Maternal Influences Upon Women's Entrepreneurial Propensity. *Entrep. Theory Pract.* **2013**, *37*, 687–711. [CrossRef]

92. Yu, W.H.; Kuo, J.C.L. The Motherhood Wage Penalty by Work Conditions: How Do Occupational Characteristics Hinder or Empower Mothers? *Am. Sociol. Rev.* **2017**, *82*, 744–769. [CrossRef]

93. Gartner, W.B.; Shane, S.A. Measuring Entrepreneurship over Time. *J. Bus. Ventur.* **1995**, *10*, 283–301. [CrossRef]

94. Reynolds, P.D.; Hay, M.; Bygrave, W.D.; Camp, S.M.; Autio, E. *Global Entrepreneuship Monitor Executive Report 2001*; Global Entrepreneurship Monitor: London, UK, 2002.

95. Deane, J. *Self-Employment Review: An Independent Report*; Department for Business, Innovation and Skills: London, UK, 2016.

96. McCollum, D.; Liu, Y.; Findlay, A.; Feng, Z.; Nightingale, G. Determinants of Occupational Mobility: The Importance of Place of Work. *Reg. Stud.* **2018**, *52*, 1612–1623. [CrossRef]

Permissions

All chapters in this book were first published in MDPI; hereby published with permission under the Creative Commons Attribution License or equivalent. Every chapter published in this book has been scrutinized by our experts. Their significance has been extensively debated. The topics covered herein carry significant findings which will fuel the growth of the discipline. They may even be implemented as practical applications or may be referred to as a beginning point for another development.

The contributors of this book come from diverse backgrounds, making this book a truly international effort. This book will bring forth new frontiers with its revolutionizing research information and detailed analysis of the nascent developments around the world.

We would like to thank all the contributing authors for lending their expertise to make the book truly unique. They have played a crucial role in the development of this book. Without their invaluable contributions this book wouldn't have been possible. They have made vital efforts to compile up to date information on the varied aspects of this subject to make this book a valuable addition to the collection of many professionals and students.

This book was conceptualized with the vision of imparting up-to-date information and advanced data in this field. To ensure the same, a matchless editorial board was set up. Every individual on the board went through rigorous rounds of assessment to prove their worth. After which they invested a large part of their time researching and compiling the most relevant data for our readers.

The editorial board has been involved in producing this book since its inception. They have spent rigorous hours researching and exploring the diverse topics which have resulted in the successful publishing of this book. They have passed on their knowledge of decades through this book. To expedite this challenging task, the publisher supported the team at every step. A small team of assistant editors was also appointed to further simplify the editing procedure and attain best results for the readers.

Apart from the editorial board, the designing team has also invested a significant amount of their time in understanding the subject and creating the most relevant covers. They scrutinized every image to scout for the most suitable representation of the subject and create an appropriate cover for the book.

The publishing team has been an ardent support to the editorial, designing and production team. Their endless efforts to recruit the best for this project, has resulted in the accomplishment of this book. They are a veteran in the field of academics and their pool of knowledge is as vast as their experience in printing. Their expertise and guidance has proved useful at every step. Their uncompromising quality standards have made this book an exceptional effort. Their encouragement from time to time has been an inspiration for everyone.

The publisher and the editorial board hope that this book will prove to be a valuable piece of knowledge for researchers, students, practitioners and scholars across the globe.

List of Contributors

Soogwan Doh
Faculty of Department of Public Administration, School of Social Sciences, University of Ulsan, Ulsan 44610, Korea

Ana Venâncio and Inês Pinto
ISEG-Lisbon School of Economics and Management, Universidade de Lisboa, and ADVANCE/CSG, 1200-781 Lisbon, Portugal

Jaana Seikkula-Leino
RDI and Business Operations, Tampere University of Applied Sciences, Kuntokatu, 33520 Tampere, Finland

Maria Salomaa
RDI and Business Operations, Tampere University of Applied Sciences, Kuntokatu, 33520 Tampere, Finland
Lincoln International Business School, University of Lincoln, Brayford Pool, Lincoln LN6 7DQ, UK

Inés Ruiz-Rosa
Departamento de Economía, Contabilidad y Finanzas, Facultad de Economía, Empresa y Turismo, Universidad de La Laguna, 38071 San Cristóbal de la Laguna, Santa Cruz de Tenerife, Spain

Desiderio Gutiérrez-Taño and Francisco J. García-Rodríguez
Departamento de Dirección de Empresas e Historia Económica, Facultad de Economía, Empresa y Turismo, Universidad de La Laguna, 38071 San Cristóbal de la Laguna, Santa Cruz de Tenerife, Spain

Pawel Dobrzanski
Department of Mathematical Economics, Wroclaw University of Economics and Business, 53-345 Wroclaw, Poland

Sebastian Bobowski
Department of International Economic Relations, Wroclaw University of Economics and Business, 53-345 Wroclaw, Poland

Jia-Ning Guo and Jia-Qi Hu
College of Business Administration, Huaqiao University, Quanzhou 362021, China

Xue-Liang Pei
College of Business Administration, Huaqiao University, Quanzhou 362021, China
East Business Management Research Centre, Huaqiao University, Quanzhou 362021, China

Tung-Ju Wu
School of Management, Harbin Institute of Technology (HIT), Harbin 150001, China

Maria-Ana Georgescu
Faculty of Sciences and Letters, "George Emil Palade" University of Medicine, Pharmacy, Sciences and Technology of Tirgu-Mures, 540139 Tirgu Mures, Romania

Emilia Herman
Faculty of Economics and Law, "George Emil Palade" University of Medicine, Pharmacy, Sciences and Technology of Tirgu-Mures, 540139 Tirgu Mures, Romania

Murude Ertac and Cem Tanova
Faculty of Tourism, Eastern Mediterranean University, 99628 Gazimagusa, North Cyprus, via Mersin 10, Turkey

Paloma Escamilla-Fajardo, Juan Manuel Núñez-Pomar and Josep Crespo
Department of Physical Education and Sport, Faculty of Physical Activity and Sport Sciences, University of Valencia, Gascó Oliag 3, 46010 Valencia, Spain

Vanessa Ratten
La Trobe Business, La Trobe University, Plenty Rd & Kingsbury Dr, Bundoora VIC, Melbourne 3086, Australia

Wafa Alwakid
Department of Business, Universitat Autònoma de Barcelona, Edifici B Campus UAB, Bellaterra (Cerdanyola del Vallès), 08193 Barcelona, Spain
Department of Business Administration, Jouf University, Al Jouf 75471, Saudi Arabia

Sebastian Aparicio
Durham University Business School, Durham University, Mill Hill Lane, Durham DH1 3LB, UK
Fundación ECSIM, Medellin, Colombia

David Urbano
Department of Business and Centre for Entrepreneurship and Social Innovation Research (CREIS), Universitat Autònoma de Barcelona, Edifici B Campus UAB, Bellaterra (Cerdanyola del Vallès), 08193 Barcelona, Spain

Eunju Jung
Graduate School of Education, Sejong University, Seoul 05006, Korea

Yongjin Lee
Department of Liberal Arts, Hansei University, Gunpo, Gyeonggi-do 15852, Korea

Nicholas Litsardopoulos and Chris Hand
Kingston Business School, Kingston University London, Kingston Hill KT2 7LB, UK

George Saridakis
Kent Business School, University of Kent, Canterbury CT2 7FS, UK

Index

Printed in the USA
CPSIA information can be obtained
at www.ICGtesting.com
JSHW051411091023
49903JS00006B/377